C000023634

Praise for *Breaking the Code of Project Management*

"Many of us have been preaching for some years that the traditional analytical tools of project management, best exemplified by CPM scheduling, have tiny impact on project success and failure. It's actually all about the behavior and interactions of people. Dr. Laufer has brought into one book an account of all the people factors, considered perhaps for the first time as a whole system. The perceptions and scholarship are inspiring and the breadth of supporting data and opinion impressive.

Getting a large body of differently skilled and differently motivated people to work together to achieve a single goal whilst everybody is constantly assaulted by the unexpected is the real project management challenge. This book will be a tremendous help to the profession in meeting the challenge."
—Dr. Martin Barnes, president, Association for Project Management; former chairman, Council of the International Project Management Association

"This is an extraordinary book and an exceptional resource for project managers. The experience I had in reading *Breaking the Code* was repeated flashes of 'that's it!' A series of 'nuggets of wisdom' that I would want to pass on to protégé project managers. Fairly simple concepts that are not necessarily difficult to implement, but are not intuitive and typically learned only through trial by fire. It reads like the combined wisdom and experience of hundreds of years, distilled down into the important 1 percent and presented as a workable model of project management mastery. It should be revisited on a regular basis to inform every project manager's changing reality, so be prepared to see dog-eared copies of this book on desks everywhere."
—Scott Tibbitts, managing director, SpaceDev Inc.; founder, Starsys Research Inc.

"This is a significant book. Anyone who has read the typical offerings on project management should read this one as an antidote. Anyone who hasn't studied the standard works should start here and skip the others. 'Breaking the code' means overcoming the standard procedures for managing projects. It also means figuring out how to really be successful. The book does both.

Laufer helps us let go of the convenient fictions about well-ordered situations. Managers should be so lucky. Laufer shows that a 'permanent white water' mentality is more apt. The tools that fit well-ordered situations aren't of much use in turbulent and complex environments. Fortunately, Laufer provides a set of strategies that is much more suited to the challenges facing project managers. And he gets this all across with a continuous stream of real-life stories."
—Dr. Gary Klein, author of *Sources of Power: How People Make Decisions*

"All white-collar work today is project work. Experienced and less experienced project managers alike have all been waiting too long for this breakthrough in project management. In giving us the 'real story' of project management, *Breaking the Code of Project Management* combines the *rigor* of *Good to Great* with the *conviction* of *Organizing Genius* and the *spirit* of *In Search of Excellence*. No project manager can afford not to read and re-read this superb book."
—Dr. Edward J. Hoffman, director, NASA Academy of Program and Project Engineering and Leadership

"This book is the breakthrough in project management we've all been waiting for—real principles illustrated by real stories told by real people. Unlike other books on the subject, *Breaking the Code of Project Management* tackles central issues and dilemmas in the complex reality of today's project environments. By using stories drawn from the experiences of master project managers, Dr. Laufer provides us with cutting-edge guidelines for dealing with multiple and conflicting demands and adeptly demonstrates how they all work together to get the best results. *Breaking the Code* is the ultimate handbook in project management and a must read for practitioners as well as for students."
—Gregory A. Howell, cofounder and COO, Lean Construction Institute

"Agile programmers and non-software project managers alike, take note. In this book, Dr. Laufer synthesizes from within the field of classical project management the results of modern agile and lean software development, and more. He shows project management to be the human-centered, creative, and determined activity that it should be. For me, this book gives hope to the project management profession as a whole as well as to the future of software project management."
—Dr. Alistair Cockburn, president, Humans and Technology; coauthor of the *Manifesto for Agile Software Development*

"*Breaking the Code* is an important and timely book. It presents fresh concepts that are uniquely packaged and thought provoking for both master project managers and beginners. Some books are valuable to practitioners within a specific industry, while others provide 'truths' that are so basic that they transcend all boundaries. *Breaking the Code* definitely falls in the latter category. It will help project managers everywhere to understand their own practices and to think through their problems with sharper insight."
—Ian Mitroff, professor emeritus of business policy, University of Southern California; author or coauthor of 26 books, including *The Essential Guide to Managing Corporate Crisis* and *The Unbounded Mind*

"Dr. Laufer's Results-Focused Leadership model is a simple, yet powerful and elegant, tool for successful project managers in their struggle to remain agile and responsive to our dynamic and globally competitive environment. His five eloquently presented principles are grounded in reality and provide practical and insightful advice and guidance for inspired leadership, effective communication, and the 'unlearning' of outdated concepts. A must read for all project managers."
—Sylvia V. Baca, vice president for social investment programs and strategic partnerships, BP America

"Dr. Laufer not only understands that project management must evolve to meet current needs, but recognizes that the key to identifying cutting-edge concepts is to extract and document the tacit knowledge of competent practitioners. As in his earlier works, Dr. Laufer departs from conventional wisdom to provide real solutions for forward-looking organizations in the twenty-first century."
—Hugh Woodward, former chair, Project Management Institute

"*Breaking the Code of Project Management* focuses on the future of project management—a future in which the ability to take action early, reflect on those actions, and adapt quickly will lead to success. Rather than the traditional 'corrective action,' the future is one of 'adaptive action.' Laufer's work, which is deeply aligned with agile principles, provides us with a fresh approach to the real dilemmas of project management."
—Jim Highsmith, author of *Agile Project Management: Creating Innovative Products*

"Dr. Laufer has painted a masterpiece in the art of project management. By combining his research, personal experiences, and real-life stories, he has created a pallet of skills that both new and experienced project managers can use to evaluate and improve their own pallets so that they too can consistently deliver highly successful projects."
—W. Scott Cameron, global project management process owner, The Procter & Gamble Company

Breaking the Code of Project Management

Alexander Laufer

BREAKING THE CODE OF PROJECT MANAGEMENT
Copyright © Alexander Laufer, 2009.

All rights reserved.

First published in 2009 by PALGRAVE MACMILLAN® in the United States – a division of St. Martin's Press LLC, 175 Fifth Avenue, New York, NY 10010.

Where this book is distributed in the UK, Europe and the rest of the world, this is by Palgrave Macmillan, a division of Macmillan Publishers Limited, registered in England, company number 785998, of Houndmills, Basingstoke, Hampshire RG21 6XS.

Palgrave Macmillan is the global academic imprint of the above companies and has companies and representatives throughout the world.

Palgrave® and Macmillan® are registered trademarks in the United States, the United Kingdom, Europe and other countries.

ISBN-13: 978-0-230-60803-0   (hardcover)
ISBN-10: 0-230-60803-5   (hardcover)
ISBN-13: 978-0-230-61351-5   (paperback)
ISBN-10: 0-230-61351-9   (paperback)

Library of Congress Cataloging-in-Publication Data

Laufer, Alexander.
  Breaking the code of project management / Alexander Laufer.
    p. cm.
  Includes bibliographical references.
  ISBN 0-230-60803-5
  1. Project management.   2. Leadership.   I. Title.

HD69.P75L378 2009
658.4'04—dc22   2008031120

A catalogue record of the book is available from the British Library.

Design by Macmillan Publishing Solutions

First edition: March 2009

10 9 8 7 6 5 4 3 2 1

Printed in the United States of America.

Contents

List of Exhibits

List of Tables

Acknowledgments

My primary research objective throughout the years has been to capture the proven practices of some of the most competent project managers, to uncover their tacit knowledge, and to explicitly articulate it. This book is based on case studies and stories collected from over 150 successful practitioners affiliated with 15 advanced organizations. There are too many of them to name each here. However, I am eternally grateful to all my friends who have so willingly shared their expertise and insights with me throughout the years.

I am particularly indebted to those who assisted me in the actual writing of this book. First and foremost, my heartfelt thanks go to a very special friend and colleague—Dr. Dora Cohenca-Zall. A true professional, Dora has been working with me on research projects for many years, during which time I have grown to rely on her sound judgment and keen insight. Throughout the writing of this book, Dora reviewed the manuscript several times and contributed remarkable suggestions as well as incisive questions. Her dedication and ownership are unparalleled. Special thanks are also due to Sharon Woodrow, who edited the text meticulously with her professional touch and uncanny ability to understand the meaning behind the words. Her artistry helped to make this book more readable and interesting. Last, but not least, is Laurie Harting, my executive editor at Palgrave Macmillan, who through her extensive personal involvement and exceptional skill was able to streamline this book and significantly enhance the quality of the final product.

Finally, my greatest gratitude is to my beloved wife, Yochy, my most precious and cherished friend who always finds the time to listen and offer her true, unbiased opinion and advice. She truly makes our home a haven of love and serves as a role model for the entire family.

Dr. Alexander Laufer: A Profile

Dr. Laufer is a chaired professor of civil engineering at the Technion-Israel Institute of Technology, where he also served as the dean of the faculty. Currently, he serves as the director of the Center for Project Leadership of Columbia University and as a member of the editorial review board of the *Project Management Journal.* During the last 20 years, Dr. Laufer has conducted research and taught at three U.S. universities. In his studies he has attempted to uncover, formulate, and articulate the "tacit" knowledge of competent project managers. In the last decade, Dr. Laufer has authored or coauthored three books on project management. He has served as the editor-in-chief of the NASA Academy of Program and Project Leadership Magazine, *ASK, Academy Sharing Knowledge,* and also as a member of the advisory board of the NASA Academy of Program and Project Leadership.

Introduction

The Real Story of Project Management: Results-Focused Leadership

All Work Is Project Work

A project may be defined as a temporary endeavor undertaken to create a unique product or service. It can be as simple as the plan for an off-site retreat or as complex as the development and production of a space shuttle. In the project method, instead of grouping people in the traditional functional units based on means (work processes, knowledge, or skills), they are grouped in cross-functional units based on ends (product or customer).

There is growing recognition that the project method is the keystone of the modern organization. While the Industrial Revolution brought greater specialization and narrowing of skills and tasks, the current information revolution is generating greater task complexity, which demands broader skills and better integration at the task level. Starting in the mid-1990s, the project method has emerged as the predominant management strategy for structuring organizations and defining the manager's roles and tasks.[1] In most companies today, managers spend much of their time focusing on projects, thus making their roles more general and lateral. The project culture, which fosters responsiveness to customers, has enabled organizations to easily migrate from the producer-dominated market of yesterday to the more complex customer-driven market of today.

Paradoxically, this sharp increase in the popularity of the project method has been accompanied by an increasing dissatisfaction with current project management practices and results. In this introduction, I first describe my own research voyage—how, together with the most competent practitioners, I have attempted to break the code of project management over the last two decades. As part of this description,

I briefly explain the rationale for the unique makeup of this book, which is composed of practitioners' stories and the results of academic research. Finally, I present the outcome of this voyage: the principles of Results-Focused Leadership.

Project Management Reform Is Required

The following four items reflect or contribute to the growing discontent with project management practices and results, underscoring the acute need for a major overhaul in our fundamental approach to project management:

1. Deep changes introduced by three leading organizations
2. The consistently poor results of a wide spectrum of projects
3. The flawed foundation of a major project management tool
4. The emerging paradigms in research and practice

Real-Life Examples of Deep Changes

The three stories that follow represent the significant changes that have taken place in recent years in the private and public sectors, at both the institutional and project levels. The first two focus on the institutional level, at NASA and Procter & Gamble (P&G), while the third focuses on the project level at the U.S. Air Force.

The first story, related by Dr. Edward Hoffman, director of the NASA Academy of Program and Project Engineering and Leadership, derives from a two-week training course for experienced project managers:

The person quickly approaching me looked serious. He told me to return imme-diately to the classroom—my instructor had just died! As I started to run, I asked if an emergency medical crew had been called. That's when he told me that my instructor had not physically died, but was being devoured by a class of 23 students who were very unhappy with the lesson plan.

. . . I arrived at the classroom, and . . . two things were clear. First, the group possessed remarkable knowledge . . . Second, those relatively new project managers in the group wanted guidance on how to manage projects. A regula-tion-style, bureaucratic, hard-edged policy statement of directives was the last thing they wanted. They were complaining that the existing policy document was overly constrictive and out of touch with the flexibility needed to successfully manage modern projects.

At that time, there was a major effort under way to rewrite the existing NASA policy document on Program and Project Management . . . I told the students that, if they wanted, I would let NASA's senior leadership know that the group would like to join that effort and present their recommendations for improvement . . . After considerable discussion, the students decided to accept the challenge.

The team spent four months conducting interviews in and out of NASA and developing recommendations and finally gave a presentation at NASA Headquarters in Washington, D.C. Their effort led to a significant change in NASA's Project Management Procedures. For example, as a result of their input, NASA was willing to abolish the "one best way" approach and to allow project teams to tailor project procedures to the unique context of their project.[a,2]

The second story, as told by Scott Cameron, the global process owner of project management at P&G, focuses on a major streamlining effort and its results:

I have noted during my career that there is a never-ending amount of rules and restrictions forced upon project managers under the guise of helping them "be successful" in managing their projects. It appears to be a one-way street; many regulations are added, but few (if any) are removed . . . I had the opportunity to assist in cleaning out such a closet [of standard procedures] as part of a project management leadership team I was part of.

Cameron reports that although the "cleaning out" required three consecutive review cycles, eventually they were able to sharply cut the number of their standard procedures. Instead of 18 technical standards and 32 standard operating procedures, project managers at P&G are now employing only four of each.[b]

The third story is shared by Terry Little, a program director for the U.S. Air Force, who was requested to abruptly leave his current project to head an ongoing, extremely challenging project. Upon assuming his new position he found that

the immediate objective was to award contracts to two competitors who would spend the next two years designing a system that would be continuously evaluated. At the end of the two years, the government would award production of the missile to one contractor.

Little was told that the previous project manager "wasn't up to the task," and he soon realized that success would require a radical change. This is how Little explained to the team what he expected of them and what they should expect of him:

First you need to put aside all of your paradigms and all of your ideas about how exactly we are going to do this and start with one basic assumption: that it's going to be done in six months . . . I am empowering you, as a group, to go figure out how to do this. My job, as the leader here, is to facilitate things, to do whatever's necessary to make the bureaucracy move out of our way, so that it parts like the Red Sea parted for Moses—that's my job.

Later on, Little explained how he actually "helped" the team to change the paradigm:

The truth is that I pulled the number "six" out of my hat. I would have been happy to be on contract at the end of seven months, or even eight months.

What I wanted to do was set something that would challenge these folks to look at things in an entirely new way. I didn't want a schedule that they felt they could achieve just by working on weekends or figuring out a handful of inventive ways to do things. I wanted something so outrageous that it would cause them, first, to essentially give up, but then—once they figured out that giving up wasn't an option—to step back and examine all their assumptions, all their beliefs, all the things that were in their heads as a result of their experiences and what they had been told in the past, and to ask themselves with a clean slate: "What do I really need to do to achieve this goal?"

What we achieved was something even better than six months. At the end of the day, we completed the source selection in less than five months . . . When we talked about it afterwards, what the team discovered was that they hadn't known how capable they could be if they just quit thinking about things in the way they had always thought about them.[c]

These three stories, which illustrate deep change, share one common characteristic: an emphasis on empowering people. This empowerment was achieved by reducing the role of bureaucracy and standard procedures, by enhancing flexibility and trust, and by challenging the team to think "out of the box."

The Poor Statistics of Project Results

Research covering a wide variety of projects consistently demonstrates poor project performance, as manifested by cost overruns. For example, a Rand Corporation study that examined 52 extremely large projects found that the projects suffered from an average cost growth of 88 percent.[3] A recent study of megaprojects found that "cost overruns of 50 per cent to 100 per cent in real terms are common, and overruns above 100 per cent are not uncommon."[4]

However, not only large projects are prone to failure. Even when all projects, regardless of size, are lumped together, the results are alarming. In their 1987 summary of all the publicly available reports on project overruns, Morris and Hough concluded that "the track record of projects is fundamentally poor . . . Projects are often completed late or over budget . . . [In] cases, representing some 3,500 projects drawn from all over the world in several different industries, overruns are the norm, being typically between 40 and 200 per cent."[5]

Results of software projects have received great attention in this regard. For example, in their study of software project failure, Keil and his colleagues reported that "based on a survey of 376 CEOs, the consulting firm CSC Index, Cambridge, MA, reports that roughly 50% of all information technology projects fail to meet chief executive expectations."[6]

The Standish Group has been doing surveys on information technology projects since 1994. Their research shows that overrunning budgets is common and that delivering projects late is normal. Delivering less functionality than was originally planned is also nothing out of the ordinary. In short, project failure in the IT world is almost standard operating procedure.

Here are some unsettling statistics: for 2001, the Standish Group database showed that a staggering 31 percent of projects were canceled before completion and 53 percent of projects cost almost double their original estimates. The proportion of projects completed on time and on budget was only 16 percent. However, even when these projects were completed, many were a mere shadow of their original requirements, with only 42 percent of completed projects preserving the originally proposed features and functions.[7]

In another study by the Standish Group in 1995, the U.S. government and private businesses spent approximately $81 billion on canceled software projects, in addition to $59 billion for budget overruns. In that study, only about one-sixth of all projects were completed on time and within budget, nearly one-third were canceled outright, and well over half were considered "challenged." Of the challenged or canceled projects, the average project ran 189 percent over budget, 222 percent behind schedule, and contained only 61 percent of the originally specified features![8]

The Flawed Foundation of PERT

One of the most well-known building blocks of project management is the PERT method.[9] In his comprehensive review of the development of project management, Morris reports, "Polaris developed a management control procedure [in 1957], PERT; this, together with CPM, was the progenitor of the management systems which over the next 20 years were to become (almost too) synonymous with project management."[10]

What evidence was provided about the effectiveness of this scheduling methodology to ensure that it would become almost a household word when discussing project management? This is how Morris describes the publicity of PERT: "Admiral Raborn and the SPO [Special Projects Office of the U.S. Navy] public relations machinery began publicizing PERT, hailing it as 'the first management tool of the nuclear and computer age.' So effective was the publicity that when the first Polaris missile was launched in 1960, press coverage of PERT was almost as great as the coverage of the launch itself. By 1962, the U.S. Government had issued 139 different documents and reports on the technique. By 1964, the bibliography on PERT comprised nearly 1000 books and articles . . . There is, however, considerable evidence that the method was deliberately over-sold, with the aim of keeping Congressional and other external critics at arm's length. Raborn used PERT as a tool to control his external environment."[11]

One of the sources that Morris used for his analysis was a detailed study of the development of the Polaris system conducted by Harvey Sapolsky. Here are some of the surprising results of this study, as reported by Sapolsky: "In interviews with contractor executives reviewing their experience with the original PERT system, not one of them said he had used the data generated by that system . . . Instead, many thought it was the SPO technical officers and engineers who actually had used the PERT system data. The technical officers and engineers, in turn, denied ever using PERT data . . . they thought it was the program evaluators . . . who made use of the PERT system . . . Persons who held positions in Plans and Programs, however, . . . never used the system; rather they thought that it was . . . the plant representatives who worked with the PERT reports. The plant representatives were similar in their response: 'No, it must have been someone else.'"[12]

Sapolsky concludes by "putting the myth in perspective": "An alchemous combination of whirling computers, brightly colored charts, and fast talking public relations officers gave the Special Projects Office a truly effective management system. It mattered not whether the parts of the system functioned or even existed. It mattered only that certain people for a certain period of time believed that they did . . . The Special Projects Office won the battles for funds and priority. Its program was protected from the bureaucratic interferences of the comptrollers and the auditors."[13] Polaris was a success, but what really stood behind its success? Davies and Hobday highlight the real practices that contributed to Polaris's success: "PERT was not actually used to build the system. . . Instead Polaris's success was the result of inspired leadership, good management and a shared spirit of commitment . . . PERT . . . was a deeply flawed management tool . . . used primarily to impress visitors . . . and to build up a myth of management effectiveness."[14]

Stout addresses the wider and long-lasting implications of disseminating the myth, the rational method, while at the same time ignoring the real soft practices that led to Polaris's success: "What is retained is not an understanding of the actual practices, but the magic and symbolism of 'the system' . . . The assumed effectiveness of PERT was not based on an evaluation of its role in Polaris; rather it was a matter of inference. The inference took the symbolic form: Polaris was a success; PERT was used; therefore, PERT was at least partially responsible for the success. Even if the second claim was true, and it is not, the inference is still questionable. But it is on this that PERT has achieved its popularity."[15]

The impact of fashion is not limited to the project world. Researchers in general management have also wrestled with this thorny issue. For example, how long do management fashions stay alive? A study examining 16 management fashions that have emerged over the past 50 years found that "PERT, a fashion of the 1950s, appears to have experienced a much longer life cycle than did quality circles, a fashion of the 1970s, and reengineering, a fashion of the 1990s."[16] Another interesting, related question is, where do management fashions come from? Similar to the above analysis regarding the PERT case, studies have found that the corporate culture rhetoric developed in the popular management press has shaped the rhetoric of the academic press, rather than vice versa.[17] In turn, this flawed academic press has a devastating impact on practice, as stated by Ghoshal: "Kurt Lewin argued that 'nothing is as practical as a good theory.' The obverse is also true: Nothing is as dangerous as a bad theory . . . bad management theories are, at present, destroying good management practices."[18]

Emerging New Paradigms in Research and Practice

In recent years, the academic press in project management has also focused on bad theories and their impact on practice. Williams concludes that "conventional methods [of project management] can exacerbate rather than alleviate project problems."[19] Melgrati and Damiani strongly criticize the prevailing project management paradigm, arguing that "project management ideology is paradoxical, because it focuses on repetitive aspects and 'marginalizes' the uniqueness and originality that should instead characterize the project."[20]

Nissen and Snider criticize the narrow orientation of the official Project Management Body of Knowledge (PMBOK® Guide): "In gross departure from the kind of centralized, static and explicit knowledge formalized through the PMBOK® Guide, we instead view theory as decentralized throughout the practice of project management—reflecting an inherently dynamic concept—that recognizes the importance of tacit knowledge."[21] Cicmil et al. admit that "what is needed to improve project management practice is not more research on what should be done . . . while a great deal is written about traditional project management we know very little about the 'actuality' of project based working and management."[22]

In their paper "The Underlying Theory of Project Management Is Obsolete," Koskela and Howell analyze the theories of planning, execution, and control and present empirical evidence that focuses on anomalies and unanticipated results. They concluded that "the present evidence is strong enough for the claim that a paradigmatic transformation of the discipline of project management is needed."[23]

One group of practitioners—software developers—took the initiative and developed, formalized, and implemented a new project management approach called the Agile method. A group of proponents of this method created a document named the Agile Manifesto through a process described by one of the group as follows: "In February 2001, a group of seventeen software pundits got together in Snowbird UT to discuss the growing field of what used to be called lightweight methods. We decide to use the term 'agile' to describe this new breed of agile methods. We also wrote the Manifesto for Software Development, setting out the values and principles of these agile processes. I was one of these self-elected visionaries."[24]

The Manifesto for Agile Software Development introduces four values that are further defined by 12 principles: "We are uncovering better ways of developing software by doing it and helping others do it. Through this work we have come to value:

1. Individuals and interactions over processes and tools
2. Working software over comprehensive documentation
3. Customer collaboration over contract negotiation
4. Responding to change over following a plan

That is, while there is value in the items on the right, we value the items on the left more."[25]

Comparing Agile methods with the traditional plan-driven methods, Boehm and Turner explain that "in general, Agile methods are very light-weight processes that employ short interval cycles; actively involve users to establish, prioritize, and verify requirements and rely on tacit knowledge within a team as opposed to documentation."[26]

The four values and 12 principles constitute a new project management paradigm that significantly differs from the classic paradigm underlying the plan-driven methods. More than a few of the underlying assumptions that led to the Agile Manifesto are quite similar to the assumptions that I have uncovered in my own studies. The Agile methods will be further discussed in this book.

Thus far we have presented the following:

- Examples of deep changes introduced by three leading organizations.
- Statistics of consistently poor results of a wide spectrum of projects.
- The flawed foundation of a major project management tool.
- The emerging call from the research community for a paradigm shift, as well as a new paradigm initiated and developed by practitioners.

These four aspects of the growing dissatisfaction with current project management practices and results all clearly point to the acute need for project reform.

Generating Knowledge: Learning from the Best Practitioners

For more than two decades, I have worked with one goal in mind: attempting to break the code of project management. In this long learning pursuit, I alternately employed two different, yet complementary, research approaches:

1. Field studies in advanced organizations using structured research tools, in particular interviews and observations of practitioners.[27]
2. Case studies and stories collected via face-to-face interviews with individual practitioners or with project teams or secured from presentations and discussions at knowledge-sharing meetings. All these studies first focused on identifying the most competent practitioners and then on uncovering, formulating, and articulating their "tacit" knowledge.[28]

What was my rationale for adopting a research practice that focuses on "advanced organizations" and on "the most competent practitioners"?

In sharing their research methodology for *Organizing Genius*, Bennis and Biederman explain why they chose to exclusively concentrate on "great groups," when the majority of working groups we typically encounter in our daily lives are not so great: "The reason is our conviction that excellence is a better teacher than mediocrity." They further assert that the lessons of the ordinary are everywhere. However, "truly profound and original insights are to be found only in studying the exemplary."[29] Waterman, in the opening of his book *What America Does Right*, provides a similar rationale for his work: "The theme is similar to that of everything I've written, starting with In Search of Excellence: learn from the best; find role models and emulate."[30]

Somewhat differently, McKelvey argues that one major flaw in management research is reliance on averages. He explains that in medical research, for example, "hearts, lungs, brains, and bones are mostly the same from one end to the other; and quantitative research based on sampling from populations works the same from one end to another—scientific findings reduced to averages work pretty well . . . With organizations and management I don't think this is the case . . . Practitioners live in a world of extremes—Toyota, eBay, Google, Southwest, Wal-Mart, and GE are good; Alitalia, Enron, Anderson, WorldCom, Lucent, and FBI are bad. All of the cases used in MBA classrooms are stories of good and bad examples—extremes, never averages . . . Practitioners don't give a damn about averages. They want to know how to identify good and bad leaders." This is one key reason, McKelvey concludes, why "practitioners find little value in academic research."[31]

Despite being based on intensive interactions with practitioners, the findings still had to be thoroughly tested in real-life settings before they could be proposed for actual use. I tried several approaches and concluded that consultation is often the only feasible way to test research results and to collect rich and unfiltered feedback firsthand. Therefore, I tested my research products at P&G over a period of three years, from 1991 to 1994.

The next story describes how P&G served as a real-life "laboratory" for me and how I accidentally encountered stories as a possible tool for uncovering and formulating project management knowledge:

My charter was quite broad—to use my research products in order to improve project management at P&G As it turned out, my sponsor (Mr. Gordon Denker, Manager of Global Product Supply Engineering), who encouraged me to "consult by wandering around," was the key to my ability to function both as a consultant and as a researcher. Although he set down some general guidelines, I was basically given a free hand in proposing my assignments. P&G was expecting that my "action research" role would in no way affect my commitment and service to them as a consultant.

I initiated a wide range of activities: training, review of procedures, development of tools, and many "learning-from-experience" discussions conducted in small groups. My main effort, however, focused on working directly with project teams in ongoing projects. Although their feedback was positive, I was still not satisfied.

During my third visit to Cincinnati, I realized that the conventional mode of consulting was insufficient for the quick, wide, and lasting assimilation that was essential for valid research implementation feedback.

My answer to this problem was storytelling. Why? Because I realized that my role was similar to that of an optometrist—trying to convince people that in order to change the way they viewed the world, they would have to change their eyeglasses. I also realized that people's minds are changed more through observation than through argument. I therefore thought that the telling of real-life stories by credible and successful managers, colleagues from their own company, would serve as an efficient substitute for observation.

The results of my effort at P&G exceeded my wildest expectations. At the conclusion of a workshop where project managers presented and discussed their stories, Mr. Denker commented: "I would never have believed that such a profound change in language, focus of attention, and way of thinking could have taken place within a two-year period."

For me personally, however, the most unexpected and lasting result of using stories at P&G was realizing that stories have unique power, not only for sharing knowledge but also for generating new knowledge. As a researcher, I found that this was indeed a very effective way to learn from practitioners. This eye-opening experience has completely changed my own paradigm regarding research methods in project management.[32]

Why are stories so effective for generating project management knowledge? We will start by exploring what we understand by "knowledge."

Knowledge may be compared to a spectrum. At one extreme, it is almost completely tacit—semiconscious and unconscious knowledge stored in the minds of individuals. At the other end of the spectrum, knowledge is almost completely explicit and structured and accessible to people other than the individuals originating it. Most knowledge, of course, exists between the two extremes.[33]

Project management lies somewhere between a "technology" and a "craft," though probably closer to a craft.[34] It is not like that of laboratory technicians or bookkeepers, who have highly structured practices and procedures that can be completely described and taught with the aid of formal rules. It is also not exactly like skilled trades, which are acquired mainly through demonstration and apprenticeship, such as bricklaying and carpentry. While some aspects of project management knowledge are explicit, a great deal of it, especially in a dynamic, complex, and fast-changing environment, is tacit.[35]

Now we can attempt to understand why stories are so effective for generating project management knowledge. A variety of sources dealing with the ways of capturing tacit knowledge support the view that "a good story is often the best way to convey meaningful (tacit) knowledge."[36] Weick and Browning assert that "narration, much like metaphor, has power precisely because it captures complex experiences that combine sense, reason, emotion, and imagination. Narration blends all those elements together and preserves their interaction in a compact summary."[37] Henry Mintzberg, reflecting on his own experience as a researcher, also underscored the importance of stories for theory development: "I need to be stimulated by rich description . . . I need to be stimulated by rich inputs that I see right before me. Tangible data is best . . . And stories are best of all, because while hard data may suggest some relationship, it is this kind of rich description that best helps to explain it."[38]

My research projects ascertained more than 500 stories from over 150 competent practitioners, which eventually led to the publication of the following three books and one magazine, all serving as rich sources of examples for the current book:[39]

- *In Quest of Project Excellence through Stories*: Stories by project managers from P&G (1994).
- *Project Management Success Stories: Lessons of Project Leaders:* Stories by project managers from eight agencies of the U.S. federal government (2000).
- *Shared Voyage: Learning and Unlearning from Remarkable Projects*: Stories by project managers from AeroVironment, California Institute of Technology, Johns Hopkins Applied Physics Laboratory, Lockheed Martin, NASA, Raytheon, and the U.S. Air Force (2005).
- *ASK, Academy Sharing Knowledge, the Magazine of the NASA Academy of Program and Project Leadership*: Stories by project managers from

NASA, the U.S. Air Force, and various industrial companies (launched in 2001).[40]

Although stories told by experienced practitioners provide a great opportunity for learning by uncovering tacit knowledge and converting it into explicit knowledge, the limitations of this research avenue cannot be ignored. First, people have a tendency to seek information that confirms their own ideas rather than to look for evidence that opposes them. Second, positive feedback (i.e., successful outcomes) is weighted more heavily in memory than negative feedback. Finally, the results of decisions are the consequences of actions taken in specific environments. People are frequently unaware of the structure of the environment in which such actions took place and thus may interpret the results incorrectly.[41]

In my studies, I meticulously attempted to address these risks, particularly by selecting competent practitioners and by developing an open atmosphere in which their awareness of these limitations was constantly enhanced. Whenever possible, I corroborated the information with additional sources, such as written documents or stories collected from other project participants.

The most effective measure that I adopted was to alternately employ the story-based approach and the complementary research approach of classic structured studies, such as interviews and observations of practitioners in the field,[42] always keeping in mind the unique strengths of each approach.[43] For example, by switching my focus back and forth from the generalization power of classic research to the power of story-based studies to convert tacit knowledge into explicit knowledge, I was able to formulate better questions for the next study and thus develop a better understanding of project management. Eventually, with the continuous and active help of some of the finest practitioners, this process allowed me to make significant progress toward breaking the code of project management.

Sharing Knowledge: Catering for Different Learning Styles

One may say that in my research, I applied Ashby's law of requisite variety.[44] This well-known law of cybernetics—"only variety can absorb variety"—states that the greater the variety of actions available to a control system, the greater the variety of perturbations it is able to compensate. In other words, a system cannot meet increasing variety in its environment unless it increases the range of its response repertoire. I attempted to cope with the limitations of each research approach by adopting both approaches.

However, Ashby's law of requisite variety is relevant not only for the researcher at the early stages of knowledge generation, but also for the reader at the later stages of knowledge consumption. This is the primary reason for the makeup of this book—a composition of brief stories of practitioners affiliated with a wide range of successful organizations, combined with the results of more traditional "by the book" research. However, beyond the "general" rationale of Ashby's law, there are two additional rationales more specifically suited to this format, the first related to learning and the second to unlearning.

Learning through Stories

We all know that most people love to read stories because they attract and captivate, can convey a rich message in a non-threatening manner, and are memorable.[45] The fact that most people are attracted to stories is crucial, especially in situations where the prospective learner suffers from a lack of time—which is the case with most project managers.

In his discussion on the features of good stories, Klein explains that "drama, empathy, and wisdom are key. Stories are remembered because they are dramatic. They are used because we can identify with one or more of the actors. They are told and retold because of the wisdom they contain—the lessons that keep emerging with each telling."[46] Jalongo and Isenberg emphasize the importance of stories for learning: "Narrative is the spark that illuminates our professional life . . . Even when the story 'belongs' to someone else, we can identify so strongly that it becomes intertwined with our own experience. It is when we are without any story, borrowed or lived, that learning and progress slow down or even stall."[47]

Stories are also an excellent tool for enhancing reflection.[48] In his book *Managers Not MBAs*, Mintzberg stresses that "activity becomes 'experience' only after it has been reflected on thoroughly." He cites T.S. Eliot, who wrote in one of his poems, "We had the experience but missed the meaning." He also cites Saul Alinsky, who argues, "Most people do not accumulate a body of experience. Most people go through life undergoing a series of happenings, which pass through their systems undigested. Happenings become experiences when they are digested, when they are reflected on, related to general patterns, and synthesized."[49] Organizations have long found stories useful for a variety of purposes, such as introducing change and fostering organizational identity and values.[50] In recent years, many leading organizations have started using stories to capture and disseminate knowledge, in particular when attempting to create a "learning organization."[51]

Unlearning through Stories

"Creating a 'learning organization' is only half the solution," assert Hamel and Prahalad. They recommend that in addition to the familiar "learning curve," companies should establish a "forgetting curve," referring to the rate at which a company can unlearn those habits that hinder future success. They stress, however, that pursuing unlearning is not easy. First, unlearning is more difficult than learning, and second, the real difficulty is how to be selective, that is, to decide what part of the past should be forgotten and what should not.[52] March and associates also reported that organizations do not easily abandon previously believed theories and that, in general, learning from history is conservative and tends to sustain existing beliefs.[53]

The second section of this introduction (Project Management Reform is Required) makes a strong case for unlearning outdated concepts of project management. However, unlearning that requires us to change our mind-set is difficult, often simply because we are unaware of our mind-set in the first place. Peter Drucker opens his book *Management Challenges for the 21st Century* with the question, "why do assumptions matter?"[54] He replies that basic assumptions about reality are the paradigms of management and are usually held subconsciously by scholars, writers, teachers, and practitioners. Yet, Drucker explains, "Those assumptions largely determine what the discipline—scholars, writers, teachers, practitioners—assume to be reality."[55] Peter Senge raises a related question: why are mental models so powerful in affecting what *we do*? He suggests that, in part, it is because they affect what *we see*. Senge explains, "Two people with different mental models can observe the same event and describe it differently, because they have looked at different details . . . They observed selectively."[56]

Very often stories may facilitate unlearning. As Nisbett and Ross suggest, people are more inclined to change their mind-set on the basis of vivid information. They explain that information is considered vivid when it is emotionally interesting, concrete, and imagery provoking, as well as proximate in a sensory, temporal, and spatial way.[57] Good real-life stories told by successful and credible managers usually convey vivid information and thus may facilitate changing mind-sets.[58] Moreover, such stories may serve as an efficient substitute for observation, which is more persuasive than arguments in changing people's mind-sets. In addition, the attraction of stories and their non-threatening nature is conducive to reading multiple stories that advocate the same kind of unlearning, thus enhancing the chances that stories will indeed facilitate unlearning.[59]

Catering for Different Learning and Unlearning Styles

While stories have apparently unique advantages for facilitating both learning and unlearning, research tells us that people have different learning (and unlearning) styles. David Kolb describes learning as "the process whereby knowledge is created through the transformation of experience.

Knowledge results from the combination of grasping experience and transforming it."[60] Kolb further explains that people differ in their preferred grasping style (via abstract conceptualization or concrete experience) and in their preferred transformation process (using reflective observation or active experimentation).[61] Since different people may prefer different learning means, using a variety of formats for conveying knowledge is essential for reaching a wider population.

A similar rationale is applicable when helping people to unlearn, as employing a variety of formats can also facilitate changing different mind-sets. In his book *Changing Minds,* Howard Gardner presents seven factors that can facilitate changing a mind-set. He asserts that "[since] a group of individuals can readily come up with different mental versions [of a phenomenon] . . . the potential for expressing the desired lesson in many compatible formats is crucial."[62]

Therefore, this book shares knowledge via a variety of formats, such as stories, results of classic research, and direct quotes from prominent practitioners and researchers. This variety should facilitate both learning and unlearning for readers with varying learning styles and mind-sets.

The Principles of Results-Focused Leadership

Throughout the years, I have periodically shared and discussed my interim findings with practitioners to get their feedback on the way in which I described the "how" and attempted to explain the "why" of their practices. Gradually, I was able to develop a "theory of practice" and to formulate a set of actionable principles on the basis of research carried out in a variety of areas, disciplines, and settings. These principles were tested successfully and found to be applicable to a wide spectrum of business, technology, and social projects—from modifying a management information system to new product development, and even to a hospital fund-raising project.[63]

While developing, testing, and refining the content of this "theory of practice," I came to realize that the product I am offering is first and foremost a "theory as a tool" for the practitioner. Thus, the primary purpose of the principles is not simply to mirror reality, but rather to help the practitioner shape reality.

Results-Focused Leadership can be described by five principles, each composed of three guidelines.[64] The following two figures (exhibits 0.1 and 0.2) introduce the reader to the five principles, illustrating both their independent roles as well as their complementary nature. The first exhibit, "Results-Focused Leadership: Essence of the Principles," graphically and most succinctly describes each of the principles while highlighting the unique nature of each principle. The second exhibit, "Results-Focused

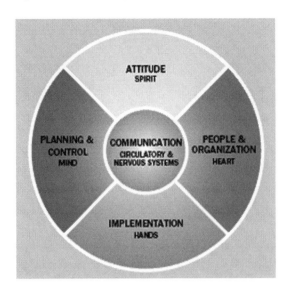

Exhibit 0.1   Results-Focused Leadership: Essence of the principles

Exhibit 0.2   Results-Focused Leadership: The human metaphor

Leadership: The Human Metaphor," shows how we, as human beings, resort to using many different, yet complementary, resources in our lives while underscoring their mutual interdependence.

The colors were selected to reflect some of the unique characteristics of each of the principles.

Green (vegetation and growth):
for planning: suggests the growing, learning-based, and evolving nature of project planning and control in a dynamic environment.

Brown (earth):
for implementation: suggests the down-to-earth, practical, and results-based focus.

Yellow (sunshine and optimism):
for attitude: suggests the spirited nature of the required "will to win" leadership.

Red (heart):
for people and organization: suggests the softer aspects of people and teams, in particular feelings, emotions, and warm and trusting relationships.

Gray (drab, fog):
for communication: suggests the endless, ongoing, non-heroic, and tedious efforts required for project communication. (It also represents the nebulous ambiguity resulting from continuous irrelevant and unclear information—a problem that frequent, intensive, and rich communication may help resolve.)

Results-Focused Leadership: Principles and Guidelines

Following are the five principles of Results-Focused Leadership, each described by three specific guidelines (Table 0.1).

This book is designed around the five principles of Results-Focused Leadership, with a chapter devoted to each principle. All five principles are equally important for project success, and during project life there is no "right" sequence for their implementation. However, from years of presenting these principles to both practitioners and graduate students, I have found that the above sequence facilitates understanding and learning. Although each of the five principles has a crucial role in project success, the two principles that most directly propel the project forward are the Yellow and the Brown principles. Therefore, the model is termed Results-Focused Leadership.

The five principles are presented separately as if they are independent of each other, when in fact they are quite interdependent. Moreover, to

Table 0.1 The five principles of Result-Focused Leadership

The green principle: Plan and control to embrace change

- The first green guideline: Define project objectives while quickly exploring the means
- The second green guideline: Employ a learning-based planning and control process
- The third green guideline: Use an appropriate amount of redundancy

The brown principle: Create a results-oriented focus

- The first brown guideline: Create and maintain a focus
- The second brown guideline: Think deliverables
- The third brown guideline: Act with agility

The yellow principle: Develop a will to win

- The first yellow guideline: Develop a sense of mission
- The second yellow guideline: Challenge the status quo
- The third yellow guideline: Persevere, but know when to retreat

The red principle: Collaborate through interdependence and trust

- The first red guideline: Take recruiting very seriously
- The second red guideline: Develop trust-based teamwork
- The third red guideline: Assess team functioning and recharge its energy

The gray principle: Update and connect through intensive communication

- The first gray guideline: Pull and push information frequently
- The second gray guideline: Employ a variety of communication mediums, with face time as top priority
- The third gray guideline: Adopt a moving about mode of communication

understand and use them correctly, all five principles must be adjusted to the unique environment of each project.

Results-Focused Leadership: Meta-Principles

In addition to the five basic principles are two meta-principles embedded within each one, thus stressing the connections between the principles themselves and between the project and its environment. Following are the two meta-principles that are highlighted in every chapter of this book:

- Embrace and apply these principles as general instructions that must be tailored to the unique context of the project (e.g., project size, stability of objectives, speed, task complexity, organizational culture, extent of top management support, and team members' experience and skills).

- The implementation of any one principle and its impact on project success depends on the implementation of all the others. To compensate for the inability to fully adhere to a principle, be prepared to modify the implementation of the others as well as to adjust project expectations.

Finally, a word on how to read this book and what to expect from it, particularly as a novice project manager. Once you have read the first two chapters and accepted the changes required in a few primary assumptions about current projects (e.g., greater uncertainty, speed, and complexity), embracing each of the five principles separately should not be too difficult. You will find that it is nothing but common sense. However, a full understanding of the meta-principles will probably require more effort. They will be fully embraced only gradually as you progress through the book.[65]

As for more experienced project managers, some of you may approach the principles as knowledge that must first be read and absorbed completely and only then implemented as a set of practices. Others may quickly attempt to implement the principles and only then find the need to fully understand the theory behind them. Yet others may alternate their focus, from learning some of the theory to implementing part of the practices and again returning to the theory.[66] I believe that all three approaches are valid and that it is largely a matter of personal preference as to which particular learning style is adopted. However, when one considers the need for unlearning as well as for learning, the alternate approach often has the most to offer, since it is more likely to bring about, gradually and naturally, the required shift in mind-set.[67]

It is my hope that both novice and experienced project managers alike will take away many things from this book. I hope that the concepts and practices, highlighted by the stories of project managers and supported by research findings, will help you, the reader, to focus on the changes required in your own environment. I hope that you will internalize the principles distilled from these stories to help guide your thoughts and actions in your own project. But, above all, I hope to instill you with the confidence that the lessons herein do not just apply to "other people." You can learn them. You can apply them. You too can become a Results-Focused Leader.

CHAPTER 1

The Green Principle: Plan and Control to Embrace Change

The First Green Guideline: Define Project Objectives While Quickly Exploring the Means

Organizations create projects to meet a variety of their business, technical, organizational, or political needs. During a project's early phases, one of the more important tasks of the project team is to translate undefined needs into clear objectives and requirements. Typically, several successive sets of objectives are developed, with each set being more detailed than its predecessor. The first set mainly focuses on the business and functional objectives, while each of the more detailed sets translates the previous set of objectives into technical requirements.

Following is an example of the requirements formulated for a hydroelectric dam project:

- To produce 80 megawatts of electric power at the start and 100 megawatts a year later
- To provide 15,000 cubic meters of irrigation water
- To provide an object of national pride
- To use local materials and labor
- To be completed by February 1, 20XX
- To be installed and begin operation at a cost of no greater than $240 million

The rationale for setting project objectives seems quite obvious, as without proper objectives the team might find itself trying to do the task right without necessarily doing the right task. The famous example from *Alice in Wonderland* articulates this very succinctly: "If you don't know where you're going, any road will get you there."

The negative implications of poorly defining requirements have been elaborately discussed in the literature. Boar asserts that "a number of 'sources of system error' studies show that 60–80% of all errors originate in [requirements] definition."[1] Davis concluded that "the top five causes for poor cost estimation all relate to the requirements process."[2]

Gause and Weinberg indicate that billions of dollars are squandered each year in building products that fail to meet requirements, primarily because the requirements were never clearly understood from the start. Using the results of a study by Barry Boehm on software development, they demonstrated the impact of late detection of an error made during the requirements phase of the project. The study shows that if the relative cost of fixing the error during the requirements phase is one unit, then fixing it would cost 3–6 units during the design phase and 30–70 units later on during the acceptance test, whereas the cost of fixing this same problem during operation would be as high as 40–1000 units.[3]

However, Gause and Weinberg claim that these numbers do not cover the entire range of potential damage resulting from poor requirements. First, Weinberg studied only completed projects, though an estimated one-third of large software projects are never completed mainly due to poor requirements definition. Second, several of the examples provided illustrate how poor requirements led to design errors in deficient products that were detected only after years of service and thus resulted in staggering damages.

It is therefore not surprising that the literature pays great attention to the development of project objectives and offers a variety of methods for eliciting the appropriate technical requirements. These methods include interviews, facilitated workshops, and focus groups, as well as the observation of similar products in use.[4] Gathering of raw data from the customer is typically followed by analysis, which may include prioritizing and establishing the relative importance of needs. At this stage, different alternatives may be offered to the customer for evaluation. Once the needed choices are made, the formal requirements specification documents can be prepared.

The prescribing literature implies that valid requirements may be ensured by systematically and carefully eliciting and documenting the complete set of requirements prior to embarking on development of the means for accomplishing them. However, the research literature and the project teams I studied suggest that one should not attempt to finalize the requirement setting process before starting to develop the means.

Project Planning as Uncertainty Reduction

The following story, told by Dr. Michelle Collins from Kennedy Space Center, raises the question of the right timing for completing the development of project requirements.

Table 1.1 Requirements for an Automatic Teller Machine

Senior Project Managers	Junior Project Managers
Functionality	Provide money in the form of $20s with no fee and warn Home Office of empty condition at least one hour in advance of becoming empty.
Reliability	With minimal annual maintenance, the ATM does not break down.
Security	The ATM communicates with the Home Office continuously including a video feed.
User-friendly	The ATM accepts at least 10 major credit cards and operates in 6 major languages with complete instructions provided where a withdrawal transaction, including printing the receipt, occurs in less than 60 seconds.

At a meeting of NASA project managers, the group was involved in an exercise on requirements. As Michelle narrates,

You are given a project to develop the software for an Automatic Teller Machine (ATM). Write four requirements . . . The group was a mix of senior and junior Project Managers (PMs). We broke into pairs to come up with the four requirements for the ATM, and then we regrouped to discuss our findings. Several of the pairs consisted of one senior PM and one junior PM . . . All three senior PMs gave requirements that were extremely brief and general; the junior PMs offered lengthy and fairly explicit requirements.

An example of a pair of responses is provided in Table 1.1.[a]

Prior to discussing the intriguing question of why the veteran project managers exhibited caution and did not rush to elaborate on the requirements, it is worthwhile to consider a personal story focusing on my own research, which was later recounted in *ASK Magazine*.

I was invited by the Construction Industry Institute (CII), a research consortium of top American companies and universities, to do research on project planning. During my research, I interviewed 39 project managers at 11 large U.S. corporations (e.g., AT&T, DuPont, Exxon, General Motors, IBM, and Procter & Gamble).

I asked each manager a series of questions about planning at the early phase of a project. Rather than confirming what I expected to hear, out of this process came something I didn't understand. Again and again, the managers I spoke with told me that they searched for potential solutions, i.e., they started engineering designs before they finalized their project objectives.

"Objectives first, means second," and "Define the problem, then solve it." That is what I had been taught as a student, and that is what I taught to my own students. But top-notch managers at well-respected companies were telling me that they didn't work that way. In almost all my interviews, I observed the same discrepancy. The objective formation process is not an isolated activity, and it is not completed before searching for alternatives begins. This astonished me or, to be honest, it shocked me.

It took me a long time before I could attain full understanding of my new observations and even longer to let go of old concepts and accept new learning. I went back through the literature and re-read pioneering works by highly respected scholars such as James March and James Thompson. I slowly found support for my new understanding of project planning. Unlearning required a lot of reinforcement.[b]

What did I learn from the CII study? First, it helped to identify two types of uncertainty: "end uncertainty" (what to do) and "means uncertainty" (how to do it). One useful definition of uncertainty for our context is "the difference between the amount of information required to perform the task and the amount of information already possessed by the project team." Both types of uncertainty must be resolved as a project moves from conception to reality. "End uncertainty" is considered to be completely resolved when project objectives and technical requirements are stable and well defined. "Means uncertainty" is considered to be completely resolved when the design and implementation plans are complete and stable.[5] Under the old paradigm, it was assumed that "end uncertainty" is completely resolved before one starts addressing "means uncertainty." The central foundation of that established paradigm is "Define the problem prior to embarking on its solution." This philosophy goes far beyond project planning. It considers the major criterion of rational decision making to be a complete separation between the setting of objectives and the selection of solutions. This has been the core principle of the problem-solving method upon which we have all been raised and educated, from first-grade arithmetic problems to graduate school research projects.

The second thing I learned from the CII study was that in today's projects "end uncertainty" is NOT completely resolved before one starts addressing "means uncertainty," and the development of a project, from concept to reality, is actually a process of uncertainty reduction. However, the CII had difficulty in accepting the notion of "uncertainty reduction" and chose instead to present my finding as "certainty enhancement."[6]

It is important to note that the CII is not unique in its reluctance to acknowledge uncertainty. In his book *Learning to Plan and Planning to Learn*, Donald Michael discusses this common attitude: "On the basis of their observations of many situations, Don Schon and Todd La Porte argue that acknowledging high levels of uncertainty to self and to others is emotionally so painful, so anxiety-producing—particularly for those who see themselves as contributing to the rationality of their organization—that people will repress their awareness that they 'know they don't know' or they will avoid situations that confront them with uncertainty; or they will treat such situations as if they were not uncertain."[7]

Together with colleagues, I subsequently verified the CII results with a sample of 93 project managers from across the United States. They were asked to rate the degree of "end uncertainty" at the beginning of construction. According to the old paradigm, one would have expected uncertainty about "what to do" to be very low in almost every case at the start of construction. However, the study showed that as late as the start of construction, approximately 80 percent of capital projects suffer from significant "end uncertainty."[8]

The issue of formulating objectives and developing the means to accomplish them has been addressed by highly recognized management scholars from various disciplines. March, who has conducted extensive research on decision making, concluded that "the argument that goal development and choice are independent behaviorally seems clearly false. It seems to me perfectly obvious that a description that assumes that goals come first and action comes later is frequently radically wrong. Human choice behavior is as much a process for discovering goals as for acting on them."[9]

In one of his studies on strategic planning, Henry Mintzberg analyzed the "design school" of strategic management, whereby strategies can be implemented only after they are first fully formulated. He concluded that "there are times when thought does, and should, precede action and guide it . . . Other times, however, especially during or immediately after a major unexpected shift in the environment, thought must be so bound up with action in an interactive and continuous process that 'learning' becomes a better label, and concept, for what happens then is 'formulation-implementation.'"[10]

In the area of software development, Cusumano concluded that in custom software projects, users often do not know what they want until they see part of the system in front of them.[11] Software development will be further discussed in Chapter 2.

Similar conclusions have been reached in elaborate empirical studies conducted worldwide. For example, a study of 308 decision processes in West Germany was able to show that the goal formation process is not completed before the beginning of the problem-solving activity. The rationale provided by the researcher was that the insight into possible solutions influences the decision makers' ideas of what they really want.[12]

Likewise, in their study of 211 R&D projects, Baker et al. concluded that "the extent to which the project's business and technical goals were well-defined and widely recognized at the time of initiation was not significantly related to the project's eventual success or failure. However, late in the life of the project the relationship was statistically significant. Business and technical goals for successful projects became better defined and more widely recognized over the life of the project than did the goals for unsuccessful projects."[13]

Now we are better equipped to reflect on and understand the opening story regarding the level of detail in the requirements given for an ATM machine, which presents striking differences between experienced and junior project managers. The experienced project managers knew that since the scenario was posed very early, at the beginning of the conceptual phase of their task, it was advisable to quickly examine the means rather than immediately attempting to formulate the requirements in great detail.[14]

How one should go about quickly examining the means is the focus of the rest of this guideline, which presents two practices employed by successful project managers:

1. Seek Input from the Implementers
2. Learn by Prototyping

First Practice: Seek Input from the Implementers

The idea that the customers should clearly know, in total and final detail, what they want before briefing the implementers—designers and manufacturers—is expecting too much. The following example demonstrates that insight into possible solutions and the available alternatives influences customers' ideas of what they really want, as well as what they can afford.

In December 1995, U.S. Air Force program director Terry Little was asked to rescue the floundering joint air-to-surface standoff missile (JASSM) program. When he was brought in to run the project, five companies competed for the contract. His first duty was to provide the companies with the requirements that should be guiding the preparation of their proposals. For the first three months, Little held weekly update meetings with representatives from each of the five companies.

When we sat down together, I would ask: Give me some feedback. Tell me specifically about this requirement. Does the path we're headed down seem right to you? Is there a requirement—or two or three or four—which you think is not going to be consistent with us getting a low-cost system? What I want to know is: Are we spinning our wheels in some area that we don't really understand, and what are the implications?

From my point of view I was trying to learn—as opposed to just trying to squeeze information out of them . . . They could tell us that this or that was a dumb requirement. We suggested a requirement, for example, to put this weapon on a number of different kinds of airplanes. A couple of the companies said, "We've looked at that, and we can do that, but it's going to take a really long time to go through all of the engineering details. If we could just start off putting it on one or two planes and get this thing built and fielded, and then modify it if we need to, we would be much better off in terms of overall cost, overall schedule, and overall performance. Give us a problem that we can work, and then add this additional scope after that."

Little's strategy challenged his government team and industry partners to completely rethink existing paradigms of acquisition reform. As he boldly suggested,

The general view in the government was that this wasn't the way you should do things at this stage of a program. Once you decide on your requirements, then you call in the contractor and say, "Here is exactly what we are going to do, we've got it all figured out, and now it is up to you to respond." I didn't think that was the way to get the most bang for the buck. I wanted the five companies who were going to bid to be involved in the process of refining the requirements. Since they were the ones who had to respond to whatever innovations we pitched, it didn't seem to me to be in their best interest—or ours—to say, "Okay, this is what we're going to do, and you companies are going to learn how to adjust." I thought the best way to improve our chances of getting a quality product was to allow for some give-and-take at this stage when our vision for the missile was still in flux.

We sometimes have a problem in DOD in that we establish a requirement without understanding: What does it really mean to try and satisfy that requirement? Until you understand the implications of what you are asking for, in terms of what it costs and how it affects schedule, it can't possibly be a firm requirement. The fact of the matter is that most requirements are just things someone made up. It starts off as somebody's opinion or view of what would be good; but what often happens is that everybody then begins to march as if it's a law of nature that you've got to meet this requirement. However much time it takes, and however much money it takes, it doesn't matter because the requirement is the requirement."[c]

Seeking input from the implementer can easily take place when representatives of downstream project phases are regularly involved in planning from the earliest possible moment.[15]

In my CII study, I found this to be the case in many progressive companies. Accordingly, the owner's project manager and his/her core team, which is typically created in the early stages of the feasibility studies, will be joined by the leadership of the engineering design contractor at the beginning of the conceptual planning phase. Leading owner representatives in the areas of procurement and contracts, as well as representatives from the manufacturing plant, are also brought in around that time. The leadership of the construction contractor and of the important equipment vendors will join during the conceptual planning phase or at the beginning of the project definition phase. Often, the end user (in addition to the customer who initiates, defines, and pays for the project) will also take an active part in project definition and sometimes even in earlier phases.

One particular early involvement approach that has received great attention in the construction industry is constructability. It is a process in which construction implementation, knowledge, and experience are used during project definition, preliminary design, and detailed design. Similar approaches, such as procurability, operability, and maintainability, also call for the early involvement of respective representatives in project planning.[16]

The Role of Constructability Changes throughout the Project Life

During detailed design engineering, the primary role of constructability is to expedite the transfer of information from engineering to construction. In general, early involvement of downstream representatives in upstream planning enables the timely accessing of essential information. This early transfer of information helps to better prepare the downstream team for implementation. To compete better in a relay race, the next runner starts warming up and actually starts running before the baton is handed off. The same thing happens in successful projects. Early involvement ensures that when the time comes for responsibility to be passed, there is no stop and start because the leadership of the next phase is already fully up to speed.

Earlier, during preliminary design engineering, its primary role is to trigger the development of innovative solutions, identify short cuts, trim fat, and, in general, foster the ease and expediency with which the facility can be constructed. In novel situations, optimization based on the refinement of an existing solution is neither the most promising nor the most time-effective approach. Significant and timely improvements may result from quick divergence based on identifying and addressing new problems. This can best be achieved by a team with sufficient skill diversity that includes representatives of downstream phases.

Very early, during project definition, constructability serves a key role in fulfilling the practice *seek input from the implementer*. Its primary role here is to provide quick feedback that will help to identify and prevent wrong decisions as early as possible. Many of these wrong decisions can be identified only during the development of the requirements, but certainly not earlier. The most qualified people to identify those possible future obstacles are downstream representatives who can preempt the future by providing quick answers and by asking the right questions in time.[17]

Involving representatives of downstream project phases in planning from the earliest possible moment has one more important outcome: it facilitates the vertical integration of the project organization. This subject will be discussed in Chapter 4.

Second Practice: Learn by Prototyping

Ends and means are typically developed successively, in a chain. For example, the contractor's work serves as the means for accomplishing the client's ends, while the supplier's work serves as the means for accomplishing the contractor's ends. In this means-ends chain, each transition demands requirements to be specified and agreed upon between the two involved parties. The following example, taken from the JASSM project, focuses on the agreement that had to be developed between the contractor and its suppliers.

> The JASSM project was based on competition in two phases. During the first phase (which was discussed earlier), in which five companies competed, two won. In the second phase (which is the focus of the current example), following a 24-month program definition and risk reduction phase, one company was awarded the contract for the full-scale engineering and production.

> *When it came out to choosing which company would be awarded the contract, we would have liked for it to have been a difficult decision. However, it was not a difficult choice. One company was clearly the stronger of the two. The one that lost didn't do a bad job . . . Their suppliers complained that the prime was unwilling to give them the money to build prototypes . . . [they explained to the prime contractor] "Unless you give us the money to do some prototyping, we aren't going to be able to give you a firm price."*

> Terry Little (JASSM's program director) explains why learning via prototyping is not so common:

> *You do prototyping up front and then see if something works like you think it will. Sometimes it will, most of the time it won't, but then you learn from that. In many respects, that is the best way to learn. Unfortunately we don't do enough of that type of learning because we would like to believe that if we get enough smart people together, we can just run through the numbers, put them in the model, do the simulation, and it will all come out just like it is supposed to. But in the real world, it rarely happens the way we predict with our models. Unfortunately prototyping is not cheap—in terms of money or the time required to do it. It is messy and sometimes you are embarrassed with the results, but eventually you reach your goal. In the long run, it saves you money.*

> And Little comes back to the selection of the contractor for JASSM:

> *The company who won was not afraid to learn from its mistakes, and prototyping was an essential part of their strategy.*[d]

The next example, from NASA, presents an innovative and efficient way for developing prototypes and demonstrates how prototyping can increase the active participation of the users in project definition.

It was time to buy the next-generation data storage system for the Mission Control Center at Johnson Space Center. The traditional way of soliciting proposals from contractors yielded a very high price tag of $3 million. Steve Gonzales, who led this effort, had a better idea:

I realized that we had to learn first-hand to be better buyers, so I came up with the idea of inviting storage area network vendors to come on site and show us their capabilities and products. I hoped that by "test driving" the latest, greatest technology, our civil servants would be smarter buyers when it came time to choose a system . . . We cleared out two rooms, reached agreements with several companies, and then, one-by-one, put their storage systems through the paces that would enable them to be installed at Mission Control—in essence, testing out a series of prototypes of the systems we hoped to acquire . . . Our prototype project allowed us to better understand our requirements before investing in a system. One of the things we learned about was clustering capabilities that would enable us to better support the Space Station's 24-hour operation . . . While our people were brought up to speed on the latest technologies available, the companies got a heads-up on our requirements.

Eventually, one of the vendors did get the work.

Using the prototype concept, NASA got a better system for less money than had been thought possible ($750,000). And in the process, we became smarter customers and smarter buyers of new technology.[c]

At times, the best way to gauge the customer's needs is to build a working model of the crucial elements of the ultimate product. This is true even in more traditional industries, like construction, where customers have greater familiarity and more experience with the final product. This approach was adopted to define the requirements for the interior design of the corporate headquarters building of Procter & Gamble (P&G) in downtown Cincinnati. The large number of new offices meant that the design team needed to be certain about their decisions. If they made one mistake in the workstation design, for example, they could potentially repeat it 3,000 or more times.

The team decided that their best bet was to create a mock-up of the building's interior and to use it as a tool for learning. Therefore, they rented the entire sixth floor of a building which had the same column-bay spacing as was planned for the new building and which was within walking distance of the existing corporate headquarters.

With the understanding that their customers wanted an open-space office system, the team began constructing different furniture systems and decorating them with a variety of carpets, paints, lighting schemes, and window treatments. They even had people "occupy" the various office mock-ups in order to collect early feedback on the different settings. As the models were built, the design team developed cost and schedule implications for each design option.

Finally, the customers were invited for several cycles of reviews and mock-up changes resulting from their feedback. Eventually, when the customers fully understood the final product and its cost and schedule implications, and were satisfied with it, the final decisions regarding interior design requirements were made.[f]

The underlying reasons for prototyping some of the uncertain elements of a project are as follows:

- Prototyping increases the active participation of the user in project definition. It recognizes the user's preeminence in setting project requirements.
- Many users are not familiar with the technical terminology. Graphic and narrative documentation techniques are insufficient for communicating all of the users' requirements. Prototyping permits everybody to generate specifications in a familiar medium.
- Often the users being called upon to provide specifications for project definition are not professionals in that area, nor do they find specifying interesting or exciting. They often require assistance in defining their own needs. A working prototype provides physical anchors to enhance the appreciation of their needs. It also provides early feedback on the implications of their decisions.
- Prototyping helps to clarify difficult-to-describe items or intangibles, such as aesthetics, appearance, ambiance, etc.
- To be able to understand and critique some elements of the ultimate product, they must actually be experienced hands-on by the user, not just read or discussed.
- The real-world problems of ultimate acceptability can be tested and verified quickly by prototyping prior to the extensive commitment of resources.

To summarize, the two primary benefits of prototyping are as follows:

- Creating a real, one-to-one model of a project's critical elements and involving the user in the fine-tuning allows the user to learn directly and quickly what he/she really needs.
- While this process consumes time and resources, it ensures valid and reliable feedback from the user. In the final analysis, it brings about the early completion of stable requirements, which require few changes.[18]

Deliberate Planning and Deliberate Learning

The preceding analysis of the stories and the research literature demonstrates that effective definition of project objectives requires both deliberate planning and deliberate learning. Typical deliberate planning may include part or all of a chain of activities comprising information search and analysis, development of alternatives, analysis and evaluation of the alternatives, and choice making. Under the deliberate planning perspective, it is assumed that project requirements are thoroughly thought through before being implemented; in other words, learning stops before acting starts. However, the deliberate learning perspective of setting project objectives claims that learning requires acting and relies on an ongoing interaction between thinking and acting.

In the first practice, seek input from the implementers, learning takes place when the "thinkers and actors" interact early on while thinking has not as yet been completed. This allows the thinkers to seek direct input from the actors. In the second practice, learn by prototyping, learning is the direct result of the interaction of thinking and acting. The learning is termed "deliberate" because it is pursued intentionally and systematically in a "planned" manner. The project team is aware of its missing knowledge and information and pursues learning by employing constructability and prototyping as a routine practice.

Deliberate planning and deliberate learning are required throughout the project life, as will be demonstrated in the next guideline (Employ a Learning-Based Planning and Control Process).[19]

Before concluding the first guideline, three central questions should be raised. The first question is about balance. **What should be the right mix of planning and learning?** In other words, when should the team engage in more planning and when in more learning? There is no "one best answer" that will fit all projects. Rather, the application of planning and learning must be tailored to the unique context of each project. Project contextual factors, such as uncertainty, complexity, speed, and organizational culture, determine the right mix. The impact of project context on its management is crucial to the application of all five project principles, and it will be discussed throughout this book.[20]

The second question concerns speed. According to the current guideline, we should quickly explore the means to reduce end uncertainty. But what is the exact meaning of "quickly"? **How fast should we attempt to reduce uncertainty?** How fast should we freeze the requirements and stop engaging in both deliberate planning (e.g., stop developing rigorous specifications) and deliberate learning (e.g., stop prototyping)? The response to this question, however, is highly interrelated with the third question.

The third question is about change. In the current guideline, we focused on the innate difficulty of defining project objectives and technical requirements due to our inability "to discover our goals without first starting to act on them," or "deciding what we want before we see part of the system in front of us." Yet, in our dynamic environment, business needs may change significantly and rapidly. **What is the impact of change in business needs on project objectives and their technical requirements?** The impact of this additional source of uncertainty on project development will be discussed in the next guideline.

As already indicated, the second and third questions are highly inter-related and thus the second should be rephrased as follows: how fast should we try to reduce end uncertainty emanating from both changes in business needs and the innate difficulties in defining objectives? How long can we allow the changes in project requirements to continue before they destroy our chances of producing a meaningful and rela-tively stable project plan? For example, a turbulent environment cou-pled with a compressed timetable (not a rare situation nowadays) may often necessitate a significant overlap of project phases, pushing design engineering to begin before project definition is frozen. If this happens, the real question is at what point would we start experiencing the very same problems we discussed at the opening of this guideline, that is, the negative implications of poor requirements. This question will be addressed in Chapter 2.

The Second Green Guideline: Employ a Learning-Based Planning and Control Process

Planning is a decision-making process whereby interdependent decisions are integrated into a system of decisions. As Ackoff, one of the early pioneers of corporate planning, concluded, "The principal complexity in planning derives from the interrelatedness of the decisions rather than from the decisions themselves."[21]

Integrating decisions requires systematic effort, but what makes effec-tive project planning particularly challenging is that it entails an antici-patory decision-making process relating to what actions to perform at some point in the future and how to perform them. In today's dynamic environment, anticipation becomes more difficult, leaving project teams to wrestle with such questions as the plan's time horizon and its appropriate level of detail.[22]

Project planning fulfills multiple purposes, including setting project objectives, providing a basis for contractual commitments between the various parties, facilitating coordination and communication, and pro-viding a yardstick for monitoring project execution. Above all, its rai-son d'etre is to provide the guidelines for project execution.[23] One of the classic roles of project planning is to facilitate project control: "If planning establishes the targets and the course to reach them, control is the process that ensures the course of action is maintained and desired targets are reached. Control involves measuring and evaluating perform-ance, and the taking of corrective action when performance diverges from plans."[24]

In most of the classic books on project management "planning and control" was portrayed as the backbone for delivering successful projects. However, major changes, primarily outside the project world, have brought about a change in both the centrality of planning and control and the methods of carrying it out. While planning and control is still critical to project success, it is only one of several crucial factors. The changes in its centrality and its interaction with the other factors are addressed throughout this book, and the changes in planning and control practices are the focus of this guideline.[25]

Underestimating the Impact of the Project's Dynamic Environment

Various tools and procedures are used for project planning and control. The most notable among them is the critical path method (CPM), as illustrated in the following story.[26]

> U.S. Navy Lieutenant Commander Jim Wink was assigned a project with an extremely tight time schedule. To meet the deadline, he allowed the contractor to start work immediately rather than first having him submit a CPM schedule for approval, as required by navy policy.
>
> The project team, composed of the contractor, the engineering and construction staff, and the customer, began almost from the beginning to resolve problems as they arose. Important systems were redesigned to meet new building code requirements, and critical building elements were reengineered and constructed. Upon final project acceptance, the team proudly counted the over 200 action items that were resolved on time. However, one of the most critical issues—the CPM schedule—was never submitted. This is how Wink describes how he managed the project:
>
> *By all accounts, the project was a major success: timely completion and quality workmanship within budget. This success, without a network project schedule, went against the grain of traditional project management. The contractor made several attempts to put together a CPM. Each one, however, was made obsolete before submission by the fast pace of construction in the field. Given that astute schedule management is critical to success, how was this project able to be completed on time in the absence of a CPM?*
>
> *Long after the project was completed, I reflected on this situation. I remembered how adamantly we had demanded a CPM from the contractor. I also recalled how well the contractor and the rest of the team coordinated and scheduled major project events without the CPM. Not a week went by without my asking the contractor for a CPM, followed by a promise to deliver one ASAP. Fortunately for everyone involved, we moved on to solving those other issues and didn't let the lack of a CPM become a major point of contention.*
>
> *The more I reflect on it, it seems to me that with so many open issues and uncertainties arising from the nature and pace of the project, it was impossible to submit a comprehensive, detailed and useful plan. Only through the systematic, collaborative efforts of the team to identify areas of uncertainty, and then to solve them immediately, was the project a success.*

Wink adds that the contractor did manage to submit several CPM schedules that were not complete, and they proved valuable to the team even if they lacked all the data. According to Wink, the partial schedules, together with the weekly planning and review meetings, contributed to the success of the project.[g]

So what is the lesson of this story? The answer has to do with both the limitations of the tool itself and the constraints imposed by the dynamic conditions of the environment.

In the introduction to this book, we presented various sources that addressed the effectiveness of the pioneering project scheduling tool, PERT—a tool that was developed at approximately the same time that the CPM was developed and is in many ways similar to it. For example, Davies and Hobday concluded that "PERT . . . was a deeply flawed management tool."[27] We presented considerable evidence that the method was deliberately oversold, with the aim of keeping congressional and other external critics at arm's length. Intensive public relation efforts were able to create a myth of management effectiveness and as a result the "[U.S.] Department of Defense required that PERT be used for weapons system development contracts—actually coercing the dissemination of an innovation."[28] We also discussed the logic that drives organizations and practitioners to be locked into procedures that are not validated by experience while reassuring themselves that "after all, it [PERT] must be useful because many organizations use it!"[29]

Most practitioners, and probably many project management experts and researchers, are unaware of the severe shortcomings of this earlier project scheduling tool. However, they will all probably raise the natural question, why should it be relevant to Wink's case? Aren't today's scheduling tools more effective than the original PERT tool? As we will show later in this guideline, today's scheduling tools are obviously more sophisticated, but since the paradigm underlying their creation has not changed significantly, they are not necessarily more effective.[30]

The Three Major Factors
To better understand this "old paradigm," we must first understand the environment surrounding today's projects. Today's project environment, whose impact is still largely ignored or underestimated by the "old paradigm" of project management, is influenced by three major factors: project uncertainty, project speed, and the manager's scarcity of attention.

The first factor—uncertainty   In the First Green Guideline (Define Project Objectives While Quickly Exploring the Means), we presented research evidence demonstrating that very often project objectives (what to do) are not fully defined, even late in project life. We also presented a variety of sources explaining that this phenomenon, which we termed "end uncertainty," is an **innate problem**, since "insight into possible solutions influences the decision-makers' ideas of what they really want." As such, "human choice is as much a process for discovering objectives as for acting on them. "

However, in our "permanent white water" era, the difficulty of defining project objectives is due to additional factors, all stemming from the dynamic environment of the project. Therefore, very often "end uncertainty" is not fully resolved by the practices presented in the First Green Guideline. In his book *Learning as a Way of Being: Strategies for Survival in a World of Permanent White Water*, Peter Vaill argues that permanent white water conditions—a metaphor he uses to describe today's "sociotechnical systems"—are full of surprises and tend to produce novel problems that were not anticipated or imagined by those concerned with the system. Thus, due to market and/or technological uncertainty, very often project ends (what to do) and project means (how to do) are unstable, and both may remain unstable throughout the duration of the project.[31]

It is widely recognized that, to a great extent, this situation is the result of the significant transformation that industry and business have undergone in recent decades. In his analysis of the reasons for this transformation in the American market, Ian Mitroff asserts that in the past raw materials were relatively cheap and easily obtainable, the domestic market was strong and foreign markets were given scant attention, intercontinental bulk transportation was slow, the effects of business events in faraway places had only slight impact, and finally, production time and product life were stretched out, allowing a leisurely inception and planning pace. However, today, communication is instantaneous as computers have taken over, intercontinental transport takes a few hours by air as compared with the weeks or months of surface shipping, market restrictions have been reduced or eliminated, and any number of events occurring anywhere in the world can now instantly influence each of the other factors. In short, the world has become a village.[32] This may very well explain the adage, "The trouble with our time is that the future is not what it used to be."

Yet, the impact of these wide-ranging global changes on the theory of project management has been largely underestimated. In a comprehensive review of the history of the development of project management, published in 1994, Morris concluded, "Modern project management . . . emerged . . . in a period that was more inflexible and less complex and where events changed less rapidly than today."[33] He also argued that "it is [the theory of project management] in many respects still stuck in a 1960s time warp."[34]

The second factor—speed Since the mid-1980s, speed has become essential to business—to such an extent that many authorities argue that speed is the single most significant basis for competitive advantage in the years ahead. There are several reasons why speed has become a competitive requirement:

- Dramatic increase in global competition.
- Accelerated pace of technological development.
- Market share and profit margins are both increased by being first in the market.[35]

Hewlett-Packard has conducted studies demonstrating that while an engineering cost overrun of 50 percent impacts overall profitability by just 4 percent, a time delay of six months in project completion can result in a 32 percent loss in after-tax profit.[36] Davidow and Malone discussed the speed with which Japanese auto manufacturers develop new cars and compared it with that of their American and European counterparts: "Typically, from design to first delivery, a car takes forty-six months and 1.7 million engineering hours in Japan versus sixty months and 3 million engineering hours in the United States and Europe. The Japanese have used this time advantage to design cars that more closely track the ever-changing desires of customers . . . by focusing upon time in their race to dominated markets, the Japanese car manufacturers have managed to be industry leaders and specialty suppliers at the same time."[37]

While speed fever was originally confined to the industrial sector, today—with better and faster communications and with customers becoming more sophisticated—speed is demanded everywhere. In manufacturing and services alike, business, technical, and social projects are expected to be implemented at an ever-increasing pace. Customers want the product or service that is right for them, and they want it NOW!

Already in 2002, Charles Handy described the mounting speed fever: "A year in a day is exactly how it feels sometimes." And he explains, "All of the world's trade in 1949 happens in a single day today, all of the foreign exchange dealings in 1979 happen now in a single day, as do all the telephone calls made around the world in 1984."[38] This factor of speed is a direct obstacle to the fulfillment of "classic project planning," simply because a great deal of time is required for information gathering and for the systematic development and evaluation of alternatives.[39]

The third factor—scarcity of attention Insufficient time for planning is not a new phenomenon. One of the oldest observations about organizational decision making and planning is that managers' time and attention are scarce resources.[40] Planning is not only time consuming, but it also—and more importantly—requires quality time. This means that to facilitate the deliberation and pondering process, time must be free of any external stress. Moreover, since it is difficult to interrelate the incremental decisions that are made at different times, planning must be carried out within the protective wall of large blocks of uninterrupted time.

We have more than enough evidence, however, to indicate that managers do not have the kind of free time necessary for proper planning. Research shows that managers' activities are typified by brevity, variety, and fragmentation. Half of the activities of American executives were found to last less than nine minutes, and only 10 percent exceeded one hour. In a similar study made in Britain, it was found that middle and top managers were able to work without interruption for half an hour or more only once every two days.[41] Empirical studies portray the typical manager's life as leaving little time for reflection and analysis amid the pressure of short-term, interrupted, and somewhat chaotic activity.

The attention issue is at the center of a book by Davenport and Beck, who present a variety of examples demonstrating the growth of available information: "The Sunday New York Times contains more factual information in one edition than in all the written material available to a reader in the fifteenth century . . . Until the beginning of the twentieth century, most people still had enough wherewithal to learn an enormous percentage of the information available to them. In 1900, a well educated person could still grasp the existing knowledge in almost every field of science and art . . . Then the size of humanity's information base zoomed sharply upward."[42] They argue that the most obvious law of supply and demand in the attention economy is that "as the amount of information increases, the demand for attention increases. As Herbert Simon, a Nobel prize-winning economist, put it, 'what information consumes is rather obvious: it consumes the attention of its recipients. Hence a wealth of information creates a poverty of attention.'"[43] Not surprisingly, recent advances in information technology have not ameliorated the problem and in fact have done more to increase the information overload than to reduce it.[44]

The manager's shortage of time will be more severe under conditions of high uncertainty, since more information must be processed during execution.[45] The speed factor will naturally impose even more constraints on the project manager's available time. Thus, the three factors—uncertainty, speed, and scarcity of attention—are very much interrelated: the greater the uncertainty, the greater the degree of scarcity of attention; moreover, the greater the speed, the greater the uncertainty and the degree of scarcity of attention.

We are not yet ready to answer the question of why Wink's contractor was not able to produce and use the CPM tool. We may argue, however, that planning and control in today's dynamic environment requires much more than tools. Practice-based evidence shows that when one does not overlook or underestimate uncertainty, speed, and scarcity of attention, one must develop a new planning and control outlook. Generally, we tend to think that planning is solely aimed at developing stability. However, this new planning outlook, which places ongoing learning at its core, is aimed at developing both stability and the capability of responding quickly to change. Indeed, it embraces change.[46] This new planning and control outlook consists of the following two practices:

First Practice: Conduct Learning-Based Reviews
Second Practice: Employ an Evolving and Feedback-Based Planning Process

First Practice: Conduct Learning-Based Reviews

Project reviews are seen primarily as a means of control by the client and upper management. Brian Muirhead from NASA, who led the design, development, and launch of the flight system for the Pathfinder mission to Mars, describes the atmosphere prevailing during the review process: "The routine is daunting. The members of the board sit at a horseshoe-shaped table, the chairman in the middle. A team member stands up in front of them and launches into his presentation. It usually isn't very long before one of the review board members interrupts the presenter with a question—rather like an attorney presenting oral arguments before the Supreme Court. The skeptical expressions, the intense looks, the scowls and smiles, are giveaways. And just as at the Supreme Court, the questions are generally polite, occasionally harsh, but all with a clear aim of probing for the truth."[47]

Since project reviews are perceived as primarily serving the needs of upper management, there is insufficient attention paid to the overall needs of the project team, and in particular, to the negative implications of the preparations required for the review. Muirhead discusses the time leading up to a project review during the Pathfinder mission: "Formal project reviews come with a clear, but unavoidable, downside. Done well, the preparations can take an enormous amount of time for the team. Preparations for a formal board review can take too many of us—me and the project's top managers plus a number of key managers and engineers at the next level down—off the line for as much as six weeks. Necessary to the overall process, but a significant distraction; and even worse, a significant loss in momentum."[48]

Dissatisfaction with the perceived role and the actual practice of project reviews at NASA was shared by two other project managers, who took steps to radically change the situation.

> Marty Davis's project was once again up for review. Marty believed that project reviews should be for the benefit of the one being reviewed and not for the reviewer, and this time he was prepared to find better ways to approach the review process. First, he pushed for the creation of a review team made up of some internal technical staff as well as some external specialists. It was his view that the review process should provide feedback from

independent and supportive experts and should encourage joint problem solving rather than just reporting. Second, he requested that the same people participate in the various review milestones throughout the project life cycle in order to provide consistency and eliminate the need to revisit issues unless absolutely critical.

What I wanted was something more like how External Reviews are conducted, where you give a half to a full day of presentation and then the review team identifies where they want to meet one-on-one. You're being reviewed to a greater depth in selective areas. Something in the presentation that piques their interest is identified as something to review in more detail.

Marty was assigned an internal cochair and recommended an external cochair. He told both cochairs that they could have seven members each and that neither of them could duplicate the same technical specialties.

Some of our management at Goddard thought I was too involved in specifying what the composition of the review team should be. Indeed, I did specify the composition, but getting good people was the whole point as far as I was concerned.

Finally, Marty decided to go ahead and immediately incorporate his proposed approach into the review process. His next review lasted for two days, with one day of presentation and one day of one-on-one sessions, followed by a caucus with the review team. The independent experts identified areas of potential concern. The issues were discussed, and many of them were closed after being worked out in real time through one-on-one meetings with the specialized staff of the project and with the technical specialists on the review team side. The issues that remained open were assigned a request for action (RFA). Eventually, Marty was left with just five RFAs.

Many people regard reviews as something onerous, a crack review team can help you identify problems in your project, and that may make the difference between mission failure and mission success.[h,49]

In the following example, Susan Motil, a project manager from NASA, reports her own experience while employing Davis's model:

The Concept Review had not gone well, and my entire team was in the dumps . . . I told my supervisor that I would like to have some control over how the next review was done . . . A couple of weeks later, my supervisor came to me and said, "Read this article and let me know what you think." It was a story in ASK Magazine about reviews by Marty Davis, a project manager at Goddard Space Flight Center. I got hold of Marty in his office and told him what had happened with our review . . . He affirmed my own feeling that the project manager has to be involved in the selection of the review board. This doesn't mean that the panel is going to be less independent or that you're trying to hide a problem. It means that you're looking for particular expertise . . . Following Marty's lead, I asked for input before assembling the new review board . . . I wanted a panel with handpicked expertise and management approval, and that's what I got . . . I tailored my review similarly in that I had two sets of reviews, one for each subsystem, and then one for the system. It was amazing how well it worked . . . They would come in and sit around a table and have a dialogue with the engineers. The engineers could show the reviewers hardware, show them test data, and the reviewers could ask anything they wanted . . . Having the right reviewers on the panel is important, but I can't emphasize enough the importance of one-on-one communication . . . With every comment that the review panel made, they gave us valuable suggestions.

Finally, Motil compared the direct outcomes of the two review processes, the first unsuccessful Concept Review and the second review based on Davis's model. She found that following the second review, the team spent significantly less time and effort dealing with the RFAs. Estimating the cost of the two reviews, she found that the second review cost the project about $200,000 as compared with the $700,000 price tag for the first review.[i]

Changing mind-set and viewing reviews as a vital learning opportunity is not easy. While it is often the case that the reviewing organization refuses to abandon the "review as control" perspective, the reviewed organization may be equally resistant to changing its approach to reviews, either because of overconfidence or skepticism. In the following two examples, winning or losing a project was largely determined by whether the contractors were willing to be open and learn from project reviews.

The first example is shared by Ray Morgan, vice president of AeroVironment, and Jenny Baer-Riedhart, NASA's program manager of environmental research aircraft and sensor technology (ERAST).

In 1994, NASA initiated the ERAST program. ERAST was to be focused on converting high-altitude, long-endurance unmanned aerial vehicles (UAVs) into research platforms. Because of the extraordinary difficulty in controlling the risks involved, UAV industry development lagged far behind the interest in and knowledge of how to improve the technology.

To mitigate the risks and attempt to stimulate the industry, NASA adopted a radically different approach and formed a joint sponsored research program with four of the main players in the industry. ERAST required only nominal cost sharing by the companies. In exchange, NASA offered not only the rights to commercialize, but also ownership of all the hardware developed.

Following is Ray Morgan's account of AeroVironment's reviews, as one of the four companies participating in ERAST:

Because ERAST was a different way of doing business, we had to tailor almost everything about the program, and that included how we did reviews. In a typical NASA contract, you wouldn't rely on the contractor saying, "We're good to go," while NASA nods its head and says okay—but that's what we did. The companies could take NASA's advice, or they could ignore it altogether. The other alliance members had less experience than we did in developing UAVs, and they probably didn't have as much appreciation for processes and learning from the past . . . For the ERAST reviews, NASA would bring in people with experience in a particular area of aircraft development and testing, even though they often had no prior background with UAVs specifically . . . Even though they were not familiar with these particular types of light-wing structures, these were still experts in physics and engineering, and the atmosphere we were operating in was the same. Many times they provided the most value by simply asking questions.[j]

Jenny Baer-Riedhart, NASA's program manager of ERAST, describes the huge negative implications for one of the companies that did not take advantage of the reviews:

The companies who were not as open about accepting NASA's advice faired worse in this alliance. One of these companies we will call X. On paper, X was a superb company. Man for man, employee for employee, every one of them was a genius in his own right. Still, despite their superior IQs, they crashed their UAV—twice, actually . . . Had X been open to what NASA's experts pointed out during the reviews, they might well have kept from crashing . . . They chose not to discuss their problems, share information, or see reviews as something that they might learn from.[k]

The following example, taken from the JASSM project of the U.S. Air Force, focuses on the selection of the contractor. Terry Little, JASSM's program director, explains how two major underlying factors clearly distinguished between the two finalists. One factor, using prototyping, was already addressed in the First Green Guideline. Little's story below illustrates the second factor of using learning-based reviews:

The one that lost didn't do a bad job. They had good engineers, they used disciplined processes, but when they got feedback from the government, instead of listening to us and looking at what they were doing, they argued—"But you just don't understand." It was as though they had their plan and nothing was going to cause them to deviate from that. The other company listened to our feedback, and after their reviews would go back and decide. What is it that we need to change? Where is it that we need to put more emphasis? Where is it that we need to get rid of people? Where is it that we need to spend more money? Every time they got feedback, they saw it as an opportunity to adapt. There was no doubt; by the time we got to the last review, everybody knew who was going to win.[l]

The learning-based reviews are also highly regarded in industries that engage in more traditional projects, such as the design and construction of manufacturing facilities. One approach that naturally facilitates a learning rather than a control focus of the review is establishing review panels composed of peers, rather than senior managers or experts, who are expected to report to senior managers following the review. In praise of the peer review practice employed at P&G (see Exhibit 1.1), Scott Cameron asserts, "The most successful method we have found to improve project performance is to conduct anywhere between one and five peer reviews throughout the life of a project."

Exhibit 1.1 Peer review practice

Purpose of the Peer Review

To gain as much valuable input in the shortest amount of time to improve the chances for a successful project and avoid disasters and known (by others) problems.

Whom to Invite

Just peers, no hierarchy. The most successful peer reviews I have attended consisted of diverse groups of people: technical engineering, project managers, construction managers, purchasing managers, finance managers, research and development personnel, and contractors. Ten to twenty people are enough—any more than that becomes unmanageable, as each person will bring his/her own agenda.

What Protocol to Use

Peer review protocol is relatively simple. It requires the project team and the project manager to concisely communicate their technical and execution strategies. The floor is then opened to all the invited guests (peers) for comments, critique, and clarifying questions. Prework can be sent out to the peers to review prior to the meeting. Peers are required to be open, honest, and engage in the communication or not bother to attend the review.

How Long Should It Be

A maximum of six to eight hours, including lunch and breaks. The project manager usually runs the meeting and has to insure that all the "peers" are contributing ideas. There are a lot of topics to cover, but the project manager must go over them quickly to avoid one or more individuals grandstanding.

How to Summarize the Discussion

Take copious notes and display them on the wall during the meeting. In the last peer review I attended, there must have been 30–40 pages of flip-chart paper capturing all the ideas/comments on a $50MM project. These were then typed and distributed to all the participants with a note to them and their boss thanking them for their contributions and for helping improve the success of the project.

What to Expect of a Peer Review

Out of the 30–40 pages of notes on flip-chart paper, there were only five to ten "nuggets" that the project team went on to use and helped them to improve the technical, cost, and schedule aspects of the project. Implementing these nuggets more than made up for the cost of the peer review. As we have conducted more peer reviews, we've noted that the invited peers are beginning to take one or two "nuggets" they had not considered back to their projects and programs.[m]

Second Practice: Employ an Evolving and Feedback-Based Planning Process

As previously mentioned, managers' activities are typified by brevity, variety, and fragmentation, making it difficult to find the quality time needed for proper planning (i.e., integrating many interdependent decisions). This problem has led to the development of a new role, the staff specialist (i.e., a planner), who has more time for planning and can also develop better expertise in mastering the planning tools that are constantly improving and becoming more sophisticated. Yet, it is not always clear how much of the planning responsibility should be delegated to the planner.

As early as 1970, this issue was addressed by Ackoff: "If a unit of this type [departmental planning unit] is given complete responsibility for preparing a plan . . . then in most cases planning has been given the kiss of death . . . The value of planning for managers lies more in their participation in the process than in their consumption of its product."[50] However, given the chronic lack of time faced by today's project manager, it might be advisable to revisit Ackoff's recommendation. Therefore, the focus of the following two stories, the first told by Don Margolies, a project manager from NASA, and the second told by Scott Cameron, a project manager from P&G, is on how the project manager and the staff specialist can share the planning responsibility in the modern dynamic environment. Margolies states,

I went to visit my contractor, and met with the scheduler and project manager. We went into their war room, and there were schedules all over the wall. They were wonderful, as detailed as can be, and so I had to ask, "Who developed the schedule?" The scheduler said, "I did." And so I asked another question, "Did the people doing the work have input?" He said, "No."

The next day I notified the contractor that I wanted the project manager and his scheduler removed from the project, and I told the contractor to start building schedules that were representative of the work that really needed to be done. Here were these wonderful schedules, detailing every single thing you ever wanted to know about the project—and they were totally false. They had no basis in reality whatsoever.

As a project manager, there are certain things you can dictate: the end date, maybe certain review period dates, but in terms of everything else that you have to do, you've got to ask the people who are doing the job . . . When you're starting a project from scratch, you build a schedule that's appropriate by working with your team. You talk to the people doing the work. You find out what they have to do and how long it's going to take. Now, even if you do it that way, your schedules can be fallible, but at least you'll have something that everybody has bought into because they helped to develop it.[n]

Cameron tells us,

A lot of times when I talk to people about doing schedules, they ask me what scheduling program I use. To be quite honest, I use a pencil and paper most of the time to sketch out the critical path as I see it, which in an electronic age probably says I'm an old fogy. The schedule is just a tool to align the project team to what they have to do by when in order to be successful. How you prepare or draw the schedule is more a philosophical debate because there are many good software programs. The key is getting your project team members to be honest as to how long their work is going to take and how much time the schedule will allow them to accomplish their tasks . . . When you ask people how long something is going to take, their response always results in the initial schedules being two to three times longer than the time you have. That's why I believe if it's a six-week or two-year schedule, every day matters and aligning the team to this fact early in the life of a project will help insure its success. When you start off on a two-year project, you tend to feel like nothing is restricting the schedule at that point, but those initial days are days which are hard to recover or very expensive to recover later in the project's life.[o]

These two stories reaffirm Ackoff's recommendation that project managers must be involved in the planning process. Even in the face of a severe time shortage, planning cannot be solved just by employing full-time specialists. While the specialists may play a major role in facilitating the planning, they themselves cannot do the planning. Project planning activities should be performed by the project team, composed of the managers and the various professionals who will ultimately be responsible for implementing the plans.[51]

These two stories together underscore two complimentary aspects of project scheduling:

1. Developing a useful schedule is probably less dependent on the specific tools and techniques used and more dependent on honest input from the people who will actually be doing the work.
2. Adhering to the schedule is more likely when the people who need to execute the project have been involved in preparation of the schedule.

Plan for Three Time Horizons

Now we turn our attention to the impact of uncertainty on the timing of planning. Since we are always less certain of the future than of the present, we find that uncertainty increases (and usually at an accelerated rate) as the time span between planning and implementation expands.[52] In addition, certain information regarding future activities is available only after other preparatory activities are completed. Therefore, uncertainty has a crucial impact on the accuracy and timing of planning. Operationally, planning accuracy may be defined as the degree to which the planned action corresponds to the action eventually executed. The greater the uncertainty at planning time, the less the planning accuracy or the degree to which the plans will be realized.

The relationship between uncertainty and accuracy for cost estimating is well established, as it is widely accepted that the level of estimating accuracy is a function of when the estimate was made. Usually, estimates prepared during the early stages of the project can be expected to vary by 40 percent or more from actual costs, whereas estimates that are updated immediately before implementation should be capable of zeroing in to within 5–15 percent of actual costs. It is important to note that this relationship between uncertainty and planning accuracy is equally valid in all other areas of planning as well.[53]

At the same time, it is also well accepted that early planning, relative to implementation, is desirable. Early planning allows more time for planning and gives the team greater influence over project resources and constraints, thereby enhancing the quality of the plan and the chances that it will actually be implemented.[54] Given these conflicting considerations, the dilemma regarding planning timing is obvious: should one plan well ahead of implementation and benefit from wielding greater influence or should planning be postponed until implementation is closer at hand in order to secure greater planning accuracy?

The answer is both. Planning should be done both early and late, but the planning horizon and degree of detail should differ. If we define the time span between planning and implementation as a planning horizon, we find that the degree of detail in the plans varies inversely with the planning horizon. Thus, short-term plans (e.g., two-week Action Plans) are very detailed, both in the number of activities pertaining to each task and in the completeness of the specifications describing each activity. Medium-term plans (e.g., 60/90-day Look-Ahead Plans) are less detailed in comparison, and long-term plans (Master Plans), which cover the duration of the entire project, are quite general, presenting only aggregate activities.[55]

Steven Pender presents an approach along this line termed the "rolling wave": "The 'rolling wave' approach to projects is increasing in acceptance and practice. This approach recognizes that firm commitment cannot sensibly be made on incomplete knowledge. Initially, firm (binding) commitments are only made on the first phase of the project, and budgetary (non-binding) commitments made on subsequent phases. As the project rolls through to the end of one phase, a firm commitment is made on the next phase."[56]

In the following section, each of these three types of plans—Action or short-term plan, Look-Ahead or medium-term plan, and Master or long-term plan—will be described.

Action plan An Action Plan, which involves firm commitments, is characterized by a short time horizon and a very high level of detail.[57] Action Plans focus on limited areas within the project that are usually the responsibility of low-level supervisors. Delegating action planning to those who are closer to the detailed work results in plans that are more responsive. Delegation also builds ownership and commitment to the plan and distributes the planning effort more evenly among management levels, thus helping to alleviate the scarcity of attention problem.

Look-ahead plan A Look-Ahead Plan, which involves tentative commitments, is characterized by a medium time horizon and a moderate degree of detail. The time horizon covered by the plan varies with management level, typically ranging from two to three weeks for a field supervisor and from two to six months for the project manager. Its purpose is to assure the effectiveness of subsequent Action Plans by allowing enough lead time to influence the future.

By preparing a plan with a two-to-six month time horizon, the project manager creates a probable plan that, in typically uncertain conditions, provides the right balance between planning accuracy and ability to influence the future. That is, with this lead time it is neither too early to establish a relatively accurate plan nor too late to influence the future with sufficient impact. Thus, by preparing and studying the implications of such a plan early on, the project manager is able to ensure the effectiveness of subsequent Action Plans.[58] Another crucial role of look-ahead planning is that of learning, which will be discussed later in this practice.[59]

Master plan A Master Plan is characterized by a long time horizon and contains limited details at a highly summarized level. The time horizon of this plan stretches into the future, up to the end of the project or to the end of its major phase.

Even though the Master Plan is based on senior management guidelines and customer constraints, which are translated into objectives and milestones, it is not really a plan of documented decisions. It is primarily a forecast of estimated project performance at specified future milestones, which renders it distinctively different from the other two types of plans. That is, the Master Plan is primarily a forecast of future results, whereas the Action Plan, and to some extent the Look-Ahead Plan, are commitments for action that specify the work process and the allocation of resources.[60] Preparing and presenting the Master Plan require more formal and sophisticated procedures than those required for the Action Plan and the Look-Ahead Plan.

Unfortunately, the illusion that better "control" is available at a greater detail level often leads clients to require overly detailed and comprehensive Master Plans. Contractors must comply and are forced to go through the ritual of applying sophisticated tools to produce cumbersome plans in the form of scheduling networks. Marketed as symbols of managerial professionalism and the key to project success, these unmanageable and cluttered networks are in fact more likely to obscure the overview of the project.[61]

Control by Learning

We may now proceed and expand the partial answer we provided earlier regarding the navy project managed by Wink. As we said above, "Today's scheduling tools are obviously more sophisticated [than the original PERT tool], but since the paradigm underlying their creation has not changed significantly, they are not necessarily more effective." Though undoubtedly many improvements have been introduced to the original PERT and CPM tools, most modern scheduling tools usually fail to acknowledge or cater to the impact of the current dynamic environment. Their failure to accommodate change is probably one of the major reasons for the repeated failure of Wink's contractor to submit a complete updated and detailed schedule.

The network model for project scheduling is promoted, to a great extent, on the premise that it can accommodate changes in a responsive manner. That is, once a plan is created, its updating should be relatively quick and simple. The use of such a model is predicated on the assumption that most changes to the plan will be focused on the duration of project activities. However, in most projects, and particularly in those that suffer from high uncertainty, the network logic itself is constantly undergoing significant and unpredictable changes. Namely, the sequence of and the relationships between activities must be modified frequently, and often the scope of the activities is considerably expanded or reduced and new activities are added. Given these parameters, updating is neither simple nor quick. Rather, in most real-life situations, major revisions occur so often that they more closely simulate plan development than routine updating. This is unfortunately true even when the team is employing the "rolling wave" practice and ties the degree of planning detail to the planning horizon. This practice usually supports a stable Action Plan, but beyond the short horizon, the rest of the project still has to cope with frequent major revisions.[62]

If such frequent major revisions to the plan indeed more closely simulate plan development than routine updating, then what is the role of project control? Can one still say that the primary role of project control is measuring project performance and then, if necessary, taking corrective action to adjust performance to the plan? The following metaphor may help us realize the need for a re-examination of this classic definition of project control.

An admiral in the U.S. Navy stood on the bridge of his flagship. Suddenly a little blip appeared on the radar screen. He turned to the ensign and said,

"Tell that ship to change course 15 degrees."
The radio responded, "You change your course 15 degrees."
The admiral bellowed in anger, "Tell that ship that we are the U.S. Navy and to change its course 15 degrees, immediately."
"You change your course 15 degrees," the radio repeated.
The admiral himself then got on the radio, "I am an admiral in the U.S. Navy. I order you to change your course 15 degrees."
"You may be an admiral in the U.S. Navy," came the response. "But I am a lighthouse."[63]

Classic concepts of control were developed for stable environments, involving permanent organizations and repetitive activities, in which it was expected that planning would be fairly accurate and implementation would largely adhere to the plan. Accordingly, the primary role of control was to identify deviations from the plan and adjust execution to conform to the plan (and only rarely to adjust the plan to project objectives). Today, the typical project has to cope with frequent changes and missing information and thus must contend with many unexpected "lighthouses." Therefore, when a deviation from the plan is detected, the repertoire of responses cannot be limited to "adhering to plan," but should also include "adjusting plans while adhering to original objectives" and sometimes even "adjusting objectives and plans to circumstances."

So what, then, is the role of project control in temporary organizations (projects) that are operating in a dynamic environment with activities of short duration and little repetition? Under conditions of high speed, high uncertainty/frequent changes, and scarcity of attention, the role of control is primarily to provide quick feedback for further planning. As project uncertainty increases, control functions less as a "governor" of execution for ensuring that implementation conforms to plan and instead assumes more of a data collection function for continuous planning. Its emphasis, therefore, should be on looking ahead with anticipation rather than looking back for justification. That is, in uncertain conditions the main question should not be "why didn't your performance yesterday conform to the original plan?" Rather, it should be "what kind of feedback can help you learn faster and perform better tomorrow?"[64]

This kind of project control is primarily accomplished as part of the look-ahead planning process through its learning role. We explained earlier that by preparing and studying the implications of the Look-Ahead Plan, the project manager is able to influence the future and ensure the effectiveness of subsequent Action Plans. However, to influence the future in uncertain situations, the look-ahead planning process should not only focus on studying the future implications of a tentative Look-Ahead Plan, but also on learning from the performance of recently completed Action Plans. Collecting fast feedback on the actual performance of recent Action Plans enables the team to verify and update uncertain or incomplete information. This systematic, yet largely informal, process of learning from experience ensures that subsequent Look-Ahead Plans will be more effective.

Evidence that ongoing learning is crucial for successful performance has been presented by researchers from a variety of fields. Neely and Al Najjar, who focus on permanent organizations, not projects, conclude that "the true role of performance measurement is to provide a means of management learning, rather than simply a means of management control."[65] In their paper "Learning Is the Critical Success Factor in Developing Truly New Products," Lynn and his colleagues conclude that "in a learning-driven strategy, the emphasis is not on the first step . . . but on subsequent, better-informed steps . . . The key . . . is the degree to which teams are able to learn from prior steps—frequently in unpredictable ways—and act on this information."[66] Pich, Loch, and Meyer, who focus on uncertain projects, argue that "learning comes from signals . . . that are incompatible with project team's predictions . . . As project teams monitor their projects, they must recognize that observed signals are incompatible with their model of the world and be willing to change their representation of the world"[67] Puddicombe, who studied construction projects, concludes that "the ability to manage change on an ongoing basis, rather than the ability to plan, appears to be the key to project management success . . . Project management is less about control and more about acknowledging limitations. Once limitations are recognized, project management becomes a process of ongoing learning."[68]

In a fast-moving and changing project, timing is the key to the effectiveness of control as a data collection function for continuous planning.

Therefore, formal reports can quickly become "old news" and completely useless.[69] As a result, the format employed for a Look-Ahead Plan can be vastly simplified. Mature companies have found that the most effective and clear communication tool for providing guidelines to busy managers is the bar-chart format.[70] Moreover, in highly uncertain situations, medium-term items are often addressed in planning meetings. The decisions made at those meetings are usually recorded as semiformal meeting protocols rather than as formal plans.[71]

The classic Experiential Learning model proposed by David Kolb can help us to better understand the ongoing learning that takes place during these project planning and control meetings.[72] According to Kolb, "[Experiential] learning is the process whereby knowledge is created through the transformation of experience. Knowledge results from the combination of grasping experience and transforming it."[73]

Accordingly, the project manager and the project team are engaged in a continuous cycle of four activities: experiencing (during the implementation of the recent cycles of Action Plans), reflecting (on the implementation of the most recent cycles of Action Plans), thinking (planning the next Look-Ahead Plan), and acting (implementing the coming cycles of Action Plans). The first and fourth activities are "doing" activities (as part of implementing the Action Plans), while the middle two activities are "planning/thinking" activities (as part of the look-ahead planning process). Thus, Action Plans and Look-Ahead Plans are inextricably intertwined, forming the learning-based, evolving project planning process.[74] This tight connection between planning and doing also underscores the point made earlier that staff specialists cannot do the planning by themselves and that effective project planning requires high involvement of the project team.

As mentioned above, the Master Plan is distinctively different from the other two types of plans, primarily functioning as an overall forecast of future results rather than as specific commitments to action. Therefore, while the ongoing "control" of the evolving plan does not attempt to adjust execution to the plan, control assumes its classic role when it comes to the Master Plan. That is, periodically (e.g., monthly), on the basis of recent performance, a new overall forecast (i.e., a new Master Plan) is prepared and compared with the previous one. If, for example, a cost overrun is detected, then the project team will attempt to change the execution plan, cut the scope of the work, or secure additional funding. The staff specialist has a central role in monitoring overall project performance, comparing performance with the plan, analyzing the results, and preparing the updated plan.[75]

In both practices of the current guideline, control is achieved primarily via learning. While "control as learning" is very effective when operating under uncertain conditions, it is, of course, not the only means for controlling project outcomes. The term "control" has many connotations in organizational life. Simons, for example, asserts that "control in organizations is achieved in many ways, ranging from direct surveillance to feedback systems to social and cultural controls."[76] Indeed, each and every one of the 14 other guidelines covered in this book contributes directly to controlling the project, thereby ensuring project success.[77] Both practices of the current guideline can be fully successful only in a culture that is conducive to learning from errors. Such a culture requires a high level of trust. This point will be discussed in the Second Red Guideline: Develop Trust-Based Teamwork.

Control by Scanning the Project Environment
Successful project leaders do not limit their attention to events occurring within the boundaries of their project. They know that in a dynamic environment, projects will succeed only through constant monitoring of changes in the external environment, both inside and outside the parent company. The information about external changes plays the same role as the information about deviations between execution results and plans. Thus, the external changes will also be fed back to serve as input for further planning. If those external changes are not detected quickly enough, then adjusting the plan will be costly. Therefore, project leaders must continuously scan the project's external environment as well as maintain constant communication with all the project's stakeholders.

Cameron, from P&G, asks us "to think of the project manager's job in terms of an hourglass. In this analogy, the top of the hourglass is the PM's hierarchy, the bottom the project team, and the connecting tube the PM." He continues and argues that one of the things the project manager must keep in mind if he wants to "improve his hierarchical IQ" is the following: "Hierarchy has information about future events that can impact the PM's project. The PM must gain the hierarchy's trust and confidence to obtain this information as soon as possible."[P] This role of the project manager is the focus of the First Gray Guideline: Pull and Push Information Frequently.[78]

Scanning the environment is often accomplished with the aid of a formal procedure—critical assumptions review (CAR) (see Exhibit 1.2 below). Project objectives and plans are always based on various planning assumptions, such as the following:

- We will receive capital in quantities and on schedule, as laid out in March.
- We can finish the technical feasibility study of the auxiliary equipment by the end of October.
- We will have sufficient skilled construction labor throughout next summer.

In an era of uncertainty, many of these planning assumptions are not stable. When such an assumption becomes invalid, it often requires an adjustment to the plan or even to the objectives. Successful project teams are aware of the instability of planning assumptions and thus employ this systematic, yet very simple, procedure on large projects. Using the CAR, they can articulate the assumptions and are able to identify changes in the assumptions early on in the process, when coping with the impact of the changes is still quick and easy.[79]

Exhibit 1.2 Critical Assumptions Review (CAR) procedure

1. The project team generates the initial list of critical assumptions at the beginning of the project. The list should be updated when major changes occur, but at least at the beginning of every major project phase.

2. The initial list of assumptions is then reduced to include only those that are most critical. A critical assumption is both important to the success of the project (i.e., project objectives and major decisions are strongly dependent on the validity of each critical assumption) and judged by the team to suffer from a considerable degree of uncertainty (i.e., most prone to fluctuate). The judgment of criticality—degree of dependence and uncertainty—is purely subjective.

3. The team then assigns ownership to each assumption and to the person responsible for its monitoring.

4. The team reviews the list periodically, verifying the validity of the assumptions, revising or deleting them when necessary, and deciding whether adjustments to project execution, plans, or objectives are required.

The benefit of using the CAR goes beyond just detecting a change in a specific assumption and making a timely response. Periodic review of the critical assumptions serves as a constant reminder to project participants that their decisions are based on shaky assumptions and not on solid facts. Research has proven that people often underestimate or even ignore uncertainty.[80] This underestimation occurs before the project begins, but even more so during project execution. People working under a tight timetable tend to develop "tunnel vision." They focus inwardly on making progress, while ignoring changes in the external project environment and their impact on the project. In addition, experienced project managers who are not satisfied with merely scanning the external environment can attempt to influence the environment by challenging "given" constraints. This practice is discussed in the Second Yellow Guideline (Challenge the Status Quo).[81]

Periodic review of the critical assumptions also invariably draws everyone's attention to current uncertainties. Thus, the CAR is helpful in developing awareness of uncertainty not only within the project team, but also at the upper management level. An uncertainty previously neglected (whether intentionally or unintentionally) can thus be brought up for review with management in an atmosphere of receptiveness and responsiveness.

The following story, by Hugh Woodward from P&G, illustrates how using the CAR was instrumental in getting management's attention and cooperation to clarify the uncertainty surrounding the objectives of a small, but extremely unclear, project.

> *Following a seven-year drought, the city demanded that the company plant reduce water consumption by 20% . . . Because of the significant number of questions about how they were going to achieve this goal, management funded only the scope considered low-risk—approximately 70% of the requested amount.*

When the project team met to kick off the design work, it was obvious that the objectives were fuzzy and suffered from a high level of uncertainty. For example, the base from which the water reduction was calculated was unclear. In addition, a second production line was to be started up during the project period, adding an unknown water demand. Moreover, the company's commitments to the city were not clear. Hugh understood that action was required to get management to understand the problems and clarify the objectives.

> *While formulating project objectives and precisely restating the water-reduction commitments in millions of gallons per day, we developed a set of critical assumptions on which the objectives and the execution strategy were based. Some of them were: "The water consumption of the new production line is outside the scope of the current reduction objectives"; "City water quality remains constant"; and "It is possible to achieve reduction objectives without negative impact on product reliability . . . While earlier it had been difficult to get management's attention for this small and unclear environmental-type project, we could now present many "what-if" questions and receive management's attention and answers. Suddenly, everything was discussable. For example, we could clearly define the conditions that would enable us to receive the remaining 30% of the requested funding. Most important, we could also confirm our assumption that the new production line was not part of the current project.*

Hugh also points out that in addition to helping clarify the project's objectives and constraints, using the CAR facilitated a greater degree of openness when discussing uncertainty issues with management.[9,82]

Anticipate . . . Anticipate . . . Anticipate . . . but Things Still Go Wrong

Early identification of critical planning assumptions and systematic review of their validity allow the project team to anticipate many surprises before they occur, leaving sufficient time to attenuate and often eliminate their impact on the project. However, as we will see, both Allan Frandsen and Christian Zazzali believe that no planning procedure can completely remove the element of surprise. Thus, anticipating does not necessarily mean predicting and forestalling, but rather being on the lookout, knowing that the most you can do is to be highly responsive when the next surprise hits you.

Allan Frandsen, from the California Institute of Technology, describes the essence of his project management philosophy as follows:

> *In running a project, I have always tried to anticipate problems. To lead a project effectively, one has to establish and maintain the flexibility to take appropriate action when needed. If I had to write down the ABCs of project management, "A" would signify anticipation. But it is not just a planning activity that needs to take place at the beginning. It is also an ongoing thought process that reviews plans over various time intervals. A manager needs to work all the time to avoid losing control of events and operating only in the reactive mode . . . Of course, a good project manager already knows, at least in general terms, what is supposed to happen next—but all too often it doesn't. So what are the alternatives? Are there sensible work-arounds? What can I do now to lay the groundwork or facilitate matters should something go wrong? These and other questions make up the ongoing process of anticipation. And because it is an ongoing process, the "A" in the ABCs of project management could just as well stand for "anticipate . . . anticipate . . . anticipate."*

[Frandsen went on to explain that B stands for building a good team and C for communicating upwards, downwards, and sideways.][r]

Frandsen first explains his problem, which is that he cannot totally rely on the planning and control system to alert him about all upcoming problems. ("Of course, a good project manager already knows, at least in general terms, what is supposed to happen next—but all too often it doesn't.")[83] Frandsen then shares his solution: he must anticipate constantly and develop a readiness to respond ("anticipate . . . anticipate . . . anticipate").

The need for responsiveness is at the center of the Third Brown Guideline (Act with Agility).[84] Following is how Christian Zazzali, who serves as a project manager of commercial construction projects for HITT Corporate Interiors, describes the effectiveness of project planning and the need for responsiveness (his story will be discussed in the Third Brown Guideline):

> *I build a project a hundred times in my head before we start work on it. I put formal plans into writing, but I also try to work through every scenario I can think of in advance to have everything lined up like dominoes, with all the details in place. But things still go wrong.*[s]

This premise of "expecting the unexpected" is discussed by three prominent scholars of decision making and uncertainty, Kahneman,

Slovic, and Tversky: "Uncertainty is a fact with which all forms of life must be prepared to contend . . . uncertainty about the significance of signs or stimuli and about the possible consequences of actions . . . action must be taken before uncertainty is resolved, and a proper balance must be achieved between a high level of specific readiness for the events that are most likely to occur and a general ability to respond appropriately when the unexpected happens."[85]

As mentioned above, Vaill argues that today's permanent white water conditions are full of surprises and tend to produce novel problems. Thus, employing planning and control practices that are designed to embrace change is crucial for project success in dynamic conditions. However, these practices alone are clearly insufficient for coping with change. The next guideline—the Third Green Guideline (Use an Appropriate Amount of Redundancy)—presents another approach for minimizing the impact of change and instability.

The Third Green Guideline: Use an Appropriate Amount of Redundancy

If we were to examine a project in which most tasks started with a fairly low level of uncertainty, we would find that in time, the relatively few uncertain tasks would begin to proliferate, introducing uncertainty into all the components of the project. This insidious growth is caused by the strong connections that typically exist between the various project tasks, creating a condition similar to the "one rotten apple" syndrome.

When the project starts with a higher level of uncertainty—a common case in our era of permanent white water—the interconnectedness of project tasks may quickly destabilize project plans even if the Second Green Guideline (Employ a Learning-Based Planning and Control Process) is adopted. Successful project teams are acutely aware of this phenomenon and constantly attempt to maintain plan stability by decoupling project tasks or by containing uncertainty to limited areas of their project. Thus, right from the beginning of the project, they pay particular attention to the organization and to the grouping of tasks within the project and the connections between them. At times, however, the best way to maintain the stability of the plan is by adding a duplicate system as a backup.

Decoupling project tasks, containing uncertainty, or adding a backup system is never without cost. These activities require the acquisition and use of redundant resources. According to the dictionary, redundancy is the provision of a duplicate system or equipment as a backup. The current guideline argues that redundancy, which is usually regarded as a "liability," can provide an extraordinary measure of "reliability" to projects with high uncertainty.[86] The notion of deliberately and systematically using limited redundant resources is totally incompatible with the concept of efficiency that has been advocated for almost a century by the scientific management school. Yet, in our era of uncertainty and speed, the most effective way to proceed is not necessarily the most efficient way. In this guideline, we will show how successful teams are able to form a **stable and adaptable** project plan that would absorb future changes through a careful slackening of resources.

The Third Green Guideline consists of the following two practices:

First Practice: Loosen Connections between Uncertain Tasks.
Second Practice: Use Backup Systems.

First Practice: Loosen Connections between Uncertain Tasks

The Second Green Guideline demonstrates how successful project teams **reduce** uncertainty by acquiring more complete and stable information and by postponing decisions. The practice presented here further suggests that when it is no longer possible to postpone decisions, these teams can absorb uncertainty by carefully adding slack resources. Ray Longino, a project manager from P&G, illustrates a typical case in which the uncertainty from one portion of a project was absorbed and isolated to allow planning for the rest of the project to proceed without delay.

Ray's team was given the task of building a new plant in a foreign country in the shortest possible time. They planned to accomplish their task by working simultaneously in two parallel paths: starting engineering and acquiring a site. While the selection of the engineering contractor was completed on time, site identification got bogged down. Despite government assurances that a site would be available on time, final agreements were never reached and the location was moved several times. Every change in location meant a change in engineering design as well, forcing the team back to square one with no resolution in sight. As a result, the lump-sum contractor who had been hired for construction execution was reluctant to start without a firm location. Eventually, Ray and his team decided to develop a plan that allowed design to proceed independently of site identification.

We then drew up a site layout which could be rotated to suit ingress and egress locations. For example, the new plant had to have a place of worship for the workers, facing a specific direction. We solved this problem by designing an octagonal building. The consequences . . . were extremely favorable. We gained a full six months on the start-up date, which would have been impossible had we waited for final site identification.[t]

This example shows how absorbing the uncertainty of one component of the project enabled the project team to prepare a robust project plan and maintain rapid progress. However, there is no free lunch (in this case, an octagonal building is more expensive). That is, the team must build in redundancy to absorb uncertainty. In today's fast-paced projects, it may be necessary to absorb uncertainty several times throughout project life and not only for one highly uncertain task. The following story told by John Wysocki, a project manager from P&G, is a typical example.

> Conflicts between contractors were common during the design phase of the project. For example, piling and foundation design were often stalled by uncertainties and pending decisions related to design of the equipment for the large hot-air systems.

> *As project manager, I tackled this problem by establishing a planning process which brought the concerned parties together in order to agree on an arrangement and a set of design assumptions well before the equipment uncertainty could actually be resolved. At these meetings, we reached agreement about such issues as maximum loads or location "envelopes," which were the general, agreed-upon areas within the construction site for the location of a particular piece of equipment. Such understandings eliminated the contractors' major uncertainties and eliminated delays. As a result, the foundation design and construction work could proceed while studies to determine the best equipment continued. We employed the same process to decouple the interdependence between several critical and uncertain tasks. This way we were able to maintain an accelerated schedule, while the additional costs of redundant resources had little effect on the overall cost.*[u]

The two preceding stories demonstrate how redundant resources were employed to contain a specific source of uncertainty within the project. By dealing with specific uncertain tasks, the successful project teams were able to create a stable project plan. It is important to point out the distinct difference between these absorption measures and the common practice of adding a contingency allowance to the project cost estimate. Contingency allowance, which is a provision for unforeseen elements of cost, is usually added as one global amount to the total project budget.[87] One of the primary reasons for providing this allowance is to ensure that the project team will not have to return to the financing organization for additional funding. Thus, from the financing organization's point of view, providing a contingency allowance is an effective approach to absorbing the uncertainty of individual projects and to establishing a stable annual budget for the organization as a whole.[88] However, it does very little to absorb uncertainty within the project itself.[89]

These two stories demonstrated how to ensure that uncertainty concentrated in a few tasks would not spill over and destabilize the entire plan. The following story, presenting the use of time buffers, shows how successful teams maintain plan stability in situations where many tasks are clouded by uncertainty. Prior to presenting the story, we will elaborate on the rationale for loosening the connection between uncertain tasks.

Two extreme ways to structure a project are by a complete network or by a hierarchy (see Exhibit 1.3 below). In the complete network, each task is connected to every other task. In the hierarchical structure, each of the tasks, except one—the node task "f"—is connected to only one other task. Assume that task "a" suffers from considerable environmental uncertainty. In the complete network, all connections between task "a" and the other tasks, and most probably other connections within the network as well, will have to be reexamined and possibly changed. Similar environmental uncertainty within the hierarchical structure, on the other hand, will require only one change—between task "a" and node task "f."

It is thus clear that the hierarchical structure is simpler, less sensitive to uncertainty, and maintains its stability with greater facility. Yet, most projects cannot be structured into a hierarchy, forming instead complex structures that are composed of networks of tasks or clusters of networks. What factors, then, influence the stability of a plan composed of a network of tasks, many of which suffer from uncertainty? Research in ecology, cybernetics, and military systems has established that as a structure's complexity grows, its stability weakens.[90] It was found in particular that for a constant level of uncertainty, the structure of a given number of tasks will be more stable when there are fewer connections between them and when their connections are loosened. Conversely, a structure with many tight connections and a high level of uncertainty is quickly destabilized.

The two previous stories demonstrated how to ensure that uncertainty concentrated in a few tasks will not spill over and destabilize the entire plan. The following story shows how successful teams maintain plan stability in situations where many tasks are clouded by uncertainty. This example, involving a project manager who was asked to remodel the basketball arena at a university, illustrates how time buffers between uncertain tasks can help to maintain plan stability by loosening tight connections between the tasks.

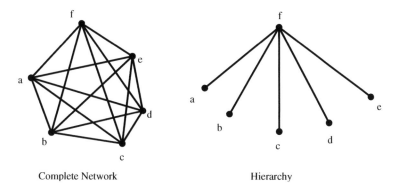

Complete Network   Hierarchy

Exhibit 1.3   Extreme possibilities for a project structure

The project manager was told that there was only a small window of opportunity— the last three weeks of summer vacation—to complete the job and that this timeline was non-negotiable. The project manager presented the initial plan to the school's administrators for approval. The plan had the last day free for any emergency that might arise (see Exhibit 1.4). The administrators, based on their experience with previous remodeling jobs, asked for a revised plan with two days at the end for emergencies. What he gave them instead was a plan with no free days at the end.

Why? After meeting with potential contractors, he found that it was impossible to accurately estimate the time needed for some of the remodeling tasks until the work had actually started. If one contractor exceeded the estimated time, for example, that would delay the start of the next contractor's work. The contractor who followed the first would not sit idle; instead he would move to another job, further delaying his start time and rendering the entire schedule useless . . .

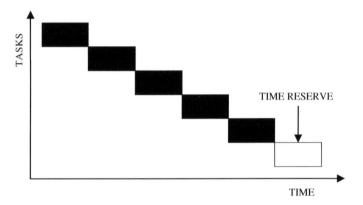

Exhibit 1.4   Proposed initial schedule

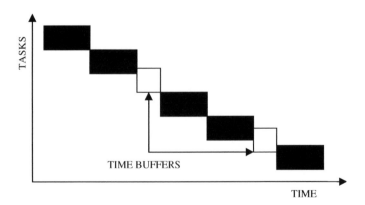

Exhibit 1.5   The checkerboard schedule

The schedule had to absorb changes as work progressed without collapsing. He did this by inserting time buffers—a half- or full-day between tasks—to follow tasks that were on or close to the critical path and had a high probability of time overrun. These would allow him to absorb schedule changes without stressing the overall timeline. A bar chart depicting the project schedule would look like a checkerboard, with black squares representing planned tasks and white squares representing the time buffers (see Exhibit 1.5).

The result was excellent. While he did use some of the time buffers, he never had to change the scheduled start time of any of the contractors.[v]

This example shows that in a world of uncertainty, it is unwise to schedule individual project tasks as fail safe. Rather, by incorporating time buffers, each task can be scheduled as safe to fail, meaning that even if it is late (fails), the entire plan is still on time (safe).[91] These time buffers enhance the resilience of the entire plan by building in a greater degree of flexibility, making it both stable and adaptable.[92] In other words, **the whole is more reliable than its parts.**

Time buffers are a widely accepted means for loosening tight connections.[93] Galbraith, a leading authority on the management of uncertainty, argued in 1972, "A good schedule is not one that loads the shop at 100 per cent 'efficiency' . . . A good schedule recognizes interactions among individual tasks by allowing access time for each task . . . An 'optimal' schedule is thus not a perfectly 'efficient' one, since it takes into account not only the cost of direct resources but also the resources used for coordination."[94]

Today's working environment is considerably more uncertain and dynamic than in 1972, and time buffers are required now more than ever. Indeed, there is much evidence that time buffers are very common throughout project life. In their research on Microsoft, Cusumano and Selby report that "in application products, buffer time typically constitutes 20 to 30 percent of the schedule . . . Since systems products have relatively longer schedules and less divisible feature sets, these projects tend to need more buffer time."[95]

Loosening connections between uncertain tasks is a typical measure often employed by successful teams. Their efforts to maintain plan stability always start with a continuous and focused monitoring of the uncertain tasks. This is easily explained by referring back to Exhibit 1.3. Think of the complete network presented as a schedule network for a project that starts at "c" and ends at "f." Now assume that the critical path, which determines the shortest total length of the project, goes through tasks "c," "d," "e," and "f." In such a case, the accepted prescription in the literature calls for a close monitoring of tasks that are on the critical path (i.e., tasks "c" through "f"). Successful teams, however, will first focus on "a," which suffers from high uncertainty. They know that unless they are able either to reduce the uncertainty that affects task "a" or to isolate task "a," the entire plan will soon fall apart, rendering the current critical path and its monitoring absolutely meaningless.

A Rand Corporation study of 52 extremely large projects found that the projects suffered from an average cost growth of 88 percent.[96] The study further concluded that it was not merely the size of the megaprojects that made them especially problematic. Rather, cost growth was found to be the result of various uncertainty factors, such as regulatory disputes and project innovations. Other studies of many different industries showed the same consistent pattern of large project overruns resulting from various uncertainty factors.[97] A *Harvard Business Review* article claimed, "Big projects fail at an astonishing rate . . . by some estimates, in fact, well over half the time."[98] Another study of megaprojects found that "cost overruns of 50 per cent to 100 per cent in real terms are common, and overruns above 100 per cent are not uncommon."[99]

To maintain the stability of the project plan, successful teams typically divide a large project into several relatively independent and autonomous subprojects, grouping the tasks by discipline, by major system or component, or by geographical area.[100] In large construction projects, it is common to divide the project into geographical areas, as illustrated in the following story told by Robert Volkman from P&G.

> With a construction cost exceeding $240 million and a workforce peaking at 2,000, the project called for a different project management approach because it was many times larger than the company's usual projects.

> *Our strategy was to divide the project into geographical areas, giving us multiple smaller projects within the larger one. This strategy created distinct manufacturing, packing, warehousing, etc., "projects," each of which was now similar in size to the large projects we were accustomed to managing. Each area was assigned its own small and independent project team consisting of a superintendent, site engineer, cost engineer, buyer, etc. The construction project manager held the centralized responsibilities for the entire project. This meant there was some overlap and duplication in the different areas, which appeared to result in large staff overhead. Critics of this project strategy would say the project could have been better run if the overhead responsibilities had been centralized . . . The results of the project were outstanding. It was completed for $10 million less than estimated, and schedule and quality targets were exceeded.*[w]

There are several compelling reasons for dividing a large project into several subprojects.

- *To cope with a large number of uncertain tasks.* Mathematical models of systems composed of *connected* elements that suffer from uncertainty show that when the number of elements exceeds a certain critical value, the system demonstrates a sharp transition from stable to unstable behavior. The models further indicate that the system's stability is significantly enhanced when it is divided into several smaller independent subsystems. Stability is also considerably improved when either the number of the connections is reduced or their strength is loosened.[101]

- *To cope with a large system of information flow in uncertain situations.* Empirical studies on the relationship between uncertainty and information processing needs found that the greater the uncertainty, the greater the number of changes and exceptions flowing within the organization through formal and informal channels. This, in turn, increases the amount of information that must be processed among decision makers during task execution. Studies have also found that for uncertain tasks, the larger the number of elements relevant to decision making, the greater their dissimilarity, and the tighter their connections, the more information there is to be processed. Thus, large projects composed of many tasks that are highly uncertain, highly dissimilar, and tightly connected create an information overload. The result is delayed decision making and poor responsiveness. Dividing a large project into small, autonomous subprojects is an effective organizing tool to reduce the impact of heavy information flow.[102]

- *To cope with a large system of people, regardless of uncertainty.* The book *Small is Beautiful: A Study of Economics as if People Mattered* makes a very convincing case for achieving smallness within a large organization. The logic is that large organizations should be composed of many semiautonomous units, termed "quasi firms," with each of them having enough freedom to provide the greatest possible opportunities for creativity and entrepreneurship. This configuration will enable the organizations to deal with the simultaneous requirements for order and freedom—requirements that are even more pronounced in uncertain situations.[103]

- *To cope with the execution of a large system in extreme situations.* To achieve a "lightning-paced" project schedule, it may be worthwhile to break down a project and execute all its subprojects in parallel. On the other hand, reducing the risk of a very uncertain and large project may be best accomplished by subdividing it into smaller ones and executing them serially. In general, where different criteria may be employed for different subprojects, smaller subprojects permit flexibility in pace and method of execution. For example, subprojects can be selectively advanced according to their execution readiness or their ability to meet specific economic criteria.

Dividing a large project into small ones, however, also has the following primary negative implications:

- *It requires the use of redundant resources.* As described in Volkman's story, additional overhead is necessary to manage each of the individual subprojects. Rather than sharing one piece of equipment as a common resource that serves the entire project, each subproject would require its own equipment. Moreover, due to the frequent changes throughout the life of the project, it is more difficult to efficiently utilize fixed resources in small segments.

- *It requires the use of additional resources for defining internal boundaries and managing interfaces.* To appreciably enhance the stability of the project plan, it is necessary to reduce the interdependence between the subprojects by defining the boundaries between them as clearly as possible (see Exhibit 1.3). If each of the subprojects is represented by a single balloon, then the entire project can be represented by a person holding the strings of several balloons. However, because no project can achieve the complete isolation of its components, the balloons are not totally independent of each other.[104] Thus, there will always be a need to manage the interfaces between the subprojects, such as by reallocating scarce shared resources in accordance with changing conditions.

- *It requires the use of additional resources for overall coordination and integration.* To considerably reduce the flow of information up the hierarchy and to enable the project manager of the entire project to process the information, the decision-making autonomy of the subprojects must be extended as much as possible. Nevertheless, the project manager still must coordinate and integrate those people who have been empowered to manage the subprojects with extended autonomy. Otherwise, the project manager runs the risk that the decisions of the subunits, which are naturally dictated by local perspective, will not support the overall mission. The project manager is the only person with a global view who can integrate all the empowered subprojects to cooperate in the pursuit of the objectives of the entire project.

It is difficult to generalize about the ideal number of subunits generated from a large project, though the typical number is very often three to five.[105] Theoretically, it depends on a complex trade-off between the benefits of smaller subunits and the costs of the additional overhead, management of interfaces, and project integration. In practice, however, the number of available options from which the practitioner must choose is often quite limited. First, the internal boundaries in most projects are "naturally" defined by disciplines, systems, or geographical areas. Second, organizational constraints, such as the availability and experience of managerial and technical resources, often affect the number and size of subunits.

Second Practice: Use Backup Systems

To underscore that redundancy should be considered as a legitimate practice in the project manager's toolbox, Marty Davis, a project manager from NASA, shares a few examples of "things we did wrong and should have known better."

> *Every project has its stories. The ones we usually want to tell are the outright success stories—but the ones we also need to hear are the "things we did wrong and should have known better." The Compton Gamma-Ray Observatory (CGRO) was the heaviest astrophysical payload ever flown at the time of its launch in April 1991. Here are some key stories about backup scenarios from that project:*
>
> *The Energetic Gamma Ray Experiment Telescope used light pipes to measure time-of-flight. These were simple pieces of plastic, bent and glued together, and this appeared to be an easy task to accomplish. The catch here is that the task appeared easy. It was known to the engineers that only one person had been able to complete this task successfully so that the light pipes worked optimally. Unfortunately, this man was about to retire, and an attempt to procure the light pipes from another source failed. Only by appealing to the man to save the project and the Center's reputation did he agree to hold off his retirement to finish the work and to train a replacement. The same scenario applied to a contractor who made the photomultiplier tubes for the science instruments and who used only one of their assemblers to make the tubes. The specifications were quite rigid, and the one assembler who knew how to make the tubes had a success rate of just 40 percent. CGRO needed more tubes and this one man was on vacation. The project office put pressure on the contractor to keep the production line working. The contractor reluctantly agreed.*
>
> *Ten tubes were pushed through the manufacturing process and the yield was zero. What the one man did working at an identical station with identical parts is not known, but CGRO lost time and the contractor lost money. They informed us that from then on we should wait until their one man was available. We agreed.*
>
> *. . . The design of the digital electronics for the COMPTEL instrument was a one-person effort. The system was ahead of schedule. The prototype was finished and had undergone preliminary tests ahead of schedule. Everything sounds wonderful, right? But then the engineer was offered a better job. He gave notice and left the project. No one else was familiar with the system and how the changes identified from testing should be made. This led to six months of long days and weekend work for team members who had to fill in.*[x]

Marty tells us that project managers need to identify in advance those one-of-a-kind critical tasks for which they lack sufficient overlap in their workforce (and where proper documentation cannot serve as a substitute). However, as the following story attempts to demonstrate, identifying these critical tasks is always easier in hindsight. Bill Clegern, a project manager from P&G, shares with us his dilemma, which is common in project life: Should one take the risk or eliminate it?

> As part of construction site preparation, the existing plant's firefighting water tank needed to be relocated 100 yards across the site. No risks for lost

production could be tolerated, since the plant's entire output was already allocated. Since there was no other reliable source of water, the tank had to be moved, reconnected, tested, and started up during a long weekend, when production was down.

Our basic scheme was to use two 50-ton cranes to pick, set, and walk the tank across a newly cleared pathway covered by a bed of compacted limestone gravel. The contractor's construction manager was absolutely sure the plan would work; so was I, until we came to the end of a session of "what if-ing." Every disaster scenario was worked through with an ultimate positive outcome until we wondered what would happen if a crane broke down.

The possibility of a breakdown was remote, and the contractor felt that he could repair any normal failure in the field or, in the worst-case scenario, get parts or call in another crane. Bill, on the other hand, assumed that breakdowns do happen and did not want to be in a position of failing because of an "act of God." He made the decision to bring in a standby crane, taking full responsibility for "squandering money" on a seemingly redundant piece of equipment. The outage arrived and things were going smoothly until one of the active cranes blew a 2-inch hydraulic hose. The backup was brought in and the job went on. The contractor found that he could not in fact repair the hose on-site. He had learned his lesson and immediately set his buyer to work telephoning around to rent another backup. He later acknowledged that Bill's initial decision to arrange for a backup was what allowed them to stay on schedule, despite his own miscalculation about the ability to repair the crane on-site.

Then the rains came. We couldn't believe how much water was coming out of the sky. Sewers throughout the city backed up, roads became flooded, and our people at the site were blocked from leaving. That would have been tragic enough if a crane or hose had been available, but neither were! The long weekend had attracted a lot of outage work, tying up every sizable crane in the area; the hose was just a rare bird and would have been unavailable, even on a good day. Luckily, no further disasters or unplanned events occurred . . . The plant started up as scheduled. In retrospect, the contractor's construction manager regretted not planning for the rain. If he'd prepared the pathway with swales to form a dike, he was sure he could have floated the tank into place. No cranes would have been necessary.[y]

Why didn't Bill make his choice on the basis of quantitative risk analysis?[106] For once, it is not so simple. MacCrimmon and Wehrung, two authorities on risk taking, argue that "most risky situations require a person to figure out what the possible alternatives are, instead of having them nicely presented."[107] Michael similarly stresses that the key is figuring out the situation and the variables: "Risk pertains when one believes that one knows what variables are involved in characterizing a situation; hence, one can assign probabilities to outcomes . . . Uncertainty pertains when one believes that one has either too much or too little information to feel confident about what variables define the situation. In this situation, no probability of outcome can be honestly assigned."[108]

Brian Muirhead from NASA, who led the design, development, and launch of the flight system for the Pathfinder mission to Mars, describes his team's approach: "[We asked] two questions: What's the probability of failure? And what's the likelihood that a failure would result in losing the mission? . . . Many people simplistically assign numbers to this analysis— implying a degree of accuracy that has no connection with reality."[109] Since the essence of project planning is integrating decisions (see Second Green Guideline), and since the variables (resources, decisions, tasks, external conditions, etc.) are very often highly interconnected, it becomes very difficult to identify the variables and to clearly define the risks in today's permanent white water conditions.

Moreover, in projects that are by definition unique endeavors, it is usually not possible to accumulate sufficient historical data to develop reliable probabilities, even when the risky situation can be clearly defined.[110] Therefore, successful project teams most often resort to continuous and evolving planning on the basis of uncertainty reduction, as described in the Second Green Guideline, rather than relying on a quantitative, formal, and design-like risk analysis.[111] Flyvbjerg et al., who studied the actual situation in the field, found that risk analysis is not a common practice, even in very large projects, which are known to suffer from significant cost overruns: "In a World Bank study of ninety-two projects, only a handful was found to contain 'thoughtful' risk analyses showing 'good practice.'"[112]

Combining the Second and Third Green Guidelines, one can see that the risk approach adopted by successful project teams is similar to the one proposed by MacCrimmon and Wehrung. This approach, which they termed "an active approach," entails "gaining time, information and control."[113] Through the Second Green Guideline, the teams attempt to reduce uncertainty by gaining time and information, while in the Third Green Guideline they try to directly control the situation by absorbing uncertainty (e.g., adding resources like a backup system or time buffers).[114]

In today's dynamic conditions, project managers are not expected to eliminate risk. Rather, they are expected to take the right risk. Yet, as the preceding story illustrates, when the negative impact of a risk is intolerable, it is absolutely irresponsible to ignore it even if it seems remote. In effect, project managers have no choice but to eliminate risk in such situations.

To mitigate the remaining risks after all the necessary preparations have been made, redundant resources are often employed to help adjust to uncertainty. In the following three stories, backups are introduced to cope with technological uncertainty. The first story is told by Allan Frandsen, from the California Institute of Technology, who served as the project manager for the development of nine scientific instruments, five of which were quite new and thus suffered from high uncertainty.

> *I came under criticism from Goddard [location of the management of the entire project] for spending payload reserve funds early in the program. Their feeling was that at the rate the funds were being used, the money would run out even before instrument environmental testing began. I countered that I was mindful of the need to maintain reserves in case failures occurred during the test program, but that judicious use of reserves early on was important.*
>
> *At one point, we had three separate efforts under way to solve a sensor development problem . . . I kept our three development efforts going simultaneously, but on a short leash, until a fix was found. The early use of reserves made this possible. I believed in my judgment on this matter, stood my ground, and was stubborn over my prerogative to control the reserves given me . . . I always advocate spending reserves early to solve problems . . . The longer you let a problem go, the worse it gets, and the more it costs to solve later down the road.[2]*

The previous story highlights the fact that even in regard to uncertain tasks, the timing and extent of using backups is often strongly disputable. Peters and Austin would disagree with Goddard and would make project managers such as Frandsen their heroes in a world of permanent white water: "If it is a messy world, the only way to proceed is by constant experimentation . . . we need to create a climate . . . that nurtures and makes heroes of experimenters and champions."[115]

In projects suffering from high technological uncertainty and tight scheduling—two common afflictions of cutting-edge endeavors—using backups early on in the form of parallel development efforts often has the same effect as accelerating early experimentation in order to learn as fast as possible. As Muirhead asserts, it is necessary to "test your concepts early": "In any project that's breaking new grounds, the manager needs to identify high-risk elements and devise ways to put them to the test early in the project. The goal is to 'retire the risk'—wring the risk out of the project—as early as possible."[116]

Retiring the risk as early as possible is in line with the conclusion presented earlier in this guideline: "Uncertain tasks that are not intensively managed today will create the new critical path tomorrow." However, by tomorrow, these tasks can destabilize a larger section of the project, very often requiring changes to project components that have already been produced. Thus, as the next story demonstrates, parallel development efforts early on are commonly accepted as an effective project method in developing new products, where uncertainty is inherently high and the project timetable is often tight. Matthew Zimmerman, a project manager for the U.S. Army's Armament, Research, Development and Engineering Center (ARDEC), describes the competition between two contractors for development of the rifle of the future, a $750 million engineering and production project:

> Contractor AA's concept convincingly contained more innovation than Contractor BB's, but their overall system solution was questionable. We faced a tough decision. Should we rely on only sub-system component demonstrations and select contractor AA? Or should we extend the contract competition? However, the next stage of competition would require larger investments by the contractors. We would probably have to contribute resources as well. But how much money should we be willing to invest to convince both contractors to continue? . . . We decided that it was too risky to rely on only sub-system component demonstrations for the history-making down-selection; instead, we encouraged more innovation and company commitment to prove their system solution warranted continued investment . . . We also decided to award each contractor approximately $10 million to demonstrate the feasibility of their system. Now it was the contractors' turn to face the hard decisions and manage the risk . . . the two competing contractors understood that a successful demonstration of their technology would probably position them in the forefront of combat weaponry for the 21st century . . . By intelligently managing the risk and the competition, the winning contractor [BB] was able to achieve a position of leadership in a highly competitive market while enabling the Government to advance the state-of-the-art in combat weaponry.[aa]

The preceding story stresses that at times the desire to stick to the original plan and to award the contract on time, as well as without additional investment, may simply amount to gambling. In these product development projects, additional experimentation in the form of competition between contractors may elicit the best effort from the contractors, reduce project risk, and maximize technology options for the customer. While the client may view the competition as fast experimentation, the competing contractors typically operate with a product development mindset, which may often include more design and analysis than typical experiments. In this case, the stakes were high and the client (ARDEC) was willing to pay a large sum of money for the competition in order to reduce the risk. However, at the same time, the interaction between the client and the contractors during the competition facilitated a crucial change in working relations.

The following story illustrates how a unique mechanism injected into the competition helped to ensure success of the project:

> The U.S. Air Force adopted a two-phase process for the JASSM project. During the first phase, which lasted six months and ended in mid-1996,

five companies competed for the contract and two of them won it. These two companies were awarded cost-plus, fixed-fee contracts totaling $237.4 million. Following a 24-month program definition and risk reduction phase, one company was awarded a $3 billion contract for the full-scale engineering and production. The project was highly successful. For example, while the goal for the unit price back in 1996 was $700,000, the actual unit cost in 2003 was reduced to less than $400,000. Many factors contributed to the outstanding results of this project. One of them was the trust that had developed between the government and the contractor during the competition through a special mechanism of helper teams. The short-term objective of this unique mechanism was to ensure that each of the parallel efforts would have the best chances of success. The long-term goal was to build a collaborative relationship with the winning contractor for the subsequent engineering and production phase.

Brian Rutledge, financial manager with the U.S. Air Force, explains the unique role of the helpers as follows:

When we down-selected from five companies to two, I switched from being the financial lead in the government program office to being program manager on a helper team for one of the companies, McDonnell Douglas. I stayed in this position for the duration of the competition, which lasted two years. A little more than a year into the competition, McDonnell Douglas merged with Boeing, and our program office was absorbed into the Boeing organization.

The role of a helper team was to assist your company in winning the contract at the end of the two years. When we began, six government people were assigned to each of the helper teams. We all came from the JASSM program office at Eglin Air Force Base. Winning was the goal. Forget about the old goal of getting on contract in six months. We had a new goal.

Terry Little, the JASSM project manager, outlines both the short- and long-term objectives that he had in mind while devising this unique arrangement.

I picked the helpers. Their job was to support their respective company—not to look after the government's interest, not to make sure the company didn't do something stupid, not to bring home secrets to me—just to help that company win, period . . . At the end of the two years, we wanted to face a difficult decision when we selected the winning company. The government's role should be to ensure the success of the project, and the way to do that was not to oversee or second-guess the contractor—but to help the contractor . . . The companies had the ability to get rid of any government person they wanted to at any time for any reason if they thought they needed someone else with a different talent or expertise, I would do whatever I could to get it for them . . . The helper teams set the stage for what I wanted the government's role to be two years later when we got down to one contractor. When we finally got down to the one company that was going to do the job, I wanted to have already established a working relationship in which we were open, straight, candid, and—most of all—trusting of one another.[bb]

Little is not alone in his desire to use experimentation in the form of competition between contractors to improve aspects of the organization. On the basis of a study of R&D processes in the semiconductor industry, West and Iansiti concluded, "The study clearly supports the claim that what matters in competition in a dynamic environment is not the magnitude of the resources committed, nor only the stock of knowledge controlled by the firm (experience) . . . Perhaps the most notable finding to emerge is the vital role played by experimentation . . . Our evidence also suggests that experimentation 'tools' are not enough . . . Experimentation should, thus, be viewed as an organizational process, not only as a technical tool."[117]

Stability, Flexibility, and Action

The main purpose of the three Green Guidelines is to plan and control while embracing change. By its nature, the First Green Guideline (Define Project Objectives while Quickly Exploring the Means), which embraces change by mixing deliberate planning and deliberate learning, is primarily practiced at the early stages of the project. On the other hand, both the Second Green Guideline (Employ a Learning-Based Planning and Control Process) and the Third Green Guideline (Use an Appropriate Amount of Redundancy) are practiced throughout project life. By comparing these two guidelines (see Exhibit 1.6) we can learn more about their complementary nature.

	The second green guideline	*The third green guideline*
Main purpose	Building short-term stability and allowing long-term flexibility	Maintaining overall stability while allowing local changes
Treatment of uncertainty	Reducing uncertainty by collecting ongoing feedback	Absorbing uncertainty
Nature of planning	Integrating project decisions	Decoupling project tasks
Viewing resources	Striving for efficiency	Allowing redundancy
Characteristics of decisions	Multiple interconnected decisions throughout project life	A few separate decisions at the beginning of major project phases

Exhibit 1.6 Comparison of the second and third guidelines

The Second Green Guideline, like a classical planning effort, attempts first to integrate project decisions while using project resources efficiently (to the extent allowed by the dynamic context of the project). Yet, due to uncertainty (and speed and scarcity of attention), planning is not undertaken prior to the start of implementation. Rather, it is carried out throughout project life, while uncertainty is gradually reduced by collecting ongoing feedback. All this with one purpose in mind: to embrace change by building a stable short-term plan and by allowing long-term flexibility.

The Third Green Guideline, on the other hand, has very little to do with classical planning. Accomplished through separate decisions usually made at the onset of major project phases, it absorbs uncertainty by decoupling project tasks and by allowing redundancy. Its purpose is complimentary to that of the Second Green Guideline: to embrace change by maintaining overall project stability while allowing local changes.[118]

To the concepts of stability and flexibility, one must add another aspect: action.[119] Weick presents the story of the army squad lost in the wintry Alps, about to give up when a map was discovered. Stimulated into action, they found their way out, only to discover back at base camp that it was a map of the Pyrenees. Weick explains that in very uncertain situations, a plan—even a very superficial one (and in that particular case, a wrong one)—can reduce uncertainty if people think that the plan is of some value. He explains that the plan animates people and stimulates action, but that the fact of animation, rather than the plan itself, is what imposes order on the situation.[120] In an earlier paper, Weick argues that "any old map or plan will do, if it gets you moving so that you learn more about what is actually in the environment."[121] Mintzberg provides his interpretation to Weick's argument and suggests that as long as you prepare an approximate plan—a plan that will provide you with a sound broad orientation—you can feel secure in the belief that whatever occurs will be manageable. This, in turn, enables you to dismiss the uncertain future and get on with the present.[122]

The complementary nature of the Second and Third Green Guidelines finds support in the book *The Paradox Principles,* which focuses on managing change. It stresses that too much change generates skepticism and frustration, arguing that "positive change requires significant stability" and that "managers need stakes in the ground to guide change."[123] A project also purports to create change, but it may generate skepticism and frustration that could hamper its progress if too much uncertainty is present. The Third Green Guideline can provide the overall stability and stakes that will motivate the team to employ the Second Green Guideline and to proceed as planned.

In uncertain situations, a plan, even with the stability and flexibility that the Second and Third Green Guidelines provide, may not be enough to ensure effective progress. It seems that in uncertain situations, we may need stability, flexibility, AND action and that stimulating action may help to reduce uncertainty. Indeed, the focus of the next guidelines, the Brown Guidelines, is on action and how it relates to planning and results.

CHAPTER 2

The Brown Principle: Create a Results-Oriented Focus

The First Brown Guideline: Create and Maintain a Focus

Edward de Bono asserts, "If I had to choose the one motivating factor that seems to me to be operating in most successful people, it is the wish 'to make things happen.'"[1] Indeed, as one article in *Fast Company* suggests, "Nothing is more important than getting it done! Today, implementation is the real source of competitive advantage! Even the best idea is only as valuable as your ability to execute it! Ideas are critical. Innovation is the mainspring of the new economy. But as more and more companies compete in ideas, the game changes to competing in the implementation of ideas. In this next stage of competition, getting an idea gives way to getting it done."[2] The objectives "to make things happen" or "get it done," as well as other related implementation guidelines, are at the heart of the Brown Principle: Create a Results-Oriented Focus. Unfortunately, these aspects have hardly been addressed by the traditional project management literature, which has largely embraced the implementation philosophy illustrated by the practices of the "European navigator."

Lucy Suchman opens her book *Plans and Situated Actions: The Problem of Human-machine Communication* with a comparison of the different navigation methods employed by the European and the Trukese navigator. "The European navigator begins with a plan—a course—which he has charted according to certain universal principles, and he carries out his voyage by relating his every move to that plan. His effort throughout his voyage is directed to remaining 'on course.' If unexpected events occur, he must first alter the plan, then respond accordingly."

The Trukese navigator, on the other hand, "begins with an objective rather than a plan. He sets off towards the objective and responds to conditions as they arise in an ad hoc fashion." The Trukese navigator steers according to the information provided by the wind, the tide, the stars, the clouds, and the sound of the water on the side of his boat. While his objective is clear from the outset, his actual course is contingent on the unique circumstances that he cannot anticipate in advance. "His effort is directed to doing whatever is necessary to reach the objective. If asked, he can point to his objective at any moment, but he cannot describe his course."

Suchman asserts that the European navigator exemplifies the prevailing cognitive science model of purposeful action and that "the view that purposeful action is determined by plans is deeply rooted in the Western human sciences as the correct model of the rational actor . . . My own contention, however, is that as students of human action, we ignore the Trukese navigator at our peril."[3]

Adopting the European navigator's underlying philosophy of responding to implementation problems by always first updating the plans may explain another glaring omission in the classic project management literature: the fact that the detachment between planning and implementation and the division of labor between the decision makers and the doers is rarely questioned. In their book on strategic planning, Mintzberg and his coauthors term this phenomenon the "fallacy of detachment," which they explain as follows: "If the [administrative] system does the thinking, then thought has to be detached from action . . . We maintain that all this is dangerously fallacious. Detached managers together with abstracted planners do not so much make bad strategy; mostly they do not make strategy at all."[4]

In his book *Computation and Human Experience*, Philip Agre also discusses the relationship between planning and execution. First, he describes the traditional paradigm: "The distinction between thought and action, of course, has deep historical roots. The scientific management movement, for example, projected these distinctions onto the structure of organizations: planning was the responsibility of an engineering department and execution was the responsibility of the line employees who were provided with detailed instructions specifying every movement necessary for the performance of their jobs." Then, reporting on novel elements introduced by artificial intelligence researchers, Agre describes a new possibility for the relationships between thought and action: "It is as if thought and action wished to intertwine themselves and were attempting to tear down the barriers that keep them apart—not to merge into one another, but to engage in a dance of give-and-take."[5]

The concepts imported from the worlds of navigation, strategic planning, and artificial intelligence call our attention to the importance of the tight relationship between planning and implementation (and thinking and doing). The reader may recall that the Green Principle requires frequent interaction between planning and implementation. The Brown

Principle further addresses the complex relationships between planning and implementation. For example, the Brown Principle stresses that in a dynamic environment, it is wrong to think that the role of project implementation is simply to "execute the plans" and that the scope of project implementation is simply "all project activities that follow project planning." Rather, project planning and project implementation overlap and interact—and considerably so. Moreover, implementation considerations are central to project success and significantly affect project planning.

Both the Brown Principle and the Green Principle share a few major assumptions. For example, both fully recognize the impact of project uncertainty, project speed, and the manager's scarcity of attention. However, they strikingly differ in their raison d'etre. The raison d'etre of the Planning and Control Principle is to provide guidelines for project execution, while the Implementation Principle attempts to constantly remind us that the raison d'etre of a project is to deliver results. The difference between planning and implementation and the bias for delivering results is captured nicely by Karl Weick: "The argument, in a nutshell, is the one set forth by a Persian proverb: 'Thinking well is wise; planning well, wiser; doing well, wisest and best of all'"[6]

The color selected for the Implementation Principle (in the figure that presents the five principles in the introduction) is brown, since in a few key aspects it bears a resemblance to de Bono's "brown brogue action shoes" and fits the rationale provided by him for this color: "Brown brogue action is concerned with getting results. The brown brogue action mode involves practicality and pragmatism. Pragmatism means being sensitive to the situation. Flexibility is a key aspect of the brown brogue action. The general skills of doing . . . are best illustrated by the brown brogue action."[7]

Now that we have addressed the distinct and crucial role of the Brown Principle, we are ready to focus on its first guideline: Create and Maintain a Focus. Two different, yet complementary, rationales for creating a focus will be outlined together with their practical implications. This will be followed by a discussion of the difficult, but essential, need to maintain a focus throughout project life.

Establish Priorities

In his 1964 book, *Managing for Results*, Peter Drucker argues that "concentration is the key to economic results. Economic results require that . . . efforts be concentrated on the few activities that are capable of producing significant results . . . A very small number of events at one extreme—the first 10 per cent to 20 per cent at most—account for 90 per cent of all results; No other principle of effectiveness is violated as constantly today as the basic principle of concentration."[8]

Unfortunately, even 40 years after Drucker made his strong case for the adoption of the concentration principle, it has not been widely embraced. Moreover, its adoption may even require a "change of mind." In his 2004 book, *Changing Minds*, Howard Gardner chooses this very principle as an example that still requires a "change of mind": "From early childhood, most of us have operated under the following assumption: When confronted with a task, we should work as hard as we are able and devote approximately equal time to each part of the task. According to this '50/50 principle,' . . . we should spread our effort equally across the various components . . . Early in the last century, the Italian economist and sociologist Vilifredo Pareto proposed what has come to be known as the '80/20 principle' or rule. As explained by Richard Koch in a charming book, *'The 80/20 Principle*,' one can in general accomplish most of what one wants—perhaps up to 80 percent of the target—with only a relatively modest amount of effort—perhaps 20 percent of expected effort."[9]

Establishing priorities by using the concentration concept (the 80/20 principle) is crucial for project success. Don Margolies, the project manager of the advanced composition explorer (ACE) at NASA's Goddard Space Flight Center, understood this concept very well. Here is how he established clear priorities for this $141 million project:

> At the start of ACE, I had the choice of spreading the money among all the players or focusing on the elements that posed the greatest risks on the project. I responded by putting the bulk of the money into trying to identify the key risks in the development of the science instruments and mitigating these to the best extent that we could at the earliest stage possible. To do this, I had to hold back spacecraft development at the Johns Hopkins Applied Physics Laboratory (APL) . . . In holding APL back by three to six months, I knew I could be shooting myself in the foot if they were not able to recover . . . My concerns about APL being able to do the job actually were quite minimal. On the other hand, no one was certain how effectively we could mitigate the risks with those problem instruments . . . Once we secured more funding, I told APL to start ramping up on the spacecraft development. As it turned out, they were able to catch up.[a]

This large project had to cope with significant complexity and uncertainty. First, ACE included nine science instruments developed by 20 researchers, who were scattered at universities and a few government labs across the United States in addition to Switzerland and Germany. Second, five of the instruments were quite new and thus suffered from high uncertainty. By not "spreading the money among all the players" and by "focusing on the elements that posed the greatest risks," Margolies clearly showed that he avoided the 50/50 principle while instead applying the 80/20 principle.

Indeed, Margolies and his entire leadership team applied the 80/20 principle not just occasionally, but systematically. For this, they adopted the "doctrine of enough." This is how the British philosopher of management Charles Handy explains this doctrine and its impact on his own behavior: "'Roses need pruning if they are to flower,' a friend replied when I complained of being overstretched. With great reluctance, because I was enjoying the spread of my activities, although conscious that nothing much was coming out of them all, I resigned from seven different committees and groups on the same day . . . It was my first introduction to the doctrine of 'enough.'"[10]

Following is one example where Margolies explains how he systematically adopted the "doctrine of enough":

What I set out to do was to establish a mutual agreement with everyone that "good enough" is good enough. Set your requirements and stick to those requirements. Once you meet the requirements, spend no additional money to make it better.[b,11]

Sufficiency and simplicity were strongly recommended by Norman Augustine (who later held the position of chief executive officer and chairman of Lockheed Martin) in his book *Augustine's Laws*. First, Augustine explains the very serious cost implications of violating the "good enough" concept, followed by a metaphor that vividly illustrates how one can try to stick to the "good enough" concept: "The 'best is the enemy of the good' . . . The last 10 percent of performance generates one-third of the cost and two-thirds of the problems . . . The secret, if there is one for controlling the costs which are added by the pursuit of peripheral, albeit impressive, capabilities is actually quite straightforward and can be seen in the workings of a Sculptor creating a statue of a hippopotamus. How does one make a statue of a hippopotamus? Very easily; one obtains a large block of granite and chips away every piece that does not look like a hippopotamus." In other words, your objective is achieved not when there is nothing more to add, but rather when there is nothing more to takeaway.[12]

To make the point of the critical impact of simplicity on reliability, Augustine offers the following example: "A modern jetliner, for example, has about 4.5 million parts . . . If a system has one million single-string parts, each with reliability of 99.999 percent for performing some specified mission, the overall probability of the mission failing is over 60 percent . . . Thomas Paine summed it up in the 1790s when he counseled, 'The more simple anything is, the less liable it is to be disordered, and the easier repaired when disordered.'"[13]

The "doctrine of enough" has a second face, a paradoxical one. As Handy explains, "The point about enough is if you don't know what 'enough' is, you don't know what 'more than enough' is, so there is never enough . . . Only if you can say what enough is . . . you are free to do anything else."[14] To paraphrase Handy's point about knowing what "enough" is, one may use the following saying: "If everything is equally important, then nothing is important."

The "more than enough" components of successful projects are at the heart of Tom Peters's philosophy of project management. Author of *The Project 50,* Peters constantly strives to transform every project into a project that matters—a "wow project": "Life is too short for non-wow projects . . . 'Sameness' in products and services spouts from companies where most work, most projects end up being 'mediocre successes.'"[15]

All the principles of Results-Focused Leadership aim at producing a "wow project." In particular, the "doctrine of enough," which is at the heart of the Create and Maintain a Focus Guideline, is central to producing a "wow project." Following Handy's concept, the leaders of the ACE project established priorities and clearly differentiated between a "good enough" treatment, which was applied to the majority of activities, and a "more than enough" treatment, which was reserved for the minority of activities. Following is one example of how the "more than enough" treatment was employed by Margolies, the project manager. At a later stage in the project, after testing was completed, the scientists wanted the instruments to come off for calibration. Margolies considered it and, despite the strong opposition of his upper management, gave it the green light.

> *It was the first time on any NASA project that I know of when all the instruments on an observatory came off for rework or calibration after the full range of environmental tests and then were reintegrated at the launch center without the benefit of an observatory environmental retest . . . My management . . . didn't mince words. "Don, you are crazy," they told me.*

> Margolies decided, however, that since they had religiously adhered to the "good enough" approach, the project was ahead of schedule and under budget, and the team was now in a position to explore a "more than enough" avenue: "We were in a position to ask: What can we do to make the science better?"[c]

Indeed, the ACE results, as evident from the ACE home page of the California Institute of Technology, are nothing short of a big WOW: "ACE has been at the L1 point for almost 10 year. As of October 2006, 438 peer reviewed papers have been published by ACE science team members. Over 100 Science News items have been released by the ACE Science Center. On January 21, 1998, NOAA (National Oceanic and Atmospheric Administration) and the ACE project opened up the ACE Real Time Solar Wind monitoring capability to the public. The service provides 24-hour coverage of the solar wind parameters and solar energetic particle intensity. ACE's position a million miles upstream of earth gives as much as an hour's warning of CMEs (coronal mass ejection) that can cause geomagnetic storms here on earth."[16]

The calibration story calls our attention to two possible perspectives on "creating a focus": global and local. The global perspective consists of classifying project components and selecting the 20 percent of project components that will be assigned more and better resources. This act of classifying and selecting is usually applied systematically and globally to all project components. At times, however, the 80/20 principle calls for a local, more energetic kind of focus that results in a sustained "pressure," a laser-like focus that can practically be applied to only a part of that 20 percent of project components. One should be reminded, however, of Handy's observation: only if one knows what "enough" is, can one be free to do "more than enough," and only then is one able to produce a "wow project." That is, the regular application of the "classifying and selecting" focus enables the frequent, but sporadic, "laser-type" focus.[17]

Manage Attention

The previous section on establishing priorities through the 80/20 principle was focused primarily on work-related aspects, such as resources, activities, and products. The central "unit of analysis" was the project, not the project manager or the project team. This section concentrates on the project manager, the project team, and the scarcity of their attention.

It was stressed in the Green Principle that managers suffer from scarcity of attention. However, as Davenport and Beck assert in their 2001 book, *The Attention Economy,* "Previous generations of citizens didn't have an attention problem, at least not compared to ours." They argue that the most obvious law of supply and demand of the attention economy is that "as the amount of information increases, the demand for attention increases . . . Hence, a wealth of information creates a poverty of attention." As Davis and Meyer succinctly put it, "We live in a world of information glut."[18]

Maneuvering our way through this information overload means that we must cope with a bewildering array of choices competing for our attention. Contrary to the assumption that the more options the better, too much choice actually exhausts our brains—ultimately restricting instead of freeing us. In his book *The Paradox of Choice: Why More is Less,* Barry Schwartz explains, "Having the opportunity to choose is essential for our well-being, but choice has negative features, and the negative features escalate as the number of choices increases . . . It isn't this or that particular choice that creates the problem; it's all the choices, taken together."[19] Joel Spolsky, for example, counted 15 different ways to shut down a laptop running Microsoft's Vista operating system. While there was probably a good reason for adding each one, no good reason could be found for adding them all! Spolsky expressed the problem very concisely: Choices = Headaches.[20]

The nature of managerial work is not designed to easily cope with information glut and countless choices. Previous research shows that managers' activities are typified by brevity, variety, and fragmentation. A recent study of highly successful construction project managers revealed a remarkably active work style. For example, the average duration of their activities was about five minutes, and about 90 percent of the activities they performed lasted less then ten minutes. These studies, as well as other studies displaying a similar dynamic pattern of managerial behavior, are further discussed in the Third Brown Guideline.[21]

Bruch and Ghoshal reached the following conclusion: "Unfortunately, everyday managerial work is hazardous to focus."[22] David Allen, the author of *Getting Things Done: Mastering the Art of Stress-Free Productivity*, provides a vivid description of this hazard to focus: "It's Monday morning. You arrive at work. You flick on your PC—and 70 new emails greet you. Your phone's voice-mail light is already blinking, and before you can make it stop, another call comes in. With each ring, with each colleague who drops by your office uninvited, comes a new demand—for attention, for a reaction, for a decision, for your time . . . [However] the real challenge is not managing your time, but maintaining your focus. If you get too wrapped up in all of the stuff coming at you, you lose your ability to respond appropriately and effectively. Remember, you're the one who creates speed because you're the one who allows stuff to enter your life."[23]

Recognizing this "hazard to focus," Davis and Meyer offer managers the following advice: "Start paying attention to how to get people's attention and keep it . . . You must get serious about it."[24] The following two stories provide examples of two project leaders who "got serious about it" and took uncommon steps with one purpose in mind: "to get people's attention and keep it."

In the first example, Brian Rutledge, the financial manager of the U.S. Air Force project JASSM, shares with us the unusual requirement made by his project manager, Terry Little:

> *After Terry said we were going to be on contract in six months, he directed someone to make a viewgraph stating this goal: "Be on contract by 1 July 1996." That was it. He wanted it pinned up in everybody's cubicle. At first I thought: Oh man, this is goofy. I know what we're doing. I don't need to have a reminder on the wall. When I talked to other people working in the program office, I just rolled my eyes. "What's this guy thinking?" I said. "It's like we're in kindergarten." After a few months, however, I had to admit that there was something to this. I saw it there everyday when I walked up to my desk. I eventually found myself stopping to think: What am I doing to get to that point, and what can I cut out of my work that's preventing me from getting there? Whenever people took me down a rabbit trail and I started to follow them a little bit, I looked at that stupid chart and said to myself: Hold on. Am I getting distracted from this?[d]*

In the second example, Chuck Anderson, vice president of Raytheon, discusses the unique nature of the meeting that he and his 80-member advanced medium range air-to-air missile (AMRAAM) team religiously held every month:

> *The best thing about doing business this way was that the customer and the contractor had joint goals, joint visions. When you have that, problems become problems we solve, rather than problems we write claims for . . . Our jobs were to make certain that the people who worked with us shared our commitment . . . All of my team members, approximately 80 of us, met for half a day off-site at a hotel. We did this every month. We rented a ballroom, and the whole purpose of that meeting, every month, was constancy of purpose. It was to get everybody aligned.*[c]

The literature supports the underlying assumption of these two stories, that is, managing attention has a crucial impact on action and results. For example, Weick argues, "To get things done, it is more important to capture a person's attention than a person's intention. People act in response to salient concerns (e.g., deadlines). So to control action, you need to control salience."[25]

In his book *Focus: The Future of Your Company Depends on It*, Al Ries sharpens the meaning of "Create a Focus." According to the 80/20 principle, setting priorities leads to investing more resources in one part of the project and less in the other part. Ries contends, however, that at times, focusing proper attention may require setting a clear preference for one option while completely abandoning the competing alternative. Ries explains this idea through the following example: "Confucius says: Man who chases two rabbits catches neither . . . The owners Steven Marks and Harvey Nelson decided to chase one rabbit only . . . 'Instead of doing two things subpar,' says Steven Marks, 'we needed to do one thing exceptionally well . . . We had to devote our energies to that part of the business that had the best chance of success' . . . Since 1990 [their] sales have increased an average of 100 percent a year."[26]

Larry Lawson, vice president of Lockheed Martin, shares an example where a project failed, among other reasons, due to the fact that its focus and attention suffered from "chasing three rabbits," that is, from the lack of a clear preference.

> *[The government] decided to terminate the [TSSAM] program because they realized it was unaffordable. What I mean by "unaffordable" is that they could not procure the numbers of missiles they needed for the unit price they were facing: $2 million per copy . . . You can point to a number of factors as to why the government ended up in a situation where they had a system that was unaffordable, but a primary lesson learned was that there were too many services involved. It was an Air Force-Navy-Army program, with requirements to meet across each service. So when DOD looked at TSSAM to try and understand*

how best to approach JASSM, the first thing they decided was: Too many cooks in the kitchen is not effective. We have to pick someone to be in the lead. It was determined that the Air Force would be the lead service on JASSM.[f]

While the "chasing rabbits" concept attributed to Confucius is not new, the need to apply it frequently is new. David Allen, the author of *Getting Things Done: Mastering the Art of Stress-Free Productivity*, explains the recent marked rise in the need to apply this concept: "We suffer the stress of infinite opportunity: There are so many things that we could do . . . The problem is . . . You can do anything—but not everything."[27]

Thus far, two different rationales for creating a focus have been presented. The first one, Establish Priorities, can be succinctly described by the adage, "If everything is equally important, then nothing is important." The second one, Manage Attention, is best captured by the concept, "You can do anything—but not everything." We turn our attention now to the difficult, yet essential, need to maintain a focus throughout project life.

Maintain Focus: Learn to "Say No"

Maintaining a constant focus throughout project life is very crucial. In the Green Principle, we presented research results demonstrating the huge negative impact of changes in project focus late in project life. On the other hand, converging on a direction too early may result in mediocre outcomes and the failure to achieve a "wow project." Certain projects, such as software development projects and projects that involve a major change in mind-set, may require more time before converging is advisable. Identifying the right timing for switching from a Green Principle mind-set (which advocates postponing the final definition of project objectives in order to explore the means) to a Brown Principle mind-set (which advocates curbing the change in project requirements) greatly depends on the specific project context. The close interaction of timing, as well as all the other principles of Results-Focused Leadership, with project context is a recurring theme revisited throughout the remaining chapters—and one with which the reader can expect to feel more comfortable by the end of this book.[28]

Handy argues, "We have to learn to say 'no' in order to move on."[29] However, maintaining focus by "saying no" is not always readily accepted, even when the timing is supposedly very clear. Thomas Coughlin, a project manager from Johns Hopkins University, demonstrates this point in the following story:

Right from the start, I knew this project had to be schedule-driven. It became apparent that to meet the deadline we would have to freeze the requirements in place and focus on them relentlessly. The scientific community offered lots of ideas on how to change instruments or subsystems in order to yield even better information about asteroids. Had I incorporated even half of their good ideas, the spacecraft would never have been built. Only those changes that could be made with negligible or minimal disruption were even considered. As a result, we stayed on schedule and launched on the second available day.[g]

The next guideline, Think Deliverables, emphasizes the need to meet customer needs. How can we reconcile meeting customer needs with the fact that Coughlin practically ignored the requests of the scientists? At times, the best way to serve the needs of the customer is to just "say no." In this case, Coughlin knew that the NEAR spacecraft would have to be launched within a 12-day window. If they missed that window, NASA would have to wait seven years for another window. Still, the scientists did not want to accept the fact that the only way to meet this clear deadline was to stop changing the requirements. Coughlin did not have a choice but to "freeze the requirements in place and focus on them relentlessly."

It is interesting to see how the primary customer, NASA, assesses the results of this project five years after the launch of the spacecraft: "NASA's Near Earth Asteroid Rendezvous (NEAR) Shoemaker spacecraft, the first to orbit an asteroid, has met all its scientific goals . . . NEAR Shoemaker has set a high standard for low-cost planetary exploration," said Dr. Edward Weiler, associate administrator for space science, NASA Headquarters, Washington D.C. "This mission has provided answers to a range of fundamental science questions . . . and has collected 10 times more data than originally planned."[30]

In the following story, Mary Chiu, the project manager for spacecraft development at the Johns Hopkins Applied Physics Laboratory, describes the process that can accompany just "saying no":

ACE was supposed to be a simple spacecraft, and that's why we decided on a simple data handling system. Early on in the project, my lead engineer on the data handling system worked this out with Dr. Stone [the head of the science team]. In fact, it was Dr. Stone's decision to go with this type of system . . . We thought everything was settled, until some people at Goddard [NASA] suggested that we use a different data handling format. With all the really neat things being done on other spacecrafts, they asked, why were we getting this "old fashioned" data handling system? For my team at APL, the people building the spacecraft, this was no small matter. To change to a different data handling system would have required a major restructuring of the spacecraft's design. At the time this issue came up . . . we were already proceeding along with fabrication, and major changes of this sort couldn't be taken lightly.

. . . I responded by writing a paper, explaining the ramifications of such a change . . . We went round and round about that, and there was quite a bit of paper exchange "Okay," I said at last, "if you want to give us a change order, fine, I'll give you the impact statement, and it will be in cost and schedule. If you still want to change from what was agreed on, that's fine, too," but I made clear that they couldn't change requirements this radically and still maintain the original schedule . . . What we did . . . was to not just say "No,"

but "No, because if you do this it will impact this, this, and this." We ended up sticking with the original system.[h]

In his book *The Art of Project Management*, Berkun Scott maintains that "things happen when you say no . . . The problem is that if you can't say no, you can't have priorities . . . If you can't say no, you can't manage a project . . . To prepare yourself . . . you need to know all the different flavors that the word no comes in:

- No, this doesn't fit our priorities . . .
- No, only if we have the time . . .
- No, only if you make <insert impossible thing here> happen . . .
- No, next release . . .
- No. Never. Ever. Really . . . "[31]

In his study of good-to-great companies, Jim Collins found that "stop doing" lists are more important than "to do" lists.[32] Terry Little, from the U.S. Air Force, shares his strategy for coping with requested changes in project requirements:

Too often I see managers who agree to adding work without either increasing the time or money to do the work. In effect, this makes adding requirements seem "free." It is bad business and can turn a realistic schedule and budget into wishful thinking. I have found it useful—and this doesn't come easy to me—to create a very bureaucratic process for changing requirements. Basically, I say there will be no changes in requirements until (1) decision makers understand the cost and schedule implications of the change, and (2) decision makers explicitly agree to those implications. It is quite amazing to see how a process that simply establishes accountability for requirements growth promotes better discipline.[i]

However, Little is aware that project changes stem not only from changes in requirements initiated by the customer. Therefore, in addition to the preceding general process for coping with change in requirements, he recommends the following practice:

The process [of developing requirements] is flawed because there are usually too many requirements. Something about the engineering or designer mentality seems to demand hosts of requirements as an input to the technical process. Granted, it's more comforting to have someone else issue the requirements than it is to have to derive them. But, being overly constrained by too many requirements with too little wiggle-room will invariably create problems. In a perfect world, a sponsor's requirement would only be to obtain a certain capability with the detailed technical requirements derived [later] from what's truly possible . . . A program or project should start with only a few key requirements. "Few" means not more than four or five, and "key" means that if the program doesn't meet these requirements, it should be terminated.[j]

Drastically reducing the number of objectives is strongly recommended
by Peters. He cites Richard Haass (a government executive and a proliferate author), who wrote "on a little card I carried with me, the three
big things I was trying to get done. Three. Not two. Not four. Not
five. Not ten. Three." Peters has slightly modified this practice to suit
his own needs: "Truth is, I disagree with Haass. My magic number [is]
TWO. No matter. Whether it's two . . . or three . . . I surely agree
with 'not four . . . not ten.'"[33]

Reducing the number of project requirements fulfills two objectives.
First, it reduces the number of changes that result from overspecification
of objectives **too early** (before the "means are explored," as recommended
by the Green Principle). In turn, reducing the number of changes facilitates adherence to "maintaining focus." Second, by forcing more priori-
tization of requirements, it enhances the development of 80/20 mind-set
and thus facilitates adherence to "creating a focus." Embracing Little's
"bureaucratic process for changing requirements," as well as his practice
of starting a project "with only a few key requirements," should significantly help the project team to both create AND maintain project focus.

Creating and maintaining project focus also establishes the proper conditions for transitioning into actual project implementation. The current
guideline attempts to establish stability, whereas the next guideline strives
to allow flexibility. Together, they build a culture similar to the one Collins
found in good-to-great companies: "They had freedom, but freedom within
a framework . . . [and they build] a culture of discipline, a culture . . .
of freedom and responsibility, within a framework." In essence, the current and next guidelines complement each other by establishing a culture
of flexibility (Think Deliverables) within a stable framework (Create and
Maintain a Focus).[34]

The Second Brown Guideline: Think Deliverables

This guideline is at the center of a wide range of practices, all deviat-
ing from the traditional process-oriented culture. However, practicing this
guideline requires a fundamentally different way of thinking. Thus, rather
than naming this guideline by using a typical "observable behavior" (e.g.,
Produce Deliverables), it is characterized by using a "reportable attitude"
(i.e., Think Deliverables). This issue will be further explored at the end
of this guideline.

This discussion of the Think Deliverables Guideline begins with the
norms and behaviors that successful project teams exhibit while practicing a strong results- and customer-oriented culture. As will be demonstrated, a results-oriented culture does not advocate a practice free of
project processes, but rather only free of heavy processes. Finally, the fundamental transformation that must be accomplished to allow a widespread
adoption of Think Deliverables will be outlined. This transformation

requires a shift from a context-free practice to a practice that tailors project processes to the unique context of the project.

A Culture of Results and Customer Orientation

This is how Geert Hofstede, who studied organizational culture, explains some of the unique characteristics of results-oriented culture and customer-oriented culture: "In the process-oriented cultures, people perceive themselves as avoiding risks . . . each day is pretty much the same. In the results-oriented cultures, people perceive themselves as comfortable in unfamiliar situations . . . each day is felt to bring new challenges . . . in the normative units [units which perceive their task as the implementation of inviolable rules], the major emphasis is on correctly following organizational procedures, which are more important than results . . . In the pragmatic units [market-driven units], there is a major emphasis on meeting customers' needs, results are more important than correct procedures."[35]

Projects are about delivering results to customers. The following two stories demonstrate how adopting an approach that focused on both project results and project customers was critical for project success. The first story is told by Pat Tobergte from P&G:

I was the project manager for a capacity improvement project, which consisted of moving two production lines from one building to another within the plant. The goal was to start up and achieve target rate within two months . . . [However], at that time, projects had typically focused on the completion of construction as their goal.

Start-up for a manufacturing facility includes activities such as equipment testing, workers' training, and the turnover of the working facility to the customer. Pat explains that by maintaining the traditional focus on completion of construction, the team could not have achieved target rate on time. Therefore, to satisfy customer needs, the team decided to extend project boundaries and to focus on the end of start-up rather than the end of construction.

We developed a plan that integrated not only engineering, purchasing, and construction but also the training for plant technicians and raw materials . . . [We used] trained technicians to do the start-up instead of bringing in "experts" to run the equipment.

And the results? The team achieved target rate in two months.[k]

In the following story by Scott Cameron from P&G, success was achieved only after an early failure triggered a radical new implementation approach:

The plant supported six of the company's businesses and the project was designed to completely close the plant and relocate its businesses to four different sites.

The project manager for this effort was new to his position; he considered this a simple project and did not think it was necessary to involve the customers in planning the relocation.

Unfortunately, under this execution strategy, the first business relocation was 30 percent over its original capital budget, was late, and did not meet the original production goals. Following the first relocation, the project manager resigned from the company and Cameron was asked to lead the project. After reviewing the project status, Cameron determined that the project's original implementation strategy did not have the proper business focus.

Working with the customers, we defined a new execution strategy . . . This new strategy named engineering/project teams for all six businesses and treated each as a separate project with specific objectives . . . The project teams achieved the desired objectives because they could now focus on each business individually.[1,36]

Both of these examples illustrate how involving the customer and adopting a results-oriented focus triggered changes in project strategy, scope, and boundaries, which in turn led to project success. The importance of working closely with the customer and shifting the team focus outwardly is further discussed in the Red and Gray Principles.

The following two stories demonstrate how the Think Deliverables attitude affects the approach to coping with failures during project implementation. The first story is told by David Panhorst, an R&D manager at Armament Research, Development and Engineering Center (ARDEC):

I managed the development of the Army's first smart tank bullet. The projectile's built-in sensor searches the ground for targets. Upon locating a target, the sensor aims and triggers a warhead to hit and defeat the target from above, where it is most vulnerable. This fly-over, shoot-down technique differs from the hit-to-defeat method use by current tank ammunition.

Following the first two budgeted iterations of fin design tests, which failed miserably, Panhorst authorized the inclusion of additional test objectives as part of the fin retest hardware in order to contain cost growth to the contract. The problem with having so many layers of test objectives, however, was that with each fin failure, all subsequent test data were lost. Nevertheless, the team pressed on and continued to add bells and whistles to each successive fin redesign test until they had gathered enough data on other subsystems to solve the problem.

It wasn't until we stopped and regrouped that we were able to refocus on the original objective and concentrate on the fin deployment problem, which, after all, is the first thing that needs to happen. By refocusing our efforts on the primary objective, we were able to fix the problem and develop a fin that opened reliably and predictably.

As children, the first lesson we learned when we were introduced to ball sports, such as baseball or tennis, was "Keep your eye on the ball." In project management, it is no different, you must maintain project focus. In our case, we should have focused on validating the project concept rather than minimizing test cost.[m]

Terry Little from the U.S. Air Force suggests a completely different way of coping with such failures during project implementation:

We had a test where a warhead didn't go off. The flight of the cruise missile was perfect, but the warhead didn't go off. You could look at this and say, "Well that's just one little piece of it." But if the warhead doesn't go off, you don't have a weapon.

In this case, we quickly determined that there was a design problem with the fuse, and we moved on to have a successful retest—but not before we mined every bit of information that we possibly could out of that failure.

Whenever there is a failure, the first thing to do is to go through a short grieving period. On JASSM, whenever we had a failure, I allowed grieving for one day. We could grieve and mope, get drunk, wring our hands, say "ain't it awful." We could do that for one day, and then it was time to put it behind us. That's a Terry Little rule.

. . . When you have a problem on a project, all of a sudden people want to know, "What's going on? What's the problem?" Most project managers want those questions to go away, so there is a tendency to want to jump to the solution and respond, "Don't worry, we've got this in hand. It was just one of those things."

What you need to do is dig until you get to the root cause of the problem, until you are certain that you understand why this failure happened. Yes, it takes a little longer. Yes, it costs more money. In my case, a week to get to the root cause of a problem is $4 or $5 million. But you've got to do it, so that when you move forward you know that you have learned from the failure. A lot of times what caused it will be a gnat, but you should still kill it with a sledgehammer and smash it to bits until you are convinced that, though you may have other failures in the future, that particular one will never occur again—ever. You can't move forward from a failure if you're worried about repeating the same mistake.[n]

The preceding two stories present two strikingly different management philosophies. Like the European navigator discussed at the beginning of this chapter, Panhorst was too concerned with the original test plan (which called for only two iterations of fin design tests), rather than focusing on the objective of the project ("to develop a fin that opened reliably and predictably"). More importantly, he was reluctant to modify the original plan. In contrast, Little quickly modified the plan in order to spend the necessary time on mining "every bit of information" from the failure. Like the Trukese navigator, Little's primary focus was on the objectives: "If the warhead doesn't go off, you don't have a weapon." In so doing, Little exhibited a fundamental aspect of the Think Deliverables approach—a focus on results requires a readiness to modify the plans leading to those results!

The following story by Larry Lawson, vice president of Lockheed Martin, demonstrates that a focus on results often requires modifications not only of the specific plans of the project, but also of another type of "plans"—general plans that are often regarded as fixed.

I remember a meeting shortly after the first-phase source selection where Terry said, "Okay, here's the way it is. We did the last downselect 50 percent on past performance. Now the rules are different. Affordability is going to be foremost. The contractor who can provide the best price—and is somebody that we can work with—is going to win."

That was a wake-up call to me. I remember realizing that we were going down the wrong road. We were moving ahead with a performance-oriented agenda. We had to change what we were doing and drive everything toward affordability, and we did. One of our engineers was quoted a few months later as saying, "We would shoot granny for a dollar."

. . . [Acquisition reform] forced us to take a whole new look at the way we did things. For example, we normally would have built composites at our Skunk Works facility in Palmdale, California. Our Skunk Works facility and team are legendary, but because affordability meant everything, we went with a supplier instead. It would have been lower risk to do it at Palmdale, it would have been superior quality, but it was going to cost us more money.

We found a company outside of Boston that had been in the business of making baseball bats and golf club shafts. They had never built a military product, but they knew how to weave carbon fiber and were open-minded, and we were committed to making them successful. We brought this small company from being a baseball bat provider to being a cruise missile supplier, and it was a remarkable transformation. I have to give the credit to the folks at Palmdale. In spite of the fact that they were going to lose the work, they found the Boston company for us. They also helped find a supplier for our missile wings. One of the fellows at Palmdale knew about a company that built surfboards. He said, "Hey, look, I think this wing is the same kind of thing that they do with surfboards." We went down to their factory in a disadvantaged section of Los Angeles and bought the equipment for them. Now they make cruise missile wings using surfboard technology.°

The story above highlights the two levels of adaptation that at times may be required in order to deliver results to the customer in a dynamic environment:

The first level of adaptation focuses on the particular plan prepared for the current project, that is, the specific plan. The second level, which is wider and deeper, focuses on the standard practices of the organization—what may be thought of as standing plans, given their predetermined nature. This second level typically involves changes in long-held routines and habits that often require the cooperation of organizational bodies external to the project. However, a results-centered organization is one that enables its project teams to adapt standard organizational practices as needs dictate.

Think "Early and Frequent Deliverables"

Think "Early and Frequent Deliverables" recommends subdividing large projects into smaller subprojects. The reader may recall that in the Third Green Guideline (Use an Appropriate Amount of Redundancy), it is also recommended that very large projects be subdivided. However, in the Third Green Guideline the subprojects are executed in parallel, while here it is recommended that the subprojects be executed serially.[37]

A 2003 article in *Harvard Business Review,* "Why Good Projects Fail Anyway," by Matta and Ashkenas, presents a good case for executing subprojects serially: "Big projects fail at an astonishing rate . . . by some estimates . . . well over half the time . . . Managers expect they can plan for all the variables in a complex project in advance, but they can't. Nobody is that smart or has that clear a crystal ball." Only late in the project life cycle do team members sometimes realize that a critical ingredient has been missed, and by that time, it may be too late to repair the damage.

The key to avoiding this problem, say Matta and Ashkenas, "is to inject into the overall plan a series of miniprojects—what we call rapid-results initiatives—each staffed with a team responsible for a version of the hoped-for overall results in miniature and each designed to deliver its results quickly." These small projects ("early deliverables") help the project team uncover the missing pieces early on in the process when it is still simple and easy to make the required adjustments to planning and implementation.

Matta and Ashkenas share an example where the goal was to double sales revenue over two years by implementing a customer relationship management (CRM) system for the sales force: "Using a traditional project management approach, you might have one team research and install software packages, another analyze the different ways that the company interacts with customers (e-mail, telephone, and in person, for example), another develop training programs, and so forth. Many months later, however, when you start to roll out the program, you might discover that the salespeople aren't sold on the benefits. So even though they may know how to enter the requisite data into the system, they refuse."

Matta and Ashkenas then present another possible way to address the same project, this time by employing the rapid-results initiatives method. For example, a single team will take responsibility for helping a small number of users in one region to increase their revenues by 25 percent within four months: "Team members would probably draw on all the activities described above, but to succeed at their goal, the microcosm of the overall goal, they would be forced to find out what, if anything, is missing from their plans as they go forward. Along the way, they would, for example, discover the salespeople's resistance, and they would be compelled to educate the sales staff about the system's benefits . . . When they've ironed out all the kinks on a small scale, their work would then become a model for the next teams, which would either engage in further rapid-results initiatives or roll the system out to the whole organization—but now with a higher level of confidence that the project will have the intended impact on sales revenue."[38]

This incremental approach to project implementation facilitates early feedback, making it vital in today's dynamic environment.[39] Both the Second Green Guideline (Employ a Learning-Based Planning and Control Process) and the Second Brown Guideline (Think Deliverables) place ongoing learning at their core. However, learning from early deliverables—tangible intermediate products—rather than from measuring performance and analyzing the deviations between planning and performance is easier and more effective. For example, in relation to software development projects, Alan MacCormack reports clear evidence of the benefits of early release of evolving products to the customer: "The most striking result to emerge from the research concerned the importance of getting a low-functionality version of the product into the customer's hands at the earliest opportunity . . . [contributing to a] dramatic difference in performance."[40]

Moreover, since early deliverables provide feedback via a familiar medium, the customer can play an active role in this learning process. Thus, Think Deliverables significantly facilitates communication between the project team and the customer. In essence, early deliverables enjoy many of the benefits of common prototyping (i.e., rich and quick feedback that the customer can easily understand and assess), with one added and crucial benefit: they are not throwaways, but rather will eventually evolve into the delivered end product.[41]

In addition to facilitating ongoing learning, early deliverables are an asset by virtue of their generating "small wins." Weick explains the nature and role of small wins as follows: "A small win is a concrete, complete, implemented outcome of moderate importance. By itself a small win may seem unimportant. A series of wins at small but significant tasks, however, reveals a pattern that may attract allies, deter opponents, and lower resistance to subsequent proposals . . . Once a small win has been accomplished, forces are set in motion that favor another small win. When a solution is put in place, the next solvable problem often becomes more visible. This occurs because new allies bring new solutions with them and old opponents change their habits. Additional resources also flow toward winners, which means that slightly larger wins can be attempted."[42]

At times, even supposedly "small milestones" can be used as small wins. As Terry Little from the U.S. Air Force explains, he uses every successful test of the missile his team develops as a small win.

It would be nice if failures never happened, but any time you undertake some-thing that has significant risk, no matter how well you attempt to do it, no matter what the caliber of the team, no matter how much money you have to spend, there will always be times when you have failures. Therefore, every suc-cessful test that you have should be a cause for celebration. It's a big deal, a very big deal. Even though in and of itself it may be just one small milestone, there is an enormous amount of energy and effort that goes into getting to this point, a point at which all of our individual work bears fruit and becomes something bigger and better than the sum of its parts. This is how we know we are a winning team.[P]

Bill Gates asserts that subdividing large projects into subprojects that are executed serially has additional benefits. Acknowledging the high failure rate of large projects, he suggests, "Projects of only three to four months' duration are going to have much lower failure rates. With short projects, you're forced to make important trade-offs that will drive you to simplicity and focus. You'll end up with goals that can be executed."[43]

How long should the incremental process last? For most projects, this process is justified only as long as uncertainty is high and as long as the learning gained from early deliverables can significantly facilitate the planning and implementation of the following project increments. In some projects, the key consideration is motivation, and the process should last as long as the motivational gains from the small successes are crucial for overcoming resistance or energizing the team.

In software projects, the incremental process is generally applied throughout the life of the project. Here, Michael Cusumano explains the process of daily "builds" at Microsoft: "The core idea is to encourage programmers to innovate and experiment, but frequently synchronize their design with other team members by creating 'builds' (working versions) of the product as often as possible."[44] The application of the incremen-tal approach throughout the life of the project is popular in software projects, even when the projects are not large. In his book *Death March*, Edward Yourdon argues that "it often makes sense to organize the entire project around the concept of a 'daily build.' By this, I mean: compile, link, install, and test the entire collection of code produced by the team every day, as if this was the last day before the deadline and you had to ship whatever you've got to the user tomorrow morning . . . [when] the project manager [only] hears status reports delivered in a verbal fash-ion or documented in written memos . . . it is all too easy to confuse motion with progress, and effort with achievement."[45]

The Agile method of software development puts the incremental approach to project implementation at the heart of its philosophy and practices. Three of the twelve principles of the Agile Alliance focus on the incremental approach, stressing the importance of early, frequent, and continuous deliverables.

- Principle One: "Our highest priority is to satisfy the customer through early and continuous delivery of valuable software."
- Principle Three: "Deliver working software frequently, from a couple of weeks to a couple of months, with a preference to the shorter timescale."
- Principle Seven: "Working software is the primary measure of progress."[46]

Project Processes in a Results-Oriented Culture

Thus far, it has been demonstrated that the Think Deliverables Guideline can be applied in three different ways:

- As a focus on end results: The guideline is applied for the project as a whole (without subdividing the project).
- As a focus on short-term results: The project is subdivided and the incremental approach is applied for the first few cycles.
- As a focus on continuous and frequent deliverables: The project is subdivided and the incremental approach is applied throughout the life of the project.

All three possibilities are results centered and in line with the argument that "in a world of change, product enslaves process."[47] Does enslaving mean that project processes should be abandoned? The answer is no. It is true that in today's dynamic environment, projects should strongly avoid an emphasis on processes like the one reported by Hofstede at the beginning of this guideline: "The major emphasis is on correctly following organizational procedures, which are more important than results." On the other hand, successful project teams should not totally abandon the use of project processes; rather, they can make use of them following their proper adaptation to the dynamic environment.

In the introduction, we shared a story by Scott Cameron on a recent streamlining of the standard project procedures at P&G. Cameron reports that project managers at P&G have had the number of their standard procedures markedly reduced from 18 technical standards and 32 standard operating procedures to only four of each. He summarizes the impact of this streamlining as follows:

The project management community was delighted with these reductions and felt empowered by them. It gave them more flexibility to manage their projects and develop their own personal management style . . . The streamlining process enabled us to reduce the effort, costs and time required to maintain these standards.[9,48]

We have repeatedly argued that every project is unique, so why is there a need for standard procedures? The answer is that even unique operations like projects share many regular, repetitive patterns of action.[49] These practices prevent reinventing the wheel, save time and energy, and contribute significantly to the parties' ability to maintain cooperation efficiently, even in the face of uncertainty. Standard project procedures also help to create a common vocabulary. The world of project management incorporates many concepts that have no hard-and-fast definitions. In this environment of multiple disciplines, specialization, and trade or slang terminology, standard project procedures avoid ambiguity and facilitate communication.[50] Finally, standard project procedures also serve as the organizational retention system, in which the accumulated organizational knowledge about project management methodology and systems is stored for purposes of formal and on-the-job training and continuous organizational learning.

The procedure manuals in companies dominated by a results-centered culture are often prepared by the most experienced practicing project managers in the company. The procedures mainly focus on the professional practices that facilitate cooperation between the numerous parties required for the delivery of the project. The procedures are brief and simple, allowing for and even encouraging flexibility. They are presented in a friendly style and format, including tips and actual examples. Moreover, these manuals explicitly recognize that the procedures are not intended to cover all possible situations, but rather only the most common ones.[51]

However, it seems that the transition from a process-centered culture to a results-centered culture is quite slow for both project researchers and practitioners.[52] Following are brief examples shared by two very experienced project managers, who at the time of sharing these stories led the development of project management practices and processes in their respective organizations. The first story is told by Scott Cameron, the global process owner of project management at P&G:

> To come back to your question about an example [regarding the impact of speed on the way I manage projects], one project comes to mind: site clearance. Unfortunately, we have had a few brands that haven't made it and we have had to clear out everything we've put in. Site clearance to me is pretty simple. You walk in the room, you see the equipment making the product, and you say, "Here's my spec: I want all of that gone," and you're ready to bid the job. Somebody might accuse me of oversimplifying it, but that's pretty much what you want done. The interesting thing is, when you go out and you ask people to write the site clearance specification, it comes back 400 pages long . . . often what's required is unlearning of old thinking. If speed is your priority, you should approach the job differently.

The second story is told by Terry Little, the director of the Air Force Acquisition Center of Excellence. Like Cameron, Little believes that in today's dynamic environment (e.g., accelerated speed), we must unlearn the old way of thinking.

> *A lot of processes that we have . . . are built on lack of trust. When you hand somebody an 11-page specification rather than a 100-page document, however, you are sending a clear signal that you trust them to do the right thing. My own belief is that, as an individual project manager, you can go a long way in that direction by starting not with the notion that someone has to earn your trust, but starting with the presumption that they're trustworthy until proven otherwise. It allows things like an 11-page specification. My biggest disappointment in the past has been when I have given project managers the opportunity to innovate, and they don't know what to do with it. They demand processes, rigidity, templates, and prescriptions. It is as if you give them a blank check and they write it for a dollar . . . What you've got to do, I am convinced, is to "unlearn" . . . all of our processes that are not oriented toward speed or credibility, but are oriented toward not making a mistake, playing it safe.*[r]

In his book *Augustine's Laws*, Augustine discusses at length the problems of process-oriented cultures, among them too many regulations and the dangers of "playing it safe." Following is one of the arguments that Augustine presents against the growth of regulations: "The fallacy in using regulations to prevent problems is that if managers could ignore the old regulation, they can ignore the new one, too." Still, Augustine asserts, "Regulations grow at the same rate as weeds," as demonstrated in the following example: "In 1946 the US Atlantic Fleet was comprised of 778 ships and sailed under regulations contained in a 72-page pamphlet. In contrast, today's Atlantic Fleet may only have 297 ships, but it is well equipped with regulations—308 pages of them."[53]

It is clear that a shift to a results-oriented culture requires learning to trust and unlearning the "play it safe" approach. However, there is another major unlearning that both researchers and practitioners alike must first undergo, that is, abandoning the "one best way" approach and recognizing the need to adapt project processes to the unique context of each project.

Tailoring Project Processes to Project Context

Drucker argues that since the study of management began in the 1930s, several assumptions regarding the realities of management have been held by most scholars, writers, and practitioners. He further argues that today these assumptions must be unlearned. Two of these assumptions are germane to our discussion. First, "there is (or there must be) ONE right organization structure." Second, "there is (or there must be) ONE right way to manage people." Regarding the first assumption, Drucker recommends that much work must be done in organization theory and practice to help managers develop "the organization that fits the task." As for the second assumption, Drucker argues, "In no other area are the basic traditional assumptions held as firmly—though mostly subconsciously—as in respect to people and their management." More importantly, "In no other area are they so totally at odds with reality and so totally counterproductive."[54]

The following experiment demonstrates one possible "counterproductive" consequence of clinging to the "one best way" when it is at odds with reality:

> *If you place in a bottle half a dozen bees and the same number of flies and lay the bottle horizontally, with its base (the closed end) to the window, you will find that the bees will persist, till they die of exhaustion or hunger, in their endeavor to discover an opening through the glass; while the flies, in less than two minutes, will all have sallied forth through the neck on the opposite side . . . It is the bees' love of light, it is their very intelligence, that is their undoing in this experiment. They evidently imagine that the issue from every prison must be where the light shines clearest; and they act in accordance, and persist in too-logical action. To bees, glass is a supernatural mystery . . . And, the greater their intelligence, the more inadmissible, more incomprehensible, will the strange obstacle appear. Whereas the featherbrained flies, careless of logic . . . flutter wildly hither and thither, and meeting here the good fortune that often waits on the simple . . . necessarily end up by discovering the friendly opening that restores their liberty to them.*[55]

Indeed, the "featherbrained" team that employs a random search (like the flies) may perform better in a dynamic environment than the "too-systematic team," which completely lacks sensitivity to variation in project context (like the bees). The challenge is to transform the "too-systematic team" and render it context sensitive, that is, a team that applies the Results-Focused Leadership principles as general instructions that must be tailored to each unique context of the project (e.g., project size, stability of objectives, speed, task complexity, organizational culture, extent of top management support, and team members' experience and skills).[56]

Johns presents evidence that organizational researchers are inclined to downplay "the specifics of the situation" or, as it is often termed, "the context." According to Johns, it seems that context-free research is somehow perceived as being more scientific and prestigious than context-specific research.[57] Unfortunately, many practitioners also downplay the importance of the context. Leinberger and Tucker explain that "the success of analytic methods led to a consensus . . . that analytic thinking was good thinking . . . Viewed from an analytic perspective, problems were believed to be context-free; therefore, managers did not appear to need a wide range of experience or the wisdom of years."[58]

For the most part, the project management literature has not given explicit treatment to context issues and has thus implicitly endorsed the "one best way" approach.[59] Recently, however, there are some notable exceptions, especially by proponents of Agile Project Management. For example, Highsmith states, "There is no silver bullet, but there are Lone Rangers who have arsenals of bullets for different situations."[60] Beck, who is extremely critical of "taylorism" (i.e., the principles of Fredrick W. Taylor, the father of scientific management), says, "My experience is that these principles make no sense as strategies for software development, no business sense, and no human sense."[61] Royce also recommends tailoring the process: "While there are some universal themes and techniques, it is always necessary to tailor the process to the specific needs of the project at hand."[62]

In his book *Six Action Shoes*, de Bono relates pragmatism to context sensitivity. "Some people condemn pragmatism because they believe that pragmatism seems to be a way of acting without principles. Pragmatism does not mean being unprincipled: it means the pragmatic use of principles. Pragmatism is when you do what can be done to achieve an objective and put as much emphasis on practicality as on principles . . . Pragmatism means being sensitive to the situation."[63]

Recently, even some large organizations have started to develop a context-sensitive culture. In the introduction, Dr. Edward Hoffman, director of the NASA Academy of Program and Project Engineering and Leadership, shares a story about 23 students, some of them very experienced project managers, who were uncomfortable with the message delivered in their advanced project management training.

> The team spent four months conducting interviews in and out of NASA, developing recommendations, and preparing a presentation given at NASA Headquarters in Washington, D.C. Their effort led to a significant change in NASA's Project Management Procedures. For example, as a result of their input, NASA was willing to abolish the "one best way" approach and to allow project teams to tailor project procedures to the unique context of their project.[5]

Following is a brief example of how the different contexts of two information technology projects may affect their working culture.

> *One is developing the control software for an airplane. What "correct behavior" means is a highly technical and mathematical subject. FAA regulations must be followed. Anything you do—or don't do—would be evidence in a lawsuit 20 years from now. The development staff shares an engineering culture that values caution, precision, repeatability, and double-checking everyone's work.*
>
> *Another project is developing a word processor that is to be used over the web. "Correct behavior" is whatever woos a vast and inarticulate audience of Microsoft Word users over to your software. There are no regulatory requirements that matter (other than those governing public stock offerings). Time to market matters— 20 months from now, it will all be over, for good or ill. The development staff*

*decidedly does not come from an engineering culture, and attempts to talk in
a way normal for the first culture will cause them to refer to you as "damage
to be routed around."*[64]

Unfortunately, as we have seen, the prevailing project management paradigm is still more process centered than results centered, and it is not
yet context sensitive. Thus, the emphasis in most projects is still placed
on the "standard" or the "common" rather than on the "unique." Melgrati
and Damiani make this point very eloquently: "Project management ideology is paradoxical because it focuses on repetitive aspects and 'marginalizes' the uniqueness and originality that should instead characterize the
project."[65]

One of the primary missions of the current book is to help the reader
become more context sensitive (see the meta-principles in the introduction). Since stories are highly context sensitive, their extensive use
throughout this book should facilitate the required shift from a context-
free mind-set to a context-specific one.[66] Sensitivity to project context
will be further discussed throughout this book.

Think Deliverables: Why "Think"?

It is time now to revisit and elaborate more on the term chosen for
this guideline: Think Deliverables. Once one accepts the definition of a
project as a temporary endeavor undertaken to create a unique product
or service and becomes convinced (by reading the current guideline) that
in a world of change, product enslaves process, then one must also accept
that delivering (unique) results to the customer should be THE raison
d'etre of a project.

This concept runs contrary to the more traditional process-centered
paradigm, in which work is organized around the concept of tasks (or
activities).[67] The centrality of the task was proposed by Fredrick Taylor
back in 1911: "Perhaps the most prominent single element in modern
scientific management is the task idea."[68] More appropriate to today's
projects, one may paraphrase Taylor's assertion as follows: "Perhaps
one of the most prominent elements in managing projects in a dynamic
environment is the deliverable idea."[69] This transformation from a
century-old paradigm of the centrality of the task idea to the centrality of the deliverable idea demands dedicated and persistent effort
aimed at changing our mind-set— indeed, to the point that we think
differently.[70]

The meaning of Think Deliverables is simply to stress that your
thoughts should be centered on deliverables for the implementation of
any and every project.[71] In fact, it may often require more than one
project until the desired change of mind-set is achieved. Successful project teams, who have undergone the required transformation from "tasks

to deliverables," understand the complementary roles of Planning and Control (the Green Principle that underscores tasks) and Implementation (the Brown Principle that underscores deliverables) and are fully aware of their vital interaction in a dynamic environment. Therefore, it is only natural for them to focus on both tasks and deliverables. The interaction between the Green and Brown Principles will be further discussed at the end of the Third Brown Guideline.

The Third Brown Guideline: Act with Agility

In a 1994 *Harvard Business Review* article, Nohria and Berkley argue that in the 1980s, U.S. business experienced an explosion of new management concepts, all with their own special formula for how to stay competitive, yet all falling short of the mark: "The management fads of the last 15 years rarely produced their promised results . . . If business leaders want to reverse this trend, they must reclaim managerial responsibility—and pragmatism is the place to start." According to Nohria and Berkley, the "four faces of pragmatism" are sensitivity to context, focus on outcomes, openness to uncertainty, and willingness to make do. The first three "faces" were at the heart of the previous guideline, Think Deliverables. The current guideline addresses the fourth "face": willingness to make do.[72]

Willingness to Make Do

According to Nohria and Berkley, managers who make do are characterized by knowing what resources are available and how to round up more on short notice. That is, they seek pragmatic answers on the basis of the material at hand. The improvising that is so often required of project managers in today's dynamic environment is a common example of making do. Brian Muirhead, who was responsible for the development and launch of the Mars Pathfinder flight system, argues that "everybody understands the need for a plan . . . But in a world of Faster, Better, Cheaper, improvising should be seen as an inseparable part of planning, the other half of a complete process. In the fast-paced, rapidly changing world in which we now live and do business, the ability to improvise has risen to the top of the priority list of managerial skills."[73] Steve Kerr, chief learning officer of General Electric, further clarifies the growing need for improvisation: "The future is moving so quickly that you can't anticipate it . . . We have put a tremendous emphasis on quick response instead of planning. We will continue to be surprised, but we won't be surprised that we are surprised."[74]

Following are two examples of improvisations introduced in the midst of projects. The first story is told by Kenneth Szalai from NASA, who served as the chief engineer and software manager for the first digital fly-by-wire aircraft:

> *A systems engineer called me and told me that the preflight self-test had failed . . . While troubleshooting, I froze and my heart sank. The problem was far worse than some self-test tolerance setting. I discovered that a half-dozen instructions did not match the program listing! . . . the flight computer had contaminated instructions. We did not have the means to automatically check the computer memory against the accurate printed listing . . . I laughed to myself and thought: How long would it take to manually check the computer memory dump against the listing? Let's see, there are 25,000 memory locations, if we had five teams of engineers, and they could read aloud and verify one memory location every 10 seconds, five teams could verify 30 memory locations in a minute. That would take about 14 hours . . . We finished by Friday afternoon, and did not find any other errors. I guess sometimes pioneering work needs solutions rather than elegance . . . We flew on Wednesday, as Carl had asked.*[t]

Facing enormous time pressure, Kenneth came up with a spontaneous improvisation that provided a simple, albeit inelegant, solution to the problem. A results-oriented focus calls for solutions, and the process used to attain those results is irrelevant.[75]

In the next case, Leslie Shepherd shares a story about a renovation project for the U.S. federal government. Since the buildings were occupied, Leslie was required to work around the tenants and the existing site conditions, and to do it quickly.

> The roof of a fully occupied office building was being renovated, which required covering it with roofing tar. The fumes from the tar were being pulled in by the building's fresh air intakes, making it impossible to work. The building manager could have shut down the air intake system for a few hours at a time, but not for the entire day. After considering his options, Leslie decided to take a non-traditional approach to solving the problem.

> *My solution may not have been elegant, but it was effective. We hired someone to stand on the roof next to the air intakes and sniff for tar fumes. The building manager trained the new worker how to turn the air intake fans on and off. He started work the very next day, turning the fans on or off depending on his olfactory reflexes. That was his only job and the additional salary for this "Official Sniffer" was far less than the lost hours resulting from interrupted work that had to be covered by the tenants. The building manager received no more complaints about the tar fumes for the entire duration of the roofing project.*[u]

Leslie, like Kenneth in the first story, was under a great time pressure. His improvisation is characterized by spontaneity *and* creativity, demonstrating that high tech is neither the only nor always the best way to solve a problem.

These two examples demonstrate that inelegant low-tech solutions can be effective due to their simplicity and quick implementation. Still, while clearly part of the required arsenal for managing projects, these kinds of ad hoc improvised solutions are not typically practiced daily. However, as we will see in the next section, other modes of the Act with Agility Guideline are in fact applied systematically and frequently.

Maintaining Momentum

In a dynamic environment, when time is a scarce resource, acting with agility is often the norm rather than the exception. In the following story, Larry Barrett, the chief systems engineer for the Hubble control center system, describes the agile decision-making practice applied during a reengineering project at the Hubble ground system.

> We achieved a remarkable level of productivity and quality during the time we developed the new code. In my experience, it was exceptional . . . What made it work so well? For one thing, we had a stakeholder who decided that Hubble needed a new ground system, and she was willing to do whatever it took to get it done quickly. To achieve this goal, she was willing to allow Ken [Ken Lehtonen, the new NASA project manager responsible for the reengineering project] to run things the way he wanted to, including demolishing a hierarchical decision structure . . .
>
> Before Ken, I recall people quitting the project because of the lack of progress. Under Ken, instead of taking days or weeks to walk up the chain-of-command with a here-is-our-recommendation presentation and to walk back down with a here-is-our-answer document, everyone who had an interest in the selection of this capability or this software product sat down at one meeting and said, "Okay, here is everything that we know. Here is how we want this thing to work. Here is how it fits in the system." In a two-hour meeting, an Integrated Product Team of ten to fifteen people could come together to make key project decisions.[v]

This story demonstrates how timely information sharing may allow even quickly made "key project decisions" to be effective. Ken Lehtonen, the new NASA project manager, created the ease of information sharing by getting away from a hierarchical approach, flattening the organization, and cultivating an open and candid collaborative culture. As he explains, "We had become the badgeless team . . . who had the trust, confidence and openness to stop in the hallways to discuss problems."

Lehtonen summarizes the exceptional achievements of the reengineering project:

> Not only did we meet our original milestone, but we had five major releases completed on time and on schedule. During that period, we delivered over one

million lines of code. We were producing something on the order of fifteen lines of code an hour, where the accepted norm is closer to five. Our defect metrics were a third of the normal industry rate.[w]

In regard to the importance of communication and synchronization among organizational participants, Sayles and Chandler liken the "time-keeping" role of the project manager to a metronome: "The project manager is primarily dealing with rates (of times) and organizational processes, not technical variables. He cannot easily second-guess the technical prowess of his line support groups . . . What he can and must do, however, is control their organizational participants, as distinct from their technical contribution . . . The view we have obtained [regarding the role of the project manager] is best described by the analogy to a metronome, a time-keeping mechanism which is designed to keep a number of diverse elements responsive to a central 'beat' of common rhythm."[76]

However, the role of the project manager is often more involved than that of a metronome and requires active intervention and decision making. As Sayles and Chandler further explain, "He often faces conflicting technical judgments . . . while it is not realistic under most circumstances to endeavor to prove who is right. It is more important that a decision be reached so that forward momentum can be resumed . . . Thus, the project manager wants to force a choice."[77]

The next example of systematic application of the Act with Agility Guideline is taken from a recent study in which ten highly successful on-site construction project managers were each systematically observed during the course of one week. This example highlights the project manager's role as a problem solver: "The documented problems were related to different aspects of the project, and they included, for example, attending to a leaky water pipe, the absence of workers from the site, overruns in the monthly budget, collision in the superposition between the systems of the building, etc . . . It was found that managers . . . dealt with an average of 20 different problems each day, devoting an average of 4.2 activities per hour to solving them."[78] In their role as problem solvers, 95.6 percent of the problems were addressed (not necessarily solved) by the project managers during the first seven minutes following problem identification, 50.3 percent were solved immediately, 63.9 percent were solved during the first iteration, and 91.8 percent were solved during the first three iterations. On the average, 18.6 percent of the problems were not resolved the same day on which they were identified and were addressed again on the following day.[79]

The findings on the dynamic behavior patterns of these successful project managers[80] were summarized as follows: "The observation revealed a remarkably active work style displayed by the project managers, who, on average, conducted each day 42 meetings, 28 phone calls, and 17 tours to the site production areas, and devoted 17 activities to paper and computer work . . . The average duration of their activities was about 5 min, and about 90% of the activities they performed lasted less then 10 min . . . [It should be stressed, however, that] . . . the managers conducted their work largely in a calm way and with a lot of self-control (. . . in only 4% of the activities, a loud tone of voice was used) . . . the on-site project managers were all acting in a dynamic nature."[81]

In his 1999 book, *What Leaders Really Do*, John Kotter refers to the phenomenon of dynamic patterns of behavior exhibited by effective managers as "the efficiency of seemingly inefficient behavior." As he explains, "Of all the patterns visible in daily behavior, perhaps the most difficult to understand, or at least appreciate, are that the executives do not plan their days in advance in much detail but instead react and that conversations are short and disjointed. On the surface, at least, behaving this way seems particularly unmanagerial. Yet these patterns are possibly the most important and most efficient of all."[82]

In light of the dynamic nature of the environment surrounding contemporary projects, it should not come as a surprise that even very successful project managers have to cope with so many problems during project implementation. Still, it is worth reiterating here that planning alone cannot guarantee the elimination of problems. In the third edition of the book *Implementation: How Great Expectations in Washington are Dashed in Oakland*, Majone and Wildavsky present their concept of "implementation as evolution," and conclude, "The planning model recognizes that implementation may fail because the original plan was infeasible. But it does not recognize the important point that many, perhaps most, constraints remain hidden in the planning stage, and are only discovered in the implementation process."[83]

In his study of top managers, Henry Mintzberg (1973) found their behavior, like that of project managers, to be highly dynamic. He identified ten major roles that they perform and pointed to the primary role as "disturbance handler": "The manager apparently allows disturbance handling to take priority over most other kinds of activity."[84] After two decades, Mintzberg (1991) revisited the roles of the manager in terms of a system of "ambiguity in, order out": "Organizations need order. They sometimes need disorder—shaking up—but for the most part (or, at least, most of the time), efficient production of goods and services requires order. And to the managers fall the responsibility of imposing or at least ensuring that order, as Peter Vaill has commented, for example: 'the manager is a creator and restorer of order' . . . But even while seeking to impose order, managers act in a most disorderly fashion. That is the message of every empirical study, from Carlson on, that the job is one of 'calculated chaos.' It is as if order is good for everyone in the organization except the manager!"[85]

A somewhat similar view regarding the role of the manager as problem solver is provided by Sayles and Chandler in their study on project managers. Their findings add the time dimension as it relates to both progress (of the project) and speed (of response, that is, the need to Act with Agility): "In working to maintain a forward momentum, the manager seeks to avoid stalemates . . . Another penalty for waiting is that in a good many situations, corrective action is possible only during a brief 'window' . . . The heart of the matter is quickness of response."[86] The importance of maintaining a forward momentum has only increased throughout the years, as argued by Muirhead and Simon: "Maintaining momentum is a cornerstone of successful management . . . Maintaining momentum is more important than always being right."[87]

Thus far, we have seen that in today's dynamic environment, "putting out fires" occurs more often than the old mind-set of scientific management would like us to believe. Successful project managers plan and attempt to anticipate; yet, at the same time, they develop a state of readiness to respond quickly to frequent and unanticipated events. They systematically apply the Act with Agility Guideline, attempting to create and maintain momentum, to avoid stalemates, and in general to create order. Ultimately, it is their ability to make quick decisions that enables them to Act with Agility.

Making Quick Decisions

Making quick decisions is often based on a process of learning by action. The learning by action mode is adopted when uncertainty (missing information) is coupled with an increased demand for speed, which in turn brings about a greater degree of scarcity of attention. As explained in the Second Green Guideline, these conditions are very common in today's dynamic environment. The following hedge-clipping metaphor, which is often cited in the literature, illustrates how several cycles of learning by action are employed to cope satisfactorily with missing information, speed, and scarcity of attention.

"The example we shall take is that of a householder facing the 'problem' of an overgrown hedge. The central point of this example is that analytic solutions appear highly complex (and possibly only approximate), while a 'nibbling' or incremental solution is available, easy, and satisfactory. That is, we emphasize the fact that the final position of a cut branch is a rather complex function of the physical characteristics of the shrub, of the adjoining shrubs, and of the place at which the cut is made. An analytic solution of the problem of where to cut each branch thus requires both extensive well-developed theory (of the cantilever properties of cut branches and of interactions with adjacent cut branches) and extensive data collection (exact dimensions of each branch). In contrast, a strategy of repeated clipping and inspecting requires no such knowledge and rapidly converges on a solution which may be adjusted to any desired degree of fit to the intended solution—a neatly clipped hedge. Hedge-clipping, then provides a clear example of a decision problem for which a highly reflective strategy is much less satisfactory than a highly active one."[88]

Thus, when speed is of the essence and time constraints are paramount, the continuous "nibbling" approach offers two main advantages:

- No demand either for deep problem understanding or extensive data collection and analysis.
- Hugely reduced cognitive demands on the decision maker.

The hedge-clipping strategy suggested here is an example of the "act first, think later" approach. In this case, action is an uncertainty-reducing device as well as a solution to the problem.[89] Often, uncertainty can be reduced substantially after a few "nibbles." Thus, only a few iterations of small actions are carried out in order to reduce uncertainty until sufficient feedback is collected to allow the rest of the task to continue with a "think first, act later" approach (i.e., a return to the project plan).

This approach of learning by doing may account for how the site construction project managers in the study cited above were able to solve some of the different problems during the first three iterations (which amounted to 91.8 percent of the daily problems they encountered). But how could the construction project managers solve 50.3 percent of the problems immediately in only one iteration upon identification of the problem?

One explanation is intuition. Gary Klein, who studied decision making for many years, opens his 2003 book, *Intuition at Work,* with the following story: "Almost two decades ago, I conducted my first research project on decision making, studying firefighters to see how they could make high-risk decisions in just a few seconds despite all the confusion and uncertainty inherent in their work. I knew that the firefighters wouldn't make their decisions by systematically comparing all of the possible ways to put out a fire because there wasn't enough time. I expected that they would only come up with two leading options and compare these to each other. I was wrong. The firefighters, especially the more experienced ones, some with over twenty years of experience, usually just considered a single option. In fact, to hear them describe it, they didn't really consider anything; they just acted."[90]

According to Klein, people are able to make decisions rapidly without conscious awareness or effort as an outcome of their experience. Thus, intuition can be seen as a natural and direct outgrowth of experience. Klein defines intuition as the way we translate our experience into action, as exemplified by the firefighters: "In our interviews with the firefighters, one of the most common statements my research team and I heard was, 'We don't make decisions.' This amazed us because we watched them routinely making very challenging decisions, many with life-or-death implications—and yet they were unaware they were doing it . . . Our research led us to the conclusion that we are all intuitive decision makers."[91]

In his article "How to Think with Your Gut," Thomas Stewart reported, "Today the [U.S. Marine] Corps's official doctrine reads, 'The intuitive approach is more appropriate for the vast majority of . . . decisions made in the fluid, rapidly changing conditions of war when time and uncertainty are critical factors, and creativity is a desirable trait.' Conditions, in other words, not unlike those in which many business decisions are made today."[92]

Back in 1984, when Daniel Isenberg studied managers and executives to see how they solved problems and made decisions, he concluded that executives do not make formal decisions using analytical methods: "Senior managers use intuition in at least five ways. First, they intuitively sense when a problem exists . . . Second, managers rely on intuition to perform well-learned behavior patterns rapidly . . . The third function of intuition is to synthesize isolated bits of data and experience into an integrated picture . . . Fourth, some managers use intuition as a check . . . on the results of more rational analysis . . . Fifth, managers can use intuition to bypass in-depth analysis and move rapidly to come up with a plausible solution . . . Intuition is not the opposite of rationality, nor is it a random process of guessing. Rather, it is based on extensive experience, both in analysis and problem solving and in implementation, and to the extent that the lessons of experience are logical and well founded, then so is the intuition."[93]

To make quick decisions, to Act with Agility, one must accumulate extensive experience.[94] Klein argues that "there are ways of building a person's experience base. Experience can be codified as stories and analogues." Thus, being exposed to a large variety of stories (e.g., like those presented in this book) can partially compensate for lack of actual experience.[95]

Simultaneous Application of the Results-Focused Leadership Principles

While there are situations that call for a more frequent reliance on intuition, by no means should analysis be ignored. As Mintzberg suggests, "To be effective, any organization has to couple analysis and intuition in its strategy making as well as other processes."[96] Pondy terms this relationship as a "union of rationality and intuition in management action."[97] Likewise, Hubert and Stuart Dreyfus debunk the old split between intuition and analysis, recommending that beginners should rely upon analysis when learning a new skill, while experts can use analysis to sharpen and clarify their intuitive insights.[98]

In relation to problems of strategic planning, Mintzberg reaches similar conclusions about planning and implementation: "It is the disassociation of thinking from acting that lies closer to the root of the problem." Mintzberg explains that the real blame has to be laid neither on formulation (planning) nor on implementation, "but on the very separation of the two."[99]

This concept—the need to apply more than one principle simultaneously— is exemplified in the following story, *Thanksgiving Hocus Pocus*, as told by the project manager, Christian Zazzali:

> *The client... had contracted with my company to build [in Washington, D.C.] the first flagship store outside of New England... I was managing the construction project, and I thought my biggest challenge was simply finishing the work in time for start of the holiday shopping season. The store opened three weeks before Thanksgiving. Then, two days before Thanksgiving, disaster struck.*
>
> *The fire protection system was designed to prevent smoke and fire from reaching the merchandise. If a fire alarm went off anywhere in the building, the system went into a massive pressurization mode. Dampers would open and the system would pump in hundreds of cubic feet of air from outside into the store, pressurizing every square foot, preventing fire or smoke from spreading into the store. That night an unknown event tripped the alarm —. The air conditioning system was still operational as the outside air temperatures had been warm all month. That night, however, temperatures plummeted to 20 degrees. With an alarm sounding in a building complex that covers many millions of square feet, no one paid attention to the cold air flowing into the space. Pipes froze and burst. Hundreds of gallons of water came down through the drywall, soaking merchandise, the carpet and the hardwood racks. This state of the art system, which had been designed to protect, was now responsible for unthinkable damage.*
>
> *The CEO himself came down from New England. Not looking yet to blame anyone—yet!—all he wanted to know was one thing: what was going to be done to get the store open for the day after Thanksgiving?*
>
> *I told him this: "Mr. CEO, we are going to fix this. We are going to make this right, and we will worry about how it happened later. First order of business, help the client survive the shock. Done. That was enough for then.*
>
> *. . . We immediately restored one of the three HVAC systems so we could at least have some heat. Once the heat was working, we could start drying things out. We mobilized all available manpower, including project managers from other projects, and at one point we had a Vice President operating a wet/dry vacuum. There were some 100 people doing whatever they could. The day before Thanksgiving we were cutting out drywall as fast as we could, everywhere we could. We brought in 400 sheets of drywall, taped it all up, kept going, and had the painters working right behind. All that was just to make it look good for the day after Thanksgiving because it all had to come down again. It came down to the wire, but when we were done it looked presentable. None of the customers knew what happened. The client was ecstatic. And guess what? He exceeded sales goals on the order of 200%. My company could have come out of this thing looking bad.*

Instead, the client loves us. We continue to do work with him, and he's said to us, "That HVAC design stunk. You were right. Next time, please tell us what we need."[x]

Although the project manager's behavior is definitely consistent with the Act with Agility Guideline, at the same time his story demonstrates that acting with agility may require more than just developing the capability for quick responsiveness and improvisation. Very often, it can be accomplished only if another principle of the five principles of Results-Focused Leadership is simultaneously applied. In this case, the Thanksgiving Hocus Pocus resulted from simultaneously applying the Act with Agility and Develop a Sense of a Mission Guidelines. Christian Zazzali demonstrated a strong sense of ownership of the project, a sense of a mission. One can better "see" Zazzali's sense of a mission by artificially breaking his response to the crisis down into four consecutive steps:

1. First, Zazzali explicitly decided what not to do: he did not say to the client "we told you so," or "let us first sort out who is responsible for the problem." He also did not first convene a series of meetings with his own upper management, legal advisors, and insurance consultants in order to figure out what to say to the client and how to proceed.
2. His initial action was to calm the client and help him "survive the shock," with assurances that "we are going to fix this."
3. Only then could he attend to the actual preparations for the solution. The first obstacles were the extremely short timetable and awkward timing— making it necessary to improvise on the composition of the workforce. He recruited project managers outside of the project in order to use them as a substitute for the regular workers, as well as to help him manage a large workforce without prior work planning.
4. Finally, he improvised on the work itself: "We were cutting out drywall as fast as we could, everywhere we could. We brought in 400 sheets of dry wall, taped it all up, kept going, and had the painters working right behind."

Only the last step can be fully described by the Act with Agility Guideline. The first two steps are primarily the result of adopting the right attitude—attitude of ownership. The third step demonstrates that this attitude is widespread within the company as a whole, as evidenced by the willingness of the project managers to serve as common workers. These first three steps fall under the guideline Develop a Sense of a Mission. The next chapter, Adopt a Will to Win, further explains this guideline.

This concept of simultaneously applying more than one principle is true for all five principles. When one first studies the principles, the easiest way to understand them is to learn each of the five principles as if it were applied separately. However, once the individual principles are grasped, they should all be perceived as they are most often implemented— as a union of principles that are applied simultaneously. (This concept is addressed again in the epilogue to this book.)

CHAPTER 3

The Yellow Principle: Develop a Will to Win

The First Yellow Guideline: Develop a Sense of Mission

The literature suggests several ways to distinguish between leaders and managers.

> Leaders are people who do the right things, while managers do things right. Leadership means coping with uncertainty and change, while managing means coping with complexity in stable conditions. Management, on the one hand, produces a degree of predictability, focuses on systems, relies on control, organizes and staffs, accepts the status quo, and motivates people to comply with standards. Leadership, on the other hand, produces change, focuses on people, relies on trust, aligns people with a direction, challenges the status quo, and inspires people to change.

In the project domain, this dichotomy raises the question, are successful projects managed or led? On the basis of a study of 36 successful project managers, Laufer and Hoffman provided the following answer: "From the analysis . . . we can draw two significant conclusions regarding the question of leadership vs. management. First . . . successful projects require strong leadership . . . Most project management writings stress the managerial aspects of projects, failing to recognize the significance of leadership . . . accepting the recommendations of the prevailing project management literature will bring about projects which are over-managed and under-led. Second . . . project managers have to assume both roles, leadership and managerial. There is, however, a need for a change in the kind of management practiced . . . in a dynamic environment, project management is not about performing according to plan, with minimal changes. It is about meeting customer needs, while coping successfully with unavoidable changes."[1]

James Highsmith, who wrote extensively on software development, also concluded, "Unfortunately, most software development projects are managed, not led."[2]

The current principle concentrates on project leadership. However, before presenting the specific guidelines of the current principle, it is important to understand the need for project leadership in the typical project environment, as well as its unique focus.

Peter Vaill, a management scholar, chose the permanent white water metaphor to describe the complex, turbulent, changing environment in which we are trying to operate. According to Vaill, following are the five intertwining characteristics of permanent white water:

1. They are full of surprises.
2. They have complex systems that tend to produce novel problems.
3. They are "messy" and ill structured.
4. They are often extremely costly.
5. They have preexisting conditions that raise the problems of recurrence.

In addition, the practical implication is that "permanent white water conditions are regularly taking us all out of our comfort zones and asking things of us that we never imagined would be required. Permanent white water means permanent life outside one's comfort zone."[3]

Ronald Heifetz went one step further and pinpointed the main challenge stemming from the need to cope with life outside one's comfort zone, namely, coping with adaptive problems. It is essential, however, to first overcome the prevailing difficulties of identifying the difference between an adaptive problem and a technical one. This is how Heifetz explains some of the differences between these two types of problems:

"There are problems that are just technical. I'm delighted when a car mechanic fixes my car, an orthopedic surgeon gives me back a healed bone . . . That's a key question: is this a problem that an expert can fix, or is this a problem that is going to require people in the community to change their values, their behavior, or their attitudes?"[4]

"With a technical challenge, the problem and the fix are already known. So the job really is to coordinate behavior and mobilize people to perform at their best what they already know how to do . . . An adaptive challenge is primarily one that requires people to develop new ways of doing things. It requires people to suffer the losses of sifting through what DNA to discard from their past. Technical challenges don't have the same demand. They require you to know the state of the art so that you can implement and mobilize organizational expertise."[5]

This is how Heifetz explains why projects require both management and leadership:

The quality and abundance of leadership markedly impacts the project world. Yet . . . we still tend to treat projects primarily as technical efforts that require management, i.e., the authoritative organizing of systems with an emphasis on planning and control . . . People need first-rate management when they face known challenges that fit their organizational designs, norms, and expertise. But they need leadership to tackle new challenges for which adaptability becomes paramount.[6]

Highsmith also views the main issue interfering with effective project management as the need for adaptation and asserts that "adaptation depends on leadership and collaboration rather than on command and control."[7]

When faced with real-life situations, successful project managers do not distinguish between management and leadership. As the meta-principle indicates (see introduction and epilogue), all five principles of Results-Focused Leadership are tightly interdependent, and the process of their implementation in the workplace requires fusion, not fission. Despite it being very artificial to split the principles, it is very helpful to do so and to treat each one as a stand-alone entity during the learning phase. All five principles attempt to mirror reality and therefore exhibit both management and leadership characteristics.[8] The current principle, however, concentrates on the leadership elements that allow for adaptability throughout the other four principles.

The current principle is composed of the following three guidelines:

- The First Yellow Guideline: Develop a Sense of Mission
- The Second Yellow Guideline: Challenge the Status Quo
- The Third Yellow Guideline: Persevere, but Know When to Retreat

The three guidelines differ by the frequency of their application as well as by the roles of the people who apply them; yet, they are highly interrelated. The first guideline should be employed by as many people of the project team as possible and, once embraced, should be virtually applied on a continuous basis. The sense of mission should derive from within each team member with guidance by the project manager in the proper direction. The second guideline should be practiced primarily by the project leader, and though usually it is applied only infrequently, it has a real impact on the continuous use of the first guideline as well as on all the other principles of Results-Focused Leadership. The third guideline should also be applied only by the project leader and even less frequently than the second guideline. However, it affects the use of the first guideline of this principle, as well as all other principles, even more profoundly.

Coping with Adaptive Problems

In the following story, Rex Geveden from NASA tells us about the strong sense of mission exhibited by two members of the project he managed.

It was a chilly, overcast Saturday in early December, and Don Hediger, a young electrical engineer working on our project, dropped by the laboratory to see what was happening. The space instrument we were building, called the OTD (Optical Transient Detector), was being tested in a thermal vacuum chamber. The purpose of the test was to prove that the OTD could survive temperature extremes in the ice-cold vacuum of space.

. . . David Trice was the engineer on duty when Don arrived at the laboratory. Thermal vacuum tests are conducted around-the-clock, requiring at least one engineer to be on duty at all times to periodically check out the instrument and make sure things are normal.

Inside the thermal vacuum chamber the temperature was 300 degrees below zero. Since some hardware components cannot withstand such cold temperatures, the OTD had several heaters that were used to keep the sensitive components warm. Meanwhile, outside the building, the wind was picking up, the sky darkened, and the power failed. The extreme winds had blown down a pair of power lines and shorted out all power to the building. Don knew they were in real trouble, as the special lenses in the OTD could only withstand temperatures down to about 30 degrees below zero. If the lenses cracked under the extreme temperatures, there would be no time to regrind them and the project would be doomed.

Knowing that the instrument required 14 volts of power, Don wondered if a common 12-volt battery might be enough to power the OTD heaters in an emergency. He jumped into his car and raced to the Amateur Radio Club office only a mile away. As president of the club, Don knew there were two deep-cycle, 12-volt batteries on hand that were used for ham radios—just what he needed. He raced back to the test facility and hooked the batteries up to the essential power bus on the instrument.

Under the dull glow of emergency lighting, Don and David began a vigil that would last until dawn. Because of the power outage, they could not measure the instrument temperatures, but they were able to monitor the current flow in the heater circuits with a hand-held meter to determine if the heaters were on or off. They were on and the batteries were working! Now it was a waiting game.

After about three hours, the emergency generator was brought online to supply power to the building and test equipment. Finally, the instrument could be tested and the temperatures could be monitored. Don and David ran a checkout test that showed that the OTD was fine and the temperatures were all within the normal range. A crisis had been averted by Don's quick thinking.[a]

This story demonstrates that coping with surprises requires staff who are not only highly skilled and resourceful, but who are also capable of coping with adaptive problems and approach their work with a sense of mission.

Following an analysis of case studies of several successful projects, Heifetz concluded, "Leadership . . . is not restricted to people in positions of authority. We see that the adaptability of an enterprise requires that many people exercise leadership at various moments in a complex process, within and across organizational lines . . . and develop . . . a sense of mission."[9]

Indeed, most of the storytellers featured throughout this book emphasize how they have to cope with "life outside one's comfort zone," that is, with adaptive problems. These problems are not dealt with effectively via "command and control," not even with the typical reward systems, accountability systems, or empowerment programs. Enlisting the team to go outside their comfort zone requires the commitment, dedication, passion, and spirit that can only be found in teams infused with a sense of mission.

Facilitating the Development of a Sense of Mission

In their research on successful teams, Warren Bennis and Patricia Ward Biederman concluded, "Great Groups think they are on a mission from God . . . Great Groups always believe that they are doing something vital, even holy . . . everything they do seems meaningful and valuable."[10]

The stories presented here were selected for the light that they shed on the practical question of how you, as the project leader, can increase the chances that your team will indeed develop a deep sense of mission.

In the First Brown Guideline, Create and Maintain a Focus, the importance of producing a "wow project" was discussed. The following story, by Ray Morgan, demonstrates how the "wow" feature of the project led to the utmost dedication of its project manager.

> In 1980, I was hired to lead a project for AeroVironment, a small company run by a man named Paul McCready, who was known as the "Father of Human-Powered Flight" . . . McCready had gotten Du Pont interested enough in his activities to sponsor a solar airplane that would fly from Paris to London. Solar power was still in its infancy, and nothing like this had ever been tried . . . To me it was the dream of a lifetime, something I never thought I'd get a chance to do. Solar power was one of the last frontiers in aviation. It was pioneering in the truest sense of the word. I told McCready when we were negotiating my employment, "If I had another way to support my family, I would do this for free" . . . We flew the Solar Challenger from Paris to Kent, England, and Du Pont loved it . . . I couldn't pull myself away. The kinds of projects I was working on were intoxicating.[b]

In *The Soul of a New Machine*, Tracy Kidder tells the story of the creation of Data General's MV/8000 computer (the Eagle Machine) by the Eclipse Group, a group of engineers led by Tom West. The Eagle was the enhancement of the existing machine, the Eclipse. Here Tracy tells us about West's efforts to make the Eagle a "wow project": "To at least some engineers, at the outset, Eagle appeared to be a fairly uninteresting computer to build. Yet, more than two dozen people worked on it overtime, without any real hope of material rewards, for a year and a half; and afterward most of them felt glad . . . West never passed any opportunity to add flavor to the project . . . He was always finding romance and excitement in the ordinary . . . 'West,' said Alsing (the software engineer), 'took a bag on the side of the Eclipse and made it the most exciting project in the company, the most exciting thing in our lives for a year and a half. He never bored us.'"[11]

Constantly striving to transform every project into a project that matters—a "wow project"—is at the heart of Tom Peters's philosophy of project management: "The world of WOW Projects rests on but one word: REFRAMING. That is . . . every 'assignment'/'task'/'job' is merely a starting point. Your real 'job': Turn that—often apparently mundane—task/job/assignment into something cool/memorable/WOW!"[12]

Bennis and Ward Biederman concluded that "inspirational leaders can transform even mundane projects, turning them, too, into missions from God."[13] One example of a leader who was able to imbue his team with a deep sense of mission is shared by Frank Snow, ground system and flight operations manager from NASA's Goddard Space Flight Center:

> *It was eight months before launch when my second Flight Operations team lead said he was leaving the project for another job, just six months after the departure of the original lead . . . With the loss of the second lead, and only eight months to prepare . . . I was forced to rethink what qualifications I needed for the Flight Ops lead. No longer did extensive operational experience seem to be the one and only prerequisite. I needed someone who could turn eight people into a competent, cohesive, motivated team . . . I needed a leader.*
>
> *Fortunately for ACE, we already had a member of the Flight Ops team who could do the job. Jeff was good technically, but he was also respected by the other Flight Ops team members for his honesty, responsiveness, and dedication to the ACE mission . . . His enthusiasm and dedication were contagious, affecting both the Flight Ops team and the other groups that worked with him . . . especially during the last two months before launch, the Flight Ops personnel worked 10–12 hour days, as well as weekends. I never heard any serious complaints; the Ops team saw this difficult task as a unique opportunity.[c]*

Jeff's ability to render a "difficult task" into a "unique opportunity" is primarily attributed to his contagious enthusiasm and dedication. Likewise, Peters cites Benjamin Zander, the conductor of the Boston

Philharmonic, who declared, "I have no pride. I'll do anything that's necessary to get people involved. I am a dispenser of enthusiasm." Peters further explains, "Ben Zander is an extraordinary conductor. Think "symphony" . . . and you are likely to think about command and control, authoritarianism, uniformity and control. All that is true . . . to some extent. But what makes for a great symphony, Zander reminds us, is each member of the orchestra soaring to unimaginable heights. And that means . . . engagement and involvement (passion) . . . not just memorizing one's part in Beethoven's Ninth. And what does it take to get members from here to there? How about . . . Chief-Dispenser-of-Enthusiasm."[14]

Being a dispenser of enthusiasm, that is, infusing enthusiasm into others through their daily ongoing interactions, is the natural way to facilitate a sense of mission. At times, however, leaders must employ more systematic and structured means for changing their team's attitude. Chuck Anderson, the vice president of Raytheon, served as an inspiration to his team members and used the team's monthly meetings as a vehicle for instilling in them a sense of mission.

> *All of my team members, approximately 80 of us, met for half a day off-site at a hotel. We did this every month. We rented a ballroom, and the whole purpose of that meeting, every month, was constancy of purpose. It was to get everybody aligned—or brainwashed, as some said.*
>
> *"Let's remember what we're about, what our responsibility to our country is. Let's do what's right. What's right is delivering on time, making sure the design is right, making sure we meet every requirement . . . "*
>
> *Some of the people who went to these meetings never got it, and we got rid of them. Even some of my most trusted people expressed doubts that the government . . . could fulfill its part of this deal and get out of our way to let us build better missiles . . . Ultimately, they had faith in me. I was the one whose job was on the line if we screwed up, if it didn't work out— and I did my best to make it clear that I knew we were doing the right thing.*[d]

During these monthly meetings, Chuck used his position as a trusted leader to create meaning for his team members. One of the consequences of permanent white water conditions is loss of meaning. Vaill asserts, "We experience both surprising, novel, messy, costly, recurring, and unpreventable events and feelings of lack of direction, absence of coherence, and loss of meaning."[15] The British philosopher of management Charles Handy explains the recent growing search for meaning in the workplace: "We're all looking for why we do the work we do. It was easy in the past—we were doing it because we needed the money to live. Now it's clear that money—for many people . . . —is more symbolic than real. We generate more wealth than we really need to live on. And money becomes a rather crude measure of success. We're looking for something more. There is, in my view, no God-given explanation for each of us as to what success might be. I do believe that we are each of us unique. We each have something to contribute to the world, and the search for meaning is finding out what that is before we die."[16]

Bennis asserts, "Great leaders imbue even the most mundane work with meaning and turn even tedious activities into inspirational missions that people rally around."[17] Bennis and Ward Biederman present a powerful example of the impact of creating meaning. Due to security reasons, the participants in the Manhattan Project were not told at first about the unique purpose of the project, namely, the development of a weapon that could end the war. However, the project manager persisted until the army granted permission to lift the veil of secrecy. This is how the project manager describes the impact of this new understanding regarding the nature and purpose of the project on the project team: "Complete transformation. They began to invent ways of doing it better . . . They worked at night. They didn't need supervising in the night; they didn't need anything . . . The work was done 'nearly ten times as fast' after it had meaning."[18]

Following is how Tom Gillman, the contracting officer of Raytheon, assesses Chuck's attempts to create meaning and the resulting impact on the team's attitude.

A particular piece of hardware on the missile had to work 90 percent of the time. Watching flight tests over one period, we determined that there were failures that occurred less than 1 percent of the time in over 1,000 watches. Contractually, we could have said, "Not our problem, we're not going to pay attention to it." Instead, we decided it was the right thing to do to see if we could figure out what was happening. We locked some engineers in the lab for six months and had them duplicate that failure. They determined that with a simple modification of the missile we could eliminate it.

We ended up spending a couple of million dollars to fix 5,000 missiles that weren't under warranty. We could have hidden behind the specifications. Nobody paid us to do the extra work, but it was the right thing to do for the war fighter . . . In previous contractual relationships we would have said, "Since it's not in the spec, I'm not going to do anything." We could have written a proposal to the government that said something like, "We can improve this by this much and it's going to cost this much money."

All programs have problems. In the normal mode of government contracting, everybody runs to the contract and says, " What does it say on paper?" Not us. The first thing we did was ask what was the best thing to do for the war fighter. Once we determined that, then we decided on the best way to solve the problem, given our resources.[c]

Thus, as Bennis concludes, "We can do so much better than we do by reminding people of the meaning of their work."[19] The stories presented in this guideline demonstrate that enhancing the development of a sense of mission requires project leaders to nurture the following aspects of work: the task has to matter to the participants; participants with the right attitude must be recruited; and project leaders have to build meaning, passion, and commitment through their daily interactions with team members. However, at times, developing a sense of mission is not enough to guarantee success. In that case, as will be explained in the next guideline, project leaders have no choice but to challenge the status quo.

The Second Yellow Guideline: Challenge the Status Quo

In their book *Fusion Leadership*, Daft and Lengel argue that "leadership in a destabilized world means nonconformity. It means breaking tradition, boundaries, and norms. One obvious trait that distinguishes a leader from a manager is a willingness to take risks . . . Leaders do not play it safe . . . It takes courage to jump into a new way of doing things . . . Failure is the first step towards success . . . Without failure we don't learn . . . Leadership is a struggle, both within yourself and within the organization."[20]

The stories in the current guideline will demonstrate this argument by presenting a series of "challenge the status quo" examples that require risk and courage in the process of failure, learning, and struggle.[21]

Listening to Yourself

In the opening story, *Listening to the Voice Inside*, Joan Salute, a project manager from NASA, reflects on the most fundamental question, "What makes for a successful project manager?"

> *Like most of us, I've had to think hard about what makes for a successful project manager . . . Project managers need the ability to: plan, schedule, budget, monitor, control, etc., etc., etc. I don't know about you, but I have a hard time with these lists. Of course these abilities matter, but for me just one stands out as the defining characteristic of any good project manager, and this is one usually not included in the list or easily encapsulated in a single word. That characteristic is his or her willingness to challenge the conventional way of doing things.*

Joan's mission seemed straightforward enough in the beginning: to launch a vehicle modified to include experimental materials, study it as it reentered the atmosphere, and then recover it. However, after being informed by the Pentagon that the mission "appeared" to conflict with the Strategic Arms Reduction Treaty (START), it became clear that explicit Pentagon approval would have to be granted to recover the vehicle. A two-month approval process dragged on for 11 months without approval or denial.

They finally approved recovery of the vehicle, but stipulated that our data must remain classified . . . After waiting this long for the first decision, I had to decide was it worth it to fight this decision. Whereas some project managers might have gotten fed up and accepted the ruling, the status quo, I dug in my heels and said "no" . . . It was a NASA flight experiment for the Aerospace Industry and for NASA—we needed this data. I estimated the value of the mission would drop by 80 percent if the data were classified.

It's true you have to choose your battles, but if you're not willing to fight you don't win any. It was a risky strategy, perhaps a bit bold, but our team truly believed the data met the requirements for non-restricted distribution. As it turned out, we won them over.

. . . On this same mission . . . Another national lab approached us with an offer to develop and provide GPS equipment to track our reentry. They had been looking for funding for a long time to develop their GPS equipment. There was pressure on me from the Air Force to accept the offer. The Air Force had helped us out in the past and now wanted this from us. No one could believe it when I turned the offer down. The pressure to accept came down even heavier when the other lab offered us the equipment for a greatly reduced price. Again, I said "no."

. . . It was uncomfortable to be the "bad guy" in this instance, but I said no because I felt it would have diverted our personnel resources and distracted us from our mission . . . The status quo thing to do would have been to try and keep everyone happy, but I drew a straight line in my mind as to what I saw was necessary to achieve a successful mission and never wavered, and we did have a successful mission, I believe, because we remained focused . . .

You can't always do what people want you to and expect to be loyal to your own core values. There will always be somebody with a competing interest there to challenge you on a judgment call. You've got to decide who you want calling the shots for you, yourself or someone else. That's why I believe challenging the status quo means challenging yourself to "do the right thing." When you know what's right, you only need listen to yourself. [f,22]

The following story will show that "listening to yourself" may often require you to take risk and to exhibit courage. This story is about a multistage project that was behind schedule when a very experienced project manager, Rick Obenschain, was brought in to lead it. Rick found out that trying to meet the specifications for one of the instruments (the sounder) would not allow him to stay on schedule. Rick knew, however, that by following the conventional way of doing business, he would not convince his client to revisit the specifications. Thus, he embraced a more unconventional way:

I needed to understand what was really needed by the people who would be using the instrument. Our customer was the National Oceanic and Atmospheric Administration (NOAA). Unfortunately, we had about three levels between the actual user, the National Weather Service, and the people who worked with us at NOAA. One day I called up Joe Friday at the National Weather Service. I said, "Joe, what time in the morning do you get in?" He said, "I get in at 6:30 a.m." I asked him, "If I'm standing downstairs at the elevator at 6:30 tomorrow morning, can I have the first half-hour of your day?" He agreed.

I got up early and went over to his office building. When he came in and saw me waiting by the elevator, he said, "Things aren't going too well, are they, Rick?" I said, "Joe, they're not. But I'm going to make a deal with you. If you will tell me right now what's the minimum you can accept on the first spacecraft, we'll get it off the ground. Eventually, we're going to build you five space-crafts, and I promise that every one will be better than the last from the instrument standpoint. But I can't build the sounder the way you want right now. We're going crazy. I can't get agreement on the real requirements from NOAA. So, what can you accept?"

We sat down there and negotiated in thirty minutes what the sounder was going to be like on the first spacecraft. I left the building before the other NOAA people came in because I couldn't be seen there talking to the National Weather Service. I came back and said, "Okay. We've got a plan now. We know how to do this." I told the people at NOAA what we were doing, and they said, "Well, wait a minute. You're not meeting the spec."

I said, "I'm meeting your requirements." "No, we want you to meet the spec."

I said, "We're not going to meet the spec. We're going to meet the requirement. Where did that requirement come from? Do me a favor, and go back and talk to the people who are going to use this instrument and make sure that isn't what they're willing to work with."

And guess what the National Weather Service told them? They said, "Yeah, Rick's right. It's not the specification, but it's what we need." So, with NOAA's concurrence, we built our sounder and launched their satellite . . . against all odds, we delivered what was needed.[8]

In the next story, Don Margolies tells us that toward the final stages of a very complex project he initiated something that has never been done before at NASA—something that put him at odds with both his superiors and team members. Nobody forced him to challenge the standard practice and initiate this risky effort. So why did he take the risk? Apparently, Margolies "listened to himself."

You've heard the expression, "Test what you fly, fly what you test." It's hard to argue with that in theory. In this case, it was a risk I was willing to take. The ACE observatory had a suite of nine instruments . . . It was the first time on any NASA project that I know of when all the instruments on an observatory came off for rework or calibration after the full range of environ-mental tests and then were reintegrated at the launch center without the bene-fit of an observatory environmental retest. Several people on the project thought I was crazy. Why do it? We had gone through our environmental test programs successfully and everything seemed to be operational. If it's not broken, don't fix it, right?

After weighing all the considerations, Margolies decided that there was more than enough slack in the schedule as well as the budget and that this was the best way to serve his clients, the scientists:

We were in a position to ask, "What can we do to make the science better?" . . . For those who had only completed marginal calibration prior to testing, the alternative was to calibrate again in orbit. Calibration in orbit takes time, and it's not as precise as on the ground. So there really was a net benefit to the science by doing this . . .

. . . How do you know the risk is low enough to put an instrument back on without retesting it under vibration? That was the question my management put to me. When I approached them about this, they didn't mince words. "Don, you are crazy," they told me. But I knew I was going to hear this, and I was prepared to explain . . . Ultimately, I was able to get management to buy off on the decision, but not without first undergoing an independent review of our plans.

. . . There were other stakeholders . . . whom I had to convince. The one I was most concerned about was Mary Chiu [the contractor's project manager] . . . We talked about it exhaustively . . . Getting Mary's buy-in, albeit a reluctant buy-in, was a major precondition for going through with it.[h]

The end results? The ACE mission was very successful.

In the three examples presented thus far, the project manager abandoned the status quo only following negotiation and agreement with external authorities, upper management, the client, or with his project team. In the following story, told by Rex Geveden from NASA, the status quo was abandoned without any prior negotiation or agreement:

The instrument had failed its vibration test, and all of us on the team were extremely disappointed . . . The vibration test had failed because a bracket that connected our instrument to the spacecraft was not strong enough . . . At a minimum, fixing the problem would normally require going through the standard procedural steps for an engineering change.

The bracket had to be redesigned to ensure its resistance to vibration and then manufactured and inspected. Even by optimistic estimates, following procedures would delay the project by a couple of weeks—time that the project could not afford.

[My] Chief Engineer, Fred Sanders . . . had a radical idea; he himself would take the bracket and strengthen it . . . He had the knowledge, skills and tools; all he needed was flight-quality hardware. I trusted Fred and gave him the green light.

On the same afternoon of the test failure, Fred sketched a hardware modification for the bracket . . . He had our shop cut the pieces that afternoon according to his sketch. He then took the pieces along with some borrowed pins and screws to his home where he drilled and tapped the instrument bracket and fastened the panels. We were back in test the next day and were overjoyed to see that the hardware passed the vibration test.[i]

It is very illuminating that Rex Geveden, the program manager who trusted his chief engineer and allowed him to deviate from the standard procedures without getting the necessary permission first, felt confident enough to go ahead and share this story immediately following the event. Even more illuminating is the fact that Rex was promoted to the position of NASA's chief engineer and later on further promoted to the prominent role of NASA's associate administrator. Apparently, both Rex and his superiors endorse Joan Salute's conclusion: "I believe challenging the status quo means challenging yourself to 'do the right thing.' When you know what's right, you only need listen to yourself."

However, before one concludes that "listening to yourself" and rushing to take risks is always advisable, one must listen to Colonel Jeanne Sutton, a program manager from the U.S. Air Force, who likewise shares her strong conviction that successful project management requires risk taking. However, she also warns, "If you don't have common sense, you're better off not taking risks. If you're known for doing stupid things— don't take risks, you're just going to hurt yourself and others."[j] The importance of being able to exercise common sense and judgment while taking risks will be further discussed in the next guideline. In the following example, Colonel Sutton presents her own dilemma regarding risk taking: whether she should openly challenge her new boss in the presence of his guests.

After only two weeks on her new job, she was summoned downtown to her boss's office and was surprised to find that he had also invited three senior executives from the company who had been involved in her predecessor's firing. Following their cordial greetings and expressions of support for her as the new program manager, the executives proceeded to brief her boss on everything that they thought was wrong with her office's solicitation for a bid and described her staff's actions in inflammatory terms. Her boss defended her lack of background knowledge, but then gave her multiple action items. After accepting the assignments and reassuring everyone that she would handle their concerns, she had another unexpected reaction.

Now, I had a quick decision to make. I could either sit back and smile benignly, playing puppet-on-a-string to both my boss and the contractor executives, or I could stake my claim as THE program manager and demand to work one-on-one with the contractor's leadership to resolve issues at my level.

So, with a slam of my hand on the table, I informed the executives that I would not tolerate them running to my boss first and taking his valuable time for things I was hired to take care of. I shocked everyone, including my boss, with my directness. They never dared challenge my authority again.[k]

The rationale that led Colonel Sutton to her quick reaction may be nicely explained by using the boiling frog analogy. According to the boiling frog tale, a frog can be boiled alive if the water is heated slowly enough. If a frog is placed in boiling water, it will jump out, but if it is placed in cold water that is slowly heated, it will never jump out. The lesson of this tale is that people should make themselves aware of minor deviations, lest they suffer a major, often catastrophic, loss. Thus, to make sure that "they never dared challenge my authority again," Colonel Sutton had to take the risk and react immediately and decisively.[23]

Improving Courage through Practice

The Third Green Guideline (Use an Appropriate Amount of Redundancy) elaborated on coping with project risk, primarily via the planning system. Yet, the current guideline stresses on the need to take risks throughout project life. Why is it necessary? Why can't one eliminate risk altogether early on? One answer to this question is provided by Bill Townsend, who has been involved with close to 60 launches during the course of his NASA career: "It is a real fallacy that it is possible to drive risk to zero . . . Everything we do has residual risk associated with it."[1,24]

Terry Little from the U.S. Air Force goes much further, claiming that taking risks is actually vital for project success: "You have to be willing to take risks in order to be successful. This carries with it an increased likelihood of mistakes. If you're not making mistakes, you're not reaching far enough." Little values mistakes made by his staff for two reasons. First, he believes that avoiding mistakes is easy—you just don't have to do anything. Second, he believes that no learning is as powerful as that which comes from making mistakes: "You can observe other people, or read, but there's nothing like good, healthy regret to give you a little insight."[m]

Lynda Rutledge, a systems engineer who worked on Little's team, provided a concrete example of Little's philosophy that a leader must create an environment where people are not fearful of making mistakes:

After being awarded a contract, one of the companies protested a decision that she had made during the source selection and formal hearings were held:

I was on edge since I'd been called to testify, and I think that he could see that. "There's something I want you to remember," he said. "One of your virtues is that you're willing to take risks and make a decision and move forward. You get things done, and I don't want this episode to taint that or make you afraid to do things." He said this same thing had happened on one of his earlier programs. Someone he admired for her energy and determination had to face a protest in her area. She never got over it, he told me.

A lot of bosses talk the talk about letting you take risks, but when something goes wrong, they punish you. Not Terry . . . "This is a good experience for you," he said to me, "you're going to learn so much from this." His sitting down with me and saying these things restored my self-confidence. As it turned out, the protest was not sustained. Over the long run, the memory of that experience encouraged me to be willing to stick my neck out again and again.[n]

In his article "No Risk, No Reward," Keith Hammonds reminds us that "playing it safe isn't always playing it smart."[25] In their book *Play to Win*, Larry Wilson and Hersch Wilson similarly assert, "When we are deeply invested in playing not to lose, we often catch ourselves thinking—and it seems almost rational—'if I can just get to my death unscathed, I'll have made it.'" Wilson and Wilson also explain what is wrong with this philosophy: "When we choose the path of playing not to lose . . . we eliminate finding our own voice. Our voice atrophies because it is not used . . . By choosing to never go wrong, we eliminate intellectual growth because it requires experimenting and risking being wrong . . . If we choose to be comfortable above all else . . . our courage and creativity atrophy."[26]

Dan Ward and Chris Quaid from the U.S. Air Force point out that in some circles, courage and judgment in project management have apparently already atrophied: "We can't allow risk management to be a bloodless, rationalistic exercise in careful planning. It is rightly a human, subjective activity. When you get right down to it, risk management is basically an exercise in personal courage and professional judgment. Lest we be accused of making stuff up, in the name of due diligence, we searched the Risk Management Guide For DoD Acquisition, Sixth Edition (Version 1.0 Aug 2006) for the words 'courage' and 'judgment.' Neither word turned up . . . The DoD shouldn't feel too bad—we searched the online archives of a commercial journal, Risk Management Magazine, and got the same results."[27]

This is what Senator John McCain, the coauthor of *Why Courage Matters: The Way to a Braver Life*, had to say about the atrophy of courage and its dire consequences: "Over the past 30 years, American culture has defined courage down . . . Courage is like a muscle. The more we exercise it, the stronger it gets. I sometimes worry that our collective courage is growing weaker from disuse . . . That means trouble for us all because courage is the enforcing virtue, the one that makes possible all the other virtues common to exceptional leaders: honesty, integrity, confidence, compassion, and humility. In short, leaders who lack courage aren't leaders."[28]

How can you make sure that your own courage does not atrophy? What can you do to improve your risk-taking attitude? William Miller, the author of *The Mystery of Courage*, asserts, "One thing that helps [you become more courageous] is to read stories of courage. They make you wonder how you would have done compared with the hero of the tale, and you get very humble. You start self-querying and fantasizing about your own response, your own reaction. As the psalmist says, "You become what you behold."[29]

In a recent article in *Harvard Business Review*, Kathleen Reardon concludes that courage is a skill that one can improve through practice. Just as Little stresses the importance of learning from one's own mistakes, she argues that "most great business leaders teach themselves to make high-risk decisions. They learn to do it well over a period of time, often decades."[30]

Warren Bennis and Burt Nanus, who interviewed more than 100 successful leaders in preparation for their book *Leaders*, observe, "Perhaps the most impressive and memorable quality of the leaders we studied was the way they responded to failure . . . They simply don't think about failure, don't even use the word, relying on such synonyms as 'mistakes,' 'glitch,' 'bungle' or countless others." Undoubtedly, these successful leaders do have failures like everyone else, but rather than adopting the negative, limited view embedded in the word failure, they choose to view such experiences as mistakes that they can learn from.[31]

In the following story, Dougal Maclise, a project manager at NASA and another strong proponent of "zero failure equals zero progress," tells us how he attempted to help Bobby, a blind child, to become less averse to risk.

After I graduated from college, I worked for two years with the Portland Public Schools as an equipment designer for handicapped children. One of the boys I worked with was named Bobby Smith. Blind since birth, Bobby was about to start attending a new school. In Portland at that time, most of the students with disabilities were being integrated into the regular schools. My task was to help the District's Mobility Expert, Mr. Thompson, teach Bobby how to get to and from school and around the school grounds on his own.

The two started out by meeting Bobby and his mother at their house, which was located on a quiet street about four blocks from the school. The route that Bobby would have to learn to negotiate appeared to be straightforward and fairly safe.

They all sat down in the living room to map out the strategy and schedule for working with Bobby. Mr. Thompson asked Bobby to go to the kitchen and back. He went to the kitchen table, turned around, and came right back. Then Mr. Thompson asked Bobby to stand in front of him and point to the doorway of the kitchen. After some hesitation, Bobby pointed toward the kitchen, but a little to the left of the doorway. Mr. Thompson continued on,

"Where is the wall?"
Bobby pointed towards and above the couch.
"And how about the ceiling?"
Bobby said, "What's a ceiling?"
That hit me. Bobby's pointing had been skewed and not what I would have expected from a sighted child, but surely he knew what a ceiling was. Mrs. Smith said, "I guess we never talked about it, so he doesn't know what it is."
Mr. Thompson then asked Bobby to run to his room and back. "We don't allow running in the house," said Mrs. Smith.
"Where can he run?"
"In the back yard, on the lawn," she said.
"Anywhere else?"
"Sometimes we run together at the park, but usually we play on the swings."
"How about the slide?"
"I like the slide!" Bobby piped up.
"I help him," said his mother.
"Where does Bobby play on his own?" I asked.
"Usually in his room or in the kitchen, if I'm there cooking."
"I heard you say it was against the rules, but does he ever run in the house?"
"No, it's just too risky."
"We'll have to change that," said Mr. Thompson.
The next few months we all worked with Bobby to help him explore his world . . . Mrs. Smith started to let him take greater risks, but she wanted to pad all the doorways. She soon found that that was not really needed because Bobby was a cautious explorer.
It was hard to get Bobby to let go of our hand when we started to explore outside and to rehearse the route to his school. He had his cane to help "look" in front of him, but he still wanted to be in contact with a guide, usually someone with him, or a wall or fence. We managed to get him to a point where he could make it all the way around the block without holding onto someone or trailing his hand along the fences or hedges . . . Inside the school, he always went down the halls trailing a hand along one of the walls until he found his classroom. During recess he played on the jungle gym, the swings or the slide, but he was not running around with the other kids. He tried to play tag, but wouldn't stray very far from the walls or the fences.
One day I had an idea. I found a stuffed ball and a beeper. Putting the beeper in the ball and closing it up with Velcro, I had a toy that Bobby could use to play with his friends. It would occupy both his hands so he would have to let go of his "guide" to be able to play, and it was soft enough that he wouldn't be hurt by it. I hoped that play would accomplish what we had not

been able to do up to this point, to get Bobby to venture away from his known guides.

Bobby was thrilled! The next day he took it to school to show to his class. That afternoon Bobby returned home with a slight black eye. Apparently, when he was playing with one of his friends, he dropped his ball when a friend had tossed it to him. They both ran to get it and bumped heads. As Mrs. Smith was tending to his eye, she couldn't help but notice his excitement as he told her all the details of the incident.

She asked him, "Didn't it hurt?"

He said, "I guess so, but Mom, I ran! I ran right into Chris! And then we started laughing. He says we can play soccer now! Can I? Is that okay? Please?"

"I guess we'll have to find a way, won't we."

And they did. Bobby played soccer, and he played other sports too. Mrs. Smith had to let go of her own anxiety, and to her credit she did. So did other parents whose children, whether blind or disabled in some way, were integrated into playtime at the school. You could see at first they were scared to let their children go, but they helped each other to accept the risks of letting go, and eventually they shared in the joy their children felt.

I often think about this episode as I manage projects. The main part of the job seems to be managing the risks, weighing the safe choice against the more risky one. Whenever I think of the new worlds of doorways, ceilings and soccer that Bobby found by taking more risks, I wonder what I might find if I take, or allow my team to take, more risks. On the other hand, I also wonder how to tell the Mrs. Smiths elsewhere that a few black eyes won't kill the patient.[o]

The Third Yellow Guideline: Persevere, but Know When to Retreat

The current guideline is composed of two contradictory recommendations. The first component, "Persevere," is primarily a continuation of the previous guideline, "Challenge the Status Quo." The lesson of this component is embodied in the old adage: "If at first you don't succeed, try and try again!" Don't be deterred by the fact that your initial attempts to challenge the status quo were all unsuccessful, keep trying, learn from your mistakes, and eventually you will make it! The second component, "Know When to Retreat," instructs you to do just the opposite.

You would like to believe that experienced project managers will have the ability to tell the difference between the seemingly impossible and the genuinely impossible. Well, projects are highly unique—tasks, objectives, organizations, participants, and contexts—and often even experienced leaders can tell the difference only after they have attempted to achieve the genuinely impossible. They are expected, however, to be able to detect their mistake quickly and retreat as fast as possible.

Persevere

In the first example of perseverance, Tommaso Rivellini, a systems engineer from NASA, highlights the importance of developing a culture that recognizes that there is no learning without failures:

> *Here I was: 26 years old, I had never worked on a flight project before, and all eyes were on me . . . Our task was to design and build airbags for Pathfinder's landing on Mars—an approach that had never been used on any mission. Airbags may seem like a simple, low-tech product, but it was eye-opening to discover just how little we knew about them . . . Airbags seemed like a crazy idea to a lot of people. Nobody ever said that, mind you, but there seemed to be a widespread feeling that the airbags weren't going to work. "We'll let you guys go off and fool around until you fall flat on your faces." That was the unspoken message I received day after day.*
>
> *Everyone's main fear about using these giant airbags was that the lander would be buried in an ocean of fabric when the airbags deflated. I began the search for a solution by building scale models of the airbags and lander, and I played with them in my office for a couple of months. I built the models out of cardboard and plastic, and taped them up with packing tape I got from the hardware store and ribbon from the fabric store. I used a small raft inflator that I had at home to pump up my model airbags. Over and over again, I filled the miniature airbags and then let them deflate, watching what happened.*
>
> *I fooled around with a dozen or more approaches before I finally came up with something that I thought worked. Slowly but surely, I came up with the idea of using cords that zigzag through belt loops inside the airbags . . . Once we built large-scale models to conduct drop tests, we started by doing simple vertical drops, first at 30 feet, and then up to 70 feet . . . Even after we had the mechanics figured out for the airbags, a big question remained: What about the rocky Martian terrain?*
>
> *. . . To simulate conditions on Mars, we brought in large lava rocks the size of a small office desk . . . The more landscape simulations we tested, the more we started tearing up the airbags. Things were not looking good . . . We tried material after material—heavy duty Kevlars and Vectrans among them—applying them in dozens of different configurations to the outside of the airbag . . . When we finished a drop test, we knew right away whether it was a success or failure. Each test was followed by a high-pressure rush to figure out what went wrong, what test to run next, how to fix the extensively damaged bags, and how to simultaneously incorporate whatever new "experimental fix" we came up with . . .*
>
> *After doing dozens of drop tests, looking at the data, and studying what was happening, we started to realize that a single layer of heavy material wasn't the solution. Multiple layers of lightweight material might prove stronger . . . We were forced to decide on the final abrasion layer design in order to meet our scheduled Qualification drop tests. In spacecraft terms, this is supposed to be the last test that you run in order to qualify your final design . . . We had a successful drop test and were finally good to go.*[P]

Tommaso was willing to persistently challenge the status quo, fail, learn, and try again. He pursued "an approach that had never been used on any mission," and he prevailed by adopting a mind-set that allowed him to experiment and reach a solution to the problem through a process of trial and error.

Likewise, Jeffrey Pfeffer, coauthor of *The Knowing-Doing Gap*, asserts that "doing means learning. Learning means mistakes." Pfeffer elaborates further on the kind of environment needed to support the learning process: "Companies . . . need to build a forgiveness framework—a tolerance for error and failure—into their culture. A company that wants you to come up with a smart idea, implement that idea quickly, and learn in the process has to be willing to cut you some slack. You need to be able to try things, even if you think that you might fail."[32]

The surrounding culture, however, is not always supportive of those who challenge the status quo. The following two stories focus on the funding process of the environmental research aircraft and sensor technology (ERAST) program. ERAST's main objective was to convert high-altitude, unmanned aerial vehicles (UAVs) into research platforms. In the first story, Jenny Baer-Riedhart, the eventual NASA project manager of the initiative, discusses her repeated attempts to "sell" the program to NASA Headquarters. In the second story, Bob Whitehead, associate administrator for aeronautics at NASA, tells his side as the "buyer" of the project.

The "Seller" Story

I made several appearances at NASA Headquarters to brief higher-ups about the status of the ERAST program. Early on in this endeavor, I learned a key lesson in working with multiple customers: Always know the folks you're meeting with, and always tailor what you're going to say based on who you know will be there. I learned this the hard way, I'm afraid to say, after getting thrown out of people's offices.

. . . . "We've got this great UAV program back in California," I said by way of introduction at one of these meetings, and from that point on they hammered me. They didn't want to hear anything about a program aimed at developing UAVs. "This is not going to work! This is not the kind of airplane we want! Why are you telling us about this?"

From their standpoint, I was the enemy, someone who would suck up resources they needed in other areas. I should have understood this ahead of time. I had anticipated some resistance, but I naively thought that all I had to do was show up and explain how successful the program was and, voilà, they were in my pocket. Yes, I knew they were fighting for other platforms, and that they had their own constraints and clients to please, but I believed in my heart of hearts that ERAST was important for NASA and that I could convince them of that. What I failed to recognize was that people are not convinced just because the seller believes that she has a wonderful product. The seller needs to understand what the buyer wants from a product.

. . . But before I went anywhere near Headquarters again, I did some serious training. I got in shape. You might even say I went to boot camp. I found people at Dryden [her Center] who appeared regularly at NASA Headquarters to talk about their programs, and I used them as a sounding board . . . When I went back to Headquarters, it still didn't feel like I was among friends, but at least I didn't get kicked out of any offices.[q]

As Bob reports, Jenny's efforts clearly paid off:

The "Buyer" Story
Jenny and her colleagues at Dryden came back to NASA Headquarters and stuck their noses in and pushed what they had to offer—and they deserve a tremendous amount of credit for that. They showed up at Headquarters, got turned away the first time, came back with a new message, got pushed aside again, but wouldn't go away—until finally we said, "Okay, if we fit this ERAST thing into the budget, then you'd better take it and run with it." And that's exactly what they did.[r]

Jenny, like Tommaso in the previous story, was willing to persistently challenge the status quo, fail, learn, and try again.[33] In both of these cases, it was clear that the project could not have proceeded without perseverance on the part of the project manager. However, this is not necessarily always the case. In the following story, Dave Stickel, a project manager from Procter & Gamble, tells how the project could have proceeded—and proceeded very easily—without the perseverance of the project manager:

I was managing a project whose scope included the addition of several new unit operations to existing production lines. Part of my project involved adding a fabricated module similar to one another project had recently purchased on a T&M (Time & Material) basis from Company A. This company had done a good job, so prevailing wisdom dictated all we had to do for this part of the job was to adapt the design to our production lines and go.

Along with our procurement manager and the project manager of the recently completed project, I traveled to the vendor's shop where these modules were fabricated . . . As soon as I walked into Company A's shop, I started getting a sales pitch . . . I liked what I saw in the shop, even without the sales pitch. And then, on top of that, our procurement manager and the project manager from our first project took me off to the side to give me their own version of the sales pitch. They told me that sticking with Company A's current design and fabrication would make my life easier and would allow me to focus on other parts of my project.

At the end of the day, we regrouped with Company A's personnel in a conference room. The vendor's representatives said that if I would give *them the green light, they would deliver the 50+ machines I needed at about $118,000/unit. My procurement manager and fellow project manager thought this was what I should do, but I was uneasy. It just didn't make sense to me. This particular unit operation is similar to a number of other unit operations throughout the manufacturing process, and the design for this one wasn't all that dissimilar from them. I knew we had paid a lot less for those other unit operations. So I said, "I've just got to think about this."*

When I got home, I checked my phone messages. Company A's shop superintendent had left me a message. He said, "After you left today, we got together and we sharpened our pencils, and we decided that we can do your project at about $108,000 a machine." It wasn't hard to figure out the math; we would save $10,000 on each of the 50 or so machines. And I said, "Wow! All I did was say I wanted to think about it, and I saved a half a million dollars." My delay of six hours was paying dividends.

But I still wasn't satisfied. This unit operation wasn't on the critical path of my project, so there was no reason I had to make the decision immediately We bid Company A along with a number of other shops I was familiar with. A few weeks later, I received a bid from Company A for $93,000 per unit. We awarded the contract at $67,000 per unit to Company B, where I also knew the people . . . In the end, I saved more than $2.5 million.[5]

As it turned out, Dave was right in his persistence and his refusal to listen to anyone but himself. He followed his instincts and relied on his own judgment. In his book *On Leadership*, John Gardner, who served as the U.S. secretary of health, education, and welfare, defines judgment as "the ability to combine hard data, questionable data and intuitive guesses to arrive at conclusions that events prove to be correct." Gardner also observes that "there are bright people who lack judgment altogether (which may be the source of the observation that 'there's nothing worse than a stupid person with a brilliant mind')."[34]

According to Weick, many scholars equate wisdom with judgment. Weick cites William James's description: "In practical talk, a man's common sense means his good judgment, his freedom from eccentricity, his gumption. 'Gumption' is a colloquial expression that means resourcefulness, enterprise, and a quality of mind that enables one to make intelligent choices."[35] Quinn, Mintzberg, and James go one step further, claiming that judgment is the most indispensable attribute of managers. In their book *The Strategy Process: Concepts, Contexts, and Cases*, they argue that "it is simply our conclusion that among all other attributes of managers, the most indispensable is judgment because it is the integrator which guides and controls all the others . . . It illuminates and evaluates the results of thinking and acting . . . judgment is also very convoluted and complex . . . most judgment calls are not simple selections between black and white, but are between subtle shades of gray . . .

Don't expect everything to work out well the first time . . . Don't be afraid to make mistakes as long as you learn from them."[36]

Perhaps these "subtle shades of gray" can account for Dave's inability to clearly explain his decision-making process. Quinn, Mintzberg, and James also stress that judgment will improve as it is applied and modified through the process of making mistakes. It appears that there is a bidirectional link between the quality of one's judgment and the extent to which that judgment is applied in action. Gardner asserts that due to their poor judgment capabilities, "there are able analysts who cannot move from analysis to action."[37]

Know When to Retreat

As we move to the second component of this guideline, "Know When to Retreat," it will become clear that even good judgment is not always enough. The following two stories are recounted by Judy Stokley, a program director from the U.S. Air Force. In the first story, *I am Not a Quitter*, she provides an example of her perseverance while having to cut her own workforce by half. In the second story, *My Pride Had Been Hurt*, she reflects on her own feelings while coping with a blow to one of her initiatives and to her ego.

I am Not a Quitter
If they asked me to do a massive downsizing again, I know I would have to do it; but I pray to God, literally, they will find somebody else . . . To stand in front of two hundred people and tell them that we are going to be down to less than a hundred in one fiscal year, that was really excruciating . . . Many people were angry with me. There were mean e-mails that were forwarded to me, and some officials complained to my bosses in Washington . . . One thing I learned about myself is that I am not a quitter . . . I am the Program Director and I will proceed as planned with this program.[t]

My Pride Had Been Hurt
One of the things I wanted to do was to establish a reasonable cost over a long-term pricing agreement and not force the contractor to provide cost or pricing data each year . . . I believed that I had verbal approval for price based acquisition from my boss in Washington, so I pitched that to . . . Raytheon [the contractor] . . . as one of the benefits of reforming our old way of doing business. Then . . . a month before we were supposed to award the contract to Raytheon . . . my boss in the Office of the Secretary of Defense told me she wouldn't let us go forward. She wouldn't sign the waiver.
. . . I was crushed . . . But I pulled myself together that weekend, and I called Chuck Anderson [Raytheon's Vice President] at home on Sunday. "Chuck, I can't deliver on Price Based Acquisition," I said. "I'm sorry, I thought I could do

it, but I can't. I can't get approval for it." "Well Judy, if that's the way it is, I guess that's the way it is," he said. "Let's have a video conference on Monday and get everybody together to figure out what to do."

. . . I still remember that Friday night after the phone call and how I felt like driving off the road. I thought so much depended on getting Price Based Acquisition. Part of the hurt was that I thought it would damage the business, but the other part was that I took it personally. I had gotten too full of myself. I was focused on putting in place all those great reforms and that great strategy, and I expected every part of the process to fall in place. I came to understand that my pride had been hurt because I had promised people something I couldn't do.[11]

Judy retreated, but with great difficulty. She admitted that she found it difficult to completely channel her ego needs away from herself and into the larger goal of developing an excellent project. When one's ego or personal agenda is allowed to take precedence over all other considerations, judgment may be easily distorted and rendered ineffective.[38]

The next example, which is an account of two brave women crossing Antarctica, illustrates how retreating can be accomplished with good judgment and great dignity.

In 2001, the two [Ann Bancroft and Liv Arnesen] became the first women to cross Antarctica's land mass on foot. But they had intended to do more—to cross the entire continent, ice shelf and all. As the end of the Antarctic summer drew nigh, the pair found themselves with about 400 miles of ice yet to cover. They had already traveled more than 1,700 miles.

The problem was that they were in a race against the elements and running out of time. Facing blizzard conditions and round-the-clock darkness that was about to descend upon them, the two women needed to decide whether or not to press on. Extending the journey would mean risking the lives of their expedition team as well as those of the pilots who might have to rescue them in an emergency. They had spent three years planning, training, and raising funds for the journey, and victory loomed ever so large. Still, they had to consider everyone's best interests and not just their own pride and ego.

After 18 more hours of towing their sleds and a few minutes of deliberation, they decided the dream had to end . . . Bancroft says the choice was sealed not only by the weather, but also by their devotion to the three million children who had followed their progress through the team's Web site. "The trip didn't belong to us alone . . . We had a chance to honor the relationships we'd created with our community; we wanted to make difficult but responsible choices for the kids. To me, that was a valuable legacy."[39]

Truly great leaders approach their projects in a way that enables an easier retreat when necessary. In his book *Good to Great*, Jim Collins shares his insight: "We were surprised, shocked really, to discover the type of leadership required to turn a good company into a great one. Compared to the high-profile leaders with big personalities . . . the good-to-great leaders . . . are a paradoxical blend of personal humility and professional will . . . [They] channel their ego needs away from themselves and into the large goal of building a great company. It's not that [they] have no ego or self-interest. Indeed, they are incredibly ambitious—but their ambition is first and foremost to their institution, not themselves."[40]

In the following story, Terry Little from the U.S. Air Force illustrates the consequences of NOT applying the guideline Persevere, But Know When to Retreat:

> *I've made plenty of mistakes in my career, but the one that I think of as providing the greatest learning opportunities occurred while I was program manager of a large Department of Defense (DoD) project designated by Congress as an acquisition reform program. I was told I would have my department's support to try almost anything—so long as it wasn't illegal—to improve acquisition in DoD.*
>
> *One of the things that came to me was to emulate a practice used by many commercial companies, profit sharing. I wanted to establish a way for the people working for me to share in the savings of the program. As I saw it, it was a win-win situation.*
>
> *I was sure the savings were going to be enormous, and I believed it would stimulate my people to be more creative, innovative, and give them a greater sense of ownership over the outcome of the program. I said to myself, "Self, you could look really heroic if you got this approved and your people got a big fat bonus all because of your brilliant idea." Thus, I set off on my Don Quixote quest to get approval.*
>
> *When I went back to tell the people in my department, I found their reaction to be a little too cool for my tastes. Suddenly they were backing off when I started talking about pay-for-performance incentives. But that didn't matter to me. I already had fallen in love with my idea and was determined to get approval at the Pentagon no matter what. I commenced to making trips from Florida to Washington DC every week, talking to various people in the Pentagon, explaining what I had in mind and why it was such a wonderful idea. All I needed was to get approval, I believed, and there would be this big cash payment for the people who worked for me. Over the next two years, I spent almost half my time in Washington.*
>
> *So carried away did I get with my brilliant idea that I decided to try and see the Secretary of Defense himself.. I managed to get an appointment on his calendar for a 15-minute meeting. I explained my proposal. He listened and then he said, "Well, I need to talk with my staff about this." When he said this to me, I knew that I was finished because the people he was going to talk with were the same people I had talked with before I got to see him.*

I persisted at this for so long not because I was impassioned about trying to help my people. Instead, it became about keeping my ego from being bruised. I persisted because I couldn't admit that I had failed. After this was all over and I looked back and saw that it was my fault that the program experienced so many difficulties, I felt disgusted with myself. I thought constantly about what I had done, how I could be so stupid, and it took nearly a year for me to come to some kind of peace with myself. For a year, it made me draw in and not want to push anymore, it made me timid and risk-averse, and that is a crippling state of mind to be in for a project manager.

I learned . . . how critical it is when you do make a mistake—and when you are trying to do anything at all you are going to make mistakes—to forgive yourself immediately and move forward. Immediately.[v]

Through this story, Little shares with us two major mistakes he committed: First, he was too slow to retreat, and second, once he retreated he was too slow to recover. Regarding the late retreat, Little, like Judy above, also refers to his ego problem: "It became about keeping my ego from being bruised." However, he explains that it was not only an ego problem, but rather more about perceiving himself as a heroic type of leader: "Thus I set off on my Don Quixote quest to get approval."

Exercising courageous leadership does not require heroism. Here, Simons, Mintzberg, and Basu attempt to debunk the myth of heroic CEOs: "Companies need CEOs who are heroic leaders. This is another half-truth. Of course, one of the CEO's roles is to provide leadership. But the real question is: What kind of leadership? . . . heroic leadership is . . . corrosive to the connection that needs to exist between a real leader and the people who make the company work. Real leadership is connected, involved, and engaged. It's often more quiet than heroic."[41]

The next story, which is shared by Paul Espinosa, a project manager at NASA, is a personal account of his experience as a mountain climber and how he learned the lesson that good judgment sometimes means cutting one's losses to avoid losing everything.

It was June and I was in Yosemite National Park in California, 2,000 feet off the ground. I was climbing El Capitan, a majestic 3,000-foot high, mile-wide granite monolith . . . After three days of climbing on its sheer face, and having completed the most difficult part of the route, my partner and I were heading down.

. . . Retreating was made worse by the fact that this was not the first—nor the second—time I had been on this route, but the third . . . On my first attempt to climb the "Nose," I was ill prepared for the enormity of the task . . . My second attempt was two years later . . . I was well trained . . . So here I was on my third attempt, another two years later. I had trained physically for the climb, practiced numerous shorter routes, and was prepared to

climb as an equal with a new partner, one who was very competent and climbed at my level.

The climb had been going wonderfully . . . By the end of the second day, we made it to 2,000 feet. We fell asleep under the stars, looking forward to the remaining 1,000 feet of climbing we figured to take another couple days. At some point during the night, I heard raindrops. We both had waterproof covers over our sleeping bags and were prepared for a storm, as long as it didn't become too severe. Unfortunately, severe is what we got... our granite "camp" was covered with 1/4 inch of flowing water. Luckily, the lightning stayed about 5 miles away, but at 2,000 feet up the wall with all the metal of our gear around us, we still felt like sitting ducks . . .

. . . We were about halfway down the cold wet wall, coming down from out of the clouds, when the rain began easing up . . . Should we have tried to stick it out just a little longer? . . . We knew we had made the right decision to head down, but it was still hard. Good judgment sometimes means cutting your losses lest you lose everything, and in this case "everything" was no mere figure of speech.

. . . By two o'clock in the afternoon we were on the ground. I was happy to be safe and looking forward to hot cocoa and a shower. Still, I was saddened over the defeat . . . My triumph on "The Nose" route of El Capitan will come eventually, I'm sure of it, and at that point I will certainly have earned it.[w]

When Paul decided to abort his third climb, he had to relinquish a dream. Still, his recovery did not last a year, like in Little's case. His recovery was extremely quick, and immediately following the saddening defeat, he was already envisioning his future triumph. Little's slow and debilitating recovery from his defeat is what made him realize how critical it is to "forgive yourself immediately and move forward."

This rule goes hand in hand with Little's strategy for coping with failures, as we saw in the Second Brown Guideline: "The first thing to do is to go through a short grieving period . . . whenever we had a failure, I allowed grieving for one day . . . and then it was time to put it behind us. That's a Terry Little rule." Yet, how can one make sure that Little's new rule of "forgive yourself immediately and move forward" will indeed be easy to follow?

In his book *Emotional Intelligence*, Daniel Goleman discusses the importance of optimism as a motivating factor: "Optimism, like hope, means having a strong expectation that things will turn out all right in life, despite setbacks and frustrations. Optimism is an attitude that buffers people against falling into apathy, hopelessness or depression in the face of tough going." However, Goleman is quick to warn the reader: "Providing, of course, it is a realistic optimism; a too-naïve optimism can be disastrous."[42]

Collins reports similar findings. On the one hand, it is recommended to "retain faith that you will prevail in the end, regardless of the difficulties."

On the other hand, one should not be overly optimistic, building unfounded beliefs of easy and quick successes, because following several, bound-to-happen disappointments, one can lose hope altogether and thus find it very difficult to recover.[43]

The reader who by now has had an opportunity to become familiar with more than a few stories in which Little challenged the status quo must be aware that he does not suffer from lack of optimism, hope, or faith. In the current case, however, he suffers from unrealistic overoptimism: "But that didn't matter to me. I already had fallen in love with my idea . . . So carried away did I get with my brilliant idea that I decided to try and see the Secretary of Defense himself." On the other hand, Ann Bancroft, Liv Arnesen, and Paul Espinosa have all demonstrated realistic optimism. Will Steger, a world-renowned polar explorer, claims that the decision which Ann and Liv faced is the most difficult of any journey: "Doing what Ann and Liv did is much harder than reaching the peak of the mountain, flying a flag, and saying, 'We're heroes, take us to the parade.' Real leadership is not about getting to the top. In this game, leadership is about coming back alive."[44] In the project world, real leadership is about the success of the project, not the ego of its leader, and challenging the status quo is desirable only when project leaders have their head in the clouds and their feet on the ground.

One can see the contrast not only between the success of the project and personal ego, but between a current, local failure and long-term, overall success. On the basis of the prison experience of Admiral Jim Stockdale in Vietnam, Collins coined the "Stockdale Paradox." Admiral Stockdale, who was a prisoner of war in Hanoi from 1965 to 1973 and was tortured multiple times, survived due to his ability to cope with the following paradox: "You must retain faith that you will prevail **in the end** AND you must also confront the most brutal facts of your **current reality**."[45]

Moreover, according to Collins, wrestling with the Stockdale Paradox "has proved powerful for coming back from difficulties not weakened, but stronger." This point was stressed, for example, in the above story by Paul Espinosa, where his recovery was extremely quick and he was already envisioning his future triumph. According to the Stockdale Paradox, one can see the retreat as a necessary tactical move, leading eventually to the strategic win. Therefore, an alternative title for the current guideline might be Persevere, but Be Willing to Retreat in Order to Prevail in the End.

CHAPTER 4

The Red Principle: Collaborate through Interdependence and Trust

The First Red Guideline: Take Recruiting Very Seriously

In 1911, Fredrick Taylor, the father of "scientific management," said, "In the past man has been first. In the future the system must be first."[1]

In 2005, Terry Little, U.S. Air Force program manager, begs to differ. Little chooses to describe his management philosophy by declaring, "McNamara, I am not." And this is how he explains it:

> Most of my peers in program management think that the most important aspects of our job are making decisions, conducting reviews, and controlling performance. In contrast, I think my priorities are to develop collaborative relations, foster alliances, and take care of the people who work for me, giving them a sense of confidence in themselves. I have to ask, What is going to occupy my time? And for the most part, what occupies my time are people issues.
>
> As I came into program management many years ago, I stumbled into an understanding of this. At first, I gravitated toward an analytical approach because of my background in operations research. I was brought up in the Robert McNamara school of management, where everything is quantifiable—if we can't build a model of something, then it doesn't exist.
>
> It didn't take me long to figure out that this idea was bankrupt. Programs move ahead because of the activities of people, but none of the models I was using measured that. I could do the fanciest calculations in the world, but did they have anything to do with determining whether the project was going to be successful? Not at all. I had some difficulty convincing the people with whom I worked that it was not the right approach because they, like me, had been brought up to believe that a sharp analytic mind can arrive at a solution for any problem.[a]

While Little has difficulties convincing some of his peers that even today "people must still be first," there are other sources supporting his outlook. Cooke-Davies, for example, declares that "it's people who get things done!" He claims that the "literature on project management is dominated by discussions of techniques, tools, methods and processes, rather than the human dimension." Cooke-Davies also reports on a study by Thomas Lechler of 448 German projects in which Lechler found that "'people' factors accounted for 47% of the variance in project success, whereas other factors that he called 'activities' accounted for no more than 12% between them." This finding led Lechler to conclude that "when it comes to project management, it's the people that matter."[2]

In another study, Hoffman and his colleagues report that "the books published on the general subject of project management give little space and attention to the subject of team development . . . This is a mistake when we realize that many practitioners identify the human dimension of project management to be the single most important determinant of project success."[3]

In his book *Good to Great: Why Some Companies Make the Leap . . . and Others Don't,* Jim Collins attempts to present "the timeless principles of good to great. It's about how you take a good organization and turn it into one that produces sustainable great results." One of these timeless principles is **"First Who . . . Then What**. We expect that good-to-great leaders would begin by setting a new vision and strategy. We found instead that they **first** got the right people on the bus, the wrong people off the bus, and the right people in the right seats—and **then** they figured out where to drive it. The old adage 'People are your most important asset' turns out to be wrong. People are **not** your most important asset. The **right** people are."[4]

In their book *Doing what Matters,* James Kilts (former chairman and CEO of the Gillette Company) and his colleagues reach a similar conclusion: "People are the make-or-break factor in business. With the right people, almost anything is possible. With the wrong team, failure awaits."[5] Tom Peters does not refer to permanent organizations, like Collins and Kilts, but rather to projects, when he makes the following recommendation regarding the "how-to" of recruiting the right people: "Take recruiting very seriously. Make it formal. Develop a hit/target list. Go after it . . . This calls for a big (in time spent) investment."[6]

Little asserts, "If you pick the right guy, everything can be screwed up and you will still be successful. I spend a lot of time picking the right horse to ride on." He applies special measures not only when selecting his own people, but also when selecting his contractors and vendors. For example, in one case he applied the following practice for selecting the contractor: "The overall effect was that past performance [of the contractor] counted for 50 percent of the source selection decision."[7]

In the following example, Ken Schwer, a project manager from NASA, describes the great efforts that were required for recruiting his team. His story highlights how recruiting has changed from being like purchasing (of resources) by Human Resources to selling (the project) by the project manager:

> *A project manager is only as good as his/her staff, so it was important for me to concentrate on selecting my core team. Since the clock to Solar Dynamics Observatory (SDO) launch had started, I needed key individuals on board to make progress. "Hand picking" the core team is an important part of establishing a teamwork environment. I wouldn't leave staffing key positions to chance.*
>
> *I knew that it was important to work with the functional supervisors and not bypass them when it came to staffing. I needed their approval and cooperation if SDO was to be successful. To accomplish this, I spent many hours each week sitting down with individuals and small groups to go over the project and to solicit their support—again and again and again. As a result, I became a better salesperson, and I was able to select my core team with the support and approval of functional management.*[b]

While there is an almost unanimous agreement regarding the need to recruit the "right" people, there is no agreement regarding the criteria that define those "right" people.[8] When it comes to projects, however, one thing is very clear: "right" does not mean "stars." Indeed, one of the primary reasons for project "dream teams" to fail is "signing too many all-stars." As Geoffrey Covin, *Fortune*'s senior editor-at-large, explains, "If everybody is a potential CEO, it's difficult to have an effective team."[9] In his essay "Teams and Stars," Scott Berkun elaborates on the "myth of all-star teams:" "The true goal of any team is not to have the best players for each position: it's to succeed. Success comes when a team makes use of the team's abilities towards a goal, something you don't get merely by picking the best players at each position. It's a rookie mistake: you can't hire assuming people will work alone. You have to understand how each person will interact and collaborate with others and choose people that fit (or that create useful tensions that you carefully manage). This may mean passing on the stellar, but volatile, candidate and choosing someone whose skills will both amplify and be amplified by the talents of others. Instead of a 3rd star, your team might best be served by an above average person who has skills the stars lack."[10]

Moreover, in most project situations, recruiting too many stars is simply not practical. As explained by Yourdon, "Most project managers have to accept the fact that they won't be given a carte blanche to hire the world's most talented superstars, and politics within the organization may make it impossible for the project manager to steal away the best people within the organization because they're already involved in other critical projects or fiercely defended by other managers."[11]

While recruiting, the project manager must constantly think about the team as a whole, that is, making sure that the team has enough complementary skills and that the selected team members can work with each other. As explained by Katzenbach and Smith, "Teams perform well [since among other things] they bring together complementary skills and experiences that, by definition, exceed those of any individual on the team." Katzenbach and Smith also stress that team members must be selected not only on the basis of their technical, functional, or problem-solving skills, but also on the basis of their interpersonal skills. Peters puts team diversity very high on his list, explaining that diversity involves a range of perspectives, which is the key to effectiveness and creativity.[12]

In the following example, Mary Chiu, a program manager from Johns Hopkins Applied Physics Laboratory, shares some of her pragmatic considerations while selecting team members for a spacecraft development project:

> *Most of my efforts in the early stages of the project were geared toward carefully choosing the right teammates. It was a matter of going around to the group supervisors and lining up people, talking to them, getting a feel for how they approached a project, learning their ideas about working on a team, and seeing how this meshed with mine.*
>
> *Although my bias was toward youth, I knew that I needed a mix of experienced veterans as well . . . For example, I had a wonderful quality assurance engineer who had been around forever. On the other side of the equation, we had a guy who was an extraordinary young mechanical engineer. I didn't realize it at the time, but when we appointed him as lead he didn't even have his degree. At APL, that would have been unimaginable to an earlier generation. I didn't know him directly, but someone pointed him out to me, and so I talked with his group supervisor and then with him, and I knew right away that he was a winner.[c]*

In our dynamic era, when project teams have to cope frequently with many changes, the "right people" often means people with high adaptability.[13] Allan Frandsen, a payload manager from the California Institute of Technology, describes why he was looking for people with a flexible outlook and how he went about recruiting them:

> *When I accepted Dr. Stone's offer in 1990 to head up the ACE payload development, I handed off my responsibilities as Chief Engineer in NASA's Jet Propulsion Laboratory (JPL) science division and moved to an office at the California Institute of Technology (Caltech) campus. Although Caltech is only seven miles from JPL, there is a noticeable cultural difference between the two institutions. From my vantage point, Caltech was the perfect place for a relatively small, low-cost ($50 million) payload like ours to flourish. Short of choosing the wrong people or having inadequate resources, nothing will torpedo a project quicker, I think, than the wrong operating environment.*

> *. . . I began inquiries with various JPL organizations to find talented peo-*
> *ple with a flexible outlook on their job who, like me, could be loaned to the*
> *campus for the duration of ACE. I was looking for the right mix of talent and*
> *attitude, people who could flourish in a university environment.*
>
> *In searching for the right talent, I was concerned about getting people who*
> *were too imbued with the JPL way. After working on big projects for years and*
> *years, one can get to the point where you can't think any other way. Flexibility*
> *was more important than sheer brain power, so I actually told supervisors that*
> *I was looking for people who were a little bit out of the mainstream.*
>
> *I didn't want a person who would be afraid to deviate from plowing the*
> *furrow down the farmer's field. Some people want to be constrained to a har-*
> *ness and go in a familiar direction, often the one of least resistance. Following*
> *rules is fine, but you have to know when the rules need to be bent, tailored,*
> *or even broken, especially on an R&D project designed and executed within a*
> *university environment where most rules were flexible and processes generally*
> *adaptable to circumstances. When I interviewed people, I wanted to hear excite-*
> *ment in their voices. The way I saw it, they were getting an opportunity to*
> *spread their wings and be innovative, which always entails some risk both to*
> *your own sense of competency and to the project.*"[d]

The importance of attitude as the criterion for selecting the "right people" has received great interest in recent years. Following an attempt to
understand the "rules for smart hiring" applied by several successful companies, Peter Carbonara explains the importance of attitude: "They've analyzed what separates their winners from their losers, good hires from bad
hires. These companies compete in a wide range of industries—from air-
lines to steel, computers to hotels—but they all arrived at the same
answer: What people know is less important than who they are. Hiring,
they believe, is not about finding people with the right experience. It's
about finding people with the right mind-set. These companies hire for
attitude and train for skill."[14]

The attitude, the mind-set, must fit the specific context. Frandsen stresses
that he needed "talented people with a flexible outlook on their job" and
that "flexibility was more important than sheer brain power." If one accepts
the concept that people are the make-or-break factor in project success and
that with the right people almost anything is possible—while with the
wrong people, failure awaits—then one must pay even greater attention to
the selection of the right project manager. It is not surprising, therefore,
that in her article "Senior Management Perceptions of Project Management
Competence," Lynn Crawford quotes one senior manager who claimed that
"the key to project success is to pick the right project manager."[15]

In the following story, Rick Obenschain, who was brought in to lead
a very large program of NASA, a program that was in "horrible shape,"
shares with us what he did when he had to select a project manager:

> *We were having the most problems with our instruments, which were being built*
> *by one of our contractors. I knew that I had to assign someone to take charge*

of this area, and I knew who I wanted: Marty Davis. Marty was working on another project, but I had seen him in action on the Gamma Ray Observatory (GRO), and I knew he was the person I needed on my team.

I went to my Center Director and I said, "You know, John, I've just got to have somebody who can go on site and ramrod these instruments because we're not getting anywhere with them." He nodded and asked who I wanted. "You can have anybody you want," he said. "That's good," I said, "because I want Marty Davis." He said, "We can't move Marty. We just put him on another project ten weeks ago." I told him why I needed Marty and why no one else would do . . . in the end, the director put Marty on the project.

Marty was so successful that eventually he replaced Rick Obenschain to become the manager of the entire program.[e]

In the last example of this guideline, Chuck Anderson, vice president of Raytheon, explains what kind of "right" project managers he was looking for in a large program that was undergoing major organizational and cultural changes:

I surrounded myself with a team of effective leaders. I'm talking about six or seven people, all hand selected by me. I knew every one of them. You need to have real leaders on your team when you're doing something like we set out to do on AMRAAM. These were people willing to make decisions, take risks, get on with it, and not study a problem to death. We've got so many smart people in this business who can't bring themselves to make decisions because they're afraid of failing. I selected people who could make swift decisions, if that's what was required.[f,16]

The Second Red Guideline: Develop Trust-Based Teamwork

It has been widely recognized that competitiveness in global industries increasingly requires the ability to develop trusting relationships.[17] In his book *Trust: The Social Virtues & the Creation of Prosperity*, Francis Fukuyama provides a sweeping assessment of the impact of culture on economic life and success in the new global economy. Fukuyama asserts that "one of the most important lessons we can learn from examination of economic life is that a nation's well-being, as well as its ability to compete, is conditioned by a single, pervasive cultural characteristic: the level of trust inherent in the society." High-trust societies, he shows, are outstanding in their potential for forming wide-reaching and successful cooperative partnerships. Low-trust societies, by contrast, often tend to be economic disaster areas and can certainly be terrible places in which to live. In short, trust is the precondition for prosperity.[18]

In his book *New Rules for the New Economy*, Kevin Kelly presents ten rules for a "connected world." One of these rules, "Relationship Tech," argues that "the network economy is founded on technology, but can only be built on relationships. It starts with chips and ends with trust." Kelly explains that while the central economic imperative of the industrial age was to increase productivity, the central economic imperative of the network economy is to amplify relationships. He further explains that "none of this enlargement of relationships can happen unless there are vast amounts of trust all around."[19]

When we shift our focus from the overall global or national level to the particular project level, we find the same or even a stronger pattern. Indeed, in our current dynamic environment, trust is extremely crucial for project success. In the following example, Tim Flores, a project manager from NASA, uses the results of his MSc research project at MIT to demonstrate this importance:

> The aim of Tim's MSc research project at MIT was to account for the different outcomes of the Pathfinder, Climate Orbiter, and Polar Lander projects, all of which were initiated by the JPL. Although all three projects were conducted under the same guiding principle ("faster, better, cheaper"), were all of comparable scope, and shared many similar elements and even some of the same team members, they had very different end results. Pathfinder was a success, while the other two projects failed.

> *I expected to find that the Pathfinder differed from the other projects on a number of levels: resources, constraints, philosophy, and personnel. And this was, to some extent, true. But I was extremely surprised to find one fundamental element that distinguished the successful mission from the failed missions: teamwork . . . The Pathfinder team developed trusting relations within a culture of openness. They felt free to make the best decisions they could with the resources available to them, and they knew that they weren't going to be crucified for mistakes. That trust never developed in the other programs.*[g]

Developing Teamwork

The purpose of the current guideline is to demonstrate how one can develop trust-based teamwork and why trust is so crucial for project success. However, before discussing the trust issue, we should first better understand the nature of and the need for multifunctional teams. The following story by Linda Abbott, a mission business manager from NASA, describes the development of a multifunctional team and the impact of the teaming process on the ultimate success of the project:

> Spacecrafts are usually built with only a few big purchase items, but literally hundreds of small items that can make for the biggest headaches. It's the $20 connector that can halt integration, leading to a costly delay. After finishing the building of another spacecraft, it was clear to Linda that the success of the project was due to the special teamwork that combined technical know-how with procurement resources.

Procurement's whole process is bound in rules and procedures and staffed by people that know the rules, but don't know about building spacecraft . . . Procurement works as a pool, with a first in, first out procedure. It works fairly well for them and is actually relatively fair to all projects, but it's unable to respond to schedule stopping emergencies. They see their job as procurement, not building spacecraft. They don't work with any one project closely enough to understand why that twenty-dollar connector is a multi-thousand-dollar emergency. Mostly, they don't have any personal investment in our success. We needed to get procurement on our team, rather than try to override them or work around them.

To circumvent the general pool procedure, Linda managed to convince procurement to assign two procurement officers to work exclusively on her project. The officers were integrated into the work of the team and invited to staff meetings. In the process of learning about the spacecraft project, they grew to understand why the technology was difficult and why unanticipated problems were inevitable, as well as the extent of their impact.

The more she learned about our project and worked on our team, the more she wanted our project to succeed. She found ways to expedite purchases when there were real emergencies. I can't tell you how many times she saved our bacon, times that were two days here, a week there, but that would have added up to a big, and costly schedule slip.

In turn, each of the team's engineers and scientists listened to the procurement officers, learning more about the procurement process and the "why's" behind some of those pesky rules. As both sides came to understand each other's constraints, the interaction between them vastly improved, as did procurement's response to schedule-stopping emergencies:

Together procurement became more responsive to our needs, and we became more responsible in meeting procurement's needs . . . By integrating them into the team, we've changed an adversarial relationship into a group relationship. If we fail, they fail. It's that simple; it's now in their vested interest to find ways to make it happen. And they've become amazingly versatile.[h]

Linda's observation that "they don't have any personal investment in our success" most succinctly conveys why the structure of the traditional functional organization obstructs teamwork. No real teamwork can take place in an organization that maintains a traditional division of labor, given that the loyalties of the R&D, marketing, engineering, production, and procurement staff primarily lie with their respective disciplines, departments, and managers. Therefore, breaking down the organization's functional walls is the minimum requirement essential for teamwork.

However, integrating a group of people with a common assignment into an effective team may be even more difficult when the people in the group are affiliated with different organizations. This is illustrated in the next story told by Bill Clegern, a project manager from Procter & Gamble (P&G), who describes how a P&G resident engineer attempted to develop teamwork with his prime contractor:

> Pierre was the P&G resident engineer managing a major expansion at one of their plants in Europe. He was forced to work with Karl, the site manager from B&N, which was a highly reputable European contractor that won the bid for the facility work. Karl's workers had adopted a superior attitude toward all the other contractors on the site right from the start, and any team-building efforts by P&G were being undermined by B&N's incessant criticism of others and smug confidence about their own "professional" construction techniques.

> *Pierre . . . grudgingly endured the situation, looking for an effective way to take Karl and B&N down a peg and get them on the team without damaging their effectiveness. Direct appeals to Karl, based on the premise that "we're all in this together," just didn't work . . . About three months into the job . . . the "master" contractor discovered that one complete set of foundations on the south face of the facility's office expansion was located 30 cm inside the intended periphery. Over 200 lineal meters of strip foundations had just been poured in the wrong place . . . This was a serious mistake . . . Karl came, hat in hand, to Pierre to "fess up."*

> Rather than demand that B&N start over, Pierre immediately called a conference of the plant, engineering, and project leaders. Together they found a way to shift internal walls, realign halls, and adjust exterior windows in order to distribute the error without resulting in any functional or aesthetic losses. Although B&N's rework cost was considerable, it was far lower than that for a complete fix and did not ruin the company's reputation. At the same time, P&G was able to stay on schedule without compromising the project's chance for success. Pierre did not take advantage of B&N nor kick Karl "while he was down." The project was ultimately labeled a big success by all involved, and their new-found teamwork allowed B&N and P&G to collaborate on subsequent projects as well.[i,20]

These two stories stress a similar key guiding philosophy: "If we fail, they fail," (the NASA story), and "we're all in this together" (the P&G story). And in both stories the rationale facilitating the adoption of this new working philosophy is also similar: the realization that unanticipated problems are inevitable. When team members understand the inevitable constraints of dynamic projects and realize that no part of the team can perform its job without collaborating with the other members, they embrace a philosophy of mutual interdependence and mutual responsibility for project results. Without the protracted forces that pull members together, project leaders must pay inordinate and unceasing attention to team maintenance. In essence, a group of people who do not feel dependent on each other is a committee, not a team.

However, as the following story demonstrates, developing this mutual responsibility for project results may require more time and more effort when the project simply can not afford to make even an early "serious mistake." This is especially true when the key players operate under strikingly different organizational cultures. This is how Gerald Murphy, the payload systems engineer from the California Institute of Technology, describes the impact of these differences on his work with his counterpart from Johns Hopkins University Applied Physics Laboratory (APL):

> Being the systems engineer for payload meant tailoring specifications to each of nine instruments. It also required coordination with 20 coinvestigators who were scattered throughout the United States at different universities, each with its own organizational culture and its own way of doing things.

> *Initially, Judi* [on the spacecraft side] *and I tried to pretend our differences didn't exist or that they would magically go away, but there were a number of times where our differences came to a head. Vibration specification was a good example. APL had a specification that they wanted us to use to qualify all instrument boxes. "Since you are riding on our spacecraft, then you have to meet our specification," they said . . . APL's specification was based on their institutional precedents, which we felt were overly conservative in the area of vibration test levels . . . ACE was my first experience finding culture differences between institutions that actually manifested themselves into heated differences of opinion at the engineering level*

> *Judi and I are both headstrong and intelligent—and used to winning arguments. I have to say, our relationship started rocky. Here we were, two equals sort of battling each other. I think it took us the better part of the first year to realize that this was dumb. We had to ask, "Why are we battling each other when we're both trying to get the job done?" We found a way to talk through things and resolve our differences, largely because we kept talking and trying to understand each other's point of view. I'm making this sound easy—it wasn't.*

> *. . . What I think we learned was this: the fact that I did things this way and Judy did them that way . . . did not mean that any of our ways was the one true way. Even though we might argue about things and agree to disagree, we earned one another's respect, and we didn't make our differences personal.*[j]

The fact that building teamwork between these two systems engineers required time and initially involved overcoming difficulties is not surprising. In their book *The Wisdom of Teams: Creating the High-Performance Organization*, Katzenbach and Smith highlight that this process is quite common: "Real teams do not develop until the people in them work hard to overcome barriers that stand in the way of collective performance . . . Overcoming barriers to performance is how groups become teams."[21] Katzenbach and Smith further explain that "real teams learn how to deal with such concerns [i.e., different cultures and personalities] through frank and open communication."[22]

Indeed, Katzenbach and Smith then defined a team as a small number of people with complementary skills who are committed to a common purpose, performance goals, and approach for which they hold themselves mutually accountable.[23] However, nowadays this definition is incomplete. Katzenbach and Smith themselves revised their definition in their 1993 book to add that "performance in the 1990s and beyond" will require us to cope with changes, and thus in the future teamwork will be characterized by "trust based relationships."[24]

Developing Trust

The trust issue will be explained by discussing two very successful, but contrasting, scenarios. In the first one, trust was developed very quickly, while in the other, a more typical case, trust was built "inch by inch."

The first story is told by John Del Frate, who was the NASA project manager of the Pathfinder Solar-Powered Airplane. The primary technological challenge faced by NASA and the contractor, AeroVironment, was that of operating an aircraft that would be both light enough to fly and large enough to be powered by the sun and carry meaningful payloads.

I learned a lot from my relationship with AeroVironment, specifically from two people, Bob Curtin and Kirk Flittie. I wish everyone could have the opportunity to work with contractors that they trust the way I trusted these guys. Usually, with the government contracting structure, we spend an inordinate amount of time and money simply because we don't trust the contractor. There is probably a reason for every process or regulation used to govern them, but they seem ridiculous and wasteful to me. I started out treating the industrial partners like "contractors," but they soon earned my trust and respect. And it paid off for both the government and the industry partners, as we were able to do more technology development at a set level of funding. Not having to constantly monitor the contractors meant a much leaner operation; we were able to work smarter and faster. But we didn't throw the necessary checks and balances out the window. Instead, we used them at a level that allowed us to pour far more concentration into getting the job done. And because of the trust we'd established, I knew that our partners always had the best interest of the project in mind . . . we had the same goal . . . We set a number of altitude records with the UAVs, and we performed a number of "first-of-a-kind" demonstrations with payloads. The highlight for me was the world altitude record we set in 2001 with the Helios aircraft on the Hawaiian Island of Kauai. We conducted our flight operations there, flying to a record altitude of

96,863 feet—10,000 feet higher than any non-rocket propelled aircraft has ever gone. We did it on the power of the sun, and it was an unforgettable experience.[k]

The Pathfinder project enjoyed several favorable conditions that facilitated the development of trust-based teamwork rather quickly, including the relocation of the project to a remote location, a flexible contractual agreement, and the unique personalities of the two specific individuals who led the contractor's team.

In their book *Credibility*, Kouzes and Posner talk about engendering trust and explain that "trusting other people encourages them to trust us; distrusting others makes them lose confidence in us."[25] Likewise, Solomon and Flores assert that "trust is a matter of reciprocal relationships . . . Trust is transformative . . . it is a matter of changing each other and the relationship through trust."[26] Indeed, Del Frate stresses the transformative and reciprocal nature of trust in his case: "I started out treating the industrial partners like 'contractors,' but they soon earned my trust and respect."

Typically, however, developing trust entails a longer and more demanding process. On the origins of trust, Solomon and Flores claim it to be "the result of continuous attentiveness and activity . . . Trust is a social practice, not a set of beliefs. It is a 'how to,' not a "knowing that."[27] Similarly, Kelly describes the nature of trust as "a peculiar quality: It can't be bought. It can't be downloaded. It can't be instant—a startling fact for an instant culture. It can only accumulate very slowly, over multiple iterations."[28]

The following stories focus on the U.S. Air Force advanced medium range air-to-air missile (AMRAAM) program and illustrate the more common scenario whereby building a trust-based team is a relatively long process requiring continuous leadership attention and intensive involvement throughout. The opening story by AMRAAM chief engineer, George Sudan, describes the cultural context of the project and its environment:

George's experience previous to joining AMRAAM was with a complicated weapons system that no one could figure out how to fire correctly.

One of the reasons the system wasn't working was because government engineers were busy meddling with the contractor. We had individuals on our team who felt that their primary responsibility was to criticize the contractor and tell them how to do their job.

With the support of management, George was able to get the engineers focused on the specification and verification business at hand, and they were able to turn things around and get the system to work.

After joining AMRAAM, George attempted to share his experience in the other program with management, but to no avail: "They thought I was out of my mind. 'You can't trust these dirty contractors. They're all out to take advantage of you,' they told me."

Not only was there no trust or sense of teamwork between the government engineers and the contractor, there was outright competition between them:

> *They expected us to line up with the contractor as though it were a basketball game. Here's their radio frequency guy, so we've got to have a radio frequency guy. Here's their software guy, so we've got to have a software guy. If he fakes left, you fake left. For our part on the government side, we were harassing our "opponents" all the time. "Let me see your documents. Let me review this. Let me see how you did that."*[1]

When George quips that "government engineers were busy meddling with the contractor" and when he uses the "basketball metaphor," he is calling our attention to the very high transaction costs of the project. Organizations get things done through exchange. Transaction costs are those associated with the exchange itself, while production costs are those expended in making whatever is to be exchanged. Transaction costs include locating a desirable trading partner, negotiating and writing a mutually acceptable agreement, monitoring the agreement, and taking the actions necessary to ensure that each party fulfills the predetermined set of obligations. Researchers claim that transaction costs may represent as much as 35–40 percent of the costs associated with economic activity.[29]

George found it impossible to change the status quo and bring about serious reform without management support, so he welcomed the arrival of Judy Stokley as the AMRAAM program director. In the following story, Judy describes her first attempt to change the status quo.

> *I hosted a meeting [at Eglin Air Force Base in Florida] with several of the key members of the two contractors building the missile, Hughes and Raytheon . . . I wanted to talk with them about our "partnership," what was wrong with it, and what we were going to do to improve it.*

To illustrate her point about what was wrong with AMRAAM, Judy brought a copy of the "spec tree"—a document containing hundreds of pages of minute details:

> *If the contractor, for any reason, needed to change something, he had to submit an Engineering Change Proposal, and the government had to approve it. The contractor documented every change in parts, down to the lowest-level nut, bolt, or screw, and sent the change proposals all day long. The government paid him to make those changes, or they didn't get done. I used to say, "If I want my contractor to flush the toilet in Tucson, I have to write him a contract letter and pay him to do it."*

In an attempt to change this adversarial mind-set, Judy proposed taking the unwieldy spec tree and replacing it with a clear, simple set of performance specifications that the contractor would control. In turn, the government would pay the contractor a fair price for the product, making for a win-win situation on both sides. However, this progressive view was not shared by all:

> *All of a sudden, Raytheon's chief engineer stood up and spoke across the room to his vice president: "Boss, I've got to make sure that before you agree to this, you understand what she's saying. Because if you do, I don't think there's any way you'll agree to it"* . . . *"Today," he continued, "if we change something here, the government pays; but what she's telling you is that with this deal, if we change something, we pay"* . . . *This man couldn't see opportunity. He could only see risk* . . . *"Oh man, we don't want any part of this," said the Raytheon vice president. "This is too different."*

Fortunately, the Hughes vice president, Chuck Anderson, was able to see Judy's inspired vision. When Raytheon and Hughes merged a year later, Chuck stayed with the program and the Raytheon vice president took his tunnel vision elsewhere.[m]

Very often it happens that once team members stereotype other team members, prejudice shapes what they see and how they act. Thus, initial perceptions of the individuals entering the project can force the project into a spiral of increasing or decreasing trust. Therefore, if possible, one should avoid recruiting team members who trigger distrust among other key players.[30]

Judy needed to wait until Chuck had assumed the leadership position before she could initiate her proposed change, which was called total system performance responsibility (TSPR). This unique approach in government contracting basically meant that the contractor accepted the responsibility to do whatever was necessary to ensure that the product met all requirements. Accordingly, simple changes could be made as deemed appropriate by the contractor without having to go through a long drawn out approval process with the government. In the following story, Chuck Anderson, Raytheon vice president, describes his response to Judy's proposed reform:

> *Judy wanted the government to save money for the program by handing over more responsibility to the contractor. If only they could trust us—that was the big "if." Judy was willing to take that chance. She'd seen me operate, and she knew that I could be trusted.[n]*

Solomon and Flores maintain that "trust entails a lack of control, but it means entering into a relationship in which control is no longer the issue . . . [Trust is not] the free fall of dependency . . . what trust makes possible is an eminently more effective interdependency: cooperation and the expansion of possibilities." Citing the Danish philosopher Soren Kierkegaard, they further assert, "It is always, to some extent 'a leap of faith' . . . What we create through our vulnerability is the solid security of a relationship."[31]

A leap of faith is indeed what many of the government staff had to make in order to change their attitude. They did not trust the contractor to make sensible decisions and feared that short-term money-saving measures would be taken at the risk of either degraded performance or increased costs in the long run. In the following story, Judy explains how she attempted to change this overriding attitude towards the contractor:

> *We solved this issue by letting these government people actually participate in the contractor's configuration change process. As participants in the contractor's decision process, they were able to see over time that their fears were unfounded. They found that the contractor really did care about satisfying the customer, that he really did care about his reputation, that he really did have a long-term perspective, and that he really did have motivations other than next quarter's profit. They saw, in effect, that the "contractor" was not an impersonal monolith, but was a group of people just like they were—trying their utmost to do the right things. In short, they found that the contractor was trustworthy.°*

Changing mind-set (unlearning) was discussed in depth in the introduction. Among other things, it was explained that people are more inclined to change their mind-set on the basis of vivid information. Thus, allowing the government people to repeatedly participate in the contractor's configuration change process provided them with vivid information that facilitated the change in mind-set and the trust-building process.

Changing mind-set was crucial, but insufficient, and Judy had to make additional changes that were more tangible. In one of these changes, Judy made sharp cuts in the size of her own team, including a reduction in the engineering team from 80 to 12. For his part, Chuck was ready to reciprocate by reducing the size of his own workforce. On the basis of his estimate, Chuck and Judy shook hands on the number of staff needed to get the job done. This would mean displacing a significant number of people from the 400 currently working on AMRAAM so as to reach the estimated target of 100.

> *When we re-joined the group, Judy announced that we would keep 100 people on the program. I remember the look in my team's eyes. It was a look that didn't mask their discomfort. They knew that many of the people*

who had worked on the program for years would lose their jobs and that the rest of them would have to figure out how to get the job done with one-fourth of the former workforce. They also knew that a handshake was our only assurance that our customer was going to live up to the agreement. "Look, we have to trust the customer on this," I said to them. "We have to trust that they understand what kind of risk we're taking in signing up for this."[P]

A common definition of trust is "one party's confidence that the other party in the exchange relationship will not exploit its vulnerabilities."[32] In the following story, Chuck demonstrates his confidence that the client will not exploit his vulnerabilities, thereby highlighting the essence of trust:

Prior to the Hughes-Raytheon merger, Chuck decided to open the corporate books to the U.S. Air Force. Raytheon's knee-jerk reaction was to accuse him of breaking the rules by exposing confidential data to the government. However, he would not be intimidated and managed to win over Raytheon's management to his way of thinking.

At the time I entered this agreement with Judy, I still had a Hughes badge on. I actually had to get Raytheon's chief operating officer to approve it. How did I get it done? I said we could pull it off, and I was believable. My prior track record probably had something to do with it, too. The bottom line was that I had run successful programs all of my career, and it's hard to argue with success.[q]

In their book *Credibility*, Kouzes and Posner provide support for Chuck's explanation about his source of power: "A credibility check is rooted in the past. It has to do with reputation . . . Credibility, like reputation, is something that is earned over time . . . The credibility foundation is built brick by brick . . . complete trust is granted (or not) only after people have had the chance to get to know more about the person."[33] In the following story, Chuck describes his continuous effort to build credibility with the client brick by brick:

All of my team members, approximately 80 of us, met for half a day off-site at a hotel. We did this every month. We rented a ballroom, and the whole purpose of that meeting, every month, was constancy of purpose. It was to get everybody aligned—or brainwashed, as some said . . . Some of the people who went to these meetings never got it, and we got rid of them.[r]

Solomon and Flores maintain that "building trust, we suggest, begins with talk about trust—talk combined with action, to be sure, but talk first of all . . . Thinking and talking about trust will not only influence our belief but also change our behavior in the world and with one another."[34]

James Watzin, a project manager from NASA, recommended similar actions when he was brought as an expert to reflect on the failed wide-field infrared explorer (WIRE) mission. Watzin submitted the following analysis of the situation: "WIRE failed because people could not or would not communicate well with each other . . . The WIRE communication difficulties . . . were driven more by individuals who simply were uncomfortable allowing others to see their work . . . They lost the opportunity for thorough peer review (the first opportunity to catch the design defect) and in doing so they lost the entire mission . . . The real lessons from this loss is that any team member that does not participate as a true team player should be excused, and that management should watch for signs of unnecessary conflict and act to understand it before more serious problems arise."[35]

These lessons are ones that Chuck has clearly learned and is not afraid to implement. In the following story, Brock McCaman, a program manager from Raytheon, describes the first signs that the changes are starting to generate positive outcomes:

> Prior to the introduction of TSPR, the government required an exhaustive report on the smallest of repairs, whereas now the company no longer even keeps any of that data.
>
> *Today, we send them a bill once a month for a fraction of the cost of what we were doing before, and we get missiles back in the field sooner. This way of contracting works better for us, for the government, for the taxpayer, and especially for the war fighter.*[s]

Research supports McCaman's account, as reported by Dyer and Chu: "Under conditions of high trust, trading partners will spend less time and resources on monitoring to see if the other is shirking or fulfilling the 'spirit' of the agreement . . . If each exchange partner is confident that the other party will not be opportunistic, then both parties can devote fewer resources to monitoring."[36] In the following story, Jon Westphal, an AMRAAM engineer, describes his unique role in building trust with the contractor.

> Judy Stokley and George Sudan were adamant about the fact that manufacturing was the business of the contractor, not the government: *"Let them do their job. We'll work with them to provide insight—not direction, not oversight."* Jon found that the best way to do so was by supporting open communication between the two parties to help them get their job done—that is, to play the role of an "enabler." Enablers are those who are not experts in any one field, but who have a broad background and know enough across

the board to communicate with the diverse group of people involved in any given project, including contracts people, finance staff, business reps, program managers, and engineers. By acting as enablers, Jon and three of his counterparts were able to work side by side with the contractor and the government people and get them in touch with the appropriate parties to help solve any and all problems as they arose.

The first thing I did was try to convince them that even though I was from the government, I was there to help in whatever capacity I could. "Hi, I'm from the government, and I'm here to help you." Usually, that's when doors slam. But you don't convince people with just words. As they say, actions speak louder, and so we had to walk it as well as talk it.

By helping the contractor to solve a technical problem, word spread quickly at the site that Jon was truly there to help, not to tell people what to do or to report on them:

The contactor had a technical problem . . . and needed to put a special team . . . to work on it. I invited myself to join the team . . . we had identified the potential impact of [the] problem and created a plan to overcome it.

Indeed, Jon approached each new situation as if he were part of the team, rather than the customer:

How do I know I was genuinely accepted? Something happened about nine months after I started going out to the contractor's site in Tucson. I wanted to talk to the Director of Operations. When I walked down to his office, there were five or six engineers standing outside, waiting in line while he had somebody in his office. I walked up to the front of the line and was going to stick my head in the office and ask a question, but the guys in line said, "Hey, what are you doing?" And I said, "Hey guys, I'm just going to ask Rick a quick question." And they said, "Hey, come on now, there's a line here." And I said, "Yeah, but I'm the customer." And they said, "You're an enabler. Get in the back of the line."[t]

In this case, the target of unlearning is reversed, with the government attempting to change the mind-set of the contractor workforce and gain their trust. *The Fifth Discipline Fieldbook* presents the following direct and most natural way for unlearning: "Buckminster Fuller used to say that if you want to teach people a new way of thinking, don't bother trying to teach them. Instead, give them a tool, the use of which will lead them to new ways of thinking."[37] By realizing that "actions speak louder" than words, Jon Westphal, the Enabler, was able to apply Fuller's recipe: "The contractor had a technical problem . . . and needed to put a special team . . . to work on it. I invited myself to join the team . . .

we had identified the potential impact of [the] problem and created a plan to overcome it." By encouraging the contractor's team to utilize his input in solving their problems, Jon "gave them a tool" that indeed led them to a new way of thinking.

Highsmith asserts that today's dynamic environment requires a great deal of adaptation: "Adaptation depends on leadership and collaboration rather than on command and control." Both Judy Stokley and Chuck Anderson challenged the status quo and demonstrated real leadership throughout the major change that the government and the contractor took upon themselves. This process produced not only a fundamental cultural change, but also a substantial financial gain, as described by Judy: "Four years later, we found that we had managed to save the Air Force more than $150 Million."[u] Their leadership and trust-based collaboration were the two primary factors behind the success of the AMRAAM project.[38]

The Importance of Trust for Dynamic Projects

How and when does trust contribute to the bottom line? Lane explains that trust becomes more critical to success when there is a degree of interdependence between trustor and trustee and when there is a need to cope with uncertainty or risk in the exchange relationship, primarily due to problems of time, information, and vulnerability resulting from the acceptance of risk. Accordingly, the three major outcomes that take place as a result of trust-based teamwork in dynamic projects are related to interdependence, uncertainty, and risk.[39]

The first major outcome of trust is the reduction in transaction costs, which is related primarily to the interdependence between trustor and trustee. This issue was previously discussed in reference to the cost savings resulting from reduced monitoring on both the Pathfinder Solar-Powered Airplane and AMRAAM. As Del Frate told us regarding the Pathfinder, "Not having to constantly monitor the contractors meant a much leaner operation; we were able to work smarter and faster . . . we were able to do more technology development at a set level of funding."

Trust will also reduce the cost of bargaining and haggling over problems that arise during project execution. If trust is high, each party will assume that the other party is acting in good faith and will not be anticipating or looking for self-interested behavior that undermines the shared goals of the team. Moreover, trust helps in resolving conflicts as they arise due to mutual confidence that inequities will be fairly addressed. In trusting relationships, the parties can focus on making the project a winner, rather than wasting their energies on fighting each other.[40]

The second major outcome of trust is the facilitation of free exchange of information. Jones and George conclude that when the trust level is low, people will refrain from freely exchanging knowledge and information because of the uncertainty about how others will use this information and because possessing that knowledge is a source of power. When the trust level is high, however, people will be willing to share knowledge and information, since they feel assured that it "will be used for the greater good and one need not exercise power to protect one's own interests."[41]

Facilitating a full and open exchange of information becomes very crucial when coping with uncertainty (i.e., missing and changing information). Indeed, applying the Green and the Brown Principles is heavily dependent on the willingness of team members to exchange information freely. For example, in the First Green Guideline (Define Project Objectives While Quickly Exploring the Means), the client must seek input from the contractor very early in the life of the project—input that will be shared only when trust is high. The planning and control outlook in the Second Green Guideline (Employ a Learning-Based Planning and Control Process), which places ongoing learning at its core, depends primarily on the open and continuous flow of information between team members. The quick and easy information exchange between planning and implementation, which is at the center of the Third Brown Guideline (Act with Agility), can take place only when trust is high.

The third major outcome of trust, which is related to coping with risk, is enabling innovation.[42] Citing multiple sources, Das and Teng conclude that trust and risk taking form a reciprocal relationship: trust leads to risk taking, and risk taking, in turn, reinforces a sense of trust, given that the expected behavior materializes.[43] In their book on the Mars Pathfinder, Muirhead and Simon remind us about the risk associated with innovation: "The catch is this: People who innovate make mistakes."[44]

The link between trust and creativity or innovation is stressed by Solomon and Flores: "In a culture structured by power relations, commitments and promises have a different meaning than they do in a context of mutual trust . . . the most damaging, although nearly invisible, aspect of such a power culture is the loss of creativity. Control-minded autocrats tend to see creativity as threatening . . . The essential virtue of trust is its openness, its celebration of possibilities. Force and fear shut these down."[45]

Earlier in this guideline, Tim Flores provided a similar argument for the reasons behind the success of the Mars Pathfinder: "The Pathfinder team developed trusting relations within a culture of openness. They felt free to make the best decisions they could . . . and they knew that they weren't going to be crucified for mistakes."

The Third Red Guideline: Sustain Teamwork Throughout

Even in a very stable world, teamwork may naturally grow weaker with the passage of time and thus require some maintenance. Due to the evolving nature of projects, however, with key players being added and subtracted, the typical situation of most project teams is far from stable. More important, as highlighted by the Green Principle, is the fact that projects in a dynamic environment continuously suffer from a wide variety of uncertainty and change regarding their "ends" and "means." Therefore, even when the project manager is successful in "getting the right people on the bus" and in building a trust-based team, today's dynamic projects require dedicated effort to sustain the teamwork. This is how Allan Frandsen, a payload manager from California Institute of Technology, succinctly describes his managerial philosophy:[46]

> In running a project, I have always tried to anticipate problems. To lead a project effectively, one has to establish and maintain the flexibility to take appropriate actions when needed . . . Despite your best-laid plans and ongoing attention to the job, the situation can turn to manure in a hurry if a personnel matter arises. So sustaining this prized team you have recruited has to be an important part of a manager's job.[v]

Sustaining Teamwork by Focusing on the People

Nurick and Thamhain assert that "team building . . . is a never ending process . . . The project manager is continually monitoring team performance to see what corrective action to prevent or correct problems."[47] Larry Lawson, Lockheed Martin's vice president, provides an example of sustaining a multi-organizational team, the JASSM team, which was composed of people from the U.S. Air Force and from Lockheed Martin:

> Whenever Terry or I felt like his people were reverting to their traditional role of overseeing the contractor, we met with the key individuals involved to talk about it and invariably this led to an offsite with the whole team. Our offsites were crucial in maintaining the focus and reinforcing the message that we were all working together.
>
> And they were invaluable in other ways. People got to know one another and realized that they weren't slimy contractors or inconsiderate government employees. These were people with real commitments to what they were working toward, at work or home. You discovered their motivations. Were they all motivated to make this program successful? Almost universally, the answer was yes. The offsites helped to build and maintain a strong teaming relationship throughout the program.[w]

Lawson stresses that although the off-sites were primarily meant for sustaining teamwork, they were also instrumental in assuring that all the individuals involved were indeed motivated. Productive teamwork clearly cannot be sustained for a long period of time if the individual team members are not motivated to work. In his book *Peak: How Great Companies Get Their Mojo from Maslow*, Chip Conley divides motivating forces into three layers: money, recognition, and meaning, but he concludes that "money is not a primary motivator once employees have moved beyond their basic needs." He argues that in developed economies, people are motivated primarily by the intangible benefits that come from recognition and meaning. He also cites Peter Drucker who asserted, "Money alone does not motivate to perform. Dissatisfaction with money grossly de-motivates."[48]

Collins explains the role of money in good-to-great companies: "Yes, compensation and incentives are important, but for very different reasons in good-to-great companies. The purpose of a compensation system should not be to get the right behaviors from the wrong people, but to get the right people on the bus in the first place and to keep them there."[49]

How does today's common bias toward individualism get in the way of sustaining teamwork?[50] While it is important to recognize the individual's performance, projects are primarily a "team sport" and attention should be given first to the team's performance.[51] In successful teams, the tension between recognition of the individuals on the team and recognition of the team as a whole is greatly dissipated. Terry Little, who served as the U.S. Air Force director for the JASSM program discussed above by Larry Lawson, shares with us one practice for recognizing the team's performance and sustaining teamwork:

> It would be nice if failures never happened, but any time you undertake something that has significant risk, no matter how well you attempt to do it, no matter what the caliber of the team, no matter how much money you have to spend, there will always be times when you have failures. Therefore, every successful test that you have should be a cause for celebration. Even though in and of itself it may be just one small milestone, there is an enormous amount of energy and effort that goes into getting to this point, a point at which all of our individual work bears fruit and becomes something bigger and better than the sum of its parts. This is how we know we are a winning team.[x]

In Norman Augustine's comprehensive book on project management, *Augustine's Laws*, two of the lessons he offers coincide with Little's practice: The "team must think of itself as a winner," and "recognition of accomplishment is an essential form of feedback."[52] Recognition of accomplishment is also the focus of the following story by Jerry Madden, a project manager from NASA, but this time the recognition is not initiated by the project leader.

The Comptel instrument was a joint contract with a German company. The NASA representative who was stationed in Germany for the duration of the project was often treated to meals by his German counterparts.

The NASA team decided that it was important to reciprocate the Germans' generosity. When the next major review was scheduled, the members of the U.S. NASA team each brought a bottle of barbecue sauce with them in their luggage. They arranged a typical American barbecue for all the German employees working on the Comptel project, and the event was a great success.

Two weeks later, we discovered a problem with a harness, which had to be repaired promptly. We brought the harness to the floor and pleaded for quick turnaround, but were told to get in line. Our project did not have the muscle to slip in front of the work being done for other projects. The technician then asked who the harness was for. We told him it was for Comptel. "Aren't they the barbecue people?" he asked. "Give me the harness, I'll fix it for you on my lunch hour."[y]

This story demonstrates that the craving to be appreciated is a compelling motivator. It also vividly highlights the power of celebrations, as explained by Deal and Kennedy: "The truth is that celebrations are good for the soul . . . Celebrations, in their purest form, are occasions to applaud belonging to something worthwhile. We're all social animals. We want to belong to a community of other people."[53] Successful project leaders are aware of the power of team celebrations and therefore use the many natural opportunities to celebrate team accomplishments in order to develop team identity and cohesiveness.

In addition to celebrating project milestones, an uplifting atmosphere can go a long way toward instilling a good mood and sense of camaraderie. Goleman and his colleagues provide research evidence for the importance of a good mood at work and assert that "when people feel good, they work at their best . . . Good moods prove especially important when it comes to teams."[54] Frank Snow, a ground project manager from NASA, recounts how sustaining teamwork may at times require the simplest of human interactions to reveal commonalities between team members and to smooth out differences, particularly in the case that a change is being made in the composition of the team.

One member of the team was using "old school" methods that totally clashed with those of another team member who was working on the same simulation.

I made the decision to let Mr. Old School go, and I called him into my office to let him know that he was going to be reassigned to another project. The only question I had for him was where he wanted to have lunch.

He said, "there's no reason to break with tradition. The Chinese place would be fine." It was where we celebrated birthdays and project milestones, and it was also the place to go when we needed to let someone go on the project but wanted to soften any hard feelings . . .

*We started off with tea and egg rolls, and by the time the lo mein got to the table, everyone was laughing and cracking jokes. Even though Mr. Old School and his counterpart couldn't agree on work, they had plenty to talk about. It turned out that they both had teenage daughters who were driving them crazy. In some ways, this is the kind of thing that can take the edge off of other differences. I could imagine them saying when they met each other again, in the cafeteria maybe, "Hey, did that little girl of yours get her driver's license?" "Yeah, and she's still driving me crazy, but how about you?" The best way to smooth out differences between team members is to give them a glimpse of one another as people outside of their work.*²

At times, there is no choice but to let a team member go if his/her input is damaging teamwork and impeding progress. However, such a decision may affect the team as a whole, and steps must be taken to counter this possible impact. In discussing this issue, Katzenbach and Smith observe, "Theoretically, any time the membership of a team changes, the team itself has ended . . . Many teams, however, fail to think carefully about the transition caused by a change in membership."⁵⁵ By thinking and acting carefully, Snow tried to deflate any bad feelings that might have otherwise surfaced and in so doing, demonstrated his adherence to two major values: respect and adherence to tradition.

In his book *Extreme Programming (XP) Explained*, Kent Beck, one of the leaders of agile software development, stresses that in addition to the four values of XP (communication, simplicity, feedback, and courage) there is one more value: "A deeper value, one that lies below the surface of the other four—respect. If members of a team don't care about each other and what they are doing, XP is doomed."⁵⁶ By showing respect to "Mr. Old School," Snow undoubtedly reinforced this value within the team and successfully used the opportunity to enhance future teamwork.

The importance of the second value, adherence to tradition, is underscored by Bolman and Deal: "Ritual and ceremony are expressive activities . . . What transpires on the surface of such activities is not as important as the deeper communication underneath. Ritual and ceremony provide opportunities for reinforcing values, revitalization spirit, and bonding individuals to the team and to one another."⁵⁷

However, sustaining teamwork may also require radical steps that are very non-traditional. This is illustrated by Larry Goshorn, former vice president of ITT Industries, who recounts the bizarre turning point in a project that was operating 300 percent over budget:

> Following a lot of finger-pointing and no real teamwork, there was a shake-up one day with the arrival of a new manager on the program. He announced,
>
> *"I just saw in the paper this morning that somebody has brought an elephant into town, and they're offering rides." Everybody else looks around the room, thinking, "Well, what has this got to do with anything?" And then the manager says to the other senior managers around the table, "Okay, you, you, you, and I are going to go over there, and we're going to ride this elephant."*
>
> *And there was great protesting. It seemed crazy. But, in the end, they went down the street a couple of blocks and rode this elephant. Believe it or not, from that point on, they started to cooperate a lot better. It's hard to argue with somebody that you've just been hanging onto on the back of an elephant—especially when there are pictures.*
>
> Goshorn concludes the story by reminding us that *"you've got to do goofy things sometimes to get people to start working together"* and *"people working together is the only way to get out of a mess."*[aa]

There is a great deal of support in the literature for Goshorn's conclusion about doing silly things to bring people together. One of the steps proposed by Bolman and Deal for "making a team work" is to use humor and play: "Humor releases tension and resolves issues that arise from day-to-day routine or in a prevailing emergency . . . Work groups often focus single-mindedly on the task at hand, discouraging any unrelated activity. Seriousness replaces godliness as a desired virtue. Effective teams, on the other hand, balance seriousness with play and humor." Likewise, Jennifer James explains that "humor helps us deal with absurdities . . . it renews energy and renews trust in ourselves, others, and the world."[58]

Sustaining Teamwork by Focusing on the Work

So far this guideline has suggested steps that can be used to sustain teamwork by focusing only on the "people" aspect. Sustaining teamwork, however, is often best achieved through a completely different approach in which the work itself provides the stimulus to carry on.

In his book *The Soul of a New Machine*, Tracy Kidder tells the story of the dazzling success of a small group of Data General engineers, called the "Eagle Group," who outperformed all other Data General divisions to produce a new state-of-the-art computer in record time: "Presumably the stonemasons who raised the cathedrals worked only partly for their pay. They were building temples to God. It was the sort of work that gave meaning to life. That's what West [the Eagle project leader] and his team of engineers were looking for, I think. They themselves liked to say they didn't work on the machine for money . . . Many looked around for words to describe their true reward. They used such phrases as 'self-fulfillment,' 'a feeling of accomplishment,' 'self-satisfaction.' Jim Guyer struggled with those terms awhile with growing impatience. Then he said: Look, I don't have to get official recognition for anything I do. Ninety-eight percent of the thrill comes from knowing that the thing you designed works and works almost the way you expected it would. If that happens, part of you is in that machine."[59]

In their research on successful teams, Bennis and Ward Biederman reach similar conclusions: "Great work is its own reward. Great groups are engaged in solving hard, meaningful problems. Paradoxically, that process is difficult but exhilarating as well . . . The payoff is not money or even glory . . . People ache to do good work. Given a task they believe in and a chance to do it well, they will work tirelessly for no more reward than the one they give themselves."[60] White et al. explain that project teams that have to cope with high uncertainty must exert a great deal of energy to accomplish their mission. This is how one of their interviewees put it: "I strongly believe that the energy invested in your job is closely related to the output you receive." In other words, "the job itself provides a reservoir of energy."[61]

It is important to note that building (and sustaining) teamwork through meaningful work was already addressed in this book. The First Brown Guideline (Create and Maintain a Focus) started with a quote from de Bono: "If I had to choose the one motivating factor that seems to me to be operating in most successful people, it is the wish 'to make things happen.'"[62] Later, the First Yellow Guideline (Develop a Sense of Mission), discussed how project leaders remind their team of the meaning of their work or, if necessary, reshape the project precisely in order to create meaning for their team. The foundations of building and sustaining teamwork through meaningful work are, therefore, fully supported by these two guidelines.

Here we can again address the question presented above: how does today's common bias toward individualism get in the way of sustaining teamwork? The answer we can now provide, on the basis of Bennis and Ward Biederman's conclusions, is much more specific: "Great groups are probably more tolerant to personal idiosyncrasies than are ordinary ones, if only because the members are so intensely focused on the work itself. That all-important task acts as a social lubricant, minimizing frictions."[63]

So how does one sustain teamwork? Is it primarily through people-oriented steps or through challenging and meaningful work? In *The Soul of a New Machine,* Tracy presents examples of sustaining teamwork through both challenging and meaningful work as well as through people-oriented steps.[64] Indeed, in most projects, sustained teamwork is achieved through a combination of the two approaches: people and work. As Katzenbach and Smith conclude, "In the final analysis, performance is both the cause and effect of teams."[65]

CHAPTER 5

The Gray Principle: Update and Connect through Intensive Communication

The First Gray Guideline: Pull and Push Information Frequently

Chester Barnard, who was a telecommunications executive and author of *Functions of the Executive*, an influential twentieth-century management book, asserted that "the first function of the executive is to develop and maintain a system of communication."[1] Similarly, Frederick Brooks, best known as the "father of the IBM System/360," argued that "the project manager's chief daily task is communication, not decision-making."[2] On the basis of a review of more than 50 studies of the communication patterns of managers at all levels, Raymond Panko concluded that "managers spend about 85% of their day communicating."[3] In a recent study of ten highly successful on-site construction project managers, who were each systematically observed on the job for one week, it was found that 76 percent of their time, on average, was dedicated to verbal communication alone (meetings, both planned and unplanned, and telephone calls).[4]

These studies highlight the central role of communication in organizational life. Given that a project functions as an ad hoc temporary organization, composed of people and units affiliated with multiple functions and different organizations, communication plays the very crucial role of strengthening and maintaining the glue that binds all parts of the organization.[5] However, the primary reason that communication is so vital to project success is the dynamic environment within which most projects have been forced to operate in recent years. When projects suffer from high uncertainty (of goals and means) and accelerated speed, the role played by project communication is much more dynamic than that of binding glue: it becomes the life blood, oxygen, and central nervous system of the project.[6]

The fact that communication dominates the time of the project manager puts the Gray Principle in a unique position vis-à-vis the other four principles. It was stressed earlier in this book that our ability to fully implement each of the five principles is dependent on our ability to implement the other four principles (see, for example, the second meta-principle in the introduction). However, since the project manager accomplishes most other principles while engaging in communication activities, the dependency of the other four principles on the Gray Principle is a bit different by virtue of its being almost continuous throughout the day and throughout the life of the project.[7] More specifically, we may view the direct impact of the Gray Principle, "Update and Connect through Intensive Communication," on the other four principles as follows: updating all project players significantly facilitates our ability to implement the Green and the Brown Principles, while connecting all players significantly facilitates our ability to implement the Yellow and the Red Principles.

Henry Mintzberg, who observed the chief executives of five organizations over a one-week period, noted two primary informational roles of these executives: "The manager serves as the focal point in his organization for the movement of nonroutine information . . . the manager emerges as the nerve center of internal information . . . and of external information as well . . . the term nerve center is chosen to encompass the many activities in which the manager receives information . . . He appears to find it most important to get his information quickly and informally . . . His special access to information allows the manager to play the important role of disseminator, sending external information into his organization and internal information from one subordinate to another."[8]

Moving from the manager role in a permanent organization 40 years ago to the role of project manager in a temporary organization within our current dynamic environment, one finds the presence of the same informational roles. However, the difference is that those roles are performed in a much more active and intensive manner, with the frequent pull and push of receiving and disseminating information.[9]

In an attempt to identify the characteristics of outstanding program managers, Cullen and Gadeken emphasize the "pulling" role of these managers to "gather information proactively." Specifically, the project manager "institutes mechanisms or develops means for collecting information on program status beyond routine methods; talks with key people and first hand sources to gather program information; seeks and gathers background information about situations, programs, etc."[10] Conversely, Randolph and Posner focus on the "pushing" role of the project manager to "inform everyone connected with the project . . . keep information flowing on a regular basis . . . One of the biggest mistakes many project managers make is not communicating with team members in a consistent, ongoing fashion."[11]

In their position at the hub of internal and external project information, project managers must pull and push information frequently in order to serve their purpose of updating and connecting. In his study of ten on-site construction project managers, Telem found that the information flow was clearly dominated by pulling and pushing activities. One aspect studied was the degree of activeness of the communication, as information flow can be conducted either actively or passively by the giver or receiver. A communication event was classified as active whenever the project managers were sharing information with others by talking or writing or when they were collecting information from others by posing questions. On the other hand, a communication event was classified as passive whenever the project managers were being questioned by others or were receiving information by listening to others. When indications of both active and passive communication were identified during the same communication event, the communication was classified as "alternately active and passive." The findings show that "during 48.5% of their time, the project managers were 'active' in relaying and absorbing information, while during 43.8% of their time, they were 'alternately active or passive.'" Only 1.7 percent of their time was spent on a passive flow of information. That is, these ten successful construction project managers exhibited a great deal of activeness in gathering (pulling) and sharing (pushing) information.[12]

The importance that these ten project managers assigned to frequent pulling and pushing information was also evident in their attitude toward frequent interruptions by unscheduled visits from their site associates, foremen, subcontractors, workers, and others who just wanted to ask or report something. Not only did the project managers show no signs of impatience and annoyance about these visits, but they even seemed to encourage spontaneous interruptions—not really regarding them as interruptions at all. They all understood the importance of constantly receiving updates (pulling information) and offering feedback (pushing information).

Thus, it is not surprising that the number of activities dedicated by these ten project managers to planned meetings (meetings scheduled at least 24 hours in advance) amounted to only 3.5 percent of all their activities, whereas the number of unplanned meetings represented 41.8 percent of all their activities. Likewise, the project managers dedicated 10.7 percent of their time to outgoing calls, while incoming calls consumed only 3.3 percent of their time. The ten project managers exhibited their preference for activeness in collecting and sharing information by also embracing the Third Gray Guideline, Communicate by Moving About, as will be described later in this chapter.[13]

Successful project managers embrace the principle of "Update and Connect through Intensive Communication" by adopting a variety of "pushing and pulling" practices. In the following example, Tony

Schoenfelder from NASA describes some of the communication practices employed by John Hodge, the first leader of the Space Station Task Force.

> *Hodge combined a number of practices and innovations that led to a unique and uninhibited atmosphere. Each day started at 8:15 AM with an unstructured 15-minute all-hands stand-up meeting. Only those who had something important to say took the floor, while everyone else crowded into the office or hallway to listen. It turned out to be a useful device in that it not only conveyed information, but also physically reunited the team each morning to reinforce the spirit of camaraderie and the sense of shared purpose . . . Hodge didn't believe in secrets. He was completely open with the staff. What he knew, they knew. Members appreciated this unusual candor and reciprocated by keeping him and the leadership well informed . . . Hodge . . . was liable to pop up unannounced anywhere at anytime . . . He not only got to know each person as a person, but also received an unfiltered heads-up as to what was going on . . . Hodge also had a unique open-door policy whereby anyone was free to visit him and discuss any matter of importance.[a]*

Hodge's practice touches upon on all the ingredients of effective communication in projects suffering from high uncertainty and accelerated speed. As Wheelwright and Clark explain, "Where markets and technologies are more dynamic and time is a more critical element of competition . . . intensive cross-functional integration is crucial . . . True cross-functional integration . . . rests on a foundation of tight linkages in time and in communication . . . between the upstream and the downstream group rich, frequent, reciprocal, and early."[14]

The concept of frequent communication is at the center of the Agile methods for software development. The introduction to this book proposed that the assumptions of its principles are similar to the "values" of the Agile methods. In their book *Balancing Agility and Discipline: A Guide to the Perplexed*, Boehm and Turner[15] compare communication in the typical plan-driven methods and in the Agile methods: "Plan-driven methods rely heavily on documented process plans (schedules, milestones, procedures) and product plans (requirements, architecture, standards) to keep everyone coordinated . . . Agile methods generally rely on more frequent, person-to-person communication."[16]

Therefore, it is only natural that the practice of a daily meeting is highly recommended by proponents of the Agile method: "The main requirement when working in Agile is to communicate . . . Have daily stand-up meetings that last only 10 minutes. Keep it to 10 minutes to allow team leaders to address daily issues."[17] Williams provides the rationale for standing during these meetings: "Every day, the development team spends a few minutes in a stand-up meeting. The team intentionally stands up in a circle during the meeting to motivate members to keep the meeting as short as possible."[18]

Sharing Interpretation and Seeking to Learn

In the following two stories, Terry Little, a program manager from the U.S. Air Force, demonstrates two other less frequent, but quite proactive, approaches to information transferring: sharing interpretation (pushing information) and seeking to learn (pulling information). In their book *The Social Life of Information*, Brown and Duguid quote the historian Brian Stock, who points out that the orthodox and the dissenters often share the same stories, but that their interpretation is what separates them. On the basis of Stock as well as other sources, Brown and Duguid conclude, "It is not shared stories or shared information so much as shared interpretation that binds people together."[19]

In his first story, *Open Newsletters*, Little explains how he uses his monthly newsletters for sharing his interpretations of events in the project with his team members:

> *The main point of starting a newsletter is to communicate with your team about the project, but if all you are communicating is dry facts, you're not using this tool wisely. Programs usually have other means of sharing facts. Your newsletter should extend beyond the boundaries of the program. For instance, you can talk about what clients feel, what upper management feels. Most often it's just the program manager or the people at the top that are interacting with clients and upper management. By sharing this information with the team, you are breaking down silos and giving everyone a stronger sense that we are all working together.*

Here are two examples of how Little used the newsletter as a tool for communicating with his team:

> ### Disappointment at Launch Delay
> *Like you, I was quite disappointed at the delay of our first launch . . . The occasion of the delay gives me an opportunity to reiterate a point that I have previously made and will continue to make . . . There are a number of reasons why schedule is so important. The most obvious is that the users have been waiting a long time to get this capability when you consider the program history; their patience is not infinite. Second, the recent events in Yugoslavia have increased schedule pressure . . . Third, we have made an absolute commitment to a 40-month development . . . No one should forget that the user does have some alternatives to JASSM if it appears that we are in major schedule trouble . . . Fourth, the Air Force's acquisition leadership has high confidence in our ability to execute. We cannot erode that confidence and expect to continue to enjoy the level of support that we have had.*

> ### Requirements Creep
> *I have previously addressed my concerns about creeping requirements and the effect that they could have on our program . . . Many see this as a user issue. However, the users we deal with have not been and are unlikely to be culprits*

in any creep. I am beginning to set my sights on others in our process as "creep culprits"—in particular the test community, aircraft program offices, and outside Government offices . . . We may choose to accept the requirements change, but it will be a collaborative, deliberate decision that considers all the ramifications of the change.[b]

In the following story, Little explains how he used his weekly meetings with the five competing companies for both pushing and pulling information:

I held weekly meetings with representatives from each of the five companies competing for the contract to give them an update on where we stood, what had changed since the last time we spoke, where we were having problems in the program office, where the requirements stood, and what approvals we still needed to get from my upper management . . . After these group meetings, I would meet with each of the five contractors separately. Not to tell them something, but to listen to what they had to say . . . When we sat down together, I would ask, "Give me some feedback. Tell me specifically about this requirement. Does the path we're headed down seem right to you? Is there a requirement— or two or three or four—which you think is not going to be consistent with us getting a low-cost system? What I want to know is: Are we spinning our wheels in some area that we don't really understand, and what are the implications?" From my point of view, I was trying to learn.[c]

Little's example of pulling information in order to learn is just one example of the systematic effort required for effective planning and control in a dynamic environment. The Second Green Guideline (Employ a Learning-Based Planning and Control Process) underlined the concept that in a dynamic environment, project planning and control is a process of ongoing learning. Moreover, the key to project success is the degree to which teams are able to learn quickly from prior steps and act on this information. This is exactly the kind of feedback that Little was attempting to "pull" during his meetings with the five companies.

Communicate Regularly with all Stakeholders

The Second Green Guideline also highlights the point that in a dynamic environment, projects are constantly affected by changes taking place both inside and outside the parent company. Therefore, project managers should not limit their attention only to events occurring within the boundaries of their project, but rather should continuously monitor the project's external environment as well. Moreover, as exemplified in this book, project managers may have to go above and beyond the mere scanning of their environment. Indeed, in cases where the success of their project requires a more favorable environment, they must take action to *create* change in their environment. This kind of proactive external orientation necessitates constant communication with all of the project's stakeholders.[20]

This is how Allan Frandsen, a payload manager from the California Institute of Technology, explains the need to "take the time" for communicating with all of the project's stakeholders.

> *The manager needs to foster communications between and among participants. You certainly don't want to hear of a problem being excused by such statements as "I didn't know I was supposed to . . ." or "I didn't know that what he was doing was incompatible with . . .", etc. And of course there are always peers as well as upper management who need to be apprised of what is going on.*
>
> *In the absence of sufficient information, they could well form a wrong opinion of the current state of affairs, or worse yet, undertake counter-productive actions based on invalid conclusions. A busy manager doesn't need any counter-productive "help" by well-intended colleagues. So the best defense is a good offense. Take the time to communicate upwards, downwards, and sideways.[d,21]*

In the following story, *Weather Reports*, Don Margolies, a NASA project manager, explains to us why and how he communicated "sideways" with his client. Margolies was located in Maryland, while his client, Dr. Edward Stone, who served as the head of the science team, was located in California.

> *Dr. Stone and I set up a schedule to talk with each other on the phone every week. In the early stages of the project, much of what was about to unfold was still up in the air. You might say the spacecraft itself was about the only thing not in the air. I thought it was crucial to the success of the project that Dr. Stone knows everything that was going on—and if something happened that involved the development of the instruments, he could be on it right away. Even if it was just to say that the weather was nice in California and there was nothing much happening here at Goddard, we always kept the appointment.[e]*

Project managers often tend to communicate with their clients only in the early stages of the project, when they must seek their input in order to formulate the project's requirements. Typically, their next opportunity to communicate again, intensive as it may be, is when a crisis erupts. In contrast, Margolies communicated on a regular basis with his client throughout the life of the project. This continuous "update and connect" practice should contribute to the reduction of crises, as well as to a better and faster response when a crisis does arise.

Scott Cameron, the global process owner of project management at Procter & Gamble (P&G), fully concurs with Frandsen's recommendation to "take the time to communicate upwards." Cameron also believes that it is helpful to view the project manager's job in terms of an hour-glass:

In this analogy, the top of the hourglass is the PM's hierarchy, the bottom the project team, and the connecting tube the PM. The hourglass sand can be anything from proposals, directions, data, and other forms of articulated communication to the unstated forms of communication, such as assumptions, perceptions, and/or prejudices that pass between the two parts. A PM's success is often determined by his or her ability to effectively manage this passage of sand! . . . Hierarchy has information about future events that can impact the PM's project. The PM must gain the hierarchy's trust and confidence to obtain this information as soon as possible . . .

I believe PMs should . . .

- *Hold regular meetings (group or 1:1) with specific members of the hierarchy to better understand each one's needs and expectations throughout the life of the project.*
- *Bring the hierarchy together on a regular basis to review the project. Too often the PM assumes the hierarchy discusses the project and the PM's concerns with one another. This is not always a safe assumption.*
- *. . . Don't allow the hierarchy to try and guess what you want from them. If you want them to do something, you should have the conviction to ask for it. If you don't want them to do anything, you should state this clearly.*[f]

In the following example, Cameron explains to us how he came to the realization that in the current dynamic environment it was necessary to make a fundamental change in his own communication practice and to be much more proactive when communicating with his clients:

I had a boss once who continually asked me what the purpose of my work was, who were my customers, and how I was keeping my customers informed about my team's work. At first I found these questions perplexing, as my customers should have known the answers. I had covered them in my monthly/quarterly reports or in my project meeting notes.

Finally, I confronted him about his questions. He acknowledged that my customers had this information, but he was hearing some disturbing comments between when I submitted my reports, comments like, "What has he done for me lately?"

I decided to take this input to heart. My ideas about communications norms needed a major overhaul. The communication norms I was comfortable with were becoming outdated. I realized the written and verbal communications response time was suddenly being measured in days or minutes. I decided I needed to change my "communications game" and began developing a proactive communications strategy to maintain the high credibility of the team and market their excellent work . . . I implemented a "Blurb" approach. What is a "Blurb"? It's a sound bite or a small piece of information explaining some excellent work someone is doing. The intent is to continually remind people the team is credible and very much in control. It also serves the dual purpose of sharing information throughout various organizations so they can benefit from what one team has learned and hence not waste time trying to reinvent the wheel.[g]

The stories throughout the current guideline underscore the fact that in a dynamic environment, timeliness is vital. This is true whether the communication is upwards, downwards, or sideways. Because the value of information is directly related to timeliness, it is more important to get partial or approximate information, so long as it is timely, than to get it complete and precise, but late.[22]

The Second Gray Guideline: Employ a Variety of Communication Mediums with Face Time as Top Priority

The fundamental communication dilemma that project managers in our era must constantly wrestle with is that of "high tech or high touch." The current guideline will first elaborate on the importance and benefits of "face time." It will be followed by a discussion of the need to employ other communication media as well. Toward the end of the guideline, the "high tech or high touch" issue will be revisited.

In the following story, *The Join-Up Meeting*, Scott Cameron, the global process owner of project management at P&G, describes the "high tech or high touch" dilemma:

I recently took on a new assignment and, as is my norm, I scheduled a series of one-hour, 1:1 join-up meetings with the various lead personnel on the team . . . During one of these meetings, the person I was meeting with informed me how pleasantly surprised she was that I had scheduled this meeting as very few individuals took the time anymore to have them.

I was shocked. I was taught that establishing a 1:1 relationship with the people on your team is critical to the project's success . . . Later I was talking to [another] project manager . . . and he indicated he had finished his join-up meetings with every person in his new organization . . . Again, I was shocked. When I reflected on these two experiences, I realized a very negative trend might be emerging in our fast-paced, schedule-driven, 500-e-mail-per-day, cell-phone-ringing, 24/7-communication, multi-tasking work lives: NO FACE TIME![h]

The Multiple Benefits of Face-to-Face Communication

In the following story, *Small Wins Make for Big Gains*, Frank Snow, the NASA manager of the Ground System and Flight Operations, describes his communication difficulties while attempting to propose an idea to another member of his team, a member who was located about 2,300 miles away.

It occurred to me that the Flight Operations team, which I managed, should get involved in the data analysis after launch . . . [they] knew the ground system we were using inside and out, and I thought that they should, at the very least, train the people out at Caltech on how to use it. So I offered our help.

One of the Co-Investigators at Caltech, however, was terribly suspicious of the Goddard project office. Almost any help we offered to make his life easier was, he believed, a ruse to take control of his instrument. As appreciation for my offer, he sent me a blistering email that basically said, in 300 words no less, "Hell no!" At that point, I decided to fly across the country to Caltech to talk with him. Maybe I'd have better luck in a face-to-face meeting.

I went there and listened to his concerns, I empathized with him, and then assured him that no one in the project office was trying to take anything away from him or from Caltech. In fact, we were actually interested in expanding Caltech's responsibilities, if they wanted this, to include flight operations.

Moreover, I told him that I would put it into the operational plan to move the total operations of the spacecraft over to Caltech after launch.

He never formally acknowledged it, but I think he saw that what we were offering was not such a bad idea after all. He allowed the Flight Ops team to come to Caltech and provide training in the ground system.

Clearly, face-to-face communication went a long way towards dispelling his suspicions about my intentions. I don't recall after this ever getting another 300-word email from him of the "no-thank-you-and-please-go-away" variety. As a matter of fact, I think I could even say that this was the beginning of a fruitful relationship that lasted for the rest of the project.[i]

No doubt that listening to his host's concerns and empathizing with him contributed to the success of Snow's trip. However, there was more to it. Influencing people and changing their mind is always difficult (especially if they are "terribly suspicious"), but it is impossible without first getting their attention. Therefore, the fundamental purpose for taking this 2,300-mile trip was simply to get the attention of the coinvestigator from Caltech.

In their 2001 book, *The Attention Economy: Understanding the New Currency of Business*, Davenport and Beck contend that "managing attention is now the single most important determinant of business success." This is how Davenport and Beck explain their assertion: "Previous generations of citizens didn't have an attention problem, at least not compared to ours . . . The Sunday New York Times contains more factual information in one edition than all the written material available to a reader in the fifteenth century . . . As the amount of information increases, the demand for attention increases. As Herbert Simon, a Nobel prize-winning economist put it, 'What information consumes is rather obvious: it consumes the attention of its recipients. Hence a wealth of information creates a poverty of attention.'"[23]

From a study of 22 managers and professionals, primarily associated with communication, internet, and design related businesses, Nardi and Whittaker concluded that engaging attention is crucial for effective communication and that engaging attention can be facilitated by face-to-face communication. Following are the observations of two of their interviewees: "Wanda describes how speakers use eye contact and body language to engage the others in the room . . . [Ashley reported that] the best way to interact with people is to look them in the eye and talk to them, and you can't do that over the telephone as easily. Certainly not email."[24] Other research has shown that differences in initial positions can be negotiated in face-to-face talks more rapidly than in electronically mediated teams.[25]

In the next story, *Semantic Differences*, Barry Smith, a project manager from P&G, underlines the decisive advantage of face-to-face communication in situations prone to misunderstanding and equivocation.

> *The U.S.-based . . . structural engineers needed specific loading information from the machine vendor, who was located in Sweden, very early in the machine-design process. The Swedish machine vendor promised to send the information on time to comply with the design contractor's timetable, but consistently failed to deliver. Despite innumerable teleconferences . . . the design firm was not getting what it needed and time was running out.*
>
> *We finally decided there was only one solution: send a structural engineer to the vendor's office in Sweden. The problem was solved very quickly. We discovered there had been a major misunderstanding about the accuracy of the data that was needed. The structural engineers kept asking for "final machine loading and dimensional data" . . . which, to a machine designer, implies loads within a tolerance of one-pound and dimensions to a fraction of an inch. The engineering contractor had actually needed more approximate loading and dimensional data. To supply the "final" information, the machine vendor had tried in vain to shorten its normal design process, which resulted in the schedule slips and data revisions we experienced.*
>
> *We also found that no amount of "high-tech" communication could replace simple "high-touch" personal meetings between the knowledgeable people involved.[j]*

This story underscores the fact that how well you communicate is determined by how well you are understood and not necessarily by how well you express yourself.[26] Peter Drucker explains how information is translated into communication: "For communication to be effective there must be both information and meaning. And meaning requires communion. If somebody whose language I do not speak calls me on the telephone, it doesn't help me at all that the connection is crystal clear. There is no 'meaning' unless I understand the language—the message the meteorologist understands perfectly is gibberish to a chemist . . . I know is the catalyst that converts 'information' into 'communication.'"[27]

When there is a language barrier and a cultural gap, as in the preceding story, face-to-face communication becomes particularly important. Research findings support the extensive use of face-to-face communication in ambiguous situations as an effective and quick method of clarifying the meaning.[28] First, face-to-face communication captures the full spectrum of human interaction. It covers all the senses—sight, hearing, smell, taste, and touch—that provide the channels through which individuals receive information. Eye contact, body movements, and facial expressions communicate a deeper meaning beyond the verbal message.[29] For example, a sarcastic versus enthusiastic tone of voice adds essential meaning to verbal statements. Facial expressions usually communicate emotions, with the eyes expressing happiness, sadness, or surprise, while the lower face, brows, and forehead reveal anger.[30] In one study of face-to-face communication, only 7 percent of the content was transmitted verbally, whereas the remaining 93 percent of received information was contained in the tone of voice and facial expressions.[31]

Second, the structure of face-to-face interaction offers a valuable opportunity for interruption, repair, feedback, and learning. In contrast to interactions through other media that are largely sequential, face-to-face interaction makes it possible for two people to send and receive messages simultaneously. The cycle of interruption, feedback, and repair possible in face-to-face interaction is so quick that it is virtually instantaneous. By seeing how others are responding to a verbal message even before it is complete, the speaker can alter it midstream to clarify it. When interaction takes place in a group setting, the number of verbal and non-verbal "conversations" that can be conducted simultaneously is almost impossible to replicate with other media. Thus, face-to-face communication is the best medium for quick resolution of ambiguity. Its immediate feedback allows understanding to be checked, interpretation to be corrected, and multiple cues to be observed simultaneously.[32]

In the previous two stories, face-to-face communication was associated with a high cost of traveling and thus was initiated only after prior attempts to solve a problem through other means of communication— e-mail in the first one and teleconferencing in the second one—had failed. In the following story, *Oral Presentations*, Lynda Rutledge, a project manager from the U.S. Air Force, had to work hard to introduce face-to-face communication prior to any specific failure in communication. However, her challenge was to modify the inclination to communicate through written proposals and responses by sheer "force of habit."

When I first started working for the Air Force, I had a hard time understanding how we make our source selections. We hand the contractors a Request for Proposal (RFP), and we don't talk to them a lot after that. They come back and hand us their proposal; we take it and evaluate it. We write down what we think is wrong with the proposal—again, we don't talk to them—and after they review our comments, they hand us back a written response . . .

Personally, I think it's absurd to choose a contractor without talking to them and finding out who they are, what their strengths are, and how you're going to team with them. Let's face it, a contract is like a marriage, and to do that sight unseen, I mean, I just think that a decision worth billions of dollars should not rely on pieces of paper.

When I finally got a program of my own to manage . . . I decided I wanted to do things differently . . . Following a long campaign for convincing my upper management and industry partners I was finally given the green light for having real face-to-face presentations . . . First, we did a dry run. Each of the three contractors competing for the award had the opportunity to give an eight-hour briefing, just as they would when the stakes were for real . . .

In the dry run, we gave them candid feedback. We told them what we thought they had done wrong, what they misunderstood in the RFP . . . There were two things we got out of that. Number one, the contractors better understood what we were asking for. Number two, we understood better how they were interpreting our RFP, so that we could clarify our document . . .

I chose to use this approach in part because I like to talk to people and look them in the eye . . . It sets the tone for the kind of relationship I want to have with my contractors after the selection, and I think it has an impact on results, too. Communication is the key to success; so why wait to get the talking started?[k]

On the surface, the disagreement between Lynda and upper management focused on the merits of a specific communication medium. However, as the following discussion will reveal, their disagreement was fundamentally a question of their divergent perceptions regarding the nature of the entire source selection process.

To understand their different perceptions of the situation, it is useful to apply the concept of rich versus lean communication channels. Face-to-face communication is generally regarded as the richest medium because of the capacity for timely feedback, the ability to convey multiple cues, the degree to which the message can be personalized, the variety of language that can be used, and the range of meaning that can be conveyed. That richness declines as people move to interaction by telephone, written personal communiqués (letters and memos), written formal communiqués (bulletins), and numerical formal communiqués (printouts). The increasing role of non-physical face-to-face communication, that is, videoconferencing in virtual teams, will be discussed later in this guideline.[33]

One of the practical implications of the variations in richness of communication channels is their suitability to different situations. Rich channels are more suitable for non-routine messages, whereas lean channels are more suitable for routine messages. Typically, non-routine messages are ambiguous, concern novel events, and pose great potential for misunderstanding. Karl Weick and Kathleen Sutcliffe conclude in their book *Managing the Unexpected: Assuring High Performance in an Age of Complexity*, "As richness is lost, so is key information."[34]

Thus, Lynda believed that the air force was misguided in its perception of the source selection process as routine and flawed in its approach to handling the process solely through lean channels of communication, namely, written proposals and responses. Lynda believed that since the situation was unique and ambiguous and posed great potential for misunderstanding, it called for adding a rich channel: face-to-face communication. Indeed, introducing the oral presentations helped in the timely identification and correction of many misunderstandings: "We told them . . . what they misunderstood in the RFP . . . we understood better how they were interpreting our RFP."

Moreover, Lynda explained that the oral presentations were meant not only to clarify and "update," but also to contribute to the second role of intensive communication, that is, "connect": "I chose to use this approach in part because I like to talk to people and look them in the eye . . . It sets the tone for the kind of relationship I want to have with my contractors after the selection."

Given the fact that most projects in today's dynamic environment must cope with high uncertainty throughout their entire course, it becomes clear that the utility of face-to-face communication extends far beyond isolated cases of non-routine events. In the following story, *The Sky Is Blue or Pink*, Don Margolies, a project manager from Goddard Space Flight Center of NASA, describes how he systematically employed face-to-face communication throughout the life of his project to "update and connect."

> *NASA's way of doing business is considerably different than APL's [Johns Hopkins University Applied Physics Laboratory, the contractor responsible for designing and building the spacecraft] . . . For a while . . . tension existed between the two organizations. If Goddard said the sky was blue, APL would say it was pink. Fortunately, the distance between Goddard and APL is about 20 minutes by car. Let me tell you, when they talk about "location, location, location," they don't just mean real estate. Having that kind of proximity to each other made all the difference in the world toward cultivating a partnership between our organizations.*
>
> *I held staff meetings at Goddard every week; Mary [APL's project manager] was always invited, and she attended most weeks. I also held monthly meetings at APL, and I brought my Goddard team with me. Each of Mary's subsystem leads stood up and gave a status report on his or her subsystem. People weren't afraid to say what was happening, and people weren't afraid to make a mistake because they understood that no one would get shot for making mistakes. Our working philosophy was: You find a mistake, you fix the mistake, and you move on.*
>
> *My staff would then get up and talk about the status of the instruments, ground system development, and so forth. I don't know how to put the value of that into dollars and cents, but I can't think of anything we did on the project that was more valuable than these meetings.*
>
> *. . . We . . . reached a point where she believed that when I said something she could take it to the bank, and I believed that when she told me something I could make a deposit as well. My being able to get out to APL in a few minutes and Mary coming over to Goddard went a long way toward establishing a trustful relationship.[1]*

This story raises the question, If proximity of "20 minutes by car" is so meaningful to the team's ability to "update and connect," then why wouldn't we eliminate the distance altogether and colocate the team?

The Multiple Benefits of Colocating Project Teams
In the following story, *Get in Bed*, Jon Bauschlicher, a project manager from NASA, shares some of the profound benefits and potential liabilities of colocation.

As Jon explains, he was always taught that "getting in bed" with the customer/supplier carried with it many occupational hazards—at best, giving the appearance of impropriety. At worst, it could compromise objectivity, cause a conflict of interest, bog down the decision-making process, and reveal information about proprietary products or design processes without the "need-to-know."

One project changed my mind about all that. Project KAFFU (Kiwi Air Force Fighter Upgrade) was a fighter retrofit program for the Royal New Zealand Air Force . . . When the contractor I was working for won the competition, the contract included sharing office space with the Royal New Zealand Air Force engineers, pilots, and maintainers . . . We sat side-by-side with these guys. They participated in every facet of the engineering development program. They helped write requirements, software, drawings, specifications, test plans, test procedures and test reports. They worked in the lab integrating and testing hardware and software . . . Aside from a few classified areas, they had full access to our entire facility . . . They were truly, fully, integrated into our engineering team.

And the results? . . . we produced . . . a better product—more capable and user-oriented—than we would have produced without the active participation of the customer's engineers, operators, and maintainers. And, in the end, we had a well-informed, well-educated customer expert in our system's uses and capabilities.

Overall, the results from "getting in bed" with the customer were nothing like I had been taught they would be. Nothing but good came from the effort, and both customer and supplier benefited—the ultimate win/win situation.[m]

Indeed, research shows that proximity not only facilitates quick and easy "update and connect," but may significantly contribute to a wide range of desirable aspects of project performance, particularly to the building of a cohesive team. In his seminal study, Tom Allen found that the communication probability between pairs of individuals declines with distance.[35] In colocated teams, many informal face-to-face interactions occur daily, most of which are unscheduled, fairly brief, relatively unstructured, spontaneous, and require little effort to initiate. The ease and frequency of such informal interactions facilitate teamwork. As Goodman and Abel observe, "Even a discussion of last night's basketball game serves an important purpose in the communication life of a work group, providing a setting for building comfort through interaction."[36]

Speed is another aspect of project performance that can benefit from colocation. Christopher Meyer, whose book primarily focuses on project speed, concluded that "without question, one of the most powerful productivity accelerators for a team-based organization is co-location." Meyer adds, "More face-to-face contact creates better personal bonds and relationships."[37] Tom Peters, who is also a great advocate of colocation, asserts that "space management may well be the most ignored—and most powerful—tool for inducing culture change, speeding up innovation projects . . . we all but ignore the key strategic issue—the parameter of intermingling."

In giving the example of an organization that had just moved to a new facility designed for colocation, Peters presents the rationale behind the design of the new facility: "The only way to break down barriers is to bring people into closer contact. The goal is . . . helping different groups accept and respect different ways of thinking and working."[38] Michael Nowik, the head of the material management group in that organization, noted a "reduced number of [formal] meetings and a less formal, more effective flow of information and dialogue. Now questions and decisions are resolved much more quickly and easily."

The positive consequences of face-to-face communication combined with colocated teams are indeed far reaching. However, as the next section illustrates, most project teams, even colocated ones, benefit from employing a variety of communication media.

Employing a Variety of Communication Media
In their book *Connections: New Ways of Working in the Networked Organization*, Lee Sproull and Sara Kiesler explain that "when information exchanges are routine and repetitive, information procedures can help regularize them . . . Information procedures make it possible to summarize, synthesize, and share vast amounts of information . . . For situations that are repetitive and explicit, reporting and requesting procedures—progress reports, financial statements . . . purchase orders . . . credit checks—move information efficiently and reliably."[39] Such information procedures specify in advance their sources and recipients as well as the format of their presentation, and the information conveyed is abstracted and organized in categories that are also specified in advance. These features make reporting procedures a more efficient vehicle for information dissemination on routine issues than face-to-face channels.[40] For example, all projects, including colocated ones, systematically employ formal and explicit time charts and schedule status reports.

Project plans are also not conveyed through face-to-face channels, but may be shared via a wide variety of formats. For example, engineering plans may take the form of flow charts, layouts, installation drawings, isometrics, interference analyses, diagrams, specifications, bills of materials, purchase requisitions, photo drawings, 3-D models, and 3-D CAD output. Likewise, execution plans are also disseminated in various formats. The most common formats used in construction projects, for example, are technical diagrams and drawings (site layout), organization charts (organizational design), time charts (scheduling), and standard forms and tables (cost estimating). Textual formats, which are less formal, such as lists, meeting protocols, and verbal instructions, are also employed.[41]

However, project teams, even colocated ones, also employ channels other than face-to-face communication for issues that are not necessarily routine and repetitive. Studying a team of computer programmers, McKenney and his colleagues found that the team employed face-to-face communication as well as e-mail and that it used the two channels for different purposes. The rich face-to-face communication was deemed more suitable for ambiguous and equivocal tasks that were open to interpretation, while the more efficient channel of e-mail was used for what they termed "organizing tasks." McKenney and his colleagues concluded that "electronic mail and face-to-face proved to be complementary channels of communication. The primary roles of electronic mail were to monitor status, send alerts, broadcast information, and invoke action. Face-to-face was used to define and discuss solutions to problems, and to maintain context by alerting the group to shifting priorities as a result of external events for improved understanding of the project over time."[42]

Colocated teams often complement their communication arsenal with "low-tech" tools, such as storyboards. In the following story, *The Storyboard's Big Picture*, Cheryl Malloy, a mission integration manager from NASA, and William Cooley, a technical analyst from Science Applications International Corporation (SAIC), explain how and why they use storyboards:

> We are using a project management tool that facilitates team communication, keeps our project team focused, streamlines work, and identifies potential issues. What did it cost us to install the tool? Almost nothing.
>
> Our tool is a storyboard. We use our storyboard to create a paper prototype of our product. Graphic sequential depictions give a quick project overview while breaking down the product into its major components . . . We tack sheets of paper on the wall in the sequence that users will likely perform their tasks . . .
>
> The storyboard process helps promote brainstorming, highlights missing tasks, and allows the team to incorporate changes prior to traveling too far down a particular path. It also helps us to stand back from our work and ask, "Is this

the most logical sequence for the way we're doing things?" We physically move pages around and put them in a different order as we resolve issues . . . Most importantly, the storyboard helps the many specialists on the team to conceptualize the relationships between their individual project tasks and the bigger picture.

During our "graffiti phase," anyone in the organization (potential users, customers, and team members alike) can . . . write down their comments directly on the sheets of paper on the wall . . . If we decide to use an idea, it becomes part of our evolving storyboard . . . By using the storyboard, we get many people involved in providing constructive feedback and, most importantly, we make certain that team members aren't going off in different directions. The storyboard keeps us all working toward the same goal.[n]

In his book *Agile Software Development*, Alistair Cockburn highly recommends the use of these storyboards, which he calls "information radiators." Cockburn explains, "Just as a heating duct blows air into a hallway . . . these posters radiate information into the hallway, onto people walking by. They are marvelous for passing along information quietly, with little effort, and without disturbing the people whose status is being reported . . . Size matters when it comes to information radiators— the bigger the better. Hallways qualify very nicely as good places for information radiators. Web pages don't. Accessing the Web page costs most people more effort than they are willing to expend, and so the information stays hidden."[43]

One reason for not employing too much face-to-face communication is simply that it may be disruptive and expensive. According to Nardi and Whittaker, the primary advantage of face-to-face communication is its ability to engender social bonding.[44] However, they emphasize that face-to-face communication has negative implications as well: "Our data show that despite the many advantages of face-to-face communication, people still sought to avoid it at certain times . . . face-to-face information is an "expensive" medium that has to be used judiciously . . . [They reported] we have all been interrupted when we were finally about to accomplish something . . . People also spoke of the emotional expense of face-to-face: the need to pay attention, engage in diverting chat, be pleasant, wear presentable clothing."[45]

Virtual Teams and Face-to-Face Communication

In recent years, there has been a clear rise in the use of virtual teams, whereby team members use technology to interact with one another across geographic, organizational, and other boundaries.[46] This is how Hinds and Kiesler explain the rise in the use of virtual teams, which they term "distributed work": "Technological advances and changes in the global economy are motivating and enabling an increasing geographic distribution of work . . . Joint ventures and multi-organizational projects are pervasive and entail work in many places . . . in mergers of companies or acquisitions of new companies, it may be infeasible to bring all employees to a single site, perhaps because key personnel refuse to move or perhaps because of the expense involved in orchestrating a move . . . Some organizations distribute work purposely as a way to establish a presence in multiple locations and increase the global appeal of their products . . . These and many other factors are motivating the rapid expansion in the amount of distributed work." [47]

Numerous researchers have pointed out the superiority of colocated project teams over virtual teams. For example, in comparing the effectiveness of geographically distributed teams versus teams working in physical proximity, Hinds and Kiesler conclude that "proximity has proven to be hard to simulate through modern technologies such as videoconferencing." Kiesler and Cummings reach a similar conclusion and highlight the weaknesses of virtual teams in terms of the two crucial aspects of project communication in a dynamic environment, namely, connecting ("forming collaborations") and updating ("transferring knowledge"): "Distributed workers will have more difficulty forming close collaborations, dealing flexibly with one another . . . strong ties will be more difficult to forge and to sustain in the distributed than in the co-located work group. Hansen . . . found that it was more difficult to transfer complex knowledge from one location to another when ties were weak."[48]

In his *Harvard Business Review* article, "Trust and the Virtual Organization," Charles Handy asserts that the technological possibilities of the virtual organization are seductive. However, he warns that as it becomes possible for more work to be done outside the traditional office, trust will become more difficult to build in a virtual organization: "Trust is not blind. It is unwise to trust people whom you do not know well, whom you have not observed in action over time, and who are not committed to the same goals . . . Trust needs bonding . . . Trust needs touch. Visionary leaders, no matter how articulate, are not enough. A shared commitment still requires personal contact to make it real. To augment John Naisbitt's telling phrase, high tech has to be balanced by high touch to build high-trust organizations . . . Videoconferences are . . . more productive if the individuals know each other as people, not just as images on the screen."[49] In their research on distributed work, Nardi and Whittaker likewise point to "the desirability—necessity, in some cases—of early face-to-face meetings to establish relationships . . . videoconferencing works more effectively when people already know each other."[50]

Herbsleb and Grinter describe how trust developed within a geographically distributed software development team, where part of the team was located in the UK and the other in Germany: "As the two primary sites began to work together, there was initially little trust between people at different locations . . . The situation improved considerably over time, and visits across sites seem to have been pivotal. As one developer noted, they just did not seem to make progress until they had worked together face to face. After working together, the relationships between the sites began to change. As one developer said, 'Things eased a lot when we met these people face to face . . . We worked much closer and resolved things much quicker as well.'"[51]

Herbsleb and Grinter attribute the initial distrust to differences in communication style and other cultural differences. Once the team players met face to face and were able to put their differences in context, they became more accustomed to each other and were less mystified by behavior that had previously seemed strange or out of place.

Nohria and Eccles, two professors from Harvard Business School, stress the need for maintaining sufficient face-to-face communication, asserting that "the crux of our argument is that you cannot build network organizations on electronic networks alone. At the core, the network organization depends on a network of relationships forged on the basis of face-to-face interaction. The network of relationships serves as the substrate on which the electronic network can float or . . . be 'embedded.' What the electronic network can do is accelerate as well as amplify the communication flow, but its viability and effectiveness will depend critically on the robustness of the underlying social structure . . . While nobody can tell what the future holds, we think that face-to-face interaction will remain a necessary basis for all social organizations."[52]

Nardi and Whittaker go one step further and propose a general approach for best utilizing face-to-face communication in distributed work: "We propose the design of media ecologies, where a particular mix of media is specified depending on the nature of the work and contextual aspects of the workplace situation . . . we need to devise an appropriate mix of face-to-face and other media . . . Three key elements of context for designing media ecologies are (1) the work tasks themselves, (2) the quality of the relationships between participants, and (3) the temporal flow of the work."[53]

The Meaning of Tailoring to Project Context

The first meta-principle, which was presented in the introduction, states that the principles must be tailored to the unique context of the project. In the Second Brown Guideline (Think Deliverables), the need for tailoring project processes to project context was further discussed. Following are three specific assumptions behind the concept of tailoring in the case of communication media.

First, one must recognize that there is no "one best way" for project communication. The current guideline clearly shows that in order to cope with a variety of situations (i.e., routine, non-routine, ambiguous, distributed work), projects must employ a variety of communication media. In essence, project communication in a dynamic environment appears to behave according to Ashby's law of requisite variety: "Only variety can absorb variety." That is, in order to manage increasing variety in the project's environment, the range of its communication repertoire must be increased.[54] At times, it may seem that adhering to Ashby's law may lead the team to provide more information than needed. However, as in the Third Green Guideline (Use an Appropriate Amount of Redundancy), coping with uncertain and ambiguous conditions may often require some measure of redundancy, so erring on the side of providing more information is appropriate.[55]

Second, the demand for employing a variety of communication media does not imply that "anything goes." Rather, the medium should fit the situation. Thus, for example, lean channels are employed for routine messages, whereas rich channels are employed for non-routine messages. Even when Nardi and Whittaker propose the employment of a variety of media for distributed work, they recommend the use of a particular mix of media tailored to the nature of the work and contextual aspects of the specific workplace situation. Tailoring requires high competencies in distinguishing between various workplace situations, in the judgment required for tailoring, and in the actual adaptation to the specific context. In the epilogue, the development of these competencies will be further elaborated.[56]

Third, the concept that "there is no one best way" does not imply that there are no wrong ways. The current guideline clearly shows that in a dynamic world, employing insufficient face-to-face communication is indeed one of those wrong ways. Updating and connecting in a dynamic environment requires sufficient face-to-face communication, and what is "sufficient" can only be determined by the specific context.

The Third Gray Guideline: Adopt a Moving About Mode of Communication

In their book *A Passion for Excellence*, Tom Peters and Nancy Austin attribute a very crucial managerial role to the moving about mode of communication and accordingly term it Management by Wandering Around. They assert that "the number one productivity problem in America is, quite simply, managers who are out of touch with their people."[57]

The Illusion of Control

The following story exemplifies what may happen when managers avoid practicing "moving about." This story is an abridged version of a bizarre episode taken from *Doctors*, a novel by Erich Segal.

It was to be a routine removal of a gallbladder. However, some problems, were anticipated since the patient, Mr. A, had a somewhat complex medical history and was allergic to almost everything one could imagine.

It was my first week as an intern on Surgery. I was eager and proud to be in the operating room with the chief surgeon, Dr. Aubrey, and the anesthesiologist, Dr. Nagy, who were considered to be the top specialists in their fields.

Everything seemed to be going smoothly until Dr. Nagy started reporting some problems. From then on, it seems that things deteriorated faster than lightning. One moment the blood pressure was dropping and the next, the ECG was going crazy. In spite of all their emergency procedures, within a few minutes the ECG was flat and Dr. Nagy pronounced the patient dead.

Suddenly there was silence. No one dared speak until Dr. Aubrey decided on a course of action. He ordered Dr. Nagy to continue aerating the lungs. I wondered what was going on. After all, the poor man was dead! Then, with growing disbelief, I watched as Dr. Aubrey took over from his assistant and carefully started suturing and closing the opening. When the last suture was in place, Dr. Aubrey quietly ordered, "Take him to the recovery room. I'll be there in a few moments."

I was stunned. Only after I recovered my speech did I dare ask Dr. Aubrey's assistant why they continued pumping air into the dead man's lungs. He seemed to think the answer was obvious: "That way, Mr. A will be pronounced dead after the operation by somebody in the recovery room. This explains why no patient of Dr. Aubrey's ever dies on his operating table."[58]

Doctors may be a work of fiction, but Pfeffer and Sutton found that similar bizarre experiences are quite common in a wide variety of businesses: "In our field research, we encountered example after example of measurement processes that fueled destructive behavior inside organizations."[59] Indeed, one can't ignore the vast body of empirical research on the frequency and magnitude of information filtering and distortion within organizations. Studies indicate that subordinates constantly play subversive "control" games to enable them to report favorable outcomes when the actual results are unfavorable. Moreover, the notion that objective ("formal-hard") data are more reliable or valid than subjective ("informal-soft") data is just a myth.[60] Mintzberg admonishes that the illusion of control may lead to an obsession with control.[61]

The intern in the *Doctors* explained that another reason for Dr. Aubrey's aberrant practice was to avoid the massive paperwork required by the hospital and the insurance companies. Thus, in addition to maintaining his perfect operating record, the surgeon was able to pass a time-consuming bureaucratic job onto the recovery room staff. This point illustrates that more paperwork does not necessarily ensure greater information reliability or accuracy. In fact, sometimes it only adds "non-value-added" cost, as Jerry Madden, a project manager from NASA, demonstrates in the following story, *You Can't Take Anything for Granted.*

> *Organizations use paperwork to prevent disorder. Much information can be easily transferred, but the forms must be read very carefully and sometimes that is not enough. A highly regarded vendor had large manufacturing contracts with NASA. Their manufacturing reports list the items that have been delivered to us. After going through one lengthy report, I went down to the integration floor expecting to see an assembled spacecraft. I found that many assemblies which had been listed were missing.*
>
> Jerry immediately called the vendor to report the errors and was told that they had two sets of paperwork: manufacturing reports for delivered items and integration returns for those items that were sent back for repairs or corrections. Once the item had been shipped back, the vendor closed out the manufacturing report.
>
> As Jerry realized, *"It just goes to show that you can't rely on the official sources. If a project manager wants effective control, he/she has to always be on the move and ask questions. Indeed, 'things are seldom what they seem.'"*°

This story demonstrates that managers who maintain a stationary position may be forced to make complex judgments with incomplete or misleading cues. Hence the following recommendation: "If a project manager wants effective control, he/she has to always be on the move and ask questions." As explained in the Second Green Guideline (Employ a Learning-Based Planning and Control Process), the "old school" approach to planning and control was to emphasize the role of control as facilitating adherence to plan—much like using a thermostat to maintain a predetermined standard. But today's projects are rarely so simple and stable. In today's dynamic world, a more suitable metaphor for project control would be coaching. A coach needs to see the game in order to guide the team and would hardly be effective if forced to operate from the locker room while receiving statistics via a monitor.

Solving Problems through Moving About

"Be on the move and ask questions" is a communication mode that can be useful for project managers with only one project or multiple projects. In her position as the head of the Observational Systems Division at Jet Propulsion Laboratory, NASA, Mary Bothwell was responsible for up to a dozen different projects. Yet, as she tells us in the next story, *Walking a Fine Line*, one of her projects required her to adopt the "moving about" mode.

> *My division was charged with building a suite of cameras for the Mars Exploration Rover project . . . things were not looking good . . . we had an*

instrument manager in charge who I believe has the potential to become a great manager, but when things got behind schedule, he didn't have the experience to know what was needed to catch up . . . After talking with the instrument manager's immediate supervisor, I could see that he was doing an excellent job of keeping people motivated and working despite the challenges. For the morale of the team, I decided not to replace him . . .

I met with the instrument manager and the deputy section manager every day . . . We would go around the table and discuss the schedule . . . We went over every item . . . Every day I would walk around to where members of the team were working and ask, "How's it going now? Did you get that answer yet?" . . . Once they figured out they couldn't get rid of me, they became forthcoming about the problems. If I saw someone in the hall and asked, "Hey how's it going? Are you there?" I began hearing, "Oh yeah, we're there" or "Oh no, we didn't quite make it and this is what we're doing" . . .

Because of that level of involvement, I knew what the challenges were so that I could forecast where the project might run into trouble . . . After several months, I was able to ease up, but I kept holding weekly meetings so that the team, down to the floor-level technician, knew that I remained engaged in the project . . . The cameras were completed in time to be integrated onto the spacecraft and rovers. The instrument team delivered superb cameras that satisfied their customers, the scientists. After delivery, we had a party.[P]

While moving about, one of the roles of the effective "leader wanderer" is to facilitate the work by providing direct help. Peters and Austin stress that "you can relieve the bottleneck on the spot, but only if you're there." On the basis of his observations at Toyota, Liker also supports "moving about" behavior and urges managers to "solve problems and improve processes by going to the source and personally observing and verifying data" as well as to "think and speak based on personally verified data." Moreover, he advises that even high-level managers "should go and see things for themselves, so they will have more than a superficial understanding of the situation."[62]

Moving About for Listening

Peters and Austin also emphasize the importance of the "leader wanderer" "getting it firsthand and undistorted." They add that managers must listen not only to their own people but also to their suppliers.[63] In the following story, *Not to Worry*, Terry Little, a project manager for the U.S. Air Force, explains why and how he listened to his supplier.

I visited one of the contractors' suppliers and asked him to tell me, "What is the prime making you do, or causing you to do, that you think is worthless or not value-added enough to offset the cost?" A representative from the prime was present, and so there was a little bit of nervousness on the part of the supplier.

I told the representative from the prime to go get a cup of coffee. I ended up with about three pages full of stuff that the supplier said was causing him headaches. As I was writing all this down, he asked, "What are you going to do with that?" And I said, "Not to worry."

How did I gain his trust? Well, for one thing, I was there. A government program manager does not normally go to visit the suppliers of a prime contractor. The fact that I was there and willing to spend a whole day looking at his facility, meeting his people, and talking to them about the program and how important their contributions were—that was a big deal to him . . .

Typically, the government says, "Our contract is with the prime, and we don't have a contract with these suppliers." Maybe that's true, theoretically, but . . . A large part of the success of the program depends on what the suppliers to my contractor are doing. Am I just going to close my eyes to that? . . . I believe it's important to communicate with everybody that's involved in the outcome of a program.

I gave the three pages to the prime without any explanation other than "this is what he told me." A week later, this guy from the prime came back to me and explained how they'd addressed everything on the list except for one thing, and he gave me a detailed and satisfactory explanation as to why the one thing was still important to do.[q]

Little takes pains to gain the trust of his suppliers because merely "moving about" does not guarantee that the information collected will be reliable. Indeed, when subordinates or suppliers perceive managers as "corporate policemen," they develop tactics to conceal or distort information, much like those described above in the story from *Doctors*. To ensure that moving about results in constructive guidance, rather than destructive micromanagement, it must be accompanied by mutual trust.

Understanding and Influencing through Moving About

In a recent study of ten highly successful on-site construction project managers, who were each systematically observed on the job for one week, it was found that moving about occupied almost 50 percent of their time. The project managers spent 28.2 percent of their time at the on-site production areas and 19.4 percent of their time at other on-site offices. Moreover, the project managers changed their location 4.1 times per hour, on average, moving between their personal offices, other on-site offices, on-site production areas, and off-site locations.[64]

Moving about helps project managers to affect project performance by better understanding what is going on and by influencing project performance faster. In terms of understanding, it should be stressed that managing by moving about does not serve as a substitute for the review of formal performance reports, but rather complements it. Observing, asking questions, and listening while moving about augment the information provided by formal reports and afford the manager better and faster comprehension of the overall picture.[65]

The influencing role of the project manager was discussed in the Third Brown Guideline, which highlighted the frequent need of the project manager to intervene, solve problems, and act with agility. Moving about greatly facilitates problem solving, and quickly. Clark and Wheelwright explain that project managers are able to resolve conflicts quickly by staying in motion out of the office. Peters and Waterman describe Management by Walking About as the heart of the first principle of the best companies. In this principle, "A Bias for Action," they offer that "there is no more important trait among excellent companies than an action orientation."[66]

Sayles and Chandler propose that when a problem arises "it is more important that a decision be reached so that forward momentum can be resumed . . . In working to maintain a forward momentum, the manager seeks to avoid stalemates . . . in a good many situations, corrective action is possible only during a brief 'window' . . . The heart of the matter is quickness of response." Similarly, Muirhead and Simon assert that "maintaining momentum is a cornerstone of successful management . . . Maintaining momentum is more important than always being right."[67]

While moving about enables the project manager to enjoy all the benefits of face-to-face communication highlighted in the Second Gray Guideline, it goes one step further by enhancing the manager's ability to directly influence the people involved in the project. Clark and Wheelwright argue that managers who move about are able to fulfill the crucial role of teaching. Peters and Austin suggest that this teaching is often coaching, through which the managers transmit their values and working philosophy.[68] Moving about, often interacting with one or only a small number of people, helps foster the project manager's image as one who is not detached from the actual work and workers, but rather is well informed, both with respect to the big picture as well as the small details. This image, coupled with the respect and credibility gained through moving about, helps the project manager to influence not only the work (by quickly solving specific problems) but also the workers themselves. In particular, it is through moving about that the project manager can naturally and systematically convey the required sense of mission (as described in the First Yellow Guideline) and the shift to "Think Deliverables."

It should now be easier to understand why the above mentioned ten successful construction project managers spend close to 50 percent of their time on moving about. By employing moving about they are able to directly influence both the work and the people. Thus, one can say that through moving about the project manager is able to push the work and pull the people. The concept of " pull and push" was also used in the First Gray Guideline in relation to pulling and pushing information. One may say, however, that while pulling and pushing information frequently serves primarily as preparation for the "real work," moving about *is* the real work.

Becoming a Results-Focused Leader: From Geometric Order to Living Order

I n writing *Breaking the Code of Project Management*, I attempted to conform to the following learning philosophy: "The central issue in learning is becoming a practitioner, not learning about practice."[1] This book is based on more than two decades of research attempting to capture the proven practices of some of the most competent project managers, to uncover their tacit knowledge, and to explicitly articulate it. This explicit knowledge is presented in the form of five principles of the theory of Results-Focused Leadership. The epilogue explains how this book can help you to become a Results-Focused Leader and what additional steps you need to take. First, however, it is important to understand why this book alone is insufficient for the development of your professional competence.

Context Is the Key

Tom Peters, who maintains that "all white-collar work today is project work," provides a very helpful historical perspective on the evolution of projects as a work mode: "Arguably, project work was the norm before the industrial revolution. Most activities took place in small, independent shops, and crafts and craftsmen were the economy centerpiece. The industrial revolution changed all that. Skills and tasks were narrowed. And narrowed again. Thousands of people went to work under the same roof. Now, thanks to competitive pressure, new distributive information technologies and the like, we are, arguably, returning to the craft tradition. The essence of the craft is the project. It may turn out that the 150 years from the time of Dickens to 1980 will have been the anomaly. What's normal . . . will end up being . . . the project."[2]

However, the prevailing theories of project management are, for the most part, still stuck in the past. For example, today's project managers must cope with a project environment that is much more dynamic than those of the past. Yet, the factors leading to this dynamic environment, such as project uncertainty, project speed, and the manager's scarcity of attention, are still largely ignored or underestimated by the prevailing theories of project management.

These theories of project management have also failed to give sufficient explicit treatment to the unique context of the project and have, at least implicitly, embraced the "one best way" philosophy. This point was expressed very eloquently by Melgrati and Damiani: "Project management ideology is paradoxical because it focuses on repetitive aspects and 'marginalizes' the uniqueness and originality that should instead characterize the project."[3] Peter Drucker maintains that the "one best way" assumptions underlying the discipline of management are "totally at odds with reality and . . . totally counterproductive."[4] In his seminal article, "Bad Management Theories Are Destroying Good Management Practices," Sumantra Ghoshal cites Kurt Lewin's argument that "nothing is as practical as a good theory." Ghoshal stresses, however, that the "obverse is also true: Nothing is as dangerous as a bad theory."[5] Ghoshal's conclusion is very relevant to project management, considering that the quality of the prevailing project management theories has profound implications for practice. For example, the consistently poor results of the wide spectrum of projects presented in the introduction can be largely attributed to the absence of "practical and good theories" of project management.

Taking into account the sources of the data in the current book, it is safe to assume that after you have completed the reading, you will be convinced that applying this theory would not be counterproductive or dangerous to good practices. However, unless you are already a very experienced project manager, you should not assume that mastering this "theory of practice" will, by itself, render you a results-focused leader. While reading this book and comprehending its five principles is indeed essential, it is only the first step on the road to becoming a results-focused leader. The following two meta-principles will help you to understand why studying Results-Focused Leadership is insufficient and what else is needed.

1. Embrace and apply these principles as general instructions that must be tailored to the unique context of the project (e.g., project size, stability of objectives, speed, task complexity, organizational culture, extent of top management support, team members' experience and skills).[6]
2. The implementation of any one principle and its impact on project success depends on the implementation of all the others. To compensate for the inability to fully adhere to a principle, be prepared to modify the implementation of the others as well as to adjust project expectations.

Now that you have had an opportunity to grasp the five principles and their interdependence, it is easy to see that in essence each principle serves as a context factor for all the other principles. For example, since a low-trust environment affects people's willingness to freely exchange information, as demonstrated in the Second Red Guideline (Develop Trust-Based Teamwork), the team's ability to fully apply the Second Green Guideline (Employ a Learning-Based Planning and Control Process) is severely affected. Thus, both meta-principles can be summed up in one overall meta-principle: **the application of the principles is dependent on the project context.**

There are basically two ways to cope with the unique context of the project. The first way is to tailor the project to its context, while the second way is quite the opposite, namely, to shape the context to fit the project. The first way, tailoring the principles as well as the project practices and processes to the project context, was elaborately addressed in the Second Brown Guideline (Think Deliverables) and in the Second Gray Guideline (Employ a Variety of Communication Mediums with Face Time as Top Priority), as well as in numerous examples throughout this book.

Examples of the second way, shaping the context to fit the project, were also presented throughout this book. In the Second Green Guideline (Employ a Learning-Based Planning and Control Process), Marty Davis from NASA wanted his project to enjoy the benefits of a learning-based review and was able to do so by first modifying the norms and practices outside of his project. Similarly, in the Second Red Guideline (Develop Trust-Based Teamwork), Judy Stokley from the U.S. Air Force and Chuck Anderson from Raytheon changed the culture characterizing their project from one structured by power relations to one based on mutual trust. They accomplished this by first modifying the norms and practices outside of their projects.[7]

What is common to both ways of coping with the unique context is that their successful application requires the extensive exercise of judgment. Quinn, Mintzberg, and James concluded that judgment is the most indispensable attribute of managers: "It is simply our conclusion that among all other attributes of managers, the most indispensable is judgment because it is the integrator which guides and controls all the others . . . most judgment calls are not simple selections between black and white, but are between subtle shades of gray . . . Don't expect everything to work out well the first time . . . Don't be afraid to make mistakes as long as you learn from them."[8] Michael Eraut stresses that judgment must rely on experience: "Judgment is not the same as understanding . . . Judgment involves practical wisdom, a sense of purpose . . . and its acquisition depends, among other things, on a wealth of professional experience."[9] In his discussion of context and "the priority of the particular," Bent Flyvbjerg concludes that it "operates via a practical rationality based on judgment and experience."[10] The judgment needed in specific context situations can not depend on the use of general rules and therefore can not be developed solely on the basis of reading books or participating in training seminars. Rather, it requires extensive experience.

Even carrying out the actual adaptation of the project to the specific context or the adaptation of the context to the specific project requires experience. Adapting the context to the project is usually much harder than the more frequent practice of adapting the project to its context, as the former is often associated with significant unlearning and nonconformity. However, both kinds of adaptation require the project leader to adjust the plan and align the various project participants in order to facilitate collaboration during the actual implementation of this adjustment. In a dynamic environment, frequent judgment calls and adaptations can be accomplished in a timely manner only by exercising leadership. Likewise, such leadership can not be acquired solely by reading a book or participating in training seminars, but also necessitates regular coaching and practice.[11]

From Project Development to Competence Development

Experience alone is not enough for developing competence. As Steven Kerr explains, "'Practice makes perfect' is not true. It is more true to say that 'practice makes permanent' (ineffective work practices become so ingrained that they are virtually impossible to unlearn) . . . [however] new managers found it easier to learn from experience when they had strong developmental relationships [with superiors or peers]."[12] In his book *Developing Professional Knowledge and Competence*, Eraut stresses that competence development requires both theory and experience: "Even in well-theorised areas of practice, the interpretation of theory is problematic and requires further learning from experience."[13]

Henry Mintzberg highlights another vital component for competence development: "Activity becomes 'experience' only after it has been reflected on thoroughly." He cites T.S. Eliot, who wrote in one of his poems, "We had the experience but missed the meaning." He also cites Saul Alinsky, who argues that "most people do not accumulate a body of experience. Most people go through life undergoing a series of happenings, which pass through their systems undigested. Happenings become experiences when they are digested, when they are reflected on, related to general patterns, and synthesized."[14]

Throughout this book, I showed how project development in a dynamic environment requires the integration of thinking and doing, as suggested by Weick: "We should pay more attention to simultaneity of thought and action and less attention to sequence."[15] This integration is also at the center of competence development. As Gosling and Mintzberg argue, "Management education should be restricted to practicing managers . . . These managers should stay on the job, so they can weave their education through their practice . . . The key to the learning is thoughtful reflection . . . Managers do not need the education equivalent of military drill; they need skillful reflection to drill into their own experience."[16]

Like Eraut, Mintzberg also stresses the key role of concepts and theory in competence development and explains that reflection is "experience considered in the light of conceptual ideas." He further elaborates that these conceptual ideas may be provided by educators: "The managers live in the territory while the faculty provide the map."[17] Outside the classroom, reading books and articles can also serve as an effective source for conceptual ideas. In particular, stories and case studies are highly recommended as an excellent tool for enhancing reflection. Since stories and case studies are highly context sensitive, reading and reflecting on them should facilitate the required shift from a context-free mind-set to a context-specific one.[18]

Competence development is thus composed of cycles of gaining work experience, acquiring new concepts by participation in training sessions and by reading stories, and using these concepts in reflecting on the experience. The best way to start your competence development process is by studying the principles of Results-Focused Leadership and by addressing each principle separately, as if it were context free. However, it is important to keep in mind that because these principles are actually context dependent, they are often applied simultaneously in practice. Therefore, the goal of the competence development process is to reach a level where the principles are perceived not as separate entities, but rather as a union of principles that can be easily and routinely applied at the same time.

The expected competence development can be better understood by revisiting the typical project development process in a dynamic environment with the help of a metaphor based on Henri Bergson's interpretation of uncertainty. This Nobel Prize winner claimed that there is no such thing as disorder, but rather there are two sorts of order: geometric and living.[19] Once people are able to repudiate "bad theories" and outdated assumptions (i.e., that life can be represented by geometric order), they will realize that the high uncertainty present in the early stages of a project outlines their natural "living order." While all projects aim to reach a perfectly functioning product with geometric order, most start with an unclear idea that influences nearly the entire course of the project. Gradually, some parts of the project approach a geometric order, but in an era of uncertainty and accelerated speed, the project as a whole does not assume geometric order until very late in its life.

Bergson's two types of order can also be used to better understand competence development, which moves in the opposite direction. Again, once people are able to eliminate "bad theories" and outdated assumptions, they will realize that no theory of abstract principles can be applied without the necessary adaptation to unique projects in a dynamic environment.[20] Early on in one's career, a project manager who has not undergone a sufficient number of cycles of experience, training, and reflection is only capable of managing a project with relatively low uncertainty. This project manager may master the principles of Results-Focused Leadership, but only separately, as if they represent a geometric order. In contrast, the project manager who has already completed a sufficient number of cycles of experience, training, and reflection will be able to simultaneously apply the principles of Results-Focused Leadership as a union of principles, as if they represent a living order.

Harvard's Ronald Heifetz asserts that "the real heroism of leadership involves having the courage to face reality—and helping people around you to face reality."[21] This ability to face reality, coupled with sufficient experience, training, and reflection will enable you to bring project development from a living order to a geometric order and to move your own competence development from a geometric order to a living order.

Notes and References

Introduction

Notes

1. Following are a few quotes that give expression to the central role of the project method: "Project management is evolving from a specialty into the central task of middle management." T.A. Stewart. 1995. Corporate Jungle Spawns a New Species: The Project Manager. *Fortune* (July 10): 179–80. "Project work is moving to center stage in our organizations . . . You cannot afford to be a 10 in operations and a 4 in project work." The Price Waterhouse Change Integration Team. 1995. *The Paradox Principles: How High Performance Companies Manage Chaos, Complexity and Contradictions to Achieve Superior Results*. Chicago, IL: Irwin, 270. "All white-collar work today is project work." T. Peters. 1999. The Wow Project. *Fast Company* 24 (April): 116. Dr. Martin Barnes. 2002. A Long Term View of Project Management— Its Past and its Likely Future. *16th World Congress on Project Management*, Berlin, June.

2. A need for a shift from 'taylorism' (i.e., the principles of Fredrick W. Taylor, the father of scientific management) to tailoring was also detected in the U.S. Department of Defense. Alan Beck, a professor at the Defense Acquisition University, strongly argues for developing the "it all depends" mind-set. Prof. Beck asserts that "the structured end—is where everything is controlled by rules and procedures. This can kill initiative and creativity—resulting in a 'work to the rule, do the minimum required' culture, which bogs down in detail and malaise." Thus, he concludes, "The most important skill is of inquiry. [encouraging] It all depends." A.W. Beck. 2001. Probing the 'It Depends' Variables. *Program Management* 30, 3 (May–June): 22–9.

3. E.W. Merrow. 1988. *Understanding the Outcomes of Megaprojects: A Quantitative Analysis of Very Large Civilian Projects*. Santa Monica, CA: Rand Corporation.

4. B. Flyvbjerg, N. Bruzelius, and W. Rothengatter. 2003. *Megaprojects and Risks: An Anatomy of Ambition*. Cambridge, UK: Cambridge University Press, 44.

5. P.W.G. Morris and G.H. Hough. 1987. *The Anatomy of Major Projects*. Chichester, UK: Wiley, 7.

6. M. Keil, A. Rai, J.E. Cheney Mann, and G.P. Zhang. 2003. Why Software Projects Escalate: The Importance of Project Management Constructs. *IEEE Transactions on Engineering Management* 50, 3: 251–61.

7. The Standish Group (http://www.standishgroup.com/) has been doing surveys on all types of IT projects since 1994. Its research is published under the title CHAOS.

8. L. Rain. 2005. IT Project Failures. *Purchasing Link*, August. http://www.eandi. org/ThePulse/Commentary/project.html, last accessed January 30, 2007.

9. Program Evaluation and Review Technique (PERT) is an event-oriented network analysis technique used to estimate program duration when there is uncertainty in the individual duration estimates.

10. P.W.G. Morris. 1994. *The Management of Projects*. London, UK: Thomas Telford Services, 25. Critical path method (CPM) is a network analysis technique used to predict project duration by analyzing which sequence of activities (which path) has the least amount of scheduling flexibility. A project network diagram is any schematic display of the logical relationships of project activities. The Critical Path is defined as the series of interdependent activities of a project, connected end-to-end, that determine the shortest total length of the project.

11. P.W.G. Morris. 1994. *The Management of Projects*. London, UK: Thomas Telford Services, 30–1.

12. H.M. Sapolsky. 1972. *The Polaris System Development*. Cambridge, MA: Harvard University Press, 123–4.

13. H.M. Sapolsky. 1972. *The Polaris System Development*. Cambridge, MA: Harvard University Press, 129.

14. A. Davies and M. Hobday. 2005. *The Business of Projects: Managing Innovation in Complex Products and Systems*. Cambridge, UK: Cambridge University Press, 151–2.

15. Stout continues his analysis by showing how organizations become locked into procedures not validated by experience: "Accepting a technique in the belief that it was effective in its original application can lead to an orthodoxy of innovation: A new control is tried (or so it is thought) and a judgment is made that it is useful without relying supporting evidence. The technique is then spread widely on the strength of its original 'test' and the associated inflated claims; and, finally, once the innovation has diffused widely, practitioners reassure themselves that, after all, it must be useful because many organizations use it!" R. Stout Jr. 1980. *Management or Control?: The Organizational Challenge*. Bloomington, IN: Indiana University Press, 25–6.

16. P. Phillips Carson, P.A. Lanier, K.D. Carson, and B.N. Guidry. 2000. Clearing a Path through the Management Fashion Jungle: Some Preliminary Trailblazing. *Academy of Management Journal* 43, 6: 1143–58.

17. S.R. Barley, G.W. Meyer, and D.C. Gash. 1988. Cultures of Culture: Academics, Practitioners and the Pragmatics of Normative Control. *Administrative Science Quarterly* 33, 1: 24–60. Spell also found that "fashions emerge from popular press before academic literature." C.S. Spell. 1999. Where do Management Fashions Come From, and How Long Do They Stay? *Journal of Management History* 5, 6: 334–48.

18. S. Ghoshal. 2005. Bad Management Theories Are Destroying Good Management Practices. *Academy of Management Learning and Education* 4, 1: 75–91.

19. T. Williams. 2005. Assessing and Moving on from the Dominant Project Management Discourse in the Light of Project Overruns. *IEEE Transactions on Engineering and Management* 52, 4: 497–508.

20. Melgrati and Damiani also assert that "the gap between theory and practice is sometimes obvious. For example, one of the claims of the discipline is that it fosters debureaucratization, horizontality, interfunctionality, downward delegation, and extended teamwork. Instead, however, the strong theoretical and applied prescriptiveness of its method seems in practice to generate close connivance and compliance with the

bureaucratic culture of large firms, insulating their permanent structures against the destabilizing impact of projects." A. Melgrati and M. Damiani. 2002. Rethinking the Project Management Framework: New Epistemology, New Insights. *Proceedings of PMI Research Conference*, Seattle: 371–80.

21. M.E. Nissen and K.F. Snider. 2002. Lessons Learned to Guide Project Management Theory and Research: Pragmatism and Knowledge Flow. *Proceedings of PMI Research Conference*, Seattle: 89–98.

22. S. Cicmil, T. Williams, J. Thomas, and D. Hodgson. 2006. Rethinking Project Management: Researching the Actuality of Projects. *International Journal of Project Management* 24, 8: 675–86. Richard Daft, relating to management researchers and not particularly to project management researchers, said back in 1983, "As a reviewer of papers, it becomes painfully clear that many authors have never seen or witnessed the phenomena about which they write. Authors cannot give an example to illustrate a point." R.L. Daft. 1983. Learning the Craft of Organizational Research. *Academy of Management Review* 8, 4: 539–46.

23. L. Koskela and G. Howell. 2002. The Underlying Theory of Project Management is Obsolete. *Proceedings of PMI Research Conference*, Seattle: 293–301. T. Williams, focusing on complex projects, also finds a need for a new paradigm. T.M. Williams. 1999. The Need for New Paradigms for Complex Projects. *International Journal of Project Management* 17, 5: 269–73.

24. M. Fowler. The Agile Manifesto: Where It Came From and Where It May Go. *Martin Fowler.com*, last accessed February 14, 2007. http://www.martinfowler.com/articles/agileStory.html

25. M. Fowler and J. Highsmith. 2001. The Agile Manifesto. *Software Development* (August), last accessed February 14, 2007. http://hristov.com/andrey/fhtstuttgart/The_Agile_Manifesto_SDMagazine.pdf For more on the Agile Methods, see M. Poppendieck and T. Poppendieck. 2003. *Lean Software Development—An Agile Toolkit*. Boston, MA: Addison-Wesley; A. Cockburn. 2002. *Agile Software Development*. Boston, MA: Addison-Wesley; K. Beck. 2000. *Extreme Programming Explained—Embrace Change*. Boston, MA: Addison-Wesley.

26. B. Boehm and R. Turner. 2004. *Balancing Agility and Discipline—A Guide for the Perplexed*. Boston, MA: Addison-Wesley, 16–7.

27. The companies with which I worked most intensively were AT&T, Bechtel, DuPont, Exxon, Hensel Phelps, IBM, J.A. Jones, Morrison Knudsen, Pepco, Procter & Gamble, and Stone & Webster. I also worked with Brown & Root, General Motors, Jacobs Engineering, Mobile, Motorola, Pennsylvania Power & Light, Texaco, and Turner.

28. The products include either stand-alone stories or case studies composed of a collection of stories from members of the project team, covering the entire project. As a researcher working closely with practitioners, I quickly learned to reverse the question I used to ask, "Why don't practitioners use what researchers know?" Rather, I began to ask, "Why don't researchers use what practitioners know?" This intuitive feeling was later reinforced by an article focusing on the characteristics of the new scholarship, in which Schon concludes, "The relationship between . . . academic and practice knowledge needs to be turned on its head. We should think about practice as a setting not only for the application of knowledge but for its generation. We should ask not only how practitioners can better apply the results of academic research, but what kinds of knowing are already embedded in competent practice." D.A. Schon. 1995. Knowing-in-Action: The New Scholarship Requires a New Epistemology. *Change* (November-December): 27–34. The problematic relationship

between management research in academia and practice has received much attention in recent years. See, for example, J.R. Bailey. 2002. Refracting Reflection: Views from the Inside. *Academy of Management Executive* 1, 1: 77; C.R. Hinings and R. Greenwood. 2002. ASQ Forum: Disconnects and Consequences in Organization Theory. *Administrative Science Quarterly* 4, 3: 411–21; G.P. Hodgkinson. 2001. Facing the Future: The Nature and Purpose of Management Research Reassessed. *British Journal of Management* 12/Special Issue, S1-S80; S.L. Rynes, J.M. Bartunek, and R. Daft. 2001. Across the Great Divide: Knowledge Creation and Transfer between Practitioners and Academics. *Academy of Management Journal* 44, 2: 340–55.

29. W. Bennis and P.W. Biederman. 1996. *Organizing Genius—The Secrets of Creative Collaboration.* Reading, MA: Addison-Wesley, 8.

30. R.H. Waterman. 1994. *What America Does Right: Learning from Companies that Put People First.* New York, NY: W.W. Norton & Company.

31. B. McKelvey. 2006. Van de Ven and Johnson's "Engaged Scholarship": Nice Try, But . . . *Academy of Management Review* 31, 4: 822–9.

32. This is what Scott Cameron, Global Process Owner of Project Management at P&G, said about the launching of the book and its usefulness 12 years following its publication: "Alex pushed the envelope when he asked project managers to tell and write stories. [They] thought, 'What do I have to offer?' [Then], they all wrote great stories. The stories aren't dated. They're [still] great stories." D. Lee. 2006. Are We On Track? How Stories Impact Project Management. In *Wake Me Up When the Data is Over—How Organizations Use Stories to Drive Results,* ed. Lori L. Silverman, 62–77. San Francisco, CA: Jossey-Bass.

33. D. Leonard and S. Sensiper. 1998. The Role of Tacit Knowledge in Group Innovation. *California Management Review* 40, 3: 112–32.

34. On technologies and crafts, see C.E. Lindblom. 1981. Comments on Decisions on Organizations. In *Perspectives in Organizational Design and Behavior,* eds. A. Van de Ven and W. Joyce, 245–8. New York, NY: Wiley.

35. In a recent book where Henry Mintzberg makes the point that MBA programs should admit only students with sufficient experience, he differentiates between engineering as a profession and management as a practice rather than a profession. Among other things, Mintzberg explains that engineering "can be taught in advance of practice . . . the trained expert can almost always outperform the layperson . . . [and] few of us would trust the intuitive engineer." In comparison, "most management is craft, meaning that it relies on experience—learning on the job . . . [and] we trust all kinds of managers who have never spent a day in a management classroom." H. Mintzberg. 2004. *Managers Not MBAs—A Hard Look at the Soft Practice of Managing and Management Development.* San Francisco, CA: Berrett-Koehler Publishers Inc., 10–11.

36. See: T.H. Davenport and L. Prusak. 1998. *Working Knowledge.* Boston, MA: Harvard Business School Press, 82; G. Roth and A. Kleiner. 1998. Developing Organizational Memory through Learning. *Organizational Dynamics* 27, 2 (Autumn): 43–60; I. Nonaka and H. Takeuchi. 1995. *The Knowledge Creating Company—How Japanese Companies Create the Dynamics of Innovation.* New York, NY: Oxford University Press, 69.

37. K.E. Weick and L.D. Browning. 1986. Argument and Narration in Organizational Communication. *Journal of Management* 12, 2: 243–59.

38. H. Mintzberg. 2005. Developing Theory About the Development of Theory. In *Great Minds in Management: The Process of Theory Development,* eds. K.G. Smith and M.A. Hitt, 355–72. New York, NY: Oxford University Press.

39. In the current book, most stories are not presented in their entirety. This practice allowed us to share a great variety of stories for each subject and at the same time produce a book that would not be too cumbersome.

40. A. Laufer, T. Post, and E.J. Hoffman. 2005. *Shared Voyage: Learning and Unlearning from Remarkable Projects.* Washington, D.C.: The NASA History Series. My 1994 book of project stories was coauthored with three Procter & Gamble project managers. That book comprised 70 stories told by 28 P&G project managers (A. Laufer, R.C. Volkman, G.W. Davenport, and S. Terry. 1994. *In Quest of Project Excellence through Stories.* Cincinnati, OH: Procter & Gamble). In 1998, I started my collaboration with Edward Hoffman, (Director of the NASA Academy of Program and Project Leadership) in the development of several knowledge-sharing projects. The first project was based on 70 project stories that they had collected from 36 federal government project managers. The book *Project Management Success Stories* was published in 2000 (A. Laufer and E.J. Hoffman. 2000. *Project Management Success Stories: Lessons of Project Leaders.* New York, NY: John Wiley & Sons).

41. See: R.M. Hogarth. 1980. *Judgment and Choice: The Psychology of Decision.* New York, NY: John Wiley and Sons, 87–91; J. Feldman. 1986. On the Difficulty of Learning from Experience. In *The Thinking Organization*, eds. H.P. Sims and D.A. Gioia, 263–92. San Francisco, CA: Jossey-Bass. Taylor and Wacker assert that "when a paradigm shifts as is now happening, experience is quite possibly the worst teacher in town . . . Change moves too fast, time is too compressed to draw any link with experience. Rational connections have been routed by connectivity. In a world as it now is, you can no longer discern the cause or the effect of any action." J. Taylor and W. Wacker. 1997. *The 500-Year Delta—What Happens After What Comes Next.* New York, NY: Harper Business, 16–7. See more on the subject of learning from experience in: P.M. Senge. 1990. *The Fifth Discipline: The Art and Practice of the Learning Organization.* New York, NY: Doubleday Currency and P.M. Senge et al. 1994. *The Fifth Discipline Fieldbook: Strategies and Tools for Building a Learning Organization.* New York, NY: Doubleday Currency.

42. See A. Laufer. 1989. *Owner's Project Planning: The Process Approach.* Source Document 45, the Construction Industry Institute, the University of Texas at Austin; A. Laufer and D. Cohenca. 1990. Factors Affecting Construction Planning Outcomes. *Journal of Construction Engineering and Management* 116, 1: 135–56; A. Laufer, R.L Tucker, A. Shapira, and A.J. Shenhar. 1994. The Multiplicity Concept in Construction Project Planning. *Construction Management and Economics* 11: 53–65; D. Telem, A. Laufer, and A. Shapira. 2006. Only Dynamics Can Absorb Dynamics. *Journal of Construction Engineering and Management* 132, 11: 1167–77. When available, I used classic studies performed by others to augment my understanding. See, for example, M.A. Lorell, J.F. Lowell, M. Kennedy, and H.P. Levaux. 2000. *Cheaper, Faster, Better? Commercial Approaches to Weapons Acquisition.* RAND Report No. MR-1147-AF. Santa Monica, CA: Rand Corporation.

43. Weick asserts that researchers must acknowledge the inevitable tradeoffs in inquiry and that "it is impossible for a theory of social behavior to be simultaneously general, accurate, and simple." While the classical studies usually produce simple and general results, the case studies are typically simple and accurate. K. Weick. 1979. *The Social Psychology of Organizing.* New York, NY: McGraw Hill, 35–42.

44. W.R. Ashby. 1956. *Introduction to Cybernetics.* New York, NY: John Wiley and Sons.

45. Schank, an artificial intelligence researcher at Northwestern University, convincingly argues that "human memory is story-based. Not all memories, however, are stories.

Rather, stories are especially interesting prior experiences, ones from which we learn . . . Not every experience makes a good story, but, if it does, the experience will be easier to remember." R.C. Schank. 1990. *Tell Me a Story: A New Look at Real and Artificial Memory.* New York, NY: Charles Scribner's Sons, 12. Wilkins also reports several studies supporting the conclusion that stories facilitate recall. A.L.Wilkins. 1983. Organizational Stories as Symbols to Control the Organization. In *Organizational Symbolism*, eds. L.R. Pondy, P.J Frost, G. Morgan, and T.C. Dandridge, 81–92. Greenwich, CT: JAI Press. Moreover, Nisbett and Ross present evidence that information that is more concrete and imaginable is retained more easily in memory. R. Nisbett and L. Ross. 1980. *Human Inference: Strategies and Shortcomings of Social Judgment.* Englewood Cliffs, NJ: Prentice-Hall.

46. G. Klein. 2001. *Sources of Power—How People Make Decisions.* London, UK: The MIT Press, 180.

47. M.R. Jalongo and J.P. Isenberg. 1995. *Teacher's Stories: From Personal Narrative to Professional Insight.* San Francisco, CA: Jossey-Bass Publishers, 50–1.

48. Jalongo and Isenberg's book *Teacher's Stories* presents multiple sources that clearly demonstrate how stories of practice offer a vehicle for practitioners to become more competent reflective practitioners (e.g., pages 10, 78, 143). Numagami suggests that the objective of management studies should be changed from a search for invariant laws of practical use to the encouragement of a reflective dialogue between researchers and practitioners and among practitioners and that the case study is an excellent vehicle for such a dialogue. T. Numagami. 1998. The Infeasibility of Invariant Laws in Management Studies: A Reflective Dialogue in Defense of Case Studies. *Organization Science* 9, 1: 2–15.

49. H. Mintzberg. 2004. *Managers Not MBAs—A Hard Look at the Soft Practice of Managing and Management Development.* San Francisco: Berrett-Koehler Publishers Inc., 254.

50. See J. Martin and M.E. Powers. 1982. Organizational Stories: More Vivid and Persuasive than Quantitative Data. In *Psychological Foundations of Organizational Behavior*, 2nd ed., ed. B.M. Staw, 161–8. Glenview, IL: Scott Foresman; A.L. Wilkins. 1984. The Creation of Company Cultures: The Role of Stories and Human Resource Systems. *Human Resource Management* 23, 1: 41–60; T. Peters and N. Austin. 1985. *A Passion for Excellence.* New York, NY: Random House; L.S. Myrsiades. 1987. Corporate Stories as Cultural Communications in the Organizational Setting. *Management Communication Quarterly* 1, 1: 84–120; D.M. Armstrong. 1992. *Managing by Storying Around.* New York, NY: Doubleday Currency; A. Laufer. 1996. *Simultaneous Management: Managing Projects in a Dynamic Environment.* New York, NY: AMACOM, American Management Association; N.L. Breuer. 1998. The Power of Storytelling. *Workforce* 77, 12: 36–41.

51. See A.S. Bucklerand and K.A. Zien. 1996. The Spirituality of Innovation: Learning from Stories. *Journal of Product Innovation Management* 13, 5: 391–405; G. Shaw, R. Brown, and P. Bromiley. 1998. Strategic Stories: How 3M Is Rewriting Business Planning. *Harvard Business Review* 76, 3 (May–June): 41–50, 233–44; T.A. Stewart. 1998. The Cunning Plots of Leadership. *Fortune* 138, 5 (September 7): 165–6; E. Weil. Every Leader Tells a Story. 1998. *Fast Company* (June–July): 38–40; B. Kaye and B. Jacobson. 1999. True Tales and Tall Tales: The Power of Organizational Storytelling. *Training and Development* 53, 3 (March): 44–52.

52. G. Hamel and C.K. Prahalad. 1994. *Competing for the Future.* Boston, MA: Harvard Business School Press, 59–61. Argyris and Schon term unlearning as "double-loop

learning," while Handy calls it "reframing." See C. Argyris and D.A. Schon. 1978. *Organizational Learning: A Theory of Action Perspective*. Reading, MA: Addison-Wesley; and C. Handy. 1989. *The Age of Unreason*. Boston, MA: Harvard Business School Press. Laufer and his associates focused extensively on the needed unlearning in project planning. See A. Laufer. 1990. Essentials of Project Planning: The Owner's Perspective. *Journal of Management in Engineering* 6, 2: 162–76; G.A. Howell, A. Laufer, and G. Ballard. 1993. Uncertainty and Project Objectives. *Project Appraisal* 8, 1: 37–43; A. Laufer, R.L. Tucker, A. Shapira, and A.J. Shenhar. 1994. The Multiplicity Concept in Construction Project Planning. *Construction Management and Economics* 11: 53–65.

53. J.G. March, L.S. Sproull, and M. Tamuz. 1991. Learning from Samples of One or Fewer. *Organization Science* 2: 1–13. Dee Hock, who was the founder and CEO of VISA USA and VISA International, makes a strong connection between creativity and unlearning: "The problem is never how to get new, innovative thoughts into your mind, but how to get old ones out." M. Waldrop. 1996. Dee Hock on Management. *Fast Company* 5 (October): 79.

54. P.F. Drucker. 1999. *Management Challenges for the 21st Century*. New York, NY: Harper Collins.

55. One specific unlearning issue that requires special attention is the impact of context on projects. Peter Drucker argues that since the study of management first began in the 1930s, several assumptions regarding the *realities* of management have been held by most scholars, writers, and practitioners. He further argues that today these assumptions must be unlearned. Two of these assumptions are germane to our study. First, "there is (or there must be) ONE right organization structure." Second, "there is (or there must be) ONE right way to manage people." P.F. Drucker. 1999. *Management Challenges for the 21st Century*. New York, NY: Harper Collins, 5, 17. For the most part, the project management literature has not given explicit treatment to context issues and has thus implicitly endorsed the "one best way" approach. Recently, however, there are some notable exceptions by proponents of Agile Project Management. For example, Highsmith states that "there is no silver bullet, but there are Lone Rangers who have arsenals of bullets for different situations." J.A. Highsmith III. 2000. *Adaptive Software Development—A Collaborative Approach to Managing Complex Systems*. New York, NY: Dorset House Publishing, 85. In addition, Beck, who is extremely critical of 'taylorism' (i.e., the principles of Fredrick W. Taylor, the father of Scientific Management), says, "My experience is that these principles make no sense as strategies for software development, no business sense, and no human sense." See Beck's annotated bibliography of F.W. Taylor's book *The Principles of Scientific Management*. 1998 (first edited in 1911). See also K. Beck. 2000. *Extreme Programming Explained: Embrace Change*. Boston, MA: Addison-Wesley, 172. W. Royce also recommends tailoring the process: "While there are some universal themes and techniques, it is always necessary to tailor the process to the specific needs of the project at hand." W. Royce. 1998. *Software Project Management: A Unified Framework*. Boston, MA: Addison-Wesley, 209–20.

56. P. Senge. 1990. *Fifth Discipline: The Art and Practice of the Learning Organization*. New York, NY: Doubleday Currency, 175.

57. R. Nisbett and L.Ross. 1980. *Human Inference: Strategies and Shortcomings of Social Judgment*. Englewood Cliffs, NJ: Prentice-Hall, 45–53, 188–90.

58. R. McKee. 2003. Storytelling That Moves People: A Conversation with Screenwriting Coach Robert McKee. *Harvard Business Review* 81, 6: 51–91. Charles

Handy suggests that reframing often needs some outside stimulus: "Re-framers need to walk in other people's worlds from time to time." C. Handy. 1989. *The Age of Unreason*. Boston, MA: Harvard Business School Press, 229–30. Heifetz says "Leadership is both active and reflective. One has to alternate between participating and observing." Using a dancing metaphor, he suggests that to discern the larger patterns on the dance floor *"we have to stop moving and get on the balcony."* R.A. Heifetz. 1999. *Leadership without Easy Answers*. Cambridge, MA: Harvard University Press, 252. We believe that listening, discussing, and reading stories may often serve as a substitute for "walking in other people's worlds" or "getting on the balcony."

59. In 1991, Laufer was invited to consult for Procter & Gamble (P&G). Laufer found that it was not easy to change a mind-set. He proposed the use of storytelling as the primary tool for introducing change at P&G. The book that he coauthored with three P&G project managers and that contains 70 stories told by 28 project managers is still in use at P&G. *In Quest of Project Excellence through Stories*. 1994, eds. A. Laufer, R.C. Volkman, G.W. Davenport, and S. Terry. Cincinnati, OH: Procter & Gamble.

60. D.A. Kolb. 1984. *Experiential Learning*. Englewood Cliffs, NJ: Prentice-Hall, 41.

61. D.A. Kolb. 1984. *Experiential Learning*. Englewood Cliffs, NJ: Prentice-Hall, 61–98.

62. Gardner identifies seven factors (he also terms them "levers") that may be at work during a significant change of mind: reason, research, resonance, representational redescriptions, resources and rewards, real-world events, and resistances. H. Gardner. 2004. *Changing Minds, The Art and Science of Changing Our Own and Other People's Minds*. Boston, MA: Harvard Business School Press, 16–8.

63. Throughout all these years of research, while developing the theory, refining it, and at times overhauling it, I was trying to adhere to Whetten's idea of a good theorist: "Sensitivity to the competing virtues of parsimony and comprehensiveness is the hallmark of a good theorist." Comprehensiveness addresses the question of whether all relevant factors are included, while parsimony addresses the question of whether some factors should be deleted because they add little additional value to our understanding. D.A. Whetten. 1989. What Constitutes a Theoretical Contribution? *Academy of Management Review* 14, 4:490–5.

64. In most of the classic books on project management, "planning and control" has been portrayed as the backbone of delivering successful projects, with the focus primarily on tools and practices. Since many practitioners are used to thinking about "project planning and control" in terms of practices, each guideline in the first chapter is further divided into two specific practices.

65. You will first realize that the application of the principles, each one individually and the five as a whole, is dependent on the project context, and then you will probably embrace the notion that the individual principles are interconnected and that each principle serves as a context for all the other principles. As you progress through this book, you will also realize that the principles nest inside each other, like Chinese boxes. To embrace each individual principle, you must embrace ALL five of them, like the parts of a hologram. In his explanation about "why our old pictures of the world do not work anymore," Mitroff finds the hologram to be an appropriate metaphor: "A hologram . . . has this interesting property that if any part of it is enlarged, one does not get merely an enlarged picture of the part being blown up but a fuzzier picture of the whole holographic picture! That is, a hologram has the strange property that the whole is contained in every part but not to the same degree of clarity and sharpness." I.I. Mitroff. 1985. Why Our Old Pictures of the World Do Not Work Anymore. In *Doing Research That Is Useful for Theory and Practice*, eds.

E.E. Lawler, A.M. Mohrman, Jr., S.A. Mohrman, G.E. Ledford, Jr., and T.G. Cummings and Associates, 19–45. San Francisco, CA: Jossey-Bass Publishers.

66. Eccles and Nohria argue that "knowledge and action, theory and practice, follow one another in a cycle of contemplation and application. Which comes first is often difficult to say and is in the end unimportant." R. Eccles and N. Nohria. 1992. *Beyond the Hype: Rediscovering the Essence of Management.* Boston, MA: Harvard Business School Press, 175.

67. *The Fifth Discipline Fieldbook* presents the following direct and most natural way for unlearning: "Buckminster Fuller used to say that if you want to teach people a new way of thinking, don't bother trying to teach them. Instead, give them a tool, the use of which will lead them to new ways of thinking." P.M. Senge, A. Kleiner, C. Roberts, and B. Smith. 1994. *The Fifth Discipline Fieldbook: Strategies and Tools for Building a Learning Organization.* New York, NY: Doubleday Currency, 28. Using the new tool will naturally trigger a reflection process, and the unlearning process usually requires several cycles of using the tool and reflecting on this new experience. In our case, implementing part of the principles constitutes "using a tool," yet it is a complex tool. Therefore, going to the book and reading the relevant material may greatly facilitate the required reflection. Eventually, several cycles of this process—implementing part of the principles followed by reading the relevant material—may pave the way for the required unlearning.

References

a. "Hurry to the Classroom, Your Instructor Just Died," Edward Hoffman, NASA. 2000. In A. Laufer and E.J. Hoffman, *Project Management Success Stories*, 54–7. New York, NY: John Wiley & Sons.

b. "Cleaning Out the Closet," Scott Cameron, Procter & Gamble. 2004. *Ask Magazine* 20 (November): 19–21 http://appel.nasa.gov/ask/about/overview/index.html

c. "Happy New Year," Terry Little, U.S. Air Force. 2005. In A. Laufer, T. Post, and E.J. Hoffman, *Shared Voyage: Learning and Unlearning from Remarkable Projects*, 79–81. Washington, D.C.: The NASA History Series; "Six is not Seven," Terry Little, U.S. Air Force. 2005. In A. Laufer, T. Post, and E.J. Hoffman, *Shared Voyage: Learning and Unlearning from Remarkable Projects*, 104–5. Washington, D.C.: The NASA History Series.

Chapter 1

Notes

1. B.H. Boar. 1984. *Application Prototyping.* New York, NY: Wiley, 3.

2. A.M. Davis. 1995. *201 Principles of Software Development.* New York, NY: McGraw-Hill, 48.

3. D.C. Gause and G.M. Weinberg. 1989. *Exploring Requirements: Quality Before Design.* New York, NY: Dorset House Publishing, 17.

4. R.S. Pressman. 2001. *Software Engineering: A Practitioner's Approach,* 5th ed. New York, NY: McGraw-Hill; K.T. Ulrich and S.D. Eppinger. 2000. *Product Design and Development,* 2nd ed. New York, NY: McGraw-Hill.

5. A. Laufer. 1989. *Owner's Project Planning: The Process Approach,* Source Document 45. The Construction Industry Institute, the University of Texas at Austin.

6. Project Organization Task Force. 1991. *Organizing for Project Success*, Publication 12–2. The Construction Industry Institute, the University of Texas at Austin. See also J.R. Turner and R.A. Cochrane. 1993. Goals-and-Methods Matrix: Coping with Projects with Ill Defined Goals and/or Methods of Achieving Them. *International Journal of Project Management* 11, 2: 93–102.

7. D.N. Michael. 1997. *Learning to Plan and Planning to Learn*, 2nd ed. Alexandria, VA: Miles River Press, 128. See also P.J.H. Schoemaker. 2002. *Profiting from Uncertainty*, Appendix A: The Psychology of Uncertainty. New York, NY: The Free Press, 223–31. On the basis of research literature, Schoemaker concludes that "our myopic eyes tend to narrow our range of view, and so fail to appreciate the full scale of uncertainty . . . In addition to myopic and distorted perceptions about risk, humans also tend to have rather timid souls when acting upon risk (however they perceive it)."

8. G. Howell, A. Laufer, and G. Ballard. 1993. Uncertainty and Project Objectives. *Project Appraisal* 8, 1: 37–43.

9. J.G. March. 1976. The Technology of Foolishness. In *Ambiguity and Choice in Organizations*, eds. J.G. March and J.P. Olsen, 69–81. Bergen: Universitetsforlaget.

10. H. Minzberg. 1990. The Design School: Reconsidering the Basic Premises of Strategic Management. *Strategic Management Journal* 11: 171–95.

11. M.A. Cusumano. 2004. *The Business of Software: What Every Manager, Programmer and Entrepreneur Must Know to Thrive and Survive in Good Times and Bad.* New York, NY: Free Press, 132.

12. J. Hauschildt. 1986. Goals and Problem-Solving in Innovative Decisions. In *Empirical Research on Organizational Decision-Making*, eds. E. Witte and H.J. Zimmermann, 3–19. North-Holland: Elsevier. Daniel Isenberg says, "One implication of acting/thinking cycles is that action is often part of defining the problem, not just implementing the solution." See D.J. Isenberg. 1984. How Senior Managers Think. *Harvard Business Review* 62 (November–December): 80–90.

13. N.R. Baker, S.G. Green, and A.S. Bean. 1986. Why R&D Projects Succeed or Fail. *Research Management* 29, 6 (November–December): 29–34. Pearson and Brockhoff provided data showing that most successful R&D projects move from idea to reality via an uncertainty reduction path. They start with high uncertainty in the ends and/or means and finish when both ends and means uncertainty is low. In comparison, most unsuccessful R&D projects still suffer from high ends uncertainty even at the end of the process. A. Pearson and K. Brockhoff. 1994. The Uncertainty Map and Project Management. *Project Appraisal* 9, 3: 211–5.

14. Mats Engwall discusses the "importance of imprecision" at the early stages of the project. According to Engwall, a too-detailed proposal early on in the project may render it more difficult to harness the required support from the relevant parties. See M. Engwall. 2002. The Futile Dream of the Perfect Goal. In *Beyond Project Management: New Perspectives on the Temporary—Permanent Dilemma*, eds. K. Sahlin-Andersson and A. Söderholm, 241–60. Stockholm: Lund: Liber/Abstrakt, CBS-Press.

15. G. Stalk and T.M. Hout. 1990. *Competing Against Time*. New York, NY: The Free Press; S.C. Wheelwright and K.B. Clark. 1992. *Revolutionizing Product Development*. New York, NY: The Free Press. Traditionally, factors such as competitive considerations and government regulations result in a barrier between the customer and potential suppliers until the customer finally awards a contract. Applying the practice "Seek Input from the Implementer," however, requires a different relationship between the customer and the suppliers than has historically existed. Otherwise, the potential for accelerating project speed is limited.

16. C.B. Tatum, J.A. Vanegas, and J.M. Williams. 1986. *Constructability Improvement during Conceptual Planning*, Source Document 4. The Construction Industry Institute, the University of Texas at Austin; C.B. Tatum, J.A. Vanegas, and J.M. Williams. 1987. *Constructability Improvement Using Prefabrication, Preassembly, and Modularization*, Source Document 25. The Construction Industry Institute, the University of Texas at Austin; C. Gray. 1983. *Buildability—The Construction Contribution*, Occasional Paper No. 29. Englemere, UK: The Chartered Institute of Building.

17. See, for example, A. Laufer. 1996. *Simultaneous Management: Managing Projects in a Dynamic Environment*. New York, NY: AMACOM; K. Bozdogan, J. Deyst, D. Hoult, and M. Lucas. 1998. Architectural Innovation in Product Development through Early Supplier Integration. *R&D Management* 28, 3: 163–73.

18. B.H. Boar. 1984. *Application Prototyping*. New York, NY: Wiley. The book makes a very effective case for the use of prototyping in data processing projects. B.W. Boehm, T.E. Gray, and T. Seewaldt. 1984. Prototyping Versus Specifying: A Multiproject Experiment. *IEEE Transaction on Software Engineering*, SE-10, 3: 290–303. K.B. Clark and T. Fujimoto. 1991. *Product Development Performance*. Boston, MA: Harvard Business School Press. See also M. Schrage. 2000. *Serious Play: How the World's Best Companies Simulate to Innovate*. Boston, MA: Harvard Business School Press.

19. As part of an elaborate review of the various strategy formation schools, Mintzberg presents the "Evolution of the Learning School." See H. Mintzberg, 1990. Strategy Formation: Schools of Thought. In *Perspectives on Strategic Management*, ed. J. Frederickson, 147–59. New York, NY: Harper Business. See also H. Mintzberg. 1994. *The Rise and Fall of Strategic Planning: Reconceiving Roles for Planning, Plans, Planners*. New York, NY: The Free Press.

20. One attempt to address this issue can be found in Barry Boehm and Richard Turner. 2004. *Balancing Agility and Discipline: A Guide for the Perplexed*. Boston, MA: Addison-Wesley.

21. R.L. Ackoff. 1970. *A Concept of Corporate Planning*. New York, NY: Wiley, 3.

22. K. Weick and K.M. Sutcliffe. 2001. *Managing the Unexpected*. San Francisco, CA: Jossey-Bass, 51–83.

23. A. Laufer, R.L. Tucker, A. Shapira, and A.J. Shenhar. 1994. The Multiplicity Concept in Construction Planning. *Construction Management and Economics* 11: 53–65.

24. A. Laufer and R.L. Tucker. 1987. Is Construction Project Planning Really Doing Its Job? A Critical Examination of Focus, Role and Process. *Construction Management and Economics* 5, 3: 243–66. Ackoff provides a classic definition for control: "To plan is to make decisions. Control is the evaluation of decisions . . . once they have been implemented. The process of control involves four steps:

   a. Predicting the outcome of decisions in the form of performance measures.
   b. Collecting information on actual performance.
   c. Comparing actual with predicted performance.
   d. When a decision is shown to have been deficient, correcting the procedure that produced it and correcting its consequences where possible."

   R.L. Ackoff. 1970. *A Concept of Corporate Planning*. New York, NY: Wiley, 112.

25. The basic assumption in the classic project management literature is that "the core of project management is planning the project." J. Packendorff. 1995. Inquiring

into the Temporary Organization: New Directions for Project Management Research. *Scandinavian Journal of Management* 11, 4: 319–33. This was also the case outside projects, in management of the permanent organization. Herbert Simon stated, "What part does decision making play in managing? I shall find it convenient to take mild liberties with the English language by using 'decision making' as though it were synonymous with 'managing.'" H.A. Simon. 1960. *The New Science of Management Decision.* New York, NY: Harper & Row, 1. In the first issue of *The Journal of the Academy of Management,* Paul Dauten analyzes the relationship between planning and management and asserts that "one might say that the fundamental principle underlying all of management is planning." P.M. Dauten Jr. 1958. Management Philosophy: The Time Dimensions of Planning. *Journal of the Academy of Management* 1, 1: 23–33.

26. CPM is a scheduling technique using precedence diagrams for graphic display of the work plan. This method is used to determine the length of a project and to identify activities that are critical to its completion.

27. A. Davies and M. Hobday. 2005. *The Business of Projects: Managing Innovation in Complex Products and Systems.* Cambridge, UK: Cambridge University Press, 152.

28. R. Stout Jr. 1980. *Management or Control?: The Organizational Challenge.* Bloomington, IN: Indiana University Press, 25.

29. R. Stout Jr. 1980. *Management or Control?: The Organizational Challenge.* Bloomington, IN: Indiana University Press, 26.

30. In his comprehensive review of the development of project management, this is how Morris viewed this issue: "Writing in the area of planning and control seemed livelier, but largely only because of the continuing developments in Information Technology." P.W.G. Morris. 1994. *The Management of Projects.* London, UK: Thomas Telford, 217.

31. P.B. Vaill. 1996. *Learning as a Way of Being: Strategies for Survival in a World of Permanent White Water.* San Francisco, CA: Jossey-Bass Publishers, 10–14. Leifer et al. classify uncertainty by its sources: market uncertainty (e.g., customer needs may fluctuate); organizational uncertainty (e.g., shaky commitment of the sponsoring organization); technological uncertainty (e.g., manufacturing the product involves innovative processes); and resources uncertainty (e.g., shortage of competent workers). R. Leifer, C.M. McDermott, G. Colarelli O'Connor, L.S. Peters, M.P. Rice, and R.W. Veryzer. *Radical Innovation: How Mature Companies Can Outsmart Upstarts.* 2000. Boston, MA: Harvard Business School Press, 22. Chen, Reilly, and Lynn classify uncertainty by dimension (newness vs. change) and by source (market vs. technology). J. Chen, R.R. Reilly, and G.S. Lynn. 2005. Speed: Too Much of a Good Thing? *Technology Management: A Unifying Discipline for Melting the Boundaries* (July 31–August 4): 520–32.

32. I.I. Mitroff. 1988. *Break Away Thinking.* New York, NY: John Wiley & Sons.

33. P.W.G. Morris. 1994. *The Management of Projects.* London, UK: Thomas Telford Services, 273.

34. P.W.G. Morris. 1994. *The Management of Projects.* London, UK: Thomas Telford Services, 217. Underestimation of uncertainty was reported by Howell and Ballard, who found that in 85 percent of the projects in their sample, managers underestimated the extent of uncertainty. G.A. Howell and G. Ballard. 1995. Lean Production Theory: Moving Beyond "Can-Do." *Unpublished paper, University of New Mexico, Civil Engineering Department.* Albuquerque, New Mexico. This phenomenon is true outside project management as well. March states that "there are

indications that decision makers, in effect, seek to deny uncertainty . . . Decision makers tend to exaggerate their control over their environment." J.G. March. 1994. *A Primer on Decision Making.* New York, NY: The Free Press, 37. D.N. Michael. 1997. *Learning to Plan and Planning to Learn.* 2nd ed. Alexandria, VA: Miles River Press, 144.

35. See G. Stalk. 1988. Time—The Next Resource of Competitive Advantage. *Harvard Business Review* 66, 4 (July–August): 41–51; T. Peters. 1990. Drucker, Ohmae, Porter and Peters—Management Briefing. *The Economist—Special Report No. 1202* (April): 70; P.G. Smith and D.G. Reinertsen. 1991. *Developing Products in Half the Time.* New York, NY: Van Nostrand Reinhold; C. Meyer. 1993. *Fast Cycle Time.* New York, NY: The Free Press.

36. J.D. Blackburn. 1991. *Time-Based Competition: The Next Battleground in American Manufacturing.* Homewood, IL: Business One Irwin, 201.

37. W.H. Davidow and M.S. Malone. 1992. *The Virtual Corporation.* New York, NY: Harper Business, 22.

38. C. Handy. 2002. *The Elephant and the Flea: Reflections of a Reluctant Capitalist.* Boston, MA: Harvard Business School Press, 101.

39. Lundin and Söderholm write, "For any organization, time is generally regarded as a scarce resource, as is often alluded to in terms such as 'time is money.' For a temporary organization the handling of time is more complicated, since time is literally limited: it ends." R.A. Lundin and A. Söderholm. 1995. A Theory of the Temporary Organization. *Scandinavian Journal of Management* 11, 3: 437–55. Kessler and Bierly report that "evidence from 75 new product development projects clearly indicates that speed is positively related to quality and has the greatest influence on success." E.H. Kessler and P.E. Bierly III. 2002. Is Faster Really Better? An Empirical Test of the Implications of Innovation Speed. *IEEE Transactions on Engineering Management* 49, 1: 2–12.

40. J.G. March and H.A. Simon. 1958. *Organizations.* New York, NY: Wiley; R.M. Cyert and J.G. March. 1963. *Behavioral Theory of the Firm.* New York, NY: Prentice-Hall.

41. H. Mintzberg. 1973. *The Nature of Managerial Work.* New York, NY: Harper & Row; R. Steward. 1967. *Managers and Their Jobs.* Maidenhead, UK: McGraw-Hill. It is illuminating to listen to the lessons that one scholar learned from a short period of real-life experience as a practicing executive. Professor Grayson, dean of the School of Business Administration of Southern Methodist University, served for 16 months as chair of the Price Commission in Phase II of President Richard M. Nixon's Economic Stabilization Program. His conclusions concerning management scientists and the issue of managers' insufficient time were that management scientists do not sufficiently understand the constraint of time on decision making and that their techniques are so time consuming to use that managers pass them by. C.J. Grayson. 1973. Management Science and Business Practice. *Harvard Business Review* 51, 4 (July–August): 41–8.

42. T.H. Davenport and J.C. Beck. 2001. *The Attention Economy: Understanding the New Currency of Business.* Boston, MA: Harvard Business School Press, 4–6.

43. T.H. Davenport and J.C. Beck. 2001. *The Attention Economy: Understanding the New Currency of Business.* Boston, MA: Harvard Business School Press, 11.

44. T. Roszak. 1994. *The Cult of Information: A Neo-Luddite Treatise on High Tech, Artificial Intelligence and the True Art of Thinking,* 2nd ed. Berkeley, CA: University of California Press.

45. J.R. Galbraith. 1977. *Organization Design.* Reading, MA: Addison-Wesley; P.C. Dinsmore. 1982. The Project Manager's Time Quandary Surveys Results and Suggested Solutions. *Proceedings of the Project Management Institute,* Toronto, 1–9.

46. Mintzberg argues that "somehow, planners want to retain the stability that planning brings to an organization—planning's main contribution, while enabling it to respond quickly to external changes in the environment—planning's main nemesis . . . What the writers on planning failed to address was the strategists' fundamental dilemma of having to reconcile the concurrent but conflicting needs for change and stability." H. Mintzberg. 1994. *The Rise and Fall of Strategic Planning: Re-conceiving Roles for Planning, Plans, Planners.* New York, NY: The Free Press, 184–8.

47. B.K. Muirhead and W.L. Simon. 1999. *High Velocity Leadership: The Mars Pathfinder Approach to Faster, Better, Cheaper.* New York, NY: Harper Collins Publishers, 23–4.

48. B.K. Muirhead and W.L. Simon. 1999. *High Velocity Leadership: The Mars Pathfinder Approach to Faster, Better, Cheaper.* New York, NY: Harper Collins Publishers, 86–7.

49. This approach finds support in the literature. D.L. Parnas and D.M. Weiss. 1985. Active Design Reviews: Principles and Practices. *Proceedings of the 8th International Conference on Software Engineering,* 132–6. Parnas and Weiss recommend that "the characteristics of the reviewers should be explicitly specified before reviewers are selected . . . The designers should pose questions to the reviewers, rather than vice versa." J.F. Maranzano, S.A. Rozsypal, G.H. Zimmerman, G.W. Warnken, P.E. Wirth, and D.M. Weiss. 2005. Architecture Reviews: Practice and Experience. *Software IEEE* 22, 2: 34–43. The authors argue that "a review process isn't a project's audit or evaluation against some arbitrary standard, nor it is a tutorial or evaluation of the architects' performance . . . The project members don't expect the review team to solve issues but rather to apply its expertise to uncover issues . . . A review's primary customers are the project team members and management."

50. R.L. Ackoff. 1970. *A Concept of Corporate Planning.* New York, NY: Wiley, 129–37. The idea shared by Ackoff about the value of the planning process (vs. the planning product), which was presented in the context of planning in general, found strong support in the agile approach for software projects. Boehm and Turner share an e-mail they received from Kent Beck, cocreator of XP, saying that "I think the phrase 'plan driven' [the way Boehm and Turner describe the traditional project management approaches] is the key. I would characterize XP as 'planning driven' in contrast." B. Boehm and R. Turner. 2004. *Balancing Agility and Discipline: A Guide for the Perplexed.* Boston, MA: Addison-Wesley, 34–5.

51. A. Laufer and R.L. Tucker. 1988. Competence and Timing Dilemma in Construction Planning. *Construction Management and Economics* 6, 4: 339–55; A. Laufer, R.L. Tucker, A. Shapira, and A.J. Shenhar. 1994. The Multiplicity Concept in Construction Planning. *Construction Management and Economics* 11: 53–65; J.S. Hekimian and H. Mintzberg. 1968. The Planning Dilemma: There is a Way Out. *Management Review:* 4–17.

52. J.C. Emery. 1969. *Organizational Planning and Control Systems, Theory and Technology.* London, UK: Macmillan; P.P. Le Breton and D.A. Henning. 1961. *Planning Theory.* Englewood Cliffs, NJ: Prentice-Hall; C.W. Churchman. 1979. *The Systems Approach.* New York, NY: Dell Publishing.

53. A. Laufer and R.L. Tucker. 1988. Competence and Timing Dilemma in Construction Planning. *Construction Management and Economics* 6, 4: 339–55.

54. See, for example, B.C. Paulson. 1976. Designing to Reduce Construction Cost. *Journal of the Construction Division*, ASCE 102: 587–92; J. Kelly and S. Male. 1993. *Value Management in Design and Construction*. London, UK: E.& F.N. Spon; J.R. Dixon and M.R. Duffey. 1990. The Neglect of Engineering Design. *California Management Review* 32, 2: 9–23.

55. The degree of detail does not depend only on the planning horizon; it is also adjusted to the project's degree of uncertainty. The plan should provide a correspondingly higher degree of detail if uncertainty is low—either because the technology is well established by past experience or because the project objectives are not problematic and environmental conditions are stable. When uncertainty is high, the formal plan's degree of detail for the near term is reduced and its decrease is accelerated across the planning horizon. Also, the greater the uncertainty, the lower the degree of formality in all three kinds of plans.

56. Steven Pender concludes that "the PMBOK and other reference material is based on probability-based risk management theory. Analysis of the underlying *assumptions of the probability-based approach shows it has limited applicability*." S. Pender. 2001. Managing Incomplete Knowledge: Why Risk Management is Not Sufficient. *International Journal of Project Management* 19, 2: 79–87. See also S. Lichtenberg. 1974. The Successive Principle-Procedure for a Minimum Degree of Detailing. *Proceedings of the Sixth Annual Seminar/Symposia of the Project Management Institute.* Washington, D.C., 570–8.

57. The common formats for Action Plans are standard forms, tables, and time charts, as well as drawings and sketches of production methods (when necessary). In construction, for example, the foreman/general foreman may prepare a weekly Action Plan in a simple matrix form. The individual jobs assigned to work crews are entered in the rows of the matrix, while the crew tasks for each day of the week are detailed in each one of the five columns. The following items are typically addressed in the matrix: crew assignments, materials, tools and equipment, production rates, safety hazards, coordination with other crews, and logistics. At the start-up phase of the project, the weekly Action Plan at the foreman/general foreman level is often prepared as a one-page bar chart in which 10 to 50 activities are detailed by half days or even by the hour.

58. This early preparation allows the project manager to adopt a diverging/converging planning process. In this process, the project manager first starts by diverging, that is, moving outward to gather information and ideas and to generate alternatives. Only then is the project manager ready to converge, that is, to move inward, focus, evaluate, and select.

59. The Look-Ahead Plan also provides direct guidelines for subsequent Action Plans. Thus, the three-month Look-Ahead Plan is employed by the project superintendent to prepare the monthly Action Plans, while the general foreman prepares the weekly Action Plan on the basis of three-week Look-Ahead Plan. In particular, the preparer of the Action Plan uses the Look-Ahead Plan to learn about the expected results for the coming period, as well as the major means to be utilized in achieving those results. The Look-Ahead Plan also identifies medium- or long-term issues that demand immediate attention, for example, equipment that will be installed only six months from now yet must be ordered immediately. Thus, the current Action Plan will address the equipment-ordering task.

60. This forecast, however, plays several major roles in a project's life. It serves as a basis for establishing contracts, both with external parties (contractors and suppliers) and

internal parties (other functional units). For these parties, the forecast defines the key assumptions needed for further planning; for example, on the basis of the forecast, the customer may set or revise the tenant occupancy schedule. It also provides the yardstick with which the overall project performance is evaluated and controlled throughout the project's life.

61. L.R. Sayles and M.K. Chandler. 1971. *Managing Large Systems: Organizations for the Future.* New York, NY: Harper & Row, 219; G.H.A. Morton. 1983. Human Dynamics in Project Planning. In *Project Management Handbook*, eds. D.I. Cleland and W.R. King. New York, NY: Van Nostrand Reinhold; D. Mason. 1984. The CPM Technique in Construction: A Critique. *AACE Transactions*, Montreal, Canada, E.2.1–E.2.10; A. Laufer and R.L. Tucker. 1987. Is Construction Project Planning Really Doing Its Job? A Critical Examination of Focus, Role and Process. *Construction Management and Economics* 5, 3: 243–66; D. Yahdav. 1989. Resource Management: An Imperfect Science. *PC Magazine* (May 16): 164; W.M. Dirsmith, S.F. Jablonsky, and A.D. Luzi. 1980. Planning and Control in the U.S. Federal Government: A Critical Analysis of PPB, MBO, and ZBB. *Strategic Management Journal* 1, 4: 303–29.

62. In a study that focused on a $20-million model project lasting 18 months, major revisions, which included changes in implementation methods or changes in the sequence of activities, were found to be introduced on an average of every 3.5 months. Under conditions of high uncertainty, frequency of updating was estimated to increase to an average of every 1.5 months. D. Cohenca, A. Laufer, and W.B. Ledbetter. 1989. Factors Affecting Construction Planning Efforts. *Construction Engineering and Management,* ASCE 115, 1: 70–89; A. Laufer and R.L. Tucker. 1987. Is Construction Project Planning Really Doing Its Job? A Critical Examination of Focus, Role and Process. *Construction Management and Economics* 5, 3: 243-66; A. Laufer and G. Howell. 1993. Construction Planning: Revising the Paradigm. *Project Management Journal* 24, 3: 23–33; A. Laufer, R.L. Tucker, A. Shapira, and A.J. Shenhar. 1994. The Multiplicity Concept in Construction Planning. *Construction Management and Economics* 11: 53–65; R. Stout Jr. 1980. *Management or Control?: The Organizational Challenge.* Bloomington, IN: Indiana University Press, 24–5.

63. H.L.S. Younes and R.G. Simmons. 2002. On the Role of Ground Actions in Refinement Planning. In *Proceedings of the Sixth International Conference on Artificial Intelligence Planning and Scheduling Systems*, eds. M. Ghallab, J. Hertzberg, and P. Traverso, 54–61. Toulouse, France: AAAI Press.

64. E.G. Flamholtz. 1996. *Effective Management Control: Theory and Practice.* Boston, MA: Kluwer Academic Publishers, 7. Flamholtz asserts that "many organizations mistakenly believe that planning is complete when a written plan has been developed. Unfortunately, this is merely the end of the beginning, and an effective control system is required if plans are to be fulfilled. Another way to look at it is that planning is actually a component of a control process, and not a stand-alone system, per se." Flamholtz reaches his conclusion in reference to permanent organizations. Our analysis shows that while in temporary organizations (projects), control and planning are also intertwined, very often the relative roles are reversed. That is, under dynamic conditions, control can be thought of as a component of planning. James A. Highsmith III stresses the importance of learning in the development of software projects. He argues that the assumption underlying traditional project management is that "deviations from the plan are mistakes that must be corrected."

In contrast, the new project management outlook maintains that "deviations guide us toward the correct solution." J.A. Highsmith III. 2000. *Adaptive Software Development*. New York, NY: Dorset House Publishing, 42–3. He concludes that "success is determined by the adequacy of the feedback, not by the accuracy of the feed-forward."

65. A. Neely and M. Al Najjar. 2006. Management Learning Not Management Control: The True Role of Performance Measurement? *California Management Review* 48, 3: 101.

66. G.S. Lynn, M. Mazzuca, J.G. Morone, and A.S. Paulson. 1998. Learning is the Critical Success Factor in Developing Truly New Products. *Research Technology Management* 41, 3: 45–51.

67. M.T. Pich, C.H. Loch, and A. De Meyer. 2002. On Uncertainty, Ambiguity, and Complexity in Project Management. *Management Science* 48, 8: 1008–23.

68. M.S. Puddicombe. 2006. The Limitations of Planning: The Importance of Learning. *Journal of Construction Engineering and Management*, ASCE 132, 9: 949–55. In their research on total quality management (TQM) implementation projects, Sitkin, Sutcliffe, and Schroeder found that: "the way that these basic TQM precepts have been articulated, extended, and applied has not reflected the distinct, learning-oriented requirements associated with higher levels of uncertainty." S.B. Sitkin, K.M. Sutcliffe, and R.G. Schroeder. 1994. Distinguishing Control from Learning in Total Quality Management: A Contingency Perspective. *Academy of Management Review* 19, 3: 537–64.

69. A.L. Stinchcombe. 1990. *Information and Organizations*. Berkeley, CA: University of California Press, 2.

70. See, for example, J.D. Cullen and C.W. Nankervis. 1985. Overcoming the Luddite Factor: Some Behavioral Aspects of the Field Supervisor's Role in Construction Planning. *International Journal of Project Management* 3, 3: 133–40.

71. Galbraith cites studies reporting that higher uncertainty results in a higher frequency of scheduled and unscheduled meetings. R. Galbraith. 1977. *Organization Design*. Reading, MA: Addison-Wesley. Documenting case studies in the United States and the United Kingdom, J. Nahapiet and H. Nahapiet reached a similar conclusion with specific regard to the planning process in construction projects. They found planning indeed to be frequently carried out by meetings. J. Nahapiet and H. Nahapiet. 1985. *The Management of Construction Projects: Case Studies from the USA and UK*. London, UK: Chartered Institute of Building.

72. D.A. Kolb. 1984. *Experiential Learning: Experience as the Source of Learning and Development*. Englewood Cliffs, NJ: Prentice-Hall, 30–1. Kolb based his model primarily on the work of J. Dewey, K. Lewin, and J. Piaget (J. Dewey. 1938. *Experience and Education*, Indianapolis, In: Kappa Delta Phi; K. Lewin. 1951. *Field Theory in Social Sciences*. New York, NY: Harper and Row; J. Piaget. 1971. *Psychology and Epistemology*. Middlesex, UK: Penguin Books); D.A. Kolb, R.E. Boyatzis, and C. Mainemelis. 2001. Experiential Learning Theory: Previous Research and New Directions. In *Perspectives on Cognitive, Learning, and Thinking Styles*, eds. R.J. Sternberg and L.F. Zhang, 227–48. Mahwah, NJ: Lawrence Erlbaum.

73. D.A. Kolb. 1984. *Experiential Learning: Experience as the Source of Learning and Development*. Englewood Cliffs, NJ: Prentice-Hall, 41.

74. The four activities (experiencing, reflecting, thinking, and acting) refer to different time horizons. Practices covered by the other guidelines that are performed on a day-to-day basis, and in particular the Third Gray Guideline, provide additional

occasions for collecting feedback and reflecting. Another similar learning model is the one proposed by Daft and Weick, which consists of three components: Scanning (Data Collection regarding performance and the environment), Interpretation (Data Given Meaning), and Learning (Action Taken). R.L. Daft and K.E. Weick. 1984. Toward a Model of Organizations as Interpretation Systems. *Academy of Management Review* 9, 2: 284–95.

75. If the situation surrounding the project has changed and the project has to cope with less frequent changes and as a result has become more stable, then the detailed planning may be done for a longer time horizon. Thus, ongoing incremental control of the evolving plan may assume its classic role, that is, identifying deviations from the plan and adjusting execution to conform to the plan.

76. R. Simons. 1995. *Levers of Control: How Managers Use Innovative Control Systems to Drive Strategic Renewal.* Boston, MA: Harvard Business School Press, 5. In general, control in organizations has three major meanings: curbing and restraining, directing and commanding, and regulating. F.E. Kast and J.E. Rosenzweig. 1985. *Organization and Management: A Systems and Contingency Approach*, 4th ed. New York, NY: McGraw-Hill, 508. In the classic project management paradigm, the typical focus is on regulating. Regulating, in turn, can be carried out only after monitoring and evaluating the actual performance and comparing it with a standard (the plan).

77. In particular, the Third Gray Guideline (Adopt a Moving About Mode of Communication). One may say that under uncertain conditions, the essence of project planning is uncertainty reduction, while that of control is fast learning from project experience. This new role of project control is just one more example of how causal chains of events in organizations are usually circular rather than linear. That is, the project is started by planning, which is the best way to influence and control the project. "Control" is continued throughout implementation, but its main purpose is really to facilitate continuous planning. For a discussion on circular interdependence and causal loops in organizations, see K.E. Weick. 1979. *The Social Psychology of Organizing*, 2nd ed. New York, NY: Random House, 86.

78. For more on the external role of the project manager, see the research report of B.J. Cullen and O.C. Gadeken. 1990. *Competency Model of Program Managers in the DOD Acquisition Process.* Fort Belvoir, VA: Defense Systems Management College. See also D.G. Ancona and D.F. Caldwell. 1992. Bridging the Boundary: External Activity and Performance in Organizational Teams. *Administrative Science Quarterly* 37, 4 (December): 634–65.

79. A similar risk mitigation and tracking technique, termed either Watch-list or Critical Items/Issues Lists, is a component of a typical arsenal of Risk Management. See *NASA System Engineering Handbook*. 1995. Washington D.C.: National Aeronautics and Space Administration, 44. The first publication on scanning project environment was by the World Bank. See W.E. Smith, B.A. Toolen, and F.J. Lethem. 1980. The Design of Organizations for Rural Development Projects— A Progress Report. *Staff Working Paper No. 375.* Washington, D.C.: The World Bank. See also R. Youker. 1992. Managing the International Project Environment. *International Journal of Project Management* 10, 4: 219–26. For a discussion on planning assumptions, see G. Abonyi. 1982. SIAM: Strategic Impact and Assumptions-Identification Method for Project, Program, and Policy Planning. *Technological Forecasting and Social Changes* 22, 1: 31–52; J. Glahn and L. Borg. 1988. Decision-Making before "Go"-Supported by Risk Management. *Proceedings*

of the 9th World Congress on Project Management, Glasgow. On the concept of surfacing planning assumptions in reference to strategic planning, see R.O. Mason and I.I. Mitroff. 1981. *Challenging Strategic Planning Assumptions*. New York, NY: Wiley.

80. P.W.G. Morris. 1994. *The Management of Projects*. London, UK: Thomas Telford Services, 217.

81. C.W. Choo. 2001. Environmental Scanning as Information Seeking and Organizational Learning. *Information Research* 7, 1: an electronic journal. Enacting, which is one of the four scanning modes covered in the paper, is basically an attempt to influence the environment.

82. The book *Predictable Surprises* asserts that even when leaders know a problem exists, they often prefer inaction. This is due to the human tendency to maintain the status quo. Employing an explicit procedure like the CAR may sometimes help the organization to attend early on to these future surprises. M.G. Bazerman and M.D. Watkins. 2004. *Predictable Surprises: The Disasters You Should Have Seen Coming and How to Prevent Them*. Boston, MA: Harvard Business Press.

83. Ackoff compared two kinds of mistakes: "Commission (doing what should not have been done) and omission (not doing what should have been done). Errors of omission are generally much more serious than errors of commission, but errors of commission are the only ones picked up by most accounting systems." In the project world, one may substitute Ackoff's "accounting systems" with "project control systems." R. Ackoff. 1999. On Passing Through 80. *Systemic Practice and Action Research* 12, 4: 425–30. M.T. Pich, C.H. Loch, and A. De Meyer classify uncertainty, and they term this kind of omission as "unforeseen uncertainty," or simply, "unknown unknowns." M.T. Pich, C.H. Loch, and A. De Meyer. 2002. Managing Project Uncertainty: From Variation to Chaos. *MIT Sloan Management Review* (Winter): 60–7.

84. J. Forester. 1991. Anticipating Implementation: Reflective and Normative Practices in Policy Analysis and Planning. In *The Reflective Turn: Case Studies In and On Educational Practice*, ed. D.A. Schon, 191–212. New York, NY: Teachers College, Columbia University. Forester, who studied city planners, made a very useful distinction regarding anticipation as follows: "In ordinary language to anticipate and to expect do share meanings but they diverge significantly as well . . . To anticipate a crisis (or a project, a policy) is not simply to foresee or expect it, but to take steps beforehand to meet it."

85. D. Kahneman, P. Slovic, and A. Tversky. 1982. *Judgment under Uncertainty: Heuristics and Biases*. Cambridge, UK: Cambridge University Press, 508.

86. M. Landau. 1969. Redundancy, Rationality, and the Problem of Duplication and Overlap. *Public Administration Review* 29, 4 (July/August): 346–58. The author cites studies that established that if the elements of the system are statistically independent (unrelated), "it requires only arithmetic increases in redundancy to yield geometric increases in reliability" (of the entire system).

87. Emery argues that since aggregation increases the likelihood that compensating errors will occur, aggregate requirement can be predicted with greater relative accuracy than can the requirement for a smaller subset of the activities. J.C. Emery. 1969. *Organizational Planning and Control Systems: Theory and Technology*. London, UK: The Macmillan Company, 27.

88. Great skill and art are required to determine the "right" contingency allowance. If the requested contingency is too low and turns out to be insufficient, you may be regarded as an incompetent project manager. If, however, it is quoted too high in

order to be on the safe side, you may hurt the chances of being approved. This global allowance must be treated very carefully; otherwise, it may be easily consumed without serving its purpose of absorbing uncertainty. See, for example, Y. Asiedu and P. Gu. 1998. Product Life Cycle Cost Analysis: State of the Art Review. *International Journal of Production Research* 36, 4: 883–908.

89. The de-scoping practice is a proactive approach to absorbing uncertainty, for both the financing organization and the project itself. In this practice, components of project scope are clearly identified and decoupled from the rest of the scope early on in the project. Thus, if a need to cut cost arises later in the life of the project, these de-scoped components can be actually eliminated from the project scope, easily and quickly, without destabilizing the overall project plan.

90. M.M. May. 1974. *Stability and Complexity in Model Ecosystems*. Princeton, NJ: Princeton University Press; M.R. Gardner and W.R. Ashby. 1970. Connectance of Large Dynamic (Cybernetic) Systems: Critical Values for Stability. *Nature* 228, 5273: 784. Dr. Zeev Bonen, former president, Rafael, Ministry of Defense, Israel, contributed to the development of the "complete network" versus "hierarchy" concept.

91. Allocating specific time buffers to specific tasks is meaningful and effective only for the short-term Action Plan. For the Master Plan, an overall time reserve should be added to the entire project. As the project proceeds, this global time reserve should be gradually depleted by allocating appropriate time buffers to specific short-term tasks. The Critical Chain approach to project management copes with uncertainty primarily through buffer management. For an assessment of its effectiveness, see, for example, T.G. Lechler, B. Ronen, and E.A. Stohr. 2005. Critical Chain: A New Project Management Paradigm or Old Wine in New Bottles? *Engineering Management Journal* 17, 4: 45–58; T. Raz, R. Barnes, and D. Dvir. 2003. A Critical Look at Critical Chain Project Management. *Project Management Journal* 34, 4: 24–32.

92. R.T. Pascale. 1991. *Managing on the Edge*. New York, NY: Touchstone; K.K Smith. 1984. Rabbits, Lynxes, and Organizational Transitions. In *The Challenge of Managing Corporate Transitions*, eds. J. Kimberly and J.B. Quinn, 267–94. Homewood, IL: Dow-Jones Irwin.

93. J.C. Emery. 1969. *Organizational Planning and Control Systems: Theory and Technology*. London, UK: The Macmillan Company, 26-7.

94. Galbraith concluded that one of the major benefits of the creation of slack resources is the reduction of the number of exceptions that the manager has to address during task execution. As a result, the amount of information that must be processed during task execution is reduced, which in turn prevents the overloading of the communication channels within the organization. J.R. Galbraith. 1972. Organization Design: An Information Processing View. In *Organization Planning Cases and Concepts*, eds. J.W. Lorsch and P.R. Lawrence, 49–74. Ontario: R.D. Irwin and Dorsey Press.

95. M.A. Cusumano and R.W. Selby. 1995. *Microsoft Secrets: How the World's Most Powerful Software Company Creates Technology, Shapes Markets, and Manages People*. New York, NY: The Free Press, 205. Howell, Laufer, and Ballard show that "reducing the immediacy of interactions between sub-cycles is an effective method used by supervisors to cope with the uncertainty. Reducing immediate interaction through the use of buffers . . . will be the most effective technique for eliminating performance-reducing interactions." G. Howell, A. Laufer, and G. Ballard. 1993.

Interaction between Subcycles: One Key to Improved Methods. *Journal of Construction Engineering and Management* 119, 4: 714–28. Howell and Ballard refined these concepts in their pioneering work on "lean construction." See, for example, G. Howell and G. Ballard. 1994. Implementing Lean Construction: Reducing Inflow Variation. *2nd Annual Conference on Lean Construction*, Católica Universidad de Chile, Santiago, September. For additional research on the use of buffers, see, for example, H.R. Thomas, M.J. Horman, R.E. Minchin, Jr., and D. Chen. 2003. Improving Labor Flow Reliability for Better Productivity as Lean Construction Principle. *Journal of Construction Engineering and Management* 129, 3: 251–61; S. Lee, F. Peña-Mora, and M. Park. 2006. Reliability and Stability Buffering Approach: Focusing on the Issues of Errors and Changes in Concurrent Design and Construction Projects. *Journal of Construction Engineering and Management, ASCE,* 132, 5: 452–64.

96. E.W. Merrow. 1988. *Understanding the Outcomes of Megaprojects: A Quantitative Analysis of Very Large Civilian Projects.* Santa Monica, CA: Rand Corporation.

97. P.W.G. Morris and G.H. Hough. 1987. *The Anatomy of Major Projects.* New York, NY: Wiley, 12.

98. N.F. Matta and R.N. Ashkenas. 2003. Why Good Projects Fail Anyways? *Harvard Business Review* 81, 9: 109–14.

99. B. Flyvbjerg, N. Bruzelius, and W. Rothengatter. 2003. *Megaprojects and Risks: An Anatomy of Ambition.* Cambridge, UK: Cambridge University Press, 44.

100. C.B. Tatum. 1983. Decision-Making in Structuring Construction Project Organizations. *Technical Report No. 279.* Stanford, CA: Department of Civil Engineering, Stanford University; R. Youker. 1980. *A New Look at Work Breakdown Structure, Course Note Series.* Washington, D.C.: The International Bank for Reconstruction and Development.

101. M.M. May. 1974. *Stability and Complexity in Model Ecosystems.* Princeton, NJ: Princeton University Press; M.R. Gardner and W.R. Ashby. 1970. Connectance of Large Dynamic (Cybernetic) Systems: Critical Values for Stability. *Nature* 228, 5273: 784.

102. J.R. Galbraith. 1972. Organization Design: An Information Processing View. In *Organization Planning Cases and Concepts*, eds. J.W. Lorsch and P.R. Lawrence, 49–74. Ontario: R.D. Irwin and Dorsey Press; J.R. Galbraith. 1977. *Organization Design.* Reading, MA: Addison-Wesley; R.B. Duncan. 1972. Characteristics of Organizational Environments and Perceived Environmental Uncertainty. *Administrative Science Quarterly* 17, 3: 313–27; N.M. Samelson and J.D. Borcherding. 1979. Motivating Foremen on Large Construction Projects. In Construction Productivity, *Proceedings of the American Society of Civil Engineers, Reprint 3597*, New York, NY, 1–14.

103. E.F. Schumacher. 1973. *Small is Beautiful: A Study of Economics as if People Mattered.* London, UK: Blond & Briggs; K.E. Weick. 1985. Sources of Order in Underorganized Systems: Themes in Recent Organizational Theory. In *Organizational Theory and Inquiry*, ed. Y.S. Lincoln, 106–36. Beverly Hills, CA: Sage. Weick analyzed permanent organizations and concluded that "stable segments in organizations are quite small."

104. J.C. Emery. 1969. *Organizational Planning and Control Systems: Theory and Technology.* London, UK: The Macmillan Company, 29.

105. C.B. Tatum. 1983. Decision-Making in Structuring Construction Project Organizations. *Technical Report No. 279.* Stanford, CA: Department of Civil Engineering, Stanford University.

106. For sources on risk management, see *A Guide to the Project Management Body of Knowledge (PMBOK Guide)*. 2004. 3rd ed. Newtown Square, PA: Project Management Institute, 237–54; *NASA Systems Engineering Handbook*, SP-6105. June 1995. NASA: 37–44.

107. K.R. MacCrimmon and D.A Wehrung. 1986. *Taking Risks: The Management of Uncertainty*. New York, NY: The Free Press, 21.

108. D. Michael. 1997. *Learning to Plan and Planning to Learn*, 2nd ed. Alexandria, VA: Miles River Press, 123.

109. Brian further explains the quantitative rating system they employed for risk management, which in many ways is similar to the Critical Assumption List we discussed in the Second Green Guideline. B.K. Muirhead and W.L. Simon. 1999. *High Velocity Leadership: The Mars Pathfinder Approach to Faster, Better, Cheaper.* New York, NY: Harper Collins Publishers, 37–8.

110. For overall project results, such as project cost, quantitative analysis is more common because the statistical data base may be wider and the stakes are higher. Moreover, since it is done less frequently and can be performed by a staff specialist (with only limited involvement of line people), allocating time for this analysis should not be a problem.

111. Schoemaker, who wrote extensively on decision making and planning in uncertain conditions, also discusses our ability to define the risk and asserts that "it is not just the magnitude of uncertainty that creates challenges but also its shifting nature." A.J.H. Schoemaker. 2002. *Profiting from Uncertainty: Strategies for Succeeding No Matter What the Future Brings*. New York, NY: The Free Press, 8–10. See also A. Laufer and G. Howell. 1993. Construction Planning: Revising the Paradigm. *Project Management Journal* 24, 3: 23–33. For more on the infrequent use of quantitative risk analysis techniques that are based on probability estimates, see, for example, R.J. Shonberger, who concluded that network simulation is probably not worth the added expense. R.J. Shonberger. 1981. Why Projects Are Always Late: A Rationale Based on Manual Simulation of a PERT/CPM Network. *Interfaces* 11, 5: 66–76.

112. B. Flyvbjerg, N. Bruzelius, and W. Rothengatter. 2003. *Megaprojects and Risks: An Anatomy of Ambition*. Cambridge, UK: Cambridge University Press, 76.

113. K.R. MacCrimmon and D.A Wehrung. 1986. *Taking Risks: The Management of Uncertainty*. New York, NY: The Free Press, 25.

114. There are additional factors hindering the common use of risk analysis in project management. Shapira argues that in the typical theoretical description for choice among risky alternatives, "the individual making the choice is pictured by this process as a passive agent." The actual reality, Shapira asserts, is very different: "When taken in a real setting, risky choice is a dynamic-active endeavor that often bears little resemblance to the ordered world of statistical decision theory." Shapira shows that even regarding the definition of risk itself, there is a striking difference. While "the most common definition of risk in decision theory is the variance of the probability distribution of outcomes," the managers who participated in his study saw risk differently. Among other things, "they attended more to the magnitude of possible loss than to its probability . . . they showed very little desire to reduce risk to a single quantifiable construct." Z. Shapira. 1994. *Risk Taking: A Managerial Perspective*. New York, NY: Russell Sage Foundation, 21, 43.

115. T. Peters and N. Austin. 1985. *A Passion for Excellence: The Leadership Difference*. New York, NY: Random House, 116.

116. B.K. Muirhead and W.L. Simon. 1999. *High Velocity Leadership: The Mars Pathfinder Approach to Faster, Better, Cheaper*. New York, NY: Harper Collins Publishers, 80.

117. J. West and M. Iansiti. 2003. Experience, Experimentation, and the Accumulation of Knowledge: The Evolution of R&D in the Semiconductor Industry. *Research Policy* 32, 5: 809–25.

118. Using the terminology of Staber and Sydow, one may say that the Second Green Guideline enhances "adaptation," while the Third Green Guideline adds "adaptive capacity." U. Staber and J. Sydow. 2002. Organizational Adaptive Capacity: A Structuration Perspective. *Journal of Management Inquiry* 11, 4: 408–24.

119. The concept of stability and flexibility is similar to the concept of "order and freedom" proposed by Schumacher and discussed earlier in this practice. E.F. Schumacher. 1973. *Small is Beautiful: A Study of Economics as if People Mattered*. London, UK: Blond & Briggs.

120. K.E. Weick. 1990. Cartographic Myths in Organizations. In *Mapping Strategic Thought*, ed. A.S. Huff, 1–10. New York, NY: Wiley.

121. K.E. Weick. 1985. Sources of Order in Underorganized Systems: Themes in Recent Organizational Theory. In *Organizational Theory and Inquiry*, ed. Y.S. Lincoln, 106–36. Beverly Hills, CA: Sage.

122. H. Mintzberg. 1994. *The Rise and Fall of Strategic Planning*. New York, NY: Prentice Hall, 292–3.

123. The Price Waterhouse Change Integration Team. 1996. *The Paradox Principles: How High-Performance Companies Manage Chaos, Complexity, and Contradiction to Achieve Superior Results*. Chicago, IL: Irwin Professional Publishing, 26–7.

References

a. "Lessons from NASA Project Managers," Dr. Michelle Collins, Kennedy Space Center. 2001. *Ask Magazine* 3 (June): 26–9. http://appel.nasa.gov/ask/about/overview/index.html

b. "Letting Go of Once and for All," Dr. Alexander Laufer. 2003. *Ask Magazine* 13 (August): 40. http://appel.nasa.gov/ask/about/overview/index.html

c. "Bang for the Buck," Terry Little, U.S. Air Force. 2005. In A. Laufer, T. Post, and E.J. Hoffman, *Shared Voyage: Learning and Unlearning from Remarkable Projects*, 94–7. Washington, D.C.: The NASA History Series.

d. "The Decision," Terry Little, U.S. Air Force. 2005. In A. Laufer, T. Post, and E.J. Hoffman, *Shared Voyage: Learning and Unlearning from Remarkable Projects*, 116–8. Washington, D.C.: The NASA History Series.

e. "Smart Buying," Steven A. Gonzalez, Johnson Space Center. 2003. *Ask Magazine* 13 (August): 6–9. http://appel.nasa.gov/ask/about/overview/index.html

f. "Prototyping Interior Design," Dave Rusell. 1996. In A. Laufer, *Simultaneous Management: Managing Projects in a Dynamic Environment*, 57–8. New York, NY: AMACOM, American Management Association.

g. "Meeting a Tight Project Schedule without a Comprehensive Network," Jim Wink, U.S. Navy. 2000. In A. Laufer and E.J. Hoffman, *Project Management Success Stories*, 76–8. New York, NY: John Wiley & Sons.

h. "Tangled Up in Reviews," Marty Davis, Goddard Space Flight Center. 2001. *Ask Magazine* 4 (July): 8–11. http://appel.nasa.gov/ask/about/overview/index.html

i. "So This Is Knowledge Sharing," Susan Motil, Glenn Research Center. 2003. *Ask Magazine* 10 (January): 6–9. http://appel.nasa.gov/ask/about/overview/index.html

j. "Check Your Ego at the Door," Ray Morgan, AeroVironment Design Development Center. 2005. In A. Laufer, T. Post, and E.J. Hoffman, *Shared Voyage: Learning and Unlearning from Remarkable Projects*, 130–1. Washington, D.C.: The NASA History Series.

k. "Check It Out," Jenny Baer-Riedhart, NASA Dryden Flight Research Center. 2005. In A. Laufer, T. Post, and E.J. Hoffman, *Shared Voyage: Learning and Unlearning from Remarkable Projects*, 131–2. Washington, D.C.: The NASA History Series.

l. "The Decision," Terry Little, U.S. Air Force. 2005. In A. Laufer, T. Post, and E.J. Hoffman, *Shared Voyage: Learning and Unlearning from Remarkable Projects*, 116–8. Washington, D.C.: The NASA History Series.

m. "The Hour Glass and the Project Manager," Scott Cameron, Procter & Gamble. 2001. *Ask Magazine* 4 (July): 27–8. http://appel.nasa.gov/ask/about/overview/index.html

n. "Reality Planning," Don Margolies, Goddard Space Flight Center. 2005. In A. Laufer, T. Post, and E.J. Hoffman, *Shared Voyage: Learning and Unlearning from Remarkable Projects*, 29–30. Washington, D.C.: The NASA History Series.

o. "Talks with W. Scott Cameron," Scott Cameron, Procter & Gamble. 2002. *Ask Magazine* 7 (March): 39–45. http://appel.nasa.gov/ask/about/overview/index.html

p. "The Hour Glass and the Project Manager Part 2: Improving your Hierarchical IQ," Scott Cameron, Procter & Gamble. 2001. *Ask Magazine* 5 (September): 32–3. http://appel.nasa.gov/ask/about/overview/index.html

q. "Everything is Discussable," Hugh Woodward. 1996. In A. Laufer, *Simultaneous Management: Managing Projects in a Dynamic Environment*, 243–4. New York, NY: AMACOM, American Management Association.

r. "Project Management: Easy as ABC," Allan Frandsen, California Institute of Technology. 2005. In A. Laufer, T. Post, and E.J. Hoffman, *Shared Voyage: Learning and Unlearning from Remarkable Projects*, 47–8. Washington, D.C.: The NASA History Series.

s. "One Way or Another," Christian Zazzali, HITT Corporate Interiors. 2003. *Ask Magazine* 14 (October): 21. http://appel.nasa.gov/ask/about/overview/index.html

t. "Will the Real Site Please Identify Itself," Ray Longino, Procter & Gamble. 1996. In A. Laufer, *Simultaneous Management: Managing Projects in a Dynamic Environment*, 78–80. New York, NY: AMACOM, American Management Association.

u. "Decoupling Interdependence," John Wysocki, Procter & Gamble. 1996. In A. Laufer, *Simultaneous Management: Managing Projects in a Dynamic Environment*, 80. New York, NY: AMACOM, American Management Association.

v. "Checkmate to Uncertainty," Alexander Laufer. 2004. *Ask Magazine* 17 (April): 40. http://appel.nasa.gov/ask/about/overview/index.html

w. "Overhead is Not Evil," Robert Volkman, Procter & Gamble. 1996. In A. Laufer, *Simultaneous Management: Managing Projects in a Dynamic Environment*, 90–1. New York, NY: AMACOM, American Management Association.

x. "A Good Man is Hard to Find," Marty Davis, Goddard Space Flight Center, NASA. 2003. *Ask Magazine* 15 (December): 13–5. http://appel.nasa.gov/ask/about/overview/index.html

y. "The Backup Crane," Bill Clegern, Procter & Gamble. 1996. In A. Laufer, *Simultaneous Management: Managing Projects in a Dynamic Environment*, 76–7. New York, NY: AMACOM, American Management Association.

z. "Differences," Allan Frandsen, California Institute of Technology. 2005. In A. Laufer, T. Post, and E.J. Hoffman, *Shared Voyage: Learning and Unlearning from Remarkable Projects*, 55–6. Washington, D.C.: The NASA History Series.

aa. "Weapon System Competitive 'Shoot-off,'" Matthew Zimmerman, U.S. Army. 2000. In A. Laufer and E.J. Hoffman, *Project Management Success Stories*, 65–7. New York, NY: John Wiley & Sons.

bb. "Narrowing the Competition," Air Force News. 2005. In A. Laufer, T. Post, and E.J. Hoffman, *Shared Voyage: Learning and Unlearning from Remarkable Projects*, 107. Washington, D.C.: The NASA History Series; "Mr. Government Man, Can You Lend a Helping Hand?," Brian Rutledge, U.S. Air Force. 2005. In A. Laufer, T. Post, and E.J. Hoffman, *Shared Voyage: Learning and Unlearning from Remarkable Projects*, 108. Washington, D.C.: The NASA History Series; http://proceedings.ndia.org/302D_Ward.pdf, last accessed January 10, 2007. "What is Help?," Terry Little, U.S. Air Force. 2005. In A. Laufer, T. Post, and E.J. Hoffman, *Shared Voyage: Learning and Unlearning from Remarkable Projects*, 109. Washington, D.C.: The NASA History Series.

Chapter 2

Notes

1. E. de Bono. 1984. *Tactics: The Art and Science of Success*. Boston, MA: Little, Brown and Company, 54.

2. P. Roberts. 2000. Getting It Done. *Fast Company* 35 (May): 146–60.

3. A. Suchman. 1987. *Plans and Situated Actions: The Problem of Human-machine Communication*. Cambridge, UK: Cambridge University Press, vii. Suchman refers to a story, quoted by G. Berreman, which was written by T. Gladwin in 1964. L.G. Berreman. 1966. Anemic and Emetic Analyses in Social Anthropology. *American Anthropologist* 86, 2: 346–54. T. Gladwin. 1964. Culture and Logical Process. In *Explorations in Cultural Anthropology: Essays Presented to George Peter Murdock*, ed. W. Goodenough. New York, NY: McGraw Hill.

4. Mintzberg and his coauthors also cite Wilson's "seven deadly sins of strategic planning." H. Mintzberg, B. Ahlstrand, and J. Lampel. 1998. *Strategy Safari: A Guided Tour through the Wilds of Strategic Management*. New York, NY: The Free Press, 64–9. I. Wilson. Strategic Planning Isn't Dead—It Changed. 1994. *Long Range Planning* 27, 4 (August): 12–24. "Thinking" and "acting" have not been only treated often as detached functions, they have also received strikingly different attention in the management literature. To examine it, I carried out a quick comparison of how many times two books, the first one on thinking and the second one on acting, were cited in Scholar Google. Both books were written by Edward de Bono. It turns out that his 1985 book, *Six Thinking Hats* (Little Brown, Boston), was cited more than 400 times, while his 1991 book, *Six Action Shoes* (Harper Business, New York), was cited only 14 times (comparison done in July 2008).

5. P. Agre. 1997. *Computation and Human Experience*. Cambridge, UK: Cambridge University Press, 150–1.

6. K.E. Weick. 1983. Managerial Thought in the Context of Action. In *The Executive Mind*, eds. S. Srivastba and Associates, 242. San Francisco, CA: Jossey-Bass.

7. E. de Bono. 1991. *Six Action Shoes*. New York, NY: Harper Business, 24, 63, 64, 67, 69.

8. P. Drucker. 1964. *Managing for Results: Economic Tasks and Risk-taking Decisions.* New York, NY: Harper & Row, 9–12.

9. H. Gardner. 2004. *Changing Minds, the Art and Science of Changing Our Own and Other People's Minds.* Boston, MA: Harvard Business School Press, 7–8. In his 1998 book, *The 80/20 Principle: The Secret of Achieving More with Less,* Richard Koch concludes that "the 80/20 principle is still the best-kept business secret." R. Koch. 1998. *The 80/20 Principle: The Secret of Achieving More with Less.* New York, NY: Doubleday, 50.

10. C. Handy. 1998. *The Hungry Spirit.* New York, NY: Broadway Books, 106.

11. Herbert Simon, who won the Nobel Prize in economics for his research in the area of decision making, was the first to explain the need for "good enough." One concept he developed is "satisficing." This concept suggests that in many cases when faced with decisions, people do not or should not attempt to achieve the optimal or the best solution, but rather a minimally accepted one. H.A. Simon. 1955. A Behavioral Model of Rational Choice. *Quarterly Journal of Economics* 69: 99–118. H.A. Simon. 1955. Bounded Rationality and Organizational Learning. *Organization Science* 2, 1: 125–34. Janis and Mann conclude that optimizing differs from "good enough" strategies of decision making in four different aspects: number of requirements to be met, number of alternatives generated, ordering and retesting of alternatives, and type of testing model used. See I.L. Janis and L. Mann. 1977. *Decision Making: A Psychological Analysis of Conflict, Choice, and Commitment.* New York, NY: Free Press, 29–30.

12. N. Augustine. 1986. *Augustine's Laws.* New York, NY: Viking Penguin, 101–7. Dan Ward cites a similar concept from Eric Raymond's book *The Cathedral and The Bazaar:* "Perfection [in design] is achieved not when there is nothing more to add, but rather when there is nothing more to take away." D. Ward. 2007. *The Simplicity Cycle.* www.lulu.com/RoguePress, 42. In his book *Simplicity,* de Bono argues that "complexity means distracted effort. Simplicity means focused effort . . . Simple systems are easier to set up, easier to monitor, and easier to repair." E. de Bono. 1998. *Simplicity.* London, UK: Penguin Books, 32–3.

13. N. Augustine. 1986. *Augustine's Laws.* New York, NY: Viking Penguin, 121–5. Christopher Meyer who wrote a book on the implementation of Fast Cycle Time (FCT) strategy asserts that "FCT competitors are fast not because they handle complexity a better than their competitors, but because they consistently strive to eliminate complexity whenever possible." C. Meyer. 1993. *Fast Cycle Time.* New York, NY: The Free Press, 8–9.

14. B. Ettorre. 1996. A conversation with Charles Handy: On the Future of Work and An End to the "Century of the Organization." *Organizational Dynamics* (Summer): 15–26.

15. T. Peters. 1999. *The Project 50 (Reinventing Work): Fifty Ways to Transform Every "Task" into a Project That Matters!* New York, NY: Alfred Knopf, 97–100. Though Jim Collins does not term it WOW, he reached somewhat similar conclusions regarding "being the best." In his book *Good to Great: Why Some Companies Make the Leap and Others Don't,* he argues, "To go from good to great requires transcending the curse of competence. It requires the discipline to say, 'just because we are good at it—just because we are making money and generating growth—doesn't necessarily mean we can become the best at it.' The good-to-great companies understand that doing what you are good at will only make you good; focusing solely on what you can potentially do better than any other organization is the only path to greatness."

J. Collins. 2001. *Good to Great: Why Some Companies Make the Leap and Others Don't*. New York, NY: Harper Business, 100.

16. Advanced Composition Explorer (ACE). *Caltechwww.srl.caltech.edu/ACE/ - 7k – 20* Last update: February, 2007, last accessed July 1, 2007.

17. Bruch and Ghoshal highlight the "power of energy and focus." They identify four kinds of managerial behavior according to the levels of energy and focus that the managers displayed. The desired behavior, termed "purposeful management," is "highly focused and energetic." H. Bruch and S. Ghoshal. 2004. *A Bias for Action*. Boston, MA: Harvard Business Press, 10–24.

18. T.H. Davenport and J.C. Beck. 2001. *The Attention Economy: Understanding the New Currency of Business*. Boston, MA: Harvard Business School Press, 4–11. S. Davis and C. Meyer. 1998. *Blur: the Speed of Change in the Connected Economy*. Reading, MA: Addison-Wesley, 246. It is interesting to point out that in the Green Principle, the manager has to cope with missing information, while here the challenge is information glut.

19. B. Schwartz. 2004. *The Paradox of Choice: Why More is Less*. New York, NY: Harper Collins, 222.

20. www.joelonsoftware.com/items/2006/11/21.html Accessed July 1, 2007.

21. D. Telem, A. Laufer, and A. Shapira, 2006. Only Dynamics Can Absorb Dynamics. *Journal of Construction Engineering and Management* 132, 11: 1167–77; H. Mintzberg. 1973. *The Nature of Managerial Work*. New York: Harper & Row.

22. H. Bruch and S. Ghoshal. 2004. *Bias for Action*. Boston, MA: Harvard Business Press, 10. A typical example of the "hazard to focus" for project managers is the need to plan for three time horizons (Action Plan, Look-Ahead Plan, and Master Plan). See the Second Green Guideline as well as D. Telem, A. Laufer, and A. Shapira. 2006. Only Dynamics Can Absorb Dynamics. *Journal of Construction Engineering and Management* 132, 11: 1167–77.

23. An interview with David Allen. Keith Hammonds. 2000. You Can Do Anything—But Not Everything. *Fast Company* 34 (May): 206–14.

24. S. Davis and C. Meyer. 1998. *Blur: the Speed of Change in the Connected Economy*. Reading, MA: Addison-Wesley, 246.

25. K. Weick. 1985. Sources of Order in Underorganized Systems: Themes in Recent Organizational Theory. In *Organizational Theory and Inquiry*, eds. Y.S. Lincoln. Beverly Hills, CA: Sage, 106–36. Allocation of attention and its role in decision making is addressed elaborately by James March, for example, "The allocation of attention affects the information available and thus the decision . . . Decisions happen the way they do, in large part, because of the way attention is allocated." J.G. March. 1994. *A Primer on Decision Making*. New York, NY: The Free Press, 23–4.

26. A. Ries. 1996. *Focus: The Future of Your Company Depends On It*. New York, NY: Harper Business, 14.

27. An interview with David Allen. Keith Hammonds. 2000. You Can Do Anything—But Not Everything. *Fast Company* 34 (May): 206–14.

28. One of the principles of the Agile Manifesto is, "Welcome changing requirements, even late in development. Agile processes harness change for the customer's competitive advantage." A. Cockburn. 2002. *Agile Software Development*. Boston, MA: Addison-Wesley, 220. K. Beck. 2000. *Extreme Programming Explained: Embrace Change*. Boston, MA: Addison-Wesley, 21.

29. http://www.pmforum.org/library/papers/2003/Top10WaysSoftwareProjectsRDifferent.pdf Accessed July 1, 2007. It seems that the Agile method is more suitable for small, highly qualified teams, composed of members who feel comfortable and empowered

by having many degrees of freedom. See B. Boehm and R. Turner. 2004. *Balancing Agility and Discipline—A Guide for the Perplexed*. Boston, MA: Addison-Wesley, 55–7. C. Handy. 1998. *The Hungry Spirit*. New York, NY: Broadway Books, 107.

30. http://nssdc.gsfc.nasa.gov/planetary/news/near_descent_pr_20010131.html Accessed July 1, 2007.

31. B. Scott. 2005. *The Art of Project Management*. Sebastopol, CA: O'Reilly Media, 332–42.

32. Jim Collins conducted an extensive empirical study of 11 good-to-great companies. In his book *Good to Great: Why Some Companies Make the Leap and Others Don't*, he describes what their "culture of discipline" means: "Adhere with great consistency to the Hedgehog concept, exercising an almost religious focus . . . Equally important, create a 'stop doing list' and systematically unplug anything extraneous . . . 'Stop doing' lists are more important than 'to do' lists . . . The good-to-great companies at their best followed a simple mantra: 'Anything that does not fit with our Hedgehog concept, we will not do. Period." J. Collins. 2001. *Good to Great: Why Some Companies Make the Leap and Others Don't*. New York, NY: Harper Business, 124, 134, 143.

33. T. Peters. 1997. *The Circle of Innovation*. New York: Alfred A Knopf, 482–3.

34. J. Collins. 2001. *Good to Great: Why Some Companies Make the Leap and Others Don't*. New York, NY: Harper Business, 123–4.

35. G. Hofstede. 1998. Identifying Organizational Subcultures: An Empirical Approach. *Journal of Management Studies* 35, 1 (January): 1–12. See also G. Hofstede, B. Neuijen, D. Daval Ohayv, and G. Sanders. 1998. Measuring Organizational Cultures: A Qualitative and Quantitative Study across Twenty Cases. *Administrative Science Quarterly* 35, 2 (June): 286–316.

36. By deciding to define a new execution strategy, Cameron is in line with de Bono, who argues that "sometimes it is much easier to start over again than to try and modify what exists." E. de Bono. 1984. *Tactics: The Art and Science of Success*. Boston, MA: Little, Brown and Company, 92.

37. At times, however, even when there is no attempt to adhere to the Third Green Guideline, the subdivision is still done in parallel. This is the case shared earlier in this guideline by Scott Cameron. In the Third Green Guideline, it was explained that since it is difficult to maintain the stability of the plan of a large project, the project is subdivided. Cameron's impetus for splitting his project (which was not a particularly large one) was not to enhance the **stability** of the plan, but rather to improve its **suitability**, ensuring that planning and implementation suit the particular needs of each customer.

38. F. Matta and R. Ashkenas. 2003. Why Good Projects Fail Anyway. *Harvard Business Review* 81, 9 (September): 109–14.

39. Thomke concludes that "people learn more efficiently when their actions are followed by immediate feedback . . . and long feedback delays impede learning." S.H. Thomke. 2003. *Experimentation Matters*. Boston, MA: Harvard Business Press, 104–5.

40. See A. MacCormack. 2001. Product-Development Practices That Work: How Internet Companies Build Software. *MIT Sloan Management Review* 42, 2 (Winter): 75–84. Studying approaches to technology implementation, Fichman and Moses, who also present the benefits of "results-driven incrementalism," warn, however, that this approach is beneficial only when the technology is divisible, that is, when the technology allows for the development of product components designed to accommodate "stand-alone" operations. R.G. Fichman and S.A. Moses. 1999. An Incremental Process for Software Implementation. *Sloan Management Review* 40, 2: 39–52.

41. Early Deliverables facilitates strong customer orientation already at early stages of the project and throughout its life. This is in contrast to the typical process-oriented culture, where the impact of project performance on the customer and customer satisfaction often become central only after project completion. See A.J. Shenhar, D. Dvir, O. Levy, and A.C. Maltz. 2002. Project Success: A Multidimensional Strategic Concept. *Long Range Planning* 34: 699–725.

42. K.E. Weick. 1984. Small Wins: Redefining the Scale of Social Problems. *American Psychologist* 39, 1: 40–9. See also R.H. Shaffer and H.A. Thomson. 1992. Successful Change Programs Began with Results. *Harvard Business Review* 70, 1 (January–February): 80–9. John Kotter includes "Generating Short-Term Wins" as one of the eight main steps required for creating a major change. J.P. Kotter. 1996. *Leading Change*. Boston, MA: Harvard Business School Press, 117–30; T. Peters and N. Austin. 1985 *A Passion for Excellence*. New York, NY: Random House, 151; J.M. Kouzes and B.Z. Posner. 1987. *The Leadership Challenge: How to Get Extraordinary Things Done in Organizations*. San Francisco, CA: Jossey-Bass, 219, 233.

43. B. Gates. 1999. *Business @ The Speed of Thought*. New York, NY: Warner Books, 312. See A. Taylor. 2000. IT Projects: Sink or Swim. *ITNOW* 42, 1: 24–6. Taylor found that "the smaller the project, the less likely it is to fail . . . 89.5% of successful projects were completed in 12 months . . . this is not to say that projects over 12 months should not be started, but that they should be broken into smaller projects . . . whenever possible."

44. M.A. Cusumano. 2004. *The Business of Software*. New York, NY: Free Press, 144.

45. E. Yourdon. 1997. *Death March*. Upper Saddle River, NJ: Prentice Hall PTR, 157–8.

46. A. Cockburn. 2002. *Agile Software Development*. Boston, MA: Addison-Wesley, 219–33.

47. R.D. Gilbreath. 1987. *Forward Thinking: The Pragmatist's Guide to Today's Business Trends*. New York, NY: McGraw Hill, 65.

48. A similar process is reported by Malee Lucas regarding the JDAM project: "The number of required MIL-SPECS and MIL-STDS was reduced from 87 at R&D start-up to zero at the contract award." M.V. Lucas. 1996. Supplier Management Practices of the Joint Direct Attack Munition Program. *PhD. thesis. Massachusetts Institute of Technology,* 151.

49. B.T. Pentland and H.H. Rueter. 1994. Organizational Routines as Grammars of Action. *Administrative Science Quarterly* 39, 3: 484–510. The study explores the sequential structure of work processes in a task that involves a high number of exceptions and frequent interruptions and that cannot be characterized as routine under any traditional definition. For a later review of the subject, see Markus C. Becker. 2004. Organizational Routines: A Review of the Literature. *Industrial and Corporate Change* 13, 4: 643–78.

50. Standard procedures also enhance a feeling of certainty. People are often incapacitated and paralyzed by insecurity and confusion when faced with high uncertainty. Standard procedures help to increase stability and confidence in two ways. First, order and predictability are enhanced if each party knows when and how to act and interact. Second, a standard procedure helps to establish internal stability by operating like a plan. It is a "plan" for generic actions, rather than the typical project plan that is created for specific actions. See also K.E. Weick. 1990. Cartographic Myths in Organizations. In *Mapping Strategic Thought*, ed. A.S. Huff, 1–10. New York, NY: Wiley; K.E. Weick. 1985. Sources of Order in Underorganized Systems: Themes in Recent Organizational Theory. In *Organizational Theory and Inquiry*, ed. Y.S. Lincoln, 106–36. Beverly Hills, CA: Sage; H. Mintzberg. 1994. *The Rise and Fall of*

Strategic *Planning: Reconceiving Roles for Planning, Plans, Planners*. New York, NY: Prentice Hall, 292–3.

51. De Bono asserts that "systems that seek to cover all exceptions make it immensely complicated for the bulk of people who are not exceptions." E. de Bono. 1998. *Simplicity*. London, UK: Penguin Books, 152.

52. See, for example, PMBOK Guide. 2004. *A Guide to the Project Management Body of Knowledge*. 3rd ed. Newtown Square, PA: Project Management Institute. In many permanent organizations, on the other hand, there has been a clear trend for more than two decades to minimize the reliance on standard processes. For example, one source describes an executive who started his tenure as managing director of a large company by taking a one-year "sabbatical," as he called it, to reduce the company's paperwork by 80 percent. T. Peters and N. Austin. 1985. *A Passion for Excellence*, New York, NY: Random House, 313.

53. N.R. Augustine. 1986. *Augustine's Laws*. New York, NY: Viking-Penguin, 328–43.

54. P.F. Drucker. 1999. *Management Challenges for the 21st Century*. New York, NY: Harper Collins, 9, 16. The "one best way" approach, which was the favorite phrase of Fredrick Taylor, the father of scientific management, came under sharp attack by Henry Mintzberg as well. In *The Rise and Fall of Strategic Planning*, Mintzberg discusses forms of organizations: "Throughout this book, we have repeatedly criticized the 'one best way' thinking in the management literature." H. Mintzberg. 1994. *The Rise and Fall of Strategic Planning: Reconceiving Roles for Planning, Plans, Planners*. New York, NY: Free Press, 397. The superiority of tailoring project processes over a one best way approach was reported in a recent study of new product development projects within Swedish companies. T. Olin and J. Wickenberg. 2001. Rule Breaking in New Product Development—Crime or Necessity? *Creativity and Innovation Management* 10, 1 (March): 15–25.

55. T. Peters and R.H. Waterman. 1982. *In Search of Excellence: Lessons from America's Best-Run Companies*. New York, NY: Harper & Row, 108.

56. See the meta-principles in the introduction.

57. Johns also gives examples of attributes that may define the context in organizational research, such as informational attributes (e.g., ambiguity); task attributes (e.g., autonomy); physical attributes (e.g., danger); and social attributes (e.g., norms). G. Johns. 2001. In Praise of Context. *Journal of Organizational Behavior* 22: 31–42; M. Gladwell. 2000. *The Tipping Point*. New York, NY: Little, Brown and Company, 133–92. Gladwell cites research and provides examples of how ordinary people underestimate the power of context.

58. P. Leinberger and B. Tucker. *1991. The Organization Man*. New York, NY: Harper Collins, 158.

59. See, for example, H. Pruijt. 2000. Repainting, Modifying, Smashing Taylorism. *Journal of Organizational Change Management* 13, 5: 439–51.

60. J.A. Highsmith III. 2000. *Adaptive Software Development—A Collaborative Approach to Managing Complex Systems*. New York, NY: Dorset House Publishing, 85.

61. See K. Beck. 2000. *Extreme Programming Explained: Embrace Change*. Boston, MA: Addison-Wesley, 172.

62. W. Royce. 1998. *Software Project Management: A Unified Framework*. Boston, MA: Addison-Wesley, 209–20. See also B. Boehm and R. Turner. 2004. *Balancing Agility and Discipline: A Guide for the Perplexed*. Boston, MA: Addison-Wesley: 34–5.

63. E. de Bono. 1991. *Six Action Shoes*. New York, NY: Harper Business, 67–8.

64. *The Seven Basic Principles of the Context-Driven School*. 2007. http://www.context-driven-testing.com/ Accessed July 1, 2007.

65. A. Melgrati and M. Damiani. 2002. Rethinking the Project Management Framework: New Epistemology, New Insights. *Proceedings of PMI Research Conference*, Seattle: 371–80. In his book *The Project 50*, Tom Peters discusses uniqueness (which he terms "a WOW project") versus sameness: "Life is too short for non-wow projects . . . We are trapped in a sea of sameness." T. Peters. 1999. *The Project 50 (Reinventing Work): Fifty Ways to Transform Every "Task" into a Project That Matters!* New York, NY: Alfred Knopf, 97–9.

66. In comparing a "one best way" type approach to a story-based approach, various researchers have reached similar conclusions regarding context. H. Zukier, for example, compared paradigmatic and narrative modes in goal-guided inference and found that the narrative mode is highly context sensitive. See H. Zukier. 1986. The Paradigmatic and Narrative Modes in Goal-Guided Inference. In *Handbook of Motivation and Cognition*, eds. R. M. Sorrentino and E.T. Higgins, 465–502. New York, NY: Guilford. See D.J. Clandinin and F.M. Connelly. 2000. *Narrative Inquiry: Experience and Story in Qualitative Research*. San Francisco, CA: Jossey-Bass, 32.

67. The early emphasis on the "task perspective" in the project management literature is discussed in B.J. Koltveit, J.T. Karlsen, and K. Grønhaug. 2007. Perspectives on Project Management. *International Journal of Project Management* 25: 3–9.

68. F. W. Taylor. 1997 (originally published in 1911, New York, NY: Harper & Bros). *The Principles of Scientific Management*. Reprinted Mineola, NY: Dover Publications, 39.

69. See Shaffer and Thomson, who discuss the "activity-centered fallacy." R.H. Schaffer and H.A Thomson. 1992. Successful Change Programs Begin with Results. *Harvard Business Review* 70, 1 (January–February): 80–9.

70. Highsmith similarly explains, "Adaptive development focuses not on tasks, but on the results—specifically, the primary components that deliver functionality to the user . . . The key . . . is to apply increasing rigor to the results, that is, to the work-state rather than to the workflow." Highsmith also stresses that the shift requires unlearning—as he terms it, *"breaking the workflow mindset."* J.A. Highsmith III. 2000. *Adaptive Software Development—A Collaborative Approach to Managing Complex Systems*. New York, NY: Dorset House Publishing, 235–60. For more on the need to focus on deliverables, see also J. R. Turner. 2000. Do You Manage Work, Deliverables or Resources? *International Journal of Project Management* 18, 2 (April): 83–4; D. J. Bryde and R. Joby. 2007. Product-Based Planning: The Importance of Project and Project Management Deliverables in the Management of Clinical Trials. *R&D Management* 37, 4 (September): 363–77.

71. According to Weick, "Managers think all the time . . . When managers act, their thinking occurs concurrently with action. Thinking is not sandwiched between activities; rather, it exists in the form of circumspection present when activities are executed. Managers can phone, tour, meet, write, network and build agendas with variable amount of intention, attention, care, control, pertinacity. To execute acts more thinkingly **is** to think. It is to create outcomes that are unlikely to be improved by disengaged reflection." K. E. Weick. 1983. Managerial Thought in the Context of Action. In *The Executive Mind: New Insights on Managerial Thought and Action*, eds. S. Srivastva and Associates, 221–42. San Francisco, CA: Jossey-Bass.

72. N. Nohria and J.D. Berkley. 1994. Whatever Happened to the Take Charge Manager? *Harvard Business Review* 72, 1 (January–February): 128–37.

73. B. Muirhead and W. Simon. 1999. *High Velocity Leadership: The Mars Pathfinder Approach to Faster, Better, Cheaper*. New York, NY: Harper Business, 193.

74. Cited in Y. Malhotra. 1998. Toward a Knowledge Ecology for Organizational White-Waters. Keynote Presentation at the *Knowledge Ecology Fair 98: Beyond Knowledge Management*, February, 2–27. http://www.openacademy.mindef.gov.sg/OpenAcademy/Learning%20Resources/Knowledge%20Mgmt/ecology.htm.

75. M. Pina e Cunha, J. Vieira da Cunha and K. Kamoche. 1999. Organizational Improvisation: What, When, How and Why. *International Journal of Management Review* 1, 3: 299–341.

76. L.R. Sayles and M.K. Chandler. 1971. *Managing Large Systems: Organizations for the Future*. New York, NY: Harper & Row, 207–8.

77. L.R. Sayles and M.K. Chandler. 1971. *Managing Large Systems: Organizations for the Future*. New York, NY: Harper & Row, 218.

78. D. Telem, A. Laufer and A. Shapira. 2006. Only Dynamics Can Absorb Dynamics. *Journal of Construction Engineering and Management* 132, 11: 1167–77.

79. D. Telem. 2005. The Work of Construction Project Managers—Its Characteristics and Implications for the Principles of Managing Projects in a Dynamic Environment. *Ph.D. thesis*, Technion–Israel Institute of Technology, Haifa, Israel, 108–13.

80. As elaborated in the introduction, many researchers have imparted great importance to learning from select populations and have dedicated their attention to learning from successful managers. See, for example, T. Peters and R.H. Waterman. 1982. *In Search of Excellence*. New York, NY: Warner; J.P. Kotter. 1982. *A Force for Change: How Leadership Differs from Management*. New York, NY: Free Press; J.P. Kotter. 1982. What Effective General Managers Really Do. *Harvard Business Review* 60, 6 (November–December): 156–67; R.H. Waterman. 1994. *What America Does Right*. New York, NY: W.W. Norton and Co.; J.C. Collins and J.I. Porras. 1994. *Built to Last—Successful Habits of Visionary Companies*. New York, NY: Harper Collins; W.G. Bennis and P.W. Biederman. 1997. *Organizing Genius: The Secret of Creative Collaboration*. Reading, MA: Addison–Wesley.

81. D. Telem, A. Laufer, and A. Shapira. 2006. Only Dynamics Can Absorb Dynamics. *Journal of Construction Engineering and Management* 132, 11: 1167–77. H. Mintzberg. 1973. *The Nature of Managerial Work*. New York, NY: Harper & Row.

82. As for explanation, Kotter cites the conclusions of another researcher, Chris Argyris, regarding the dynamic environment surrounding managers: "[effective managers are] adept at grasping and taking advantage of each item in the random succession of time and issue fragments that crowd their days." J.P. Kotter. 1980. *What Leaders Really Do*. Boston, MA: Harvard Business School Press, 151, 155, 162–63, 166.

83. G. Majone and A. Wildavsky. 1979. Implementation as Evolution. In *Implementation*, 3rd edition, eds. J.L. Pressman and A. Wildavsky, 163–80. Berkeley, CA: University of California Press.

84. H. Mintzberg. 1973. *The Nature of Managerial Work*. New York, NY: Harper & Row, 81–4. Delbecq and Filley, who studied project managers, concluded that "the temporary and amorphic character of the project group requires . . . proactive behavior . . . by means of problem-centered leadership." A. Delbecq and A. Filley. 1974. Program and Project Management in the Matrix Organization: A Case Study. *Monograph No. 9* (January). University of Wisconsin-Madison, 59.

85. H. Mintzberg. (1991) Managerial Work: Forty Years Later. In *Executive* Behaviour, *Reprinted with Contributions by Henry Mintzberg and Rosemary Stewart*, ed. S. Carlson. Uppsala, Sweden: Studia Oeconomiae Negatiorum 32, Uppsala Universitet.

86. L.R. Sayles and M.K. Chandler. 1971. *Managing Large Systems*: Organizations for the Future. New York, NY: Harper & Row, 218–9. One is tempted to attribute the central role that problem solving plays in the work of the project manager primarily to the current dynamic environment. However, as early as 1959, a *Harvard Business Review* article stressed the central role of "unraveling the knots": "Like the line manager, the project manager is at once a man of thought and a front man. As a man of action, his most important function will be the preservation of a sense of momentum throughout all layers of the project . . . the . . . managerial function of trouble shooting, or of unraveling the knots, will occupy a great deal of his time." P.O. Gaddis. 1959. The Project Manager. *Harvard Business Review* 37, 3 (May–June): 89–97.

87. B. Muirhead and W. Simon. 1999. *High Velocity Leadership: The Mars Pathfinder Approach to Faster, Better, Cheaper*. New York, NY: Harper Business, 76–7.

88. This hedge-clipping metaphor is from T. Connolly and G. Wolf. 1981. Deciding on Decision Strategies: Towards an Enriched Contingency Model. *Proceedings of the Academy of Management Annual Meeting*. San Diego, CA: 181–5. See also T. Connolly. 1980. Uncertainty, Action and Competence: Some Alternatives to Omniscience in Complex Problem-Solving. In *Uncertainty: Behavioral and Social Dimensions,* ed. S. Fiddle, 69–91. New York, NY: Praeger; T. Connolly. 1988. Hedge-Clipping, Tree-Felling and the Management of Ambiguity: The Need for New Images of Decision-Making. In *Managing Ambiguity and Change*, eds. L.R. Pondy, R.J. Boland, and H. Thomas, 37–50. New York, NY: Wiley.

89. H. Mintzberg argues that there are times when thought should precede action and guide it. Other times, however, especially during or immediately after a major unexpected shift in the environment, thought must be bound up with action in an interactive and continuous process. Thus, Mintzberg concludes that "'learning' becomes a better label, and concept, for what happens then is 'formulation-implementation.'" H. Mintzberg. 1990. The Design School: Reconsidering the Basic Premises of Strategic Management. *Strategic Management Journal* 11: 171–95. Weick concluded that "we should pay more attention to simultaneity of thought and action and less attention to sequence;" K.E. Weick. 1983. Managerial Thought in the Context of Action. In *The Executive Mind*, eds. S. Srivastba and Associates, 242. San Francisco, CA: Jossey-Bass. See also J.B. Quinn. 1980. *Strategies for Change: Logical Incrementalism*. Englewood Cliffs, NJ: Irwin.

90. G. Klein. 2003. *Intuition at Work*. New York, NY: Doubleday-Currency, xv.

91. G. Klein. 2003. *Intuition at Work*. New York, NY: Doubleday-Currency, xv–xvi.

92. T. Stewart. 2002. How to Think with Your Gut. *Business 2.0*, (November): 98–104.

93. Daniel Isenberg says, "One implication of acting/thinking cycles is that action is often part of defining the problem, not just implementing the solution." See D.J. Isenberg. 1984. How Senior Managers Think. *Harvard Business Review* 62, (November–December): 80–90.

94. Indeed, the experience level of the ten on-site construction project managers was high—the mean experience accumulated as project managers was 15 years, and the mean overall experience on the construction site was 21 years. Edward de Bono argues that "an expert is someone who has succeeded in making decisions and judgments simpler through knowing what to pay attention to and what to ignore." E. de Bono. 1998. *Simplicity*. London, UK: Viking, 22.

95. G. Klein. 1998. *Sources of Power: How People Make Decisions*. Cambridge, MA: MIT Press, 287. Stories were also recommended as a tool for improving the ad hoc mode of Act with Agility, that is, improvisation. Frank Barrett asks, "What practices and

structures can we implement that might emulate what happens when jazz bands improvise?" His first suggestion is, "Boost the processing of information during and after actions are implemented." He concludes that diverse stories can improve improvisation capabilities. F.J. Barret. 1998. Creativity and Improvisation in Jazz and Organizations: Implications for Organizational Learning. *Organization Science* 9, 5 (September–October): 605–22.

96. H. Mintzberg. 1994. *The Rise and Fall of Strategic Planning: Reconceiving Roles for Planning, Plans, Planners.* New York, NY: The Free Press, 329.

97. L.R. Pondy. 1983. Union of Rationality and Intuition in Management Action. In *The Executive Mind,* eds. S. Srivastba and Associates, 169–91. San Francisco, CA: Jossey-Bass.

98. H.L. Dreyfus and S.E. Dreyfus. 1986. *Mind over Machine: The Power of Human Intuitive Expertise in the Era of the Computer.* New York, NY: The Free Press.

99. H. Mintzberg. 1994. *The Rise and Fall of Strategic Planning: Reconceiving Roles for Planning, Plans, Planners.* New York, NY: The Free Press, 285. Mintzberg explores the disconnection of thinking from acting and concludes that "future planning disconnected from present action is futile . . . while thinking must certainly precede action, it must also follow action, close behind, or else run the risk of impeding it!" H. Mintzberg. 1994. *The Rise and Fall of Strategic Planning: Reconceiving Roles for Planning, Plans, Planners.* New York, NY: The Free Press, 291–3.

References

a. "Judgment Calls," Don Margolies, Goddard Space Flight Center, NASA. 2005. In A. Laufer, T. Post, and E.J. Hoffman, *Shared Voyage: Learning and Unlearning from Remarkable Projects,* 28–9. Washington, D.C.: The NASA History Series.

b. "Stopping at 'Good Enough,'" Don Margolies, Goddard Space Flight Center, NASA. 2005. In A. Laufer, T. Post, and E.J. Hoffman, *Shared Voyage: Learning and Unlearning from Remarkable Projects,* 32–3. Washington, D.C.: The NASA History Series.

c. "Test What You Fly?," Don Margolies, Goddard Space Flight Center NASA, 2005. In A. Laufer, T. Post, and E.J. Hoffman, *Shared Voyage: Learning and Unlearning from Remarkable Projects,* 69-72. Washington, DC: The NASA History Series.

d. "Goofy Pictures," Brian Rutledge, U.S. Air Force. 2005. In A. Laufer, T. Post, and E.J. Hoffman, *Shared Voyage: Learning and Unlearning from Remarkable Projects,* 98. Washington, D.C.: The NASA History Series.

e. "Constancy of Purpose," Chuck Anderson, Raytheon. 2005. In A. Laufer, T. Post, and E.J. Hoffman, *Shared Voyage: Learning and Unlearning from Remarkable Projects,* 202. Washington, D.C.: The NASA History Series. "Committed to a Big Vision," Chuck Anderson, Raytheon. 2005. In A. Laufer, T. Post, and E.J. Hoffman, *Shared Voyage: Learning and Unlearning from Remarkable Projects,* 204–5. Washington, D.C.: The NASA History Series.

f. "TSSAM Lessons Learned," Larry Lawson, Lockheed Martin Corporation. 2005. In A. Laufer, T. Post, and E.J. Hoffman, *Shared Voyage: Learning and Unlearning from Remarkable Projects,* 88. Washington, D.C.: The NASA History Series. "Behave Yourself," Larry Lawson, Lockheed Martin Corporation. 2005. In A. Laufer, T. Post, and E.J. Hoffman, *Shared Voyage: Learning and Unlearning from Remarkable Projects,* 115–6. Washington, D.C.: The NASA History Series.

g. "Unrelenting Focus," Thomas Coughlin, The John Hopkins University. 2000. In A. Laufer and E.J. Hoffman, *Project Management Success Stories,* 122–3. New York, NY: John Wiley & Sons.

h. "Keeping It Simple, Not," Mary Chiu, John Hopkins Applied Physics Laboratory. 2005. In A. Laufer, T. Post, and E.J. Hoffman, *Shared Voyage: Learning and Unlearning from Remarkable Projects*, 44–5. Washington, D.C.: The NASA History Series.

i. Terry Little, U.S. Air Force. 2005. In A. Laufer, T. Post, and E.J. Hoffman, *Shared Voyage: Learning and Unlearning from Remarkable Projects*, 96. Washington, D.C.: The NASA History Series.

j. "Requirements: The More the Better?" Terry Little, U.S. Air Force. 2003. *Ask Magazine* 14 (October): 26–7. http://appel.nasa.gov/ask/about/overview/index.html

k. "A Project Ends at End of Start-Up," Pat Tobergte, Procter & Gamble. 1997. In A. Laufer, *Simultaneous Management: Managing Projects in a Dynamic Environment*, 25–6. New York, NY: AMACOM, American Management Association.

l. "Going and Coming," Scott Cameron, Procter & Gamble. 2002. *Ask Magazine* 6 (January): 32–4. http://appel.nasa.gov/ask/about/overview/index.html

m. "Keep Your Eye on the Ball," David Panhorst, ARDEC. 2000. In A. Laufer and E.J. Hoffman, *Project Management Success Stories*, 131–3. New York, NY: John Wiley & Sons.

n. "A Terry Little Rule," Terry Little, U.S. Air Force. 2005. In A. Laufer, T. Post, and E.J. Hoffman, *Shared Voyage: Learning and Unlearning from Remarkable Projects*, 123–4. Washington, D.C.: The NASA History Series.

o. "Watch Out, Granny!" Larry Lawson, Lockheed Martin Corporation. 2005. In A. Laufer, T. Post, and E.J. Hoffman, *Shared Voyage: Learning and Unlearning from Remarkable Projects*, 113–4. Washington, D.C.: The NASA History Series.

p. "A Terry Little Rule," Terry Little, U.S. Air Force. 2005. In A. Laufer, T. Post, and E.J. Hoffman, *Shared Voyage: Learning and Unlearning from Remarkable Projects*, 124. Washington, D.C.: The NASA History Series.

q. "Cleaning Out the Closet," Scott Cameron, Procter & Gamble. 2004. *Ask Magazine* (November): 19–21. http://appel.nasa.gov/ask/about/overview/index.html

r. "Speed Merchants: A Conversation with Scott Cameron and Terry Little," 2003. *Ask Magazine* 11 (March): 26–9. http://appel.nasa.gov/ask/about/overview/index.html

s. "Hurry to the Classroom, Your Instructor Just Died!" Edward Hoffman, NASA. 2000. In A. Laufer and E.J. Hoffman, *Project Management Success Stories*, 54–7. New York, NY: John Wiley & Sons.

t. "Fly Safe, But Fly," Kenneth Szalai, NASA Dryden Flight Research Center. 2004. *Ask Magazine* 19 (August): 12–5. http://appel.nasa.gov/ask/about/overview/index.html

u. "Simple Solutions Surpass Sophistication," Leslie Shepherd, General Services Administration. 2000. In A. Laufer and E.J. Hoffman, *Project Management Success Stories*, 82–5. New York, NY: John Wiley & Sons.

v. "Radical is Temporary," Larry Barrett, Orbital Sciences Corporation. 2004. *Ask Magazine* 17 (April): 10–3. http://appel.nasa.gov/ask/about/overview/index.html

w. "Right on Time, Radically," Ken Lehtonen, Goddard Space Flight Center. 2004. *Ask Magazine* 17 (April): 6–9. http://appel.nasa.gov/ask/about/overview/index.html

x. "Thanksgiving Hocus Pocus," Christian Zazzali, HITT Corporate Interiors. 2003. *Ask Magazine* 10 (January): 17–21. http://appel.nasa.gov/ask/about/overview/index. html

Chapter 3

Notes

1. A. Laufer and E.J. Hoffman. 2000. *Project Management Success Stories*. New York, NY: John Wiley & Sons, xx–xxi.

2. J. Highsmith. 1999. *Adaptive Software Development*. New York, NY: Dorset House Publishing, 210.

3. P. Vaill. 1996. *Learning as a Way of Being*. San Francisco, CA: Jossey-Bass, 10–4.

4. J. Flower. 1995. A Conversation with Ronald Heifetz: Leadership without Easy Answers. *The Healthcare Forum Journal* 38, 4 (July-August). http://www6.miami.edu/pld/Article_on_Adaptive_change.pdf

5. J. Nelson. *An Interview with Ronald A. Heifetz*. http://www.cambridge-leadership.com/publications/pdfs/heifetz_interview.pdf Accessed August 30, 2007.

6. Ronald Heifetz in the foreword to the book *Shared Voyage*. A. Laufer, T. Post, and E.J. Hoffman. *Shared Voyage: Learning and Unlearning from Remarkable Projects*. 2005. Washington, D.C.: The NASA History Series. v; Leinberger and Tucker also concluded that "there is a shift from a structured to a flexible management style as we realize that **change** is the very essence of the Information Economy." P. Leinberger and B. Tucker. 1991. *The New Individualists: The Generation after the Organization Man*. 1991. New York, NY: Harper Collins, 345.

7. J. Highsmith. 1999. *Adaptive Software Development*. New York, NY: Dorset House Publishing, 208.

8. Even the first principle (Plan and Control to Embrace Change), which is about systems and thus naturally exhibits more management aspects, allows for a great deal of adaptability and can be practiced effectively only if it is supported by strong leadership as well. For example, one purpose of the First Green Guideline is to amplify learning at the early stages (i.e., allowing change). The purpose of the Second Green Guideline is to build short-term stability while allowing long-term flexibility, whereas the purpose of the Third Green Guideline is to maintain overall stability while allowing local changes.

9. Ronald Heifetz in the foreword to the book *Shared Voyage*. A. Laufer, T. Post, and E.J. Hoffman. *Shared Voyage: Learning and Unlearning from Remarkable Projects*. 2005. Washington, D.C.: The NASA History Series, vi.

10. W. Bennis and P. Ward Biederman. 1997. *Organizing Genius: The Secrets of Creative Collaboration*. Reading, MA: Addison-Wesley, 204.

11. T. Kidder. 1981. *The Soul of a New Machine*. Boston, MA: Little, Brown and Company, 275.

12. T. Peters. 1999. *The Project 50 (Reinventing Work): Fifty Ways to Transform Every "Task" into a Project That Matters!* New York, NY: Alfred Knopf, 25.

13. W. Bennis and P. Ward Biederman. 1997. *Organizing Genius: The Secrets of Creative Collaboration*. Reading, MA: Addison-Wesley, 25.

14. T. Peters. 1997. *The Circle of Innovation*. New York, NY: Alfred A Knopf, 480–1.

15. P. Vaill. 1996. *Learning as a Way of Being*. San Francisco, CA: Jossey-Bass, 16.

16. C. Handy. 1997. The Search for Meaning: A Conversation with Charles Handy. *Leader to Leader* 5 (Summer): 14–20. http://www.leadertoleader.org/knowledgecenter/L2L/summer97/handy.html. See also C. Handy. 1998. *The Hungry Spirit*. New York, NY: Broadway Books, 101–21. See also D. Duchon and T. D. A. Plowman. 2005. Nurturing the Spirit at Work: Impact on Work Unit Performance. *The Leadership Quarterly* 16: 807–33.

17. W.G. Bennis. 1999. *Old Dogs, New Tricks*. Provo, UT: Executive Excellence Publishing, 43.

18. W. Bennis and P. Ward Biederman. 1997. *Organizing Genius: The Secrets of Creative Collaboration*. Reading, MA: Addison-Wesley, 205. On finding and managing meaning see P. Glen. 2003. *Leading Geeks*. San Francisco, CA: Jossey Bass, 109–10, 171–2.

19. W.G. Bennis. 1999. *Old Dogs, New Tricks*. Provo, UT: Executive Excellence Publishing, 43.

20. R. Daft and R. Lengel. 1998. *Fusion Leadership: Unlocking the Subtle Forces that Change People and Organizations*. San Francisco, CA: Robert-Koehler, 156–64.

21. All the stories presented in the current guideline stress the need for project autonomy, typically by **maintaining its flexibility**. The reader may remember that allowing project flexibility is one of the primary roles of the Green and Brown Principles. However, as the current guideline will demonstrate, at times the only way to maintain project flexibility is by challenging the status quo. A.C.J. De Leeuw and H.W. Volberda. 1996. On the Concept of Flexibility: A Dual Control Perspective. *Omega, International Journal of Management Science* 24, 2: 121–39. Kamps and Pólos concluded that "organizations attempt to reduce constraints in their environment." J. Kamps and László Pólos. 1999. Reducing Uncertainty: A Formal Theory of Organizations in Action. *American Journal of Sociology* 104, 6 (May): 1774–810. Also in her book *Choices for the Manager*, Rosemary Stewart focuses on the interplay among demands, choices, and constraints. R. Stewart. 1982. *Choices for the Manager*. Englewood Cliffs, NJ: Prentice-Hall.

22. Bruch and Ghoshal compare motivation to will power, arguing, "Note that the difference between motivation and willpower matters only when the particular challenge you face is difficult. Easy and familiar tasks do not engage the human will. Ambitious goals, long-term projects, high uncertainty, extreme opposition—such circumstances both need and stimulate the forces of volition." H. Bruch and S. Ghoshal. 2004. *A Bias for Action: How Effective Managers Harness Their Willpower, Achieve Results, and Stop Wasting Time*. Boston, MA: Harvard Business School Press, 54–6.

23. A somewhat similar phenomenon, this time regarding learning from surprises, is highlighted by Karl Weick and Kathleen Sutcliffe in their book *Managing the Unexpected*. They explain that "perceptions of the unexpected are fleeting . . . You'll probably know when something unexpected happens. You'll know it because you'll feel surprised . . . Trust your feelings. They are a solid clue that your model of the world is in error." K. Weick and K. Sutcliffe. 2001. *Managing the Unexpected*. San Francisco, CA: Jossey-Bass, 41.

24. A systematic treatment of project risks is presented in the Third Green Guideline.

25. K.L. Hammonds. 2002. No Risk, No Reward. *Fast Company* 57 (April): 82.

26. L. Wilson and H. Wilson. 1998. *Play to Win*. Austin, TX: Bard Press, 147–53.

27. D. Ward and C. Quaid. 2007. The Pursuit of Courage, Judgment, and Luck: A Rogue Risk Management Rant Defense. *Defense AT&L* 36, 2 (March–April): 28–30. It is interesting to mention here a related conclusion reached by two well-known researchers on risk and decision making. March and Shapira concluded that "perhaps the most troubling feature of decision theory in this context is the invitation it provides to managerial passivity. By emphasizing the calculation of expectations as a response to risk." J.G. March and Z. Shapira. 1987. Managerial Perspectives on Risk and Risk Taking. *Management Science* 33, 11 (November): 1404–18

28. J. McCain. 2004. In Search of Courage: Finding the Courage within You. *Fast Company* 86 (September): 56. In his book *Practice What You Preach*, David Maister quotes C. S. Lewis: "Courage is not simply one of the virtues, but the form of every virtue at the testing point." D. Maister. 2001. *Practice What You Preach: What Managers Must Do to Create a High Achievement Culture*. New York, NY: The Free Press, 193. Tichy uses the term the "edge" and defines it as "the courage to see

reality and act on it." N. Tichy. 1997. *The Leadership Engine: How Winning Companies Build Leaders at Every Level.* New York, NY: Harper Business, 152–3.

29. H. Rubin. 2002. An Interview with William Ian Miller. *Fast Company* 55 (January): 96.

30. K.K. Reardon. 2007. Courage as a Skill. *Harvard Business Review*, January: 58–64. Miller reached similar conclusions: "To develop moral courage, moral courage must be habituated and practiced." R. Miller. 2005. Moral Courage: Definition and Development. *Ethics Resource Center.* http://www.ethics.org/pdfs/erc_moralcourage_rmiller.pdf

31. W. Bennis and B. Nanus. 1985. *Leaders.* New York, NY: Harper & Row, 69; Pfeffer and Sutton also conclude that "there is no learning without error." They quote Benjamin Zander, the conductor of the Boston Philharmonic, who argues that "we should celebrate our mistakes . . . only by risking hitting wrong notes that learning results." J. Pfeffer and R Sutton. 1999. *The Knowing-Doing Gap: How Smart Companies Turn Knowledge into Action.* Boston, MA: Harvard Business School, 131.

32. A. M. Webber. 2000. Why Can't We Get Anything Done? *Fast Company* 35 (May): 168. An interview with Jeffrey Pfeffer.

33. The ERAST story raises an additional important point: there are times when the role of the project leader is simply to sell the project. However, the general lesson is that projects can, and do, succeed because of politics, and they may also fail because of politics. Politics does not have to be a dirty word. If it means working closely and openly with customers and stakeholders, it is an essential approach that requires continuous dedication of time and attention.

34. J. Gardner. 1990. *On Leadership.* New York, NY: The Free Press, 49.

35. Weick, K. 1998. The Attitudes of Wisdom: Ambivalence as the Optimal Compromise. In *Organizational Wisdom and Executive Courage,* eds. S. Srivasta and D. Cooperider, 40–64. San Francisco, CA: The Lexington Press.

36. J. Quinn, H. Mintzberg, and R. James. 1988. *The Strategy Process: Concepts, Contexts, and Cases.* Englewood Cliffs, NJ: Prentice Hall, xi, 956–60. See also the reflections of John Willard Marriott Jr.: J.W. Marriott Jr. and K.A. Brown. 1997. *The Spirit to Serve: Marriott's Way.* New York, NY: Harper Business, 142.

37. J. Gardner. 1990. *On Leadership.* New York, NY: The Free Press, 49.

38. See also R. Greenleaf. 1977. *Servant Leadership: A Journey into the Nature of Legitimate Power and Greatness,* Mahwah, NJ: Paulist Press, 13.

39. C. Dahle. 2004. On Thin Ice. *Fast Company* 86 (September): 79.

40. J. Collins. 2001. *Good to Great: Why Some Companies Make the Leap and Others Don't.* New York, NY: Harper Business, 12–3, 21.

41. R. Simons, H. Mintzberg, and K. Basu. 2002. Memo to: CEOs. *Fast Company* 59 (June): 117.

42. D. Goleman. 1995. *Emotional Intelligence.* New York, NY: Bantam Books, 87–90.

43. Jim Collins. 2001. *Good to Great: Why Some Companies Make the Leap and Others Don't.* New York, NY: Harper Business, 83–7. Kouzes and Posner assert that the current business environment requires "leaders who express optimism for the future . . . Leaders must keep hope alive, even in the most difficult of time . . . Without hope there can be no courage." J.M. Kouzes and B.Z. Posner. 2002. *The Leadership Challenge.* San Francisco, CA: Jossey-Bass, 398. See also Rosabeth Moss Kanter who concludes that "confidence is real only when it is grounded in reality." R.M. Kanter. 2004. *Confidence: How Winning Streaks and Losing Streaks Begin and End.* New York, NY: Three River Press, 210.

44. C. Dahle. 2004. On Thin Ice. *Fast Company* 86 (September): 79.

45. Jim Collins. 2001. *Good to Great: Why Some Companies Make the Leap and Others Don't.* New York, NY: Harper Business, 83–7.

References

a. "Improvisation is Alive and Well," Rex Geveden, NASA. 2000. In A. Laufer and E.J. Hoffman, *Project Management Success Stories*, 79–81. New York, NY: John Wiley & Sons.

b. "Crash and Learn," Ray Morgan, AeroVironment Design Development Center. 2005. In A. Laufer, T. Post, and E.J. Hoffman, *Shared Voyage: Learning and Unlearning from Remarkable Projects*, 144-5. Washington, D.C.: The NASA History Series.

c. "Two Outs, Bottom of the Ninth," Frank Snow, Goddard Space Flight Center. 2005. In A. Laufer, T. Post, and E.J. Hoffman, *Shared Voyage: Learning and Unlearning from Remarkable Projects*, 66–7. Washington, D.C.: The NASA History Series.

d. "Constancy of Purpose," Chuck Anderson, Raytheon. 2005. In A. Laufer, T. Post, and E.J. Hoffman, *Shared Voyage: Learning and Unlearning from Remarkable Projects*, 202–3. Washington, D.C.: The NASA History Series.

e. "Just Like Buying a TV," Tom Gillman, Raytheon. 2005. In A. Laufer, T. Post, and E.J. Hoffman, *Shared Voyage: Learning and Unlearning from Remarkable Projects*, 204. Washington, D.C.: The NASA History Series.

f. "Listening to the Voice Inside," Joan Salute, Ames Research Center, NASA. *Ask Magazine* 2. http://appel.nasa.gov/ask/about/overview/index.html

g. "What Goes Around, Comes Around," Rick Obenschain, Goddard Space Flight Center, NASA. 2004. *Ask Magazine* 16 (February): 10–5. http://appel.nasa.gov/ask/about/overview/index.html

h. "Test What You Fly?," Don Margolies, Goddard Space Flight Center, NASA. 2005. In A. Laufer, T. Post, and E.J. Hoffman, *Shared Voyage: Learning and Unlearning from Remarkable Projects*, 69–72. Washington, D.C.: The NASA History Series.

i. "The Old Tired Dog," Rex Geveden, NASA. 2000. In A. Laufer and E.J. Hoffman, *Project Management Success Stories*, 13–4. New York, NY: John Wiley & Sons.

j. "Profile of Successful Project Leaders: Col. Jeanne Sutton, U.S. Air Force." 2000. In A. Laufer and E.J. Hoffman, *Project Management Success Stories*, 230–1. New York, NY: John Wiley & Sons.

k. "Nobody's Puppet," Col. Jeanne Sutton, U.S. Air Force. 2000. In A. Laufer and E.J. Hoffman, *Project Management Success Stories*, 111–2. New York, NY: John Wiley & Sons.

l. "*Ask* Talks with Bill Townsend." 2005. *Ask Magazine* 21 (Spring): 42–6. http://appel.nasa.gov/ask/about/overview/index.html

m. "Profile of Successful Project Leaders: Terry Little, U.S. Air Force." 2000. In A. Laufer and E.J. Hoffman, *Project Management Success Stories*, 222–3. New York, NY: John Wiley & Sons.

n. "Straight from the Boss," Lynda Rutledge, U.S. Air Force. 2005. In A. Laufer, T. Post, and E.J. Hoffman, *Shared Voyage: Learning and Unlearning from Remarkable Projects*, 106. Washington, D.C.: The NASA History Series.

o. "What's a Ceiling?" Dougal Maclise, Ames Research Center, NASA. 2001. *Ask Magazine* 3 (May): 18–21. http://appel.nasa.gov/ask/about/overview/index.html

p. "Dropping in on Mars," Tommaso Rivellini, Jet Propulsion Laboratory, NASA. 2003. *Ask Magazine* 13 (August): 18–21 http://appel.nasa.gov/ask/about/overview/index.html

q. "Know Thyself—But Don't Forget to Learn About Your Customer, Too," Jenny Baer-Riedhart, NASA. 2005. In A. Laufer, T. Post, and E.J. Hoffman, *Shared Voyage: Learning and Unlearning from Remarkable Projects*, 138–9. Washington, D.C.: The NASA History Series.

r. "Real Politic," Bob Whitehead, NASA. 2005. In A. Laufer, T. Post, and E.J. Hoffman, *Shared Voyage: Learning and Unlearning from Remarkable Projects*, 139–40. Washington, D.C.: The NASA History Series.

s. "Listening to That Voice Inside," Dave Stickel, Procter & Gamble. 2003. *Ask Magazine* 14 (October): 14–5. http://appel.nasa.gov/ask/about/overview/index.html

t. "*Ask* Talks with Judy Stokley." 2002. *Ask Magazine* 9 (October): 32–7. http://appel.nasa.gov/ask/about/overview/index.html

u. "Price-Based Acquisition," Judy Stokley, U.S. Air Force. 2005. In A. Laufer, T. Post, and E.J. Hoffman, *Shared Voyage: Learning and Unlearning from Remarkable Projects*, 200–1. Washington, D.C.: The NASA History Series.

v. "The Don Quixote Complex," Terry Little, U.S. Air Force. 2001. *Ask Magazine* 5 (September): 12–4. http://appel.nasa.gov/ask/about/overview/index.html

w. My Big Wall," Paul Espinosa, Ames Research Center, NASA. 2002. *Ask Magazine* 7 (March): 27–30. http://appel.nasa.gov/ask/about/overview/index.html

Chapter 4

Notes

1. R. Kanigel. 1997. *The One Best Way: Frederick Winslow Taylor and the Enigma of Efficiency*. New York, NY: The Penguin Books, 19.

2. T. Cooke-Davies. 2002. It's People Who Get Things Done. *Project Manager Today* 14, 1 (January): 16–21; Lechler T. 1998. When It Comes to Project Management, It's The People That Matter: An Empirical Analysis of Project Management in Germany. In *IRNOP III. The Nature and Role of Projects in the Next 20 Years: Research Issues and Problems*, eds. F. Hartman, G. Jergeas, and J. Thomas, 205–15. Calgary, CA: University of Calgary.

3. E.J. Hoffman, C.S.Kinlaw, and D.C. Kinlaw. 2000. Developing Superior Project Teams: A Study of the Characteristics of High Performance in Project Teams. *Proceedings of the PMI Research Conference*, June. Paris, France: 29–35. The Agile Manifesto goes a long way from Taylor and McNamara. This document, formulated in 2001 by a group of software developers, describes the four underlying values of a new project management approach called "the Agile Method":

    a. Individuals and interactions over processes and tools
    b. Working software over comprehensive documentation
    c. Customer collaboration over contract negotiation
    d. Responding to change over following a plan

    That is, while there is value in the items on the right, we value the items on the left more. M. Fowler and J. Highsmith. 2001. The Agile Manifesto. *Software Development*, (August), last accessed February 14, 2007. http://hristov.com/andrey/fhtstuttgart/The_Agile_Manifesto_SDMagazine.pdf. For more on the Agile Method, see M. Poppendieck and T. Poppendieck. 2003. *Lean Software Development—An Agile Toolkit*. Boston, MA: Addison-Wesley; A. Cockburn. 2002. *Agile Software*

Development. Boston, MA: Addison-Wesley; K. Beck. 2000. *Extreme Programming Explained—Embrace Change*. Boston, MA: Addison-Wesley.

4. J. Collins. 2001. *Good to Great: Why Some Companies Make the Leap and Others Don't*. New York, NY: Harper Business, 13–5.

5. J. Kilts. 2007. *Doing What Matters: How to Get Results That Make a Difference—The Revolutionary Old-School Approach*. New York, NY: Crown Business, 146.

6. T. Peters. 1999. *The Project 50 (Reinventing Work): Fifty Ways to Transform Every "Task" into a Project That Matters!* New York, NY: Alfred A. Knopf, 156.

7. A. Laufer and E.J.Hoffman. 2000. *Project Management Success Stories: Lessons of Project Leaders*. New York, NY: John Wiley & Sons, 115–7, 219–24.

8. One camp is probably best represented by three McKinsey consultants who published the book *The War for Talent* on the basis of a comprehensive study. They assert that talented people are scarce and that superior talent makes a huge difference in company performance. E. Michaels, H. Handfield-Jones, and B. Axelrod. 2001. *The War for Talent*. Boston, MA: Harvard Business School Press.

9. G. Colvin. 2006. Why Dream Teams Fail. *Fortune*, June. http://cnnmoney.printthis. clickability.com

10. S. Berkun. 2005. *#47. Teams and Stars. scottberkun.com*, October. http://www. scottberkun. com/essays/essay47.htm

11. E. Yourdon. 1999. *Death March: The Complete Software Developer's Guide to Surviving "Mission Impossible" Projects*. Upper Saddle River, NJ: Prentice Hall, 120–3.

12. J.R. Katzenbach and D.K. Smith. 1993. *The Wisdom of Teams: Creating the High-Performance Organization*. Boston, MA: Harvard Business School Press, 18, 120; T. Peters. 1999. *The Project 50 (Reinventing Work): Fifty Ways to Transform Every "Task" into a Project That Matters!* New York, NY: Alfred A. Knopf, 84–6.

13. Using Tom Davenport's classification of knowledge workers, one can easily see that the criteria for "right people" depend on the context and, in particular, are not the same for permanent and temporary (projects) organizations. T.H. Davenport. 2002. Can You Boost Knowledge Work's Impact on the Bottom Line? *Harvard Management Update* (November): 10–1. Campitt and DeKoch conclude that in an uncertain environment, it is not sufficient to hire very intelligent people who are low on "emotional intelligence," since only those with high "emotional intelligence" "can overcome the inevitable setbacks associated with attempting new tasks." P.G. Campitt and R.J. DeKoch. 2001. *Embracing Uncertainty: The Essence of Leadership*. Armonk, NY: M.E. Sharpe, 154.

14. P. Carbonara. 1996. Hire for Attitude, Train for Skill. *Fast Company* 4 (August): 73.

15. L. Crawford. 2005. Senior Management Perceptions of Project Management Competence. *International Journal of Project Management* 23, 1: 7–16

16. Studying four great project managers, Alan Webb asks the eternal question, "are great project managers born or made?" and his reply is "both." A. Webb. 1996. Great Engineering Project Managers: Are They Born or Made? Part 1. *Engineering Management Journal* 6, 1 (February): 33–40; A. Webb. 1996. Great Engineering Project Managers: Are They Born or Made? Part 2. *Engineering Management Journal* 6, 2 (April): 79–87. See also L. Crawford. 2005. Senior Management Perceptions of Project Management Competence. *International Journal of Project Management* 23: 7–16. L. Crawford. 2000. Profiling the Competent Project Manager. In *Project Management Research at the Turn of the Millennium: Proceedings of PMI Research Conference*, 21–4 June. Paris, France: 3–15. Sylva, NC: Project Management Institute; H. Mintzberg. 2004. Leadership and Management Development: An Afterword.

Academy of Management Executive 18, 3 (August): 140–2; J.A. Raelin. 2004. Don't Bother Putting Leadership into People. *Academy of Management Executive* 18, 3 (August): 131–5. See also two studies by O. Gadeken. 1990. A Competency Model of Program Managers in the DOD Acquisition Process. *Defense Systems Management College.* February; O. Gadeken. 1991. Competencies of Project Managers in the MOD Procurement Executive. *Royal Military College of Science,* July. Shrivenham, UK.

17. See, for example, L. Huff and L. Kelley. 2003. Levels of Organizational Trust in Individualist versus Collectivist Societies: A Seven-Nation Study. *Organization Science* 14, 1 (January–February): 81–90; J.B. Barney and M.H. Hansen. 1994. Trustworthiness as a Source of Competitive Advantage. *Strategic Management Journal* 15 (Winter): 175–90.

18. F. Fukuyama. 1995. *Trust: The Social Virtues and the Creation of Prosperity.* New York, NY: The Free Press, 7. Fukuyama proposes that it is the social capital of a given country (or even area within a country) that defines how its economy functions.

19. K. Kelly. 1999. *New Rules for the New Economy: 10 Radical Strategies for a Connected World.* New York, NY: Penguin Books, 118–39.

20. Alistair Cockburn discusses the contribution of collaboration between two parties to their formal contract and maintains that "good collaboration can save a contract situation when it is in jeopardy. Good collaboration can sometimes make a contract unnecessary. Either way, collaboration is the winning element." A. Cockburn. 2002. *Agile Software Development.* Boston, MA: Addison-Wesley, 218.

21. J.R. Katzenbach and D.K. Smith. 1993. *The Wisdom of Teams: Creating the High-Performance Organization.* Boston, MA: Harvard Business School Press, 18. Alistair Cockburn asserts that "one might think that removing all conflict from a project team should be the best, but that turns out to be not the case. People need to be able to disagree in order to identify design problems." A. Cockburn. 2002. *Agile Software Development.* Boston, MA; Addison-Wesley, 101.

22. J.R. Katzenbach and D.K. Smith. 1993. *The Wisdom of Teams: Creating the High-Performance Organization.* Boston, MA: Harvard Business School Press, 111.

23. Successful project managers pay great attention to the size of their project team. They create the smallest team possible that includes all the necessary skills. Katzenbach and Smith maintain that large numbers of people have trouble interacting constructively as a group and experience difficulties "agreeing on actionable specifics." They conclude that groups larger than 20 or 25 have difficulties becoming real teams. J.R. Katzenbach and D.K. Smith. 1993. *The Wisdom of Teams: Creating the High-Performance Organization.* Boston, MA: Harvard Business School Press, 45–7.

24. J.R. Katzenbach and D.K. Smith. 1993. *The Wisdom of Teams: Creating the High-Performance Organization.* Boston, MA: Harvard Business School Press, 211.

25. J. Kouzes and B. Posner. 1993. *Credibility: How Leaders Gain and Lose It, Why People Demand It.* San Francisco, CA: Jossey-Bass, 107.

26. R. Solomon and F. Flores. 2001. *Building Trust in Business, Politics, Relationships and Life.* New York, NY: Oxford University Press, 14.

27. R. Solomon and F. Flores. 2001. *Building Trust in Business, Politics, Relationships and Life.* New York, NY: Oxford University Press, 13.

28. K. Kelly. 1999. *New Rules for the New Economy: 10 Radical Strategies for a Connected World.* New York, NY: Penguin Books, 133.

29. O.E. Williamson. 1979. Transaction-Cost Economics: The Governance of Contractual Relations. *The Journal of Law and Economics* 22, 2: 233–61; L.T. Hosmer. 1995. Trust: The Connecting Link between Organizational Theory and

Philosophical Ethics. *Academy of Management Review* 20, 2 (April): 379–403. J.H. Dyer and W. Chu. 2003. The Role of Trustworthiness in Reducing Transaction Costs and Improving Performance: Empirical Evidence from the United States, Japan and Korea. *Organization Science* 14, 1 (January–February): 57–68. O.E. Williamson. 1985. *The Economic Institutions of Capitalism.* New York, NY: Free Press; O.E. Williamson. 1991. Comparative Economic Organization: The Analysis of Discrete Structural Alternatives. *Administrative Science Quarterly* 36, 2 (June): 269–96.

30. R. Solomon and F. Flores. 2001. *Building Trust in Business, Politics, Relationships and Life.* New York, NY: Oxford University Press, 14.

31. R. Solomon and F. Flores. 2001. *Building Trust in Business, Politics, Relationships and Life.* New York, NY: Oxford University Press, 45–6.

32. J.H. Dyer and W. Chu. 2003. The Role of Trustworthiness in Reducing Transaction Costs and Improving Performance: Empirical Evidence from the United States, Japan and Korea. *Organization Science* 14, 1 (January–February): 57–68. This is how Charles Handy defines trust: "By trust, organizations really mean confidence, a confidence in someone's competence and in his or her commitment to a goal." C. Handy. 1995. Trust and the Virtual Organization: How Do You Manage People Whom You Do Not See? *Harvard Business Review* 73, 3 (May/June): 40–50.

33. J. Kouzes and B. Posner. 1993. *Credibility: How Leaders Gain and Lose It, Why People Demand It.* San Francisco, CA: Jossey-Bass, 25.

34. R. Solomon and F. Flores. 2001. *Building Trust in Business, Politics, Relationships and Life.* New York, NY: Oxford University Press, 14, 43.

35. WIRE Case Study. Response #2 by James Watzin. http://appel.nasa.gov/node/32; http://klabs.org/richcontent/Reports/nasa_wire_lesson.pdf.

36. J.H. Dyer and W. Chu. 2003. The Role of Trustworthiness in Reducing Transaction Costs and Improving Performance: Empirical Evidence from the United States, Japan and Korea. *Organization Science* 14, 1 (January–February): 57–68.

37. P.M. Senge, A. Kleiner, C. Roberts, and B. Smith. 1994. *The Fifth Discipline Fieldbook: Strategies and Tools for Building a Learning Organization.* New York, NY: Doubleday Currency, 28.

38. J.A. Highsmith III. 2000. *Adaptive Software Development—A Collaborative Approach to Managing Complex Systems.* New York, NY: Dorset House Publishing, 206.

39. C. Lane. 1998. Introduction: Theories and Issues in the Study of Trust. In *Trust within and between Organizations: Conceptual Issues and Empirical* Applications, eds. Christel Lane and Reinhard Bachmann, 1–30. New York, NY: Oxford University Press.

40. J.H. Dyer and W. Chu. 2003. The Role of Trustworthiness in Reducing Transaction Costs and Improving Performance: Empirical Evidence from the United States, Japan and Korea. *Organization Science* 14, 1 (January–February): 57–68; B. Uzzi. 1997. Social Structure and Competition in Interfirm Networks: The Paradox of Embeddedness. *Administrative Science Quarterly* 42, 2 (June): 35–67.

41. G.R. Jones and J.A. George. 1998. The Experience and Evolution of Trust: Implications for Cooperation and Teamwork. *Academy of Management Review* 23, 3: 531–46. See also R.B. Shaw. 1997. *Trust in Balance: Building Successful Organizations on Results, Integrity, and Concern.* San Francisco, CA: Jossey-Bass Publishers, 13–5.

42. In his book *Group Genius*, Keith Sawyer makes a strong tie between collaboration and innovation. Sawyer advises us to forget about the myth of the solitary genius. Innovation, he explains, emerges from a series of sparks—not from a single flash of insight. Therefore, collaboration increases the capability of the organization to

generate more ideas and better ideas and enhances the culture of innovation. K. Sawyer. 2007. *Group Genius: The Creative Power of Collaboration.* New York, NY: Basic Books.

43. T.K. Das and B.S. Teng. 1998. Between Trust and Control: Developing Confidence in Partner Cooperation in Alliances. *Academy of Management Review* 23, 3: 491–512.

44. B.K. Muirhead and W.L. Simon. 1999. *High Velocity Leadership: The Mars Pathfinder Approach to Faster, Better, Cheaper.* New York, NY: Harper Collins Publishers, 154.

45. R. Solomon and F. Flores. 2001. *Building Trust in Business, Politics, Relationships and Life.* New York, NY: Oxford University Press, 26–7.

46. Various popular sports games are often used as metaphors for the different working styles of project teams. For example, for relatively low-uncertainty situations and when relatively large teams are employed, a common metaphor is that of a football game. Here, a strong central leadership places the players in fixed positions, with the emphasis on "scheduling and control." For high-uncertainty situations and when relatively small teams are employed, the game plan metaphor often used is that of basketball. Here, the team structure and working style are geared to promoting creative and spontaneous interaction and high adaptability within a small team tied by a fairly loose definition of roles. However, in today's dynamic environment of many projects, the rules of the game, and even the game plan itself, often change during the game, making the sustaining of teamwork even more critical. See, for example, R.W. Keidel. 1984. *Game Plans: Sports Strategies for Business.* New York, NY: Berkley Books.

47. A.J. Nurick and H.J. Thamhain. 2006. Team Development in Multinational Environments, Chapter 19. In *Global Project Management Handbook*, eds. D.I. Cleland and R. Gareis. New York, NY: McGraw-Hill.

48. C. Conley. 2007. *Peak: How Great Companies Get Their Mojo from Maslow.* San Francisco, CA: Jossey-Bass, 45–54.

49. J. Collins. 2001. *Good to Great: Why Some Companies Make the Leap and Others Don't.* New York, NY: Harper Business, 50.

50. J.R. Katzenbach and D.K. Smith. 1993. *The Wisdom of Teams: Creating the High-Performance Organization.* Boston, MA: Harvard Business School Press, 13.

51. Not recognizing individual members of the team is a grave mistake. Randolph and Posner state it very succinctly: "There is nothing so unequal as the equal treatment of unequals." However, when discussing teamwork, Augustine stresses very clearly that "this is most assuredly not to say there is no place for individualists, only that it is necessary for members of the team to suppress individual desires for the overall good of the team." P.C. Earley and C.B. Gibson. 1998. Taking Stock in Our Progress on Individualism-Collectivism: 100 Years of Solidarity and Community. *Journal of Management* 24, 3: 265–304; W.A. Randolph and B.Z. Posner. 1987. *Getting the Job Done!; Managing Project Teams and Task forces for Success.* Englewood Cliffs, NJ: Prentice Hall, 64; N.R. Augustine. 1986. *Augustine's Laws.* New York, NY: Viking-Penguin, 363–4; W. Royce. 1998. *Software Project Management: A Unified Framework.* Boston, MA: Addison-Wesley, 45

52. N.R. Augustine. 1986. *Augustine's Laws.* New York, NY: Viking-Penguin, 363–4.

53. T.E. Deal and A.A. Kennedy. 1999. *The New Corporate Cultures.* Reading, MA: Perseus Books, 244.

54. D. Goleman, R. Boyatzis, and A. McKee. 2002. *Primal Leadership: Learning to Lead with Emotional Intelligence.* Boston, MA: Harvard Business School Press, 14.

55. J.R. Katzenbach and D.K. Smith. 1993. *The Wisdom of Teams: Creating the High-Performance Organization.* Boston, MA: Harvard Business School Press, 164–5.

56. K. Beck. 1999. *Extreme Programming (XP) Explained: Embrace Change.* Boston, MA: Addison-Wesley, 34–5.

57. L. Bolman and T. Deal. 1992. What Makes a Team Work? *Organizational Dynamics* (Autumn): 34–44.

58. L. Bolman and T. Deal. 1992. What Makes a Team Work? *Organizational Dynamics* (Autumn): 34–44; T.E. Deal and A.A. Kennedy. 1999. *The New Corporate Cultures.* Reading, MA: Perseus Books, 247; J. James. 1996. *Thinking in the Future Tense: Leadership Skills for a New Age.* New York, NY: Simon & Schuster, 175.

59. T. Kidder. *The Soul of a New Machine.* 1981. Boston, MA: Little, Brown and Company: 272–3.

60. W. Bennis and P.W. Biederman. 1997. *Organizing Genius: The Secret of Creative Collaboration.* Reading, MA: Addison-Wesley, 215.

61. R.P. White, P. Hodgson, and S. Crainer. 1996. *The Future of Leadership: Riding the Corporate Rapids into the 21st Century.* Lanham, MD: Pitman Publishing, 163–7.

62. E. de Bono. 1984. *Tactics: The Art and Science of Success.* Boston, MA: Little Brown and Company, 54.

63. W. Bennis and P.W. Biederman. 1997. *Organizing Genius: The Secret of Creative Collaboration.* Reading, MA: Addison-Wesley, 203. Katzenbach and Smith reach a somewhat similar conclusion, though based on a different rationale: "Teams are not antithetical to individual performance. Real teams always find ways for each individual to contribute and thereby gain distinction." J.R. Katzenbach and D.K. Smith. 1993. *The Wisdom of Teams: Creating the High-Performance Organization.* Boston, MA: Harvard Business School Press, 14.

64. See an elaborate analysis of these people-oriented steps in L. Bolman and T. Deal. 1992. What Makes a Team Work? *Organizational Dynamics* (Autumn): 34–44.

65. J.R. Katzenbach and D.K. Smith. 1993. *The Wisdom of Teams: Creating the High-Performance Organization.* Boston, MA: Harvard Business School Press, 107.

References

a. "McNamara, I Am Not," Terry Little, U.S. Air Force. 2005. In A. Laufer, T. Post, and E.J. Hoffman, *Shared Voyage: Learning and Unlearning from Remarkable Projects,* 87–8. Washington, D.C.: The NASA History Series.

b. "Start Up," Ken Schwer, NASA. 2003. *Ask Magazine* 11 (March): 18–20. http://appel.nasa.gov/ask/about/overview/index.html

c. "Girl Sat," Mary Chiu, Johns Hopkins Applied Physics Laboratory. 2005. In A. Laufer, T. Post, and E.J. Hoffman, *Shared Voyage: Learning and Unlearning from Remarkable Projects,* 39–40. Washington, D.C.: The NASA History Series.

d. "Compliments to the Chef," Allan Frandsen, California Institute of Technology. 2005. In A. Laufer, T. Post, and E.J. Hoffman, *Shared Voyage: Learning and Unlearning from Remarkable Projects,* 35–7. Washington, D.C.: The NASA History Series.

e. "What Goes Around Comes Around," Rick Obenschain, Goddard, NASA. 2004. *Ask Magazine* 16 (February): 10–5. http://appel.nasa.gov/ask/about/overview/index.html

f. "Constancy of Purpose," Chuck Anderson, Raytheon. 2005. In A. Laufer, T. Post, and E.J. Hoffman, *Shared Voyage: Learning and Unlearning from Remarkable Projects,* 202–3. Washington, D.C.: The NASA History Series.

g. "Earthly Considerations on Mars," Tim Flores, NASA. 2003. *Ask Magazine* 12 (June): 5–8. http://appel.nasa.gov/ask/about/overview/index.html

h. "Teaming to Make a Routine of the Impossible," Linda Abbot, NASA. 2000. In A. Laufer and E.J. Hoffman, *Project Management Success Stories*, 158–62. New York, NY: John Wiley & Sons.

i. "If One Fails, We All Fail," Bill Clegern, Procter & Gamble. 1997. In A. Laufer, *Simultaneous Management: Managing Projects in a Dynamic Environment*, 144–5. New York, NY: AMACOM, American Management Association.

j. "Common Ground," Gerald Murphy, California Institute of Technology. 2005. In A. Laufer, T. Post, and E.J. Hoffman, *Shared Voyage: Learning and Unlearning from Remarkable Projects*, 59–60. Washington, D.C.: The NASA History Series.

k. "Old Journey, New Heights," John Del Frate, NASA. 2005. Ask Magazine 21 (Spring): 6–9. http://appel.nasa.gov/ask/about/overview/index.html

l. "Someone Has to Get It," George Sudan, U.S. Air Force. 2005. In A. Laufer, T. Post, and E.J. Hoffman, *Shared Voyage: Learning and Unlearning from Remarkable Projects*, 175–6. Washington, D.C.: The NASA History Series.

m. "Meeting of Minds," Judy Stokley, U.S. Air Force. 2005. In A. Laufer, T. Post, and E.J. Hoffman, *Shared Voyage: Learning and Unlearning from Remarkable Projects*, 182–4. Washington, D.C.: The NASA History Series.

n. "The Big 'If,'" Chuck Anderson, Raytheon. 2005. In A. Laufer, T. Post, and E.J. Hoffman, *Shared Voyage: Learning and Unlearning from Remarkable Projects*, 185. Washington, D.C.: The NASA History Series.

o. "Trust is Money," Judy Stokley, U.S. Air Force. 2005. In A. Laufer, T. Post, and E.J. Hoffman, *Shared Voyage: Learning and Unlearning from Remarkable Projects*, 188–90. Washington, D.C.: The NASA History Series.

p. "The Handshake," Chuck Anderson, Raytheon. 2005. In A. Laufer, T. Post, and E.J. Hoffman, *Shared Voyage: Learning and Unlearning from Remarkable Projects*, 187. Washington, D.C.: The NASA History Series.

q. "That's Confidential Data!," Chuck Anderson, Raytheon. 2005. In A. Laufer, T. Post, and E.J. Hoffman, *Shared Voyage: Learning and Unlearning from Remarkable Projects*, 197. Washington, D.C.: The NASA History Series.

r. "Constancy of Purpose," Chuck Anderson, Raytheon. 2005. In A. Laufer, T. Post, and E.J. Hoffman, *Shared Voyage: Learning and Unlearning from Remarkable Projects*, 202–3. Washington, D.C.: The NASA History Series.

s. "What Measure Matters?" Brock McCaman, Raytheon. 2005. In A. Laufer, T. Post, and E.J. Hoffman, *Shared Voyage: Learning and Unlearning from* Remarkable Projects, 191. Washington, D.C.: The NASA History Series.

t. "Enabler," Jon Westphal, U.S. Air Force. 2005. In A. Laufer, T. Post, and E.J. Hoffman, *Shared Voyage: Learning and Unlearning from Remarkable Projects*, 197–9. Washington, D.C.: The NASA History Series.

u. "Trust is Money," Judy Stokley, U.S. Air Force. 2005. In A. Laufer, T. Post, and E.J. Hoffman, *Shared Voyage: Learning and Unlearning from Remarkable Projects*, 188–90. Washington, D.C.: The NASA History Series.

v. "Project Management: Easy as ABC," Allan Frandsen, California Institute of Technology. 2005. In A. Laufer, T. Post, and E.J. Hoffman, *Shared Voyage: Learning and Unlearning from Remarkable Projects*, 47–9. Washington, D.C.: The NASA History Series.

w. "For Better or Worse," Larry Lawson, Lockheed Martin Corporation. 2005. In A. Laufer, T. Post, and E.J. Hoffman, *Shared Voyage: Learning and Unlearning from Remarkable Projects*, 118–9. Washington, D.C.: The NASA History Series.

x. "A Terry Little Rule," Terry Little, U.S. Air Force. 2005. In A. Laufer, T. Post, and E.J. Hoffman, *Shared Voyage: Learning and Unlearning from Remarkable Projects*, 123–4. Washington, D.C.: The NASA History Series.

y. "What a Little Barbecue Sauce Will Do," Jerry Madden, NASA. 2000. In A. Laufer and E.J. Hoffman, *Project Management Success Stories*, 177. New York, NY: John Wiley & Sons.

z. "The 'Tried and True,'" Frank Snow, NASA. 2005. In A. Laufer, T. Post, and E.J. Hoffman, *Shared Voyage: Learning and Unlearning from Remarkable Projects*, 62–3. Washington, D.C.: The NASA History Series.

aa. "Pulling Stories Out of the Trunk," Larry Goshorn, ITT Industries. 2003. *Ask Magazine* 15 (December): 15. http://appel.nasa.gov/ask/about/overview/index.html

Chapter 5

Notes

1. C. Barnard. 1938. *The Functions of the Executive*. Cambridge, MA: Harvard University Press, 226. In a more recent article, Young and Post reached a similar conclusion: *"The Chief Executive as Communication Champion."* M. Young and J.E. Post. 1993. Managing to Communicate, Communicating to Manage: How Leading Companies Communicate with Employees. *Organizational Dynamics* 22, 1: 31–43.

2. F. Brooks. 1995. *The Mythical Man-Month*. Reading, MA: Addison-Wesley, 240.

3. R. Panko. 1992. Managerial Communication Patterns. *Journal of Organizational Computing* 2, 1: 95–122.

4. The basic unit (for measurement and analysis) used by this study was that of activities. Activities were defined by the mode of work used by the manager (i.e., meetings, tours, telephone conversations, and so on), and the change in the composition (identity or number) of the participants in the activity. As in several other studies, the study recognized the existence of simultaneity, meaning that one single activity can accommodate more than one recorded category, such as information delivered to the manager both verbally and in writing during the same activity. Therefore, the percentages of the accumulated durations of the various communication modes totaled more than 100 percent. A. Laufer, A. Shapira, and D. Telem. 2008. Communicating in Dynamic Conditions: How Do On-Site Construction Project Managers Do It? *Journal of Management in Engineering, ASCE* 24, 2: 75–86.

5. Giles Hirst and Leon Mann assert, *"Communication processes form the building block of effective teamwork."* G. Hirst and L. Mann. 2004. A Model of R&D Leadership and Team Communication: The Relationship with Project Performance. *R&D Management* 34, 2 (March): 147–60. M. Becerra and A. Gupta. 2003. Perceived Trustworthiness within the Organization: The Moderating Impact of Communication Frequency on Trustor and Trustee Effects. *Organization Science* 14, 1 (January–February): 32–44.

6. As early as 1974, Jay Galbraith reached the conclusion that "the greater the uncertainty of the task, the greater the amount of information that has to be processed between decision makers during the execution of the task." J. Galbraith. 1974. Organization Design: An Information Processing View. *Interfaces* 4, 3 (May): 28–36.

7. Indeed, the Gray Principle is located at the center of Exhibits 1 and 2 in the introduction, surrounded by the other four principles.

8. H. Mintzberg. 1973. *The Nature of Managerial Work*. New York, NY: Harper and Row, 71; H. Mintzberg. 1971. Managerial Work: Analysis from Observation. *Management Science* 18, 2 (October): B97–B110.

9. Currently, even permanent organizations find the need to adopt a more active outlook regarding information flow. Stephan Haeckel, for example, highlights the need to cope with change and as a result to switch from "make and sell" to "sense and respond." See S. Haeckel. 1999. *Adaptive Enterprise: Creating and Leading Sense-and Respond Organizations*. Boston, MA: Harvard Business School Press, 12–3, 32–4.

10. B.J. Cullen and O.C. Gadeken. 1990. *Competency Model of Program Managers in the DOD Acquisition Process*. Fort Belvoir, VA: Defense Systems Management College, Appendix E.

11. W.A. Randolph and B.Z. Posner. 1992. *Getting the Job Done!: Managing Project Teams and Task Forces for Success*. Englewood Cliffs, NJ: Prentice Hall, 77–84.

12. A. Laufer, A. Shapira, and D. Telem. 2008. Communicating in Dynamic Conditions: How Do On-Site Construction Project Managers Do It? *Journal of Management in Engineering, ASCE* 24, 2: 75–86.

13. A. Laufer, A. Shapira, and D. Telem. 2008. Communicating in Dynamic Conditions: How Do On-Site Construction Project Managers Do It? *Journal of Management in Engineering, ASCE* 24, 2: 75–86.

14. C. Wheelwright and K.B. Clark. 1992. *Revolutionizing Product Development: Quantum Leaps in Speed, Efficiency, and Quality*. New York, NY: The Free Press, 175–7. See also K.B. Clark and T. Fujimoto. 1991. *Product Development Performance: Strategy, Organization, and Management in the World Auto Industry*. Boston, MA: Harvard Business School Press, 210–2.

15. B. Boehm and R. Turner. 2004. *Balancing Agility and Discipline—A Guide for the Perplexed*. Boston, MA: Addison-Wesley, 34–5.

16. The project manager's role of maintaining frequent two-way communication is underscored by Williams. But, in her case of XP programming, frequent means "every few minutes." L. Williams. 2003. The XP Programmer: The Few-Minutes Programmer. *IEEE Software* 20, 3 (May–June): 16–20.

17. M. David. 2007. *Extreme Project Management: Using Agile*, 01/03/07 http://business.itbusinessnet.com/articles/viewarticle.jsp?id=92814.

18. Williams also stresses the importance of being not simply communicative, but also being "communicative with everyone on the team." L. Williams. 2003. The XP Programmer: The Few-Minutes Programmer. *IEEE Software* 20, 3 (May–June): 16–20.

19. J. Seely Brown and P. Duguid. 2000. *The Social Life of Information*. Boston, MA: Harvard Business School Press, 107, 260.

20. One of the principles presented in the book *X-teams: How to Build Teams that Lead, Innovate, and Succeed* is "X-teams engage in high levels of external activities." D.G. Ancona and H. Bresman. 2007. *X-teams: How to Build Teams that Lead, Innovate, and Succeed*. Boston, MA: Harvard Business School Press, 65. See also D.G. Ancona and D.F. Caldwell. 1992. Bridging the Boundary: External Activity and Performance in Organizational Teams. *Administrative Science Quarterly* 37, 4 (December): 634–5.

21. Gilbreath discusses four levels of organizations with whom the project manager has to communicate: Level 1: Contractors, suppliers, company services; Level 2: Contractor operations, company operations, competing projects; Level 3: Customers, regulators, insurers; Level 4: Community, media, general public. See R.D. Gilbreath. 1986. *Winning at Project Management*. New York, NY: John Wiley and Sons, 280–8.

22. See, for example, Young and Post, who concur with this concept and recommend, "Communicate what you know when you know it. Do not wait until every detail is resolved." M. Young and J.E. Post. 1993. Managing to Communicate, Communicating to Manage: How Leading Companies Communicate with Employees. *Organizational Dynamics* 22, 1: 31–43.

23. T.H. Davenport and J.C. Beck. 2001. *The Attention Economy: Understanding the New Currency of Business,* Boston, MA: Harvard Business School Press, 3–11. See also the discussion about scarcity of attention in the Second Green Guideline (Employ a Learning-Based Planning and Control Process). See also M.T. Hansen and M.R. Haas. 2001. Competing for Attention in Knowledge Markets: Electronic Document Dissemination in a Management Consulting Company. *Administrative Science Quarterly* 46, 1: 1–28.

24. B.A. Nardi and S.Whittaker. 2002. The Place of Face-to-Face Communication in Distributed Work. In *Distributed Work,* eds. P. Hindsand and S. Kiesler, 95–7. Cambridge, MA: The MIT Press.

25. N. Nohria and R.G. Eccles. 1992. Face-to-Face: Making Network Organizations Work. In *Networks and Organizations,* eds. N. Nohria and R.G. Eccles, 288–308. Boston, MA: Harvard Business School Press.

26. In her article "Sharing Meaning across Occupational Communities," Beth Bechky links the misunderstandings between engineers, technicians, and assemblers on a production floor to their work contexts. B.A. Bechky. 2003. Sharing Meaning across Occupational Communities: The Transformation of Understanding on a Production Floor. *Organization Science* 14, 3 (May–June): 312–30.

27. P. Drucker. 1989. *The New Realities: In Government and Politics/In Economics and Business/In Society and World View.* New York, NY: Harper and Row, 260. In their book *Intercultural Communication: A Discourse Approach,* Ron Scollon and Susan Wong Scollon reach a similar conclusion by discussing the limitations of language. R. Scollon and S.W. Scollon. 2001. *Intercultural Communication: A Discourse Approach.* Cambridge, MA: Wiley-Blackwell, 10–11.

28. R.L. Daft and R.H. Lengel. 1984. Information Richness: A New Approach to Managerial Behavior and Organization Design. In *Research in Organizational Behavior,* eds. B. Staw and L.L. Cummings, 191–233. Greenwich, CT.: JAI Press; R.L. Daft and R.H. Lengel. 1986. Organizational Information Requirements, Media Richness and Structural Design. *Management Science* 32, 5: 554–69; N. Nohria and R.G. Eccles. 1992. Face-to-Face: Making Network Organizations Work. In *Networks and Organizations,* eds. N. Nohria and R.G. Eccles, 288–308. Boston, MA: Harvard Business School Press; J.W. Jones, C. Saunders, and R. McLeod. 1994. Information Acquisition during Decision Making Processes: An Exploratory Study of Decision Roles in Media Selection. *IEEE Transactions on Engineering Management* 41, 1: 41–9.

29. This duplication of cues inherent in the face-to-face medium provides an essential measure of redundancy. In uncertain and ambiguous situations, this redundancy significantly enhances the reliability of communication. See M. Landau. 1969. Redundancy, Rationality, and the Problem of Duplication and Overlap. *Public Administration Review* 29, 4 (July–August): 346–58. See also A. Cockburn. 2002. *Agile Software Development.* Boston, MA: Addison-Wesley, 91–5.

30. D.D. Acker. 1980. *Skill in Communication.* Fort Belview, VA: Publications Division, Defense Systems Management College.

31. A. Meherabian. 1971. *Silent Messages.* Belmont, CA: Wadsworth.

32. Alistair Cockburn asserts that "interactive, face-to-face communication is the cheapest and fastest channel for exchanging information." A. Cockburn. 2002. *Agile Software Development*. Boston, MA: Addison-Wesley, 148.

33. K. Weick and K. Sutcliffe. 2001. *Managing the Unexpected: Assuring High Performance in an Age of Complexity*. San Francisco, CA: Jossey-Bass, 168.

34. K. Weick and K. Sutcliffe. 2001. *Managing the Unexpected: Assuring High Performance in an Age of Complexity*. San Francisco, CA: Jossey-Bass, 168; R.L. Daft and D. Marcic. 1998. *Understanding Management*. Fort Worth, TX: The Dryden Press, 484–6.

35. T.J. Allen. 1977. *Managing the Flow of Technology*. Boston, MA: MIT Press. See also T.J. Allen. 2007. Architecture and Communication among Product Development Engineers. *California Management Review* 49, 2 (Winter): 23–41.

36. G.O. Goodman and M.J. Abel. 1987. Communication and Collaboration: Facilitating Cooperative Work through Communication. *Technology and People* 3: 129–145. This is how Kiesler and Cummings concluded their comprehensive review of face-to-face studies: "Research shows that face-to-face discussion has a strong impact on cooperation through its impact on bonds, social contract, and group identity. It is the most powerful medium known for coordinating work within an interdependent group . . . the frequency of spontaneous, informal communication has dramatic effects on the strength of social and work ties and on the evolution of activities that people do together and functions they serve for one another." S. Kiesler and J. Cummings. 2002. What Do We Know about Proximity and Distance in Work Groups? A Legacy of Research. In *Distributed Work*, eds. P. Hinds and S. Kiesler, 57–82. Cambridge, MA: The MIT Press. Hogel and Proserpio found that "team members' proximity is significantly related to teamwork quality." M. Hogel and L. Proserpio. 2004. Team Member Proximity and Teamwork in Innovative Projects. *Research Policy* 33: 1153–65. Allen explains that "people who work nearby come to know each other better, are much more likely to share what they are doing, and consequently coordinate their work better." T.J. Allen. 2007. Architecture and Communication among Product Development Engineers. *California Management Review* 49, 2 (Winter): 23–41. See also S. Teasley, L. Covi, M.S. Krishnan, and J.S. Olson. 2000. How Does Radical Collocation Help a Team Succeed? *Proceedings of the 2000 ACM Conference on Computer Supported Cooperative Work*. New York, NY: ACM Press, 339–46.

37. C. Meyer. 1993. *Fast Cycle Time: How to Align Purpose, Strategy, and Structure for Speed*. New York, NY: The Free Press, 133, 217.

38. T. Peters. 1992. *Liberation Management: Necessary Disorganization for the Nanosecond Nineties*. New York, NY: Alfred Knopf, 413–14. Kahn and McDonough reported about the results of research conducted at McDonnell Douglas, Ford, and Honda. All found that colocation promoted integration. K.B. Kahn and E.F. McDonough III. 1997. An Empirical Study of the Relationships among Co-location, Integration, Performance, and Satisfaction. *Journal of Production Innovation Management* 14, 3 (May): 161–78.

39. L. Sproull and S. Kiesler. 1995. *Connections: New Ways of Working in the Networked Organization*. Cambridge, MA: The MIT Press, 125–6.

40. B.L. Kirkman and J.E. Mathieu. 2005. The Dimensions and Antecedents of Team Virtuality. *Journal of Management* 31, 5 (October): 700–18.

41. A study of 18 construction sites in California found that the relative frequency of the formats for construction plans are time charts and tables (41 percent); technical and

organizational diagrams (23 percent); and textual (36 percent). See A. Laufer, A. Shapira, D. Cohenca-Zall, and G.A. Howell. 1993. Prebid and Preconstruction Planning Process. *Journal of Construction Engineering and Management, ASCE* 119, 3: 426–44.

42. J.L. McKenney, M.H. Zack, and V. Doherty. 1992. Complementary Communication Media: A Comparison of Electronic Mail and Face-to-Face Communication in a Programming Team. In *Networks and Organizations: Structure, Form, and Action*, eds. N. Nohria and R.G. Eccles, 262–87. Boston, MA: Harvard Business School Press.

43. A. Cockburn. 2002. *Agile Software Development*. Boston, MA: Addison-Wesley, 84–8.

44. Nardi and Whittaker highlight the following examples for engendering social bonding: "Touch helps create social bonds that scaffold communication . . . Eating and drinking together are perhaps the most fundamental way in which people come to feel connected." B.A. Nardi and S. Whittaker. 2002. The Place of Face-to-Face Communication in Distributed Work. In *Distributed Work*, eds. P. Hinds and S. Kiesler, 83–112. Cambridge, MA: The MIT Press.

45. B.A. Nardi and S. Whittaker. 2002. The Place of Face-to-Face Communication in Distributed Work. In *Distributed Work*, eds. P. Hinds and S. Kiesler, 83–112. Cambridge, MA: The MIT Press. See also R.E. Kraut, S.R. Fussell, S.E. Brennan, and J. Siegel. 2002. Understanding Effects of Proximity on Collaboration: Implications for Technologies to Support Remote Collaborative Works. In *Distributed Work*, eds. P. Hinds and S. Kiesler, 137–64. Cambridge, MA: The MIT Press.

46. See, for example, L.L. Martins, L.L. Gilson, and M.T. Maynard. 2004. Virtual Teams: What Do We Know and Where Do We Go from Here? *Journal of Management* 30, 6: 805–35; S.L. Jarvenpaa and D.E. Leidner. 1999. Communication and Trust in Global Virtual Teams. *Organization Science* 10, 6 (November–December): 791–815; A. Powell, G. Piccoli, and B. Ives. 2004. Virtual Teams: A Review of Current Literature and Directions for Future Research. *The DATA BASE for Advances in Information Systems* 35, 1 (Winter): 6–36; B.L. Kirkman and J.E. Mathieu. 2005. The Dimensions and Antecedents of Team Virtuality. *Journal of Management* 31, 5 (October): 700–18.

47. P. Hinds and S. Kiesler. 2002. Preface. In *Distributed Work*, eds. P. Hinds and S. Kiesler, xiii–xviii. Cambridge, MA: The MIT Press.

48. P.Hinds and S. Kiesler. 2002. Preface. In *Distributed Work*, eds. P. Hinds and S. Kiesler, xiii–xviii. Cambridge, MA: The MIT Press; S. Kiesler and J. Cummings. 2002. What Do We Know about Proximity and Distance in Work Groups? A Legacy of Research. In *Distributed Work*, eds. P. Hinds and S. Kiesler, 57–82. Cambridge, MA: The MIT Press.

49. C. Handy. 1995. Trust and the Virtual Organization. *Harvard Business Review* 73, 3 (May–June): 40–50. Handy explains that "it is easy to be seduced by the technological possibilities of the virtual organization." One explanation suggested by Brown and Hagel III, when discussing the strategic role of information technology (IT) in organizations, is that "rather than help companies understand that IT is only a tool, technology vendors have tended to present it as a panacea. 'Buy this technology and all your problems will be solved.'" J. Brown and J. Hagel III. 2003. Does IT Matter? An HBR Debate, Letters to the Editor. *Harvard Business Review* (June): 2.

50. B.A. Nardi and S. Whittaker. 2002. The Place of Face-to-Face Communication in Distributed Work. In *Distributed Work*, eds. P. Hinds and S. Kiesler, 83–112. Cambridge, MA: The MIT Press.

51. J.D. Herbsleb and R.E. Grinter. 1999. Splitting the Organization and Integrating the Code: Conway's Law Revisited. *Proceedings of the 21st International Conference on Software Engineering*. Los Angeles, CA: 85–95. See also K.V. Siakas and E. Siakas. 2008. The Need for Trust Relationships to Enable Successful Virtual Team Collaboration in Software Outsourcing. *International Journal of Technology, Policy and Management* 8, 1: 59–75.

52. N. Nohria and R.G. Eccles. 1992. Face-to-Face: Making Network Organizations Work. In *Networks and Organizations: Structure, Form, and Action*, eds. N. Nohria and R.G. Eccles, 288–308. Boston, MA: Harvard Business School Press.

53. B.A. Nardi and S. Whittaker. 2002. The Place of Face-to-Face Communication in Distributed Work. In *Distributed Work*, eds. P. Hinds and S. Kiesler, 83–112. Cambridge, MA: The MIT Press.

54. W.R. Ashby. 1956. *Introduction to Cybernetics*. New York, NY: John Wiley and Sons.

55. Bennett asserts that "redundancy works by providing additional clues to the intended meaning." J. Bennett. 1985. *Construction Project Management*. London, UK: Butterworths, 128. See also I. Nonaka. 1990. Redundant Overlapping Organizations: A Japanese Approach to Managing the Innovation Process. *California Management Review* 32, 3: 27–38.

56. Michael Tushman reports that "instead of a one best way of managing communication, these results indicate that the more successful projects tailor their communication patterns to fit the information processing demands of their work." M. Tushman. 1978. Technical communication in R&D Laboratories: The Impact of Project Work Characteristics. *Academy of Management Journal* 21, 4: 624–45. Fitting project communication to project context was also reported by Gales et. al. L. Gales, P. Porter, and D. Mansour-Cole. 1992. Innovation Project Technology, Information Processing and Performance: A Test of the Daft and Lengel Conceptualization. *Journal of Engineering and Technology Management* 9, 3–4: 303–38.

57. T. Peters and N. Austin. 1985. *A Passion for Excellence*. New York, NY: Random House, 8–9.

58. E. Segal. 1988. *Doctors*. New York, NY: Bantam Books, 303–6.

59. J. Pfeffer and R. Sutton. 1999. *The Knowing-Doing Gap: How Smart Companies Turn Knowledge into Action*. Boston, MA: Harvard Business School, 139.

60. The discussion of "Objective versus Subjective Measures" is presented in A.H Van De Ven and D. L. Ferry. 1980. *Measuring and Assessing Organizations*. New York, NY: John Wiley and Sons, 59. Mintzberg cites several studies that provide evidence for the prevailing phenomena of unintentional as well as intentional distortion of data in information systems. H. Mintzberg. 1994. *The Rise and Fall of Strategic Planning*. New York, NY: Prentice Hall, 264–6. See also S.E. Barndt. 1981. Upward Communication Filtering in the Project Management Environment. *Project Management Quarterly* 12, 1 (March): 39–43. Barndt reports on research findings showing that 25–45 percent of the information in upward communication is filtered. Subversive control games are reported by H.H. Meyer, E. Kay, and J.R.P. French. 1965. Split Roles in Performance Appraisal. *Harvard Business Review* 43, 1: 123–9.

61. H. Mintzberg. 1994. *The Rise and Fall of Strategic Planning*. New York, NY: Prentice Hall, 210. Studies show that even in chance-determined situations (e.g., lotteries), observing an early sequence of "successes" can lead people to believe that they have some control over outcomes. See R.M. Hograth and S. Markridakis. 1981. Forecasting and Planning: An Evaluation. *Management Science* XXVII, 2: 115–35.

62. J.K. Liker. 2004. *The Toyota Way: 14 Management Principles from the World's Greatest Manufacturer*. New York, NY: McGraw-Hill, 40.

63. T. Peters and N. Austin. 1985. *A Passion for Excellence*. New York, NY: Random House, 378–9. Manfred Kets De Vries highlights an important point regarding our listening habit: "There is a saying that goes: 'We have two ears and one mouth so that we can listen as much as we speak.' There is a lot of wisdom in that ratio. Most of us would benefit from talking less and listening—**really** listening—more." M.F.R. Kets De Vries. 2001. *The Leadership Mystique. A User's Manual for the Human Enterprise*. London, UK: Prentice Hall, 32.

64. A. Laufer, A. Shapira, and D. Telem. 2008. Communicating in Dynamic Conditions: How Do On-Site Construction Project Managers Do It? *Journal of Management in Engineering, ASCE* 24, 2: 75–86.

65. See K.E. Weick. 1987. Perspectives on Action in Organizations. In *Handbook of Organizational Behavior*, ed. J. Lorsch, 10–28. Englewood Cliffs, NJ: Prentice Hall. See also R.M. Baron. 1981. Social Knowing from an Ecological-Event Perspective: A Consideration of the Relative Domains of Power for Cognitive and Perceptual Modes of Knowing. In *Cognition, Social Behavior and the Environment*, ed. H.H. Harvey, 61–89. Hillsdale, NJ: Erlbaum; P.L. Knowles and D.L. Smith. 1982. The Ecological Perspective Applied to Social Perception: Revision of a Working Paper. *Journal for the Theory of Social Behavior* 12: 53–78; R.L. Daft and R.H. Lengel. 1984. Information Richness: A New Approach to Managerial Behavior and Organization Design. In *Research in Organizational Behavior*, eds. B. Staw and L.L. Cummings, 191–233. Greenwich, CT.: JAI Press.

66. K.B. Clark and S.C. Wheelwright. 1992. Organizing and Leading Heavyweight Development Teams. *California Management Review* 34, 3 (Spring): 9–28; T.J. Peters and R.H. Waterman. *In Search of Excellence*. 1982. New York, NY: Warner, 121–5.

67. L.R. Sayles and M.K. Chandler. 1971. *Managing Large Systems: Organizations for the Future*. New York, NY: Harper & Row, 218–9; B. Muirhead and W. Simon. 1999. *High Velocity Leadership: The Mars Pathfinder Approach to Faster, Better, Cheaper*. New York, NY: Harper Business, 76–7.

68. K.B. Clark and S.C. Wheelwright. 1992. Organizing and Leading Heavyweight Development Teams. *California Management Review* 34, 3 (Spring): 9–28; T. Peters and N. Austin. 1985. *A Passion for Excellence*. New York, NY: Random House, 378–92.

References

a. "The Idyllic Workplace." Tony E. Schoenfelder, NASA. 2002. *Ask Magazine* 7 (March), 22–6. http://appel.nasa.gov/ask/issues/07/07s_idyllic_schoenfelder.php

b. "Open Newsletters." Terry Little, U.S. Air Force. 2002. *Ask Magazine* 6 (January): 36–40. http://appel.nasa.gov/ask/issues/06/06_newsletters.php

c. "Bang for the Buck." Terry Little, U.S. Air Force. 2005. In A. Laufer, T. Post, and E.J. Hoffman, *Shared Voyage: Learning and Unlearning from Remarkable Projects*, 94–5. Washington, D.C.: The NASA History Series.

d. "Project Management: Easy as ABC." Allan Frandsen, California Institute of Technology. 2005. In A. Laufer, T. Post, and E.J. Hoffman, *Shared Voyage: Learning and Unlearning from Remarkable Projects*, 47–9. Washington, D.C.: The NASA History Series.

e. "Weather Reports." Don Margolies, Goddard Space Flight Center, NASA. 2005. In A. Laufer, T. Post, and E.J. Hoffman, *Shared Voyage: Learning and Unlearning from Remarkable Projects*, 31. Washington, D.C.: The NASA History Series.

f. "The Hour Glass and the Project Manager Part 2: Improving Your Hierarchical IQ," Scott Cameron, Procter & Gamble. 2001. *Ask Magazine* 5 (September): 32–4. http://appel.nasa.gov/ask/issues/05/05f_hourglass_cameron.php

g. "What Has He Done For Me Lately?" Scott Cameron, Procter & Gamble. 2002. *Ask Magazine* 9 (October): 25–7. http://appel.nasa.gov/ask/issues/09/09f_done_cameron.php

h. "The Join-Up Meeting," Scott Cameron, Procter & Gamble. 2002. *Ask Magazine* 7 (March): 31–3. http://appel.nasa.gov/ask/issues/07/07f_joinup_cameron.php

i. "Small Wins Make for Big Gains," Frank Snow, Goddard Space Flight Center, NASA. 2005. In A. Laufer, T. Post, and E.J. Hoffman, *Shared Voyage: Learning and Unlearning from Remarkable Projects*, 53–4. Washington, D.C.: The NASA History Series.

j. "Semantic Differences." Barry Smith, Procter & Gamble. 1997. In A. Laufer, *Simultaneous Management: Managing Projects in a Dynamic Environment*, 222–3. New York, NY: AMACOM, American Management Association.

k. "Oral Presentations," Lynda Rutledge, U.S. Air Force. 2005. In A. Laufer, T. Post, and E.J. Hoffman, *Shared Voyage: Learning and Unlearning from Remarkable Projects*, 102. Washington, D.C.: The NASA History Series. See also, "Say What You Mean," Lynda Rutledge, U.S. Air Force. 2004. *Ask Magazine* 16 (February): 34–7. http://appel.nasa.gov/ask/issues/16/practices/index.html.

l. "The Sky is Blue, or Pink," Don Margolies, Goddard Space Flight Center, NASA. 2005. In A. Laufer, T. Post, and E.J. Hoffman, *Shared Voyage: Learning and Unlearning from Remarkable Projects*, 42–4. Washington, D.C.: The NASA History Series.

m. "Transfer Wisdom Workshops: Get in Bed," Jon Bauschlicher, Kennedy Space Center. 2003. *Ask Magazine* 12 (June): 19. http://appel.nasa.gov/ask/issues/12/special/next.html#getinbed

n. "The Storyboard's Big Picture," Cheryl Malloy and William Cooley, NASA and SAIC. 2003. *Ask Magazine* 13 (August): 24–5. http://appel.nasa.gov/ask/issues/13/practices/index.html

o. "You Can't Take Anything for Granted," Jerry Madden, NASA. 2000. In A. Laufer and E.J. Hoffman, *Project Management Success Stories*, 86–8. New York, NY: John Wiley & Sons.

p. "Walking a Fine Line," Mary Bothwell, Jet Propulsion Laboratory, NASA. 2004. *Ask Magazine* 17 (April): 14–7. http://appel.nasa.gov/ask/issues/17/17s_fineline_bothwell.php

q. "Not to Worry," Terry Little, U.S. Air Force. 2005. In A. Laufer, T. Post, and E.J. Hoffman, *Shared Voyage: Learning and Unlearning from Remarkable Projects*, 112-3. Washington, D.C.: The NASA History Series.

Epilogue

Notes

1. J. Seely Brown and P. Duguid. 1994. Organizational Learning and Communities-of-Practice: Toward a Unified View of Working, Learning and Innovation. In *New Thinking in Organizational Behavior: From Social Engineering to Reflective Action*, ed. H. Tsoukas, 165–87. Oxford, UK: Butterworth-Heinemann.

2. T. Peters. 1992. *Liberation Management: Necessary Disorganization for the Nanosecond Nineties*. New York, NY: Alfred A. Knopf, 222.

3. A. Melgrati and M. Damiani. 2002. Rethinking the Project Management Framework: New Epistemology, New Insights. *Proceedings of PMI Research Conference*, Seattle: 371–80.

4. P.F. Drucker. 1999. *Management Challenges for the 21st Century*. New York, NY: Harper Collins, 5, 17. While for the most part the project management literature has not given explicit treatment to context issues, there are some notable exceptions by proponents of Agile Project Management. See, for example, J.A. Highsmith III. 2000. *Adaptive Software Development—A Collaborative Approach to Managing Complex Systems*. New York, NY: Dorset House Publishing; C. Kaner, J. Bach, and B. Pettichord. 2001. *Lessons Learned in Software Testing: A Context-Driven Approach*. New York, NY: John Wiley & Sons.

5. S. Ghoshal. 2005. Bad Management Theories Are Destroying Good Management Practices. *Academy of Management Learning and Education* 4, 1 (March): 75–91.

6. David Johnson points out that "context becomes conceived of in terms of constraints and limits on individual action, rather than enablers." D. Johnson. 2003. On Contexts of Information Seeking. *Information Processing & Management* 39, 5 (September): 735–60. Context factors related to projects can indeed inhibit or facilitate the implementation of the principles. Moreover, the impact of context factors may vary throughout the life of the project. For example, in the Second Yellow Guideline (Challenge the Status Quo), Don Margolies from NASA realized that his project context had changed: "[Now] towards the final stages of a very complex project . . . there was more than enough slack in the schedule as well as the budget." So Margolies took advantage of this facilitating context and conducted a comprehensive testing of all the systems and the instruments.

7. On the basis of several recent sources, David Johnson concludes that "there is an increasing tendency to suggest that individuals and groups are not only shaped by context, the classic approach *of contingency and situational perspectives, but can in turn shape contexts.*" D. Johnson. 2003. On Contexts of Information Seeking. *Information Processing & Management* 39, 5 (September): 735–60. However, even as early as 1966, Harvey (editor of the book and author of the specific chapter "Ends, Means, and Adaptability") already argued that "there are at least two ways in which a system could accommodate to deviant or pressureful environments. One way would consist of altering the environment and the other of changing the system in the direction of conformity to the direction of the environmental press." O.J. Harvey. 1966. Ends, Means, and Adaptability. In *Experience, Structure and Adaptability*, ed. O.J. Harvey, 7–8. New York, NY: Springer Publishing Company.

8. J. Quinn, H. Mintzberg, and R. James. 1988. *The Strategy Process: Concepts, Contexts, and Cases*. Englewood Cliffs, NJ: Prentice Hall, xi, 956–60.

9. M. Eraut. 1994. *Developing Professional Knowledge and Competence*. London, UK: The Falmer Press, 49.

10. B. Flyvbjerg. 2001. *Making Social Science Matter: Why Social Inquiry Fails and How It Can Succeed Again*. Cambridge, MA: University Press, 57–8.

11. Tichy discusses the question, are leaders made or born? Tichy concludes that "not everyone can be the CEO of a multibillion-dollar corporation, just as not every one can be an Olympian or win at Wimbledon, but with coaching and practice, we can all be a lot better than we are." N.M. Tichy. 1997. *The Leadership Engine*. New York, NY: Harper Business, 6. Bennis concludes that "at bottom, becoming a leader is synonymous with becoming yourself. It's precisely that simple, and it's also that difficult . . . Leadership courses can only teach skills. They can't teach character or

vision—and indeed they don't even try. Developing character and vision is the way leaders invent themselves." W. Bennis. 1989. *On Becoming a Leader.* Cambridge, MA: Perseus, 9, 42. See also the section Improving Courage through Practice in the Second Yellow Guideline (Challenge the Status Quo).

12. S. Kerr. 2004. Introduction: Preparing People to Lead. *Academy of Management Executive* 18, 3 (August): 118–20.

13. M. Eraut. 2000. Non-formal Learning and Tacit Knowledge in Professional Work. *British Journal of Educational Psychological Society* 70, 113–36. Herman van Gunsteren discusses the meaning of rules and concludes that "normative sociology mistakenly assumes that rules are absolute . . . the same for everyone . . . In contradiction to those views, everyday-life sociologists argue that . . . the meaning of rules [is determined by] other factors such as the situation . . . personal interpretations [of the situation] may be equally important . . . [rules are used] to bring prior experience to bear on new experience . . . Skills and practical know-how are essential for competent rule use." H.R. van Gunsteren. 1976. *The Quest for Control: A Critique of the Rational-central-rule Approach in Public Affairs.* New York, NY: John Wiley & Sons, 117–9.

14. H. Mintzberg. 2004. *Managers Not MBAs—A Hard Look at the Soft Practice of Managing and Management Development.* San Francisco, CA: Berrett-Koehler Publishers Inc., 254.

15. K.E. Weick. 1983. Managerial Thought in the Context of Action. In *The Executive Mind*, eds. S. Srivastba and Associates, 241. San Francisco, CA: Jossey-Bass. Eccles and Nohria conclude that "knowledge and action, theory and practice, follow one another in a cycle of contemplation and application. Which comes first is often difficult to say and is in the end unimportant." R. Eccles and N. Nohria. 1992. *Beyond the Hype: Rediscovering the Essence of Management.* Boston: Harvard Business School Press, 175.

16. J. Gosling and H. Mintzberg. 2006. Management Education as If Both Matter. *Management Learning* 37, 4: 419–28. For more on the subject of reflection on action, see M. Eraut. 1994. *Developing Professional Knowledge and Competence.* London, UK: The Falmer Press, 146–9, and W. Bennis. 1989. *On Becoming a Leader.* Cambridge, MA: Perseus, 60–71, 114–20.

17. H. Mintzberg. 2004. *Managers Not MBAs—A Hard Look at the Soft Practice of Managing and Management Development.* San Francisco, CA: Berrett-Koehler Publishers Inc, 264. While Eraut expects experience to help in the interpretation of the theory, Mintzberg expects that the maps will help in the interpretation of the experience. Weick's comment mentioned in a previous note (note 15) is relevant here as well: "We should pay more attention to simultaneity of thought and action and less attention to sequence." The crucial role of concepts and paradigms in interpreting practice is highlighted by Peter Senge. Senge asked the following question, why are mental models so powerful in affecting what we do? He suggests that, in part, it is because they affect what we see. Senge explains that "two people with different mental models can observe the same event and describe it differently because they have looked at different details . . . They observed selectively." P. Senge. 1990. *Fifth Discipline: The Art and Practice of the Learning Organization.* New York, NY: Doubleday, 175.

18. Jalongo and Isenberg present multiple sources that demonstrate how stories of practice offer a vehicle for practitioners to become more competent reflective practitioners. M.R. Jalongo and J.P. Isenberg. 1995. *Teacher's Stories: From Personal Narrative*

to Professional Insight. San Francisco, CA: Jossey-Bass Publishers, 50–1. The reader may find the following list of books of case studies useful for enhancing reflection and context-sensitive mind-set: B. Burrough. 1998. *Dragonfly: NASA and the Crisis Aboard Mir.* New York, NY: HarperCollins Publishers; W. Bennis and P. Ward Biederman. 1997. *Organizing Genius: The Secrets of Creative Collaboration.* Reading, MA: Addison-Wesley; A. Lansing. 1959. *Endurance: Shackleton's Incredible Voyage.* New York, NY: Carrol and Graf Publishers, Inc.; M. Useem. 1998. *The Leadership Moment.* New York, NY: Three River Press; B. Muirhead and W.L. Simon. 1999. *High Velocity Leadership.* New York, NY: HarperCollins Publishers; T.P. Hughes. 1998. *Rescuing Prometheus.* New York, NY: Vintage Books; B.R. Rich and L. Janos. 1994. *Skunk Works: A Personal Memoir of my Years at Lockheed.* Boston, MA: Little, Brown and Company; T. Kidder. 1981. *The Soul of a New Machine.* Boston, MA: Little, Brown and Company.

19. H. Bergson. 1911. *Creative Evolution.* New York, NY: The Modern Library, 240–58.
20. Flyvbjerg argues that "the problem in the study of human activity is that every attempt at a context-free definition of an action, that is, a definition based on abstract rules or laws, will not necessarily accord with the pragmatic way an action is defined by the actors in a concrete social situation . . . human activity cannot be reduced to a set of rules, and without rules there can be no theory." B. Flyvbjerg. 2001. *Making Social Science Matter: Why Social Inquiry Fails and How It Can Succeed Again.* Cambridge, MA: University Press, 43, 46. Weick contends, however, that these "theories of action" play a very crucial role in organization: "When people 'agree' on a paradigm, they are more likely to agree on its existence than on its rules . . . paradigms are more analogues to cultures than to philosophical systems . . . Theories of action 'are for organizations what cognitive structures are for individuals. They filter and interpret signals from the environment and tie stimuli to responses' . . . These maps constitute theories of action which organizations elaborate and refine as new situations are encountered." K.E. Weick. 1995. *Sensemaking in Organizations.* Thousand Oaks, CA: Sage Publications, 120–1.
21. R. Heifetz. 1999. The Leader of the Future. *Fast Company* 25 (May): 130.

Index

(Please note that page numbers in *italics* indicate endnotes.)